Memorial Book of the Community of Maków-Mazowiecki
(Maków Mazowiecki, Poland)

Translation of
Sefer zikaron le-kehilat Maków-Mazowiecki

Original Book Edited by: J. Brat

Originally published in Tel Aviv 1969

JewishGen
מרכז עולמי לגנאלוגיה יהודית
The Global Home for Jewish Genealogy

A Publication of JewishGen, Inc.
Edmond J. Safra Plaza, 36 Battery Place, New York, NY 10280
646.494.5972 | info@JewishGen.org | www.jewishgen.org

MUSEUM OF
JEWISH HERITAGE
A LIVING MEMORIAL
TO THE HOLOCAUST

Memorial Book of the Community of Maków-Mazowiecki (Maków Mazowiecki, Poland)
Translation of *Sefer zikaron le-kehilat Maków-Mazowiecki*

Editor of Original Yizkor Book: J. Brat
Project Coordinator: Anita Frishman Gabbay
Cover Design: Rachel Kolokoff Hopper
Layout and Name Indexing: Jonathan Wind
Photo Extraction: Sondra Ettlinger

Printed in the United States of America by Lightning Source, Inc.

Library of Congress Control Number (LCCN): 2022931515

ISBN: 978-1-954176-34-8 (hard cover: 420 pages, alk. paper)

About JewishGen.org

JewishGen, an affiliate of the Museum of Jewish Heritage - A Living Memorial to the Holocaust, serves as the global home for Jewish genealogy.

Featuring unparalleled access to 30+ million records, it offers unique search tools, along with opportunities for researchers to connect with others who share similar interests. Award winning resources such as the Family Finder, Discussion Groups, and ViewMate, are relied upon by thousands each day.

In addition, JewishGen's extensive informational, educational and historical offerings, such as the Jewish Communities Database, Yizkor Book translations, InfoFiles, Family Tree of the Jewish People, and KehilaLinks, provide critical insights, first-hand accounts, and context about Jewish communal and familial life throughout the world.

Offered as a free resource, JewishGen.org has facilitated thousands of family connections and success stories, and is currently engaged in an intensive expansion effort that will bring many more records, tools, and resources to its collections.

Please visit https://www.jewishgen.org/ to learn more.

Executive Director: Avraham Groll

About the JewishGen Yizkor Book Project

Yizkor Books (Memorial Books) were traditionally written to memorialize the names of departed family and martyrs during holiday services in the synagogue (a practice that still exists in many synagogues today).

Over the centuries, as a result of countless persecutions and horrific atrocities committed against the Jews, Yizkor Books (Sefer Zikaron in Hebrew) were expanded to include more historical information, such as biographical sketches of famous personalities and descriptions of daily town life.

Following the Holocaust, the idea of remembrance and learning took on an urgent and crucial importance. Survivors of the Holocaust sought out other surviving residents of their former towns to memorialize and document the names and way of life of those who were ruthlessly murdered by the Nazis. These remembrances were documented in Yizkor Books, hundreds of which were published in the first decades after the Holocaust.

Most of these books were published privately, or through landsmanshaftn (social organizations comprised of members originating from the same European town or region) that still existed, and were often distributed free of charge. Sadly, the languages used to document these crucial histories and links to our past, Yiddish and Hebrew, are no longer commonly understood by a significant percentage of Jews today. As a result, JewishGen has undertaken the sacred responsibility of translating these books into English so that the culture and way of life of these communities will be preserved and transmitted to future generations.

In 1986, a group of farsighted JewishGenners started a project to pool their efforts together in groups based upon their ancestors from each town and donate money to get the Yizkor books of their ancestral towns translated into English. As the translated material became available, it was made accessible for free at www.JewishGen.org/Yizkor. Hardcover copies can be purchased by visiting https://www.jewishgen.org/Yizkor/ybip.html (see below).

It is our hope that the translation of these books into English (and other languages) will assist the countless Jewish family researchers who are so desperately seeking to forge a connection with their heritage.

Director of JewishGen Yizkor Book Project: Lance Ackerfeld

About JewishGen Press

JewishGen Press (formerly the Yizkor Books-in-Print Project) is the publishing division of JewishGen.org, and provides a venue for the publication of non-fiction books pertaining to Jewish genealogy, history, culture, and heritage.

In addition to the Yizkor Book category, publications in the Other Non-Fiction category include Shoah memoirs and research, genealogical research, collections of genealogical and historical materials, biographies, diaries and letters, studies of Jewish experience and cultural life in the past, academic theses, and other books of interest to the Jewish community.

Please visit https://www.jewishgen.org/Yizkor/ybip.html to learn more.

Director of JewishGen Press: Joel Alpert
Managing Editor - Jessica Feinstein
Publications Manager - Susan Rosin

Notes to the Reader

The images in the original book were reproduced from photographs from the time of the first edition. These reproductions were already of poor quality, being pre-war and at least 30 or more years old. As a result the images in the book are the best achievable.

A reader can view the original scans of the book on the websites listed below.

The original book can be seen online at the Yiddish Book Center website:

https://www.yiddishbookcenter.org/collections/yizkor-books/yzk-nybc313877/brot-yitshak-sefer-zikaron-li-kehilat-makov-mazovyetsk

or
at the New York Public Library Digital Collections website:

https://digitalcollections.nypl.org/items/36ed2530-5b23-0133-1ffb-00505686a51c

To obtain a list of Shoah victims from Maków-Mazowiecki (Maków Mazowiecki, Poland) the reader should access the Yad Vashem web site listed below; one can also search for specific family names using family name option. These lists are continually updated by Yad Vashem, so it is worthwhile to periodically search these lists.

There is more valuable information (including the Pages of Testimony, etc.) available on this website: https://yvng.yadvashem.org/

A list of all books available from JewishGen Press along with prices is available at: https://www.jewishgen.org/Yizkor/ybip.html

Photo Credits

Front Cover:

Front cover photo: *Rabbi Efraim Fishel Nyman may he rest in peace, the author of "Beit Efraim", the grandson of the righteous Gaon R' Motelle from Maków.* [Page 429].

Back Cover:

Excerpt from: *The Blood Chronicles by Yekhezkel Itzcovitch /Tel Aviv.* [Page11].

Back cover image by: Pinchas (Sharon) Schulenrein. For more information about the artist and his work, please see the *"Sons of Makow Remembered in USA and Canada"* Appendix.

Background texture and color: Rachel Kolokoff Hopper

Background front and back cover photo: *Homage to a Winter Garden* by Rachel Kolokoff Hopper

Introduction

My Makow Odyssey
by
Dr. Joseph Schuldenrein

Beginnings (1950's)

They say that your earliest childhood memories are among your most vivid. There aren't many of them, they're not necessarily significant, yet they stick and retain a visual permanence. My earliest recollection is facing a steel blue sky, lying prone in a baby carriage with a strange woman and my mother looking down on me. I once described that memory to my mother and she concluded that the woman was probably her close friend Betty and we were walking in the park in Bad Nauheim, Germany. It was probably 1950, two years before we sailed to the United States; I was less than a year old. By age 8 memories are still vivid but more frequent, and at that age, I suppose, the child begins to string them together in cognitive fashion. These are coherent, connected and form a story. And that is when my personal Makow odyssey began.

We lived in a run-down building in New York's Upper West Side for our first decade after leaving Europe. Szulim (dad) was from Makow, Nina (mom) from Warsaw. I recall vividly that until 1958, when my brother was born, we used to drive to Brooklyn, almost every Sunday, to visit my dad's best childhood friend, Mordecai Cywiner and his family; we knew him as Modkhe (Yiddish diminutive). The two of them could not have been more different. Modkhe was Orthodox, soft-spoken, gentle, and reserved. My dad was a loud-mouth atheistic rabble rouser whose angry rants could pierce walls. After the war, Modkhe left for Israel, started a family, moved to Brooklyn and ultimately settled in Boro Park, an enclave of the few Makowers who survived. He worked as a machinist in a spacious converted warehouse on Centre Street in Lower Manhattan. Dad arrived in the U.S. having earned two degrees in engineering, the first in Warsaw before the war, and another at the University of Freiberg, Germany after liberation. Dad was an instructor at the Displaced Persons (D.P.) camp in Eschwege, where I was born.

On most Sundays, dad and Modkhe went to meetings of the United Makower Relief. This was the Makower Landsmanshaft, a community house and social service agency of the Makower group. Many of the members were impoverished, barely getting by, and while few spoke English, we gathered for Sunday meals with several of the families.

It was tough going for most of us refugees in the '50's and my dad, despite his degrees and in part because of his volatile temper, found himself intermittently unemployed. Modkhe got him work on weekends at the Centre Street machine shop and I occasionally went there on Sundays to help. Dad also taught me something about machining. I'll never forget the parts that were made there. Dad explained that they were holders for diamonds that had to be machined to micrometric specifications.

But what made the strongest impression on me was the group of machinists, helpers, laborers and even janitors that lined up along the extended rows of lathes and machines separated by aisles. The creaky wood floorboards were covered with grime and oil so thick that you could easily slip and break your neck. I kind of liked the shop because it was so different. I was drawn to the men who worked there. Many were nice and friendly, but some had eerily blank stares and said nothing. It shocked me to see how several of them were infirm. Guys with visible deformities, limps, club feet, bad teeth, mangled fingers; dad himself had bent fingers and nails that were never smooth. But most were friendly and every Sunday one or two would come up to me and say "Vuhs macht a klein yid?" (Yiddish vernacular for "How are you doing little guy?"). The quiet ones also grinned at me occasionally. They were all Makowers or refugees from surrounding Polish towns like Mlawa and Pultusk. Years later dad explained to me that, like him, these guys had gone through hell in the camps and that some had lingering infirmities, aggravated in the U.S. because of the poor conditions in the old factory shops. I was especially struck by Faivel, a sweet man with blackened gums and teeth like I had never seen before. Not, that is, until many years later when I looked through Roman Vishniac's famous photo volume "A Vanished World". There's a vivid snapshot taken with a fish-eye lens. It showed a prematurely aged Jew with an exaggerated smile in the Warsaw Ghetto. The darkened gums and teeth called to mind Faivel. Periodontal disease, a dentist told me. My mom explained that it was trench mouth, very common in the ghetto when she was a teen.

The Yizkor Book: Origins (1965-1969)

Over the years, our contact with the refugee community underwent changes as acculturation and absorption into what was then known as the "American melting pot" became a reality. We, like many other Holocaust refugees, left the tenement and moved out (and up) to the outer boroughs. By the '60's, subconsciously or not, I slowly shed my immigrant identity, leaving Yeshiva and matriculating at a high school with a diverse population. My parents transitioned as well, albeit in different ways. Dad remained close to Modkhe, but they did not see each other as often. What I did not know was that dad got very involved with United Makower Relief as the aging refugees dispersed and the older members of the Landsmanshaft began to die off.

Both Dad and Modkhe served on the U.S. Yizkor book's planning and coordinating committee in Brooklyn. Dad and his two older brothers got deeply involved in the effort, motivated by the family's prominent role in the community before the war. By the late '60's his brother Pinchas Sharon had established himself as a prominent graphic artist and he designed the book's original cover art. The senior brother, Rabbi Simcha Ben Zakkai contributed photos, including a 1935 group shot at the "Yavneh" school in Makow where he was an instructor. My grandparents were occasionally identified by name, especially on the maternal side, because of community involvement and because of "yichus" (Yiddish for "pedigree"). Yichus was a very big deal in the "shtetlach" of pre-war Eastern Europe. It originally meant that you came from the local gentry, nobility, or prominent religious lineage. Over time the term was expanded to "big shots" or "somebodies" because one's family was large, influential, rich or all three. That was the case for the "Frenkels", my maternal grandmother's side. It's gruesome and somewhat ironic, I suppose, but simply look at the names in the back of this book for the list of Kedoyshim (martyrs). The largest number of surnames mentioned...well these were the Makower families with Yichus. The list of Frenkels numbers 15.

My own participation in the book publishing effort was limited to technical or publishing related questions my dad posed to me as volume organizer. I was flattered that he appreciated my input insofar as I was the News Editor of my High School newspaper. The book's subject matter was of marginal relevance to me. That was due, in part, to the typical alienation teens felt from their parents, but also because I saw myself through the prism of "Americanization". I recall being confused, if not stunned by the shocking history of the Jewish chapter in Europe's war between Germany and the Allies. But more directly, I was embarrassed by my parents' accents and that they were so different not only from typical Americans but even from non-immigrant Jews. Those personal reactions were not unfounded. Now, over half a century later, it is known that Holocaust awareness at that time ('50's and '60's) was a sensitive topic that American Jews shied away from and the refugees themselves remained uncomfortable discussing. Makow might have been Mars as far as I was concerned.

The original Yizkor volume, released in Hebrew and Yiddish, came out in 1969. Up to that time I had never seen my father brimming with such pride as he did when he came home with the published beautifully bound volume, carefully wrapped in newspaper.

Several years after publication Modkhe passed. Szulim wept inconsolably for days. Modkhe was his nearest and dearest friend in this world as well as his closest living connection to his beloved Makow. This quiet, modest, and reserved man authored the most touching and poignant description of life in Makow before the war. If there is single piece that conveys the pre-war flavor of the shtetl it is the Cywiner chapter entitled "A Street in Makow". It is an uncanny, nostalgic portrayal of the town viewed through the lens of a child, with a vision of a time and place little short of idyllic. On the few occasions when I overheard dad and his soulmate Modkeh conversing they spoke softly of the beauty of the place, the kids they played with, the intimacy of the community, and joy of being a carefree child in this wonderful little town. They talked about games and hiding places, most notably a lovely mill on the river where they stored toys and candies for special occasions. And Dad recounted tales of his youth in Makow in wistful terms, especially in our first years in America.

Holocaust Consciousness: Awareness Across Generations (1970's and 1980's)

By the late 70's Holocaust awareness had become a cause celebre that was taken up not only by Jewish groups but on the international stage. The term "refugee" was replaced by "survivor". The Landsmanshaftn called attention to the plight of aging communities of Holocaust victims. The Second Generation (2G) movement was born, spurred on by the publication of Helen Epstein's seminal *Children of the Holocaust,* nothing less than a clarion call to survivors and their offspring. The Holocaust generation was beginning to die off, and their experiences, largely repressed during years of transition, required first-hand documentation by survivors before it was too late. As the 2G's grew into adulthood they took on initiatives to break their parents' long-held silences and recount their own experiences growing up in the shadows.

By the 1980's global Holocaust awareness was in full throttle. The trend expanded exponentially with the collapse of the Soviet Block and the reunification of Germany. In Europe the opening of sealed frontiers after post-war isolation promoted a rekindled Holocaust awareness. In 1994 an initiative was created by the YIVO as the original Yizkor Books were dusted off, removed from the shelves, and re-read by Yiddish speakers. The world was trying to make sense of the madness that seized mid-20th century Europe, resulting in the genocide of a vibrant and influential people. Translations were necessitated to make the primary sources available to the public.

In the '90's the tragic resurgence of ethnic cleansing in the Third World (Africa in Rwanda and Cambodia previously) and in Europe yet again (Kosovo and the former Yugoslavia) reinforced the fact that mass murder brought about by authoritarianism was not a thing of the past. The message of the Holocaust was timely, and its specter was not only lurking but showed signs of resurfacing if not confronted head on.

The Visit (April 1988)

Despite this revivalism, by the end of the 20th century the Landsmanschaftn were starting to shut down because of dwindling number of survivors. While remaining enclaves largely supported the goals of a renewed Holocaust mission ("We Will Never Forget") the psychological hurdles within the survivor communities were multi-faceted. Responses to the challenges of reconciling with the past met with mixed responses. That said, the 2G's went international and took up the mission. Thanks largely to their efforts, organized trips to long abandoned scenes of the crimes began in the late 1980's.

In April 1988, my late brother and I joined a Los Angeles based survivor and 2G trip to Poland and Russia. It was one of the first of many subsequent Remembrance and Commemoration trips. The timing of this trip was pivotal insofar as it occurred in advance of the collapse of the Soviet Block. Organizational protocols and logistics were crude and basic, to say the least. Post-Holocaust dialogues between the Eastern Block and the West were not yet established, the Iron Curtain countries had not yet formally acknowledged the unique nature of the anti-Semitic Genocide, and international settlements between survivor organizations and formerly complicit nations were still years if not decades away.

The Commemoration Tours were ad-hoc affairs at the time. By the tail end of our tour, I had made friends with the tour guides, in part because I assisted in translating Yiddish texts, narratives and Polish signage to the English-speaking groups. As a token of appreciation, the guides facilitated a private tour of Makow for my brother and me. We found a local filmographer, a Mr. Wieslau Pickauski, to document our Makow visit. At that time there was still a small group of Poles who had memories of the once bustling Jewish community. Several claimed to vaguely remember our family. Mr. Pickauski, weighed down by the then bulky VHS camera, popped in a tape, and orchestrated a walking tour for my brother and myself.

As we set out, I remember being rueful and teary eyed that Szulim, my dad, did not accompany us. By this time, at age 74, Dad was in an advancing stage of Alzheimer's disease. He was in no position to leave home, much less confront a past that could have disoriented him unpredictably.

The Makow visit was as stultifying as it was impactful. My immediate response to seeing this place was one of disbelief, confusion, ironic humor, and, yes, rage. It was impossible to fathom what had happened here…. that the majority ethnic population that had dominated the fabric of the town for centuries had simply vanished, almost overnight.

For all practical purposes the town looked to me like a backwater hovel, stuck in time, a relict time capsule populated by hard and grizzled denizens, most seemingly septuagenarians and older. The landscape bore no semblance to the vibrant presence that Cywiner described in his recollections of a childhood imbued with love and happiness. What my brother and I saw was an amalgam of wooden shacks in various states of disrepair, boarded up windows, littered front and backyards. As we sauntered through town an odd assortment of townsfolk accompanied us, some curious as to what in the name of God well-heeled folks like us could possibly want in their deserted corner of the world. The odd drunk wandered out from a shack here, an elderly woman tended to her tomato plants there, a lone barefoot child rode a tricycle along an unpaved stretch of road. Skinny stray dogs everywhere, scavenging for scraps and bones.

And yet, at least a few onlookers were somewhat familiar with our mission. Pickauski explained that the occasional odd group of foreigners had begun to make its way to Makow a year or two earlier. I will never forget overhearing the phrase "Jestescie Zhidzhe tutaj dzisiaj" ("the Jews are here today") as we started walking. They mumbled the words softly, but both my brother and I were taken aback. A small host of local town officials escorted us to every "landmark", patiently explaining where the baths (and the mikvah ruins) were. They made sure to lead us to Makow's most famous draw: the cemetery. It was in disrepair at the time, but one of the officials told us that restoration efforts were being implemented. That effort soon emerged as the signature objective of survivor groups, not only for former Makowers but also for survivors from any and all of the hundreds of towns in Eastern and Central Europe.

The townsfolk pointed out sites of local Jewish commercial establishments in the old "Rynek" (town square and marketplace) and noted, quite innocently, which ones belonged to Jews before the war. As we approached the Rynek, we were joined by a very elderly man, limping ahead, and leaning on a beautiful but well weathered walking stick. He moved silently while our small crowd cleared the way for him with obvious deference and respect. The group pace slowed markedly when he joined. I never got his name. He was mostly silent except for occasional utterances to individuals who leaned over to catch his every word. As we moved past the square he called out and asked me my name and when I said "Schuldenrein" and "Frenkel", he stopped and stared deliberately at the square. And then he pointed to a broken down and collapsed pile of wood and said "Tahm, tahm to biwa" ("Over there, that's where it was"). He fixed his stare on me and said "Dobreh ludzie" ("Good people"), then turned abruptly and limped away. That said it all, as far as I was concerned. As he sidled off the younger people and our filmographer Pickauski emphasized that he was the Town Elder. I was given to understand that in his own unobtrusive way he made it a point to introduce himself to all who came to Makow on what eventually became a semi-regular Jewish pilgrimage. As I wrote these words, I thought of him and paused…. suspecting that he may have lived another few years, but that he took with him the last living memories of pre-Holocaust Makow.

As we proceeded along the banks of the River Ozycz, we saw it. The mill. I spotted it immediately. No warning nor explanation necessary. It was exactly where it was supposed to be from Szulim's description. Whenever dad spoke about Makow he invariably mentioned the mill, as if it was a natural fit to the calmness of the landscape and the peace he drew from it as a child. To be truthful, I cannot recall the structure's form in detail. It was growing dark, and we had to move on. We got there at dusk. The combined effect of the mill against the fading sunset reminded me of the mid-19th century paintings typical of the Hudson River school in New York state, just north of the city. It seemed fitting that this landmark signaled the final stages of our tour, at dusk. Perhaps it was staged that way?

Shortly thereafter, Mr. Pickauski handed me the VHS tape, hesitated for a brief second, and then invited my brother and our tour guides to his house where we drank tea in a tall glass. That's the way we drank it at home, in New York, up until the day my mother died; two lumps of sugar. It seemed so familiar. Mr. Pickauski was a joyful yet serious and uniquely perceptive man. His moods that day were nothing short of absolute empathy. He appreciated both the somberness of our mission and the relief my brother and I felt. Our relief was borne of finally visiting this place and projecting the reality to a distant past which was meaningful to us. It provided a backdrop to the individual our dad became and the part of him that was passed on to Alan and me as part of our family heritage.

I remember speaking with Pickauski's lovely wife for at least fifteen minutes while we sipped our tea. She expressed an urge to go to America and kept saying that everything would be changing in Poland in the next few years. As if she knew that the days of the Eastern Block were numbered. And that the future would be better and maybe, just maybe, this ramshackle, dirty town might look forward to happier days. As we were talking, Pickauski motioned me aside and asked for the VHS tape that he had handed me earlier. He excused himself saying he wanted to review the footage and clean it up in his processing studio. A half hour later he returned. We bade our farewells, and his parting words were "I'd appreciate it if you looked at this shortly upon your return to America. Please make sure that everything is OK". I felt intimately connected to this fine man and his family. We embraced and said our goodbyes, my promising him that I would view the film directly after arriving home.

The urgency of his words was compelling, and I took it to heart. As soon as we returned my brother, and I sat down to watch the film. Our new Polish friend edited it masterfully and in a way which placed Alan and me in the center of the presentation. His edit had the effect of conveying not only our instinctive responses but also our intense and sometimes playful conversations with the locals. I always found that viewing films (first VHS, now digital) is cathartic, especially in new places. It's because the process of filming is so consuming that it is not possible to digest the sights, sounds and indeed the novelty of an unfamiliar setting. It just goes by so fast. Various folks who accompanied us pointed out historic sites in the background that I could not fully take in. Even though my Polish was good the rapidity of the conversation coupled with the new sights and sounds made the experience difficult to process. But in repeated viewings at home, it all came together somehow. I saw things I missed in real time. There were, for example, several well preserved and quite majestic buildings in the background. Repeated viewings accentuated the serenity of the landscape that echoed dad's descriptions from his childhood. He often spoke of the gentle flow of the river and its almost passive prominence across rolling fields and farmland. You could tell from his recounting that these memories brought a unique peace to him that we rarely witnessed as kids growing up. The film almost transmitted his memories to us.

And then...... the coup de gras.

It was the video's last segment, and it spanned the bridge crossing over the river Ozycz. Pickauski had deliberately slowed the panoramic filming to highlight every architectural detail of the bridge moving east to west. The film's sharp color transitioned to a grainy black and white, almost seamlessly, while the recording speed slowed, gradually, deliberately. For the briefest of seconds, I suspected an artistic transition until the view passed to a pole capped by a flag with a black swastika offset against a white background. Before my mind's eye could process it, the film had reached the other side of the river, where the scene picked up a crowd of people wearing black, gray, and white clothing, sporting light patches with a Jewish star on their upper arms......

It was footage from the Makow Ghetto. Pickauski spliced the segment onto the film while we were at his house. It was a ten-minute clip, visibly, clearly orchestrated and recorded by the Gestapo. The staging was so clumsy, the sub-text so clear. Wan faces, some perplexed, some aping and smiling, darting in and out of view. Older and younger folks gesticulating with their hands so unnaturally; the occasional improvised pose and an individual, an Orthodox elder, gray beard and payess (side-locks) with an awestruck perplexed look on his face. If you did not know better, you'd say "What the hell is this about?"

But we know better. So much better.

Coming Home (September 1989)

A year and a half later, in the fall of 1989, I had just taken over the ground floor of our family's house to start up my own business. My mother Nina had passed three years earlier and dad was rapidly sinking into debilitating dementia. He lived upstairs at the time, but I moved him up and down to my place since he required near full-time attention.

I remember doing a minor repair in the bathroom of the apartment while listening to "All Things Considered", the expanded news coverage of National Public Radio (NPR) then (and now). It came on at 4 PM and typically began with a long feature piece after a brief summary of the day's news headlines. This day was no different. No different, that is until the leading piece began with "September 1, 1939. The town of Makow Mazowiecki awoke to the sounds of sirens......" I froze, turned up the volume and sat, transfixed... I checked the date. September 1, 1989. Yes, indeed. 50 Years after the formal beginning of World War II. And it was clear. Makow, on the Polish-Prussian border, was one of the first towns invaded by Hitler's ground forces and the Luftwaffe bombings on that fateful day. If I am not mistaken, it was NPR correspondent Noah Adams who hosted that especially long feature piece. My gut reaction was to run upstairs and get Szulim to listen to the broadcast. I brought him down, slowly, making sure that he would not slip accidentally. I sat him down on a chair and moved the radio to within earshot.

Dad smiled, almost blankly, as he gazed. occasionally drifting into a snooze. It was obvious that most of the broadcast went past him. NPR did interviews of older residents of Makow, including, I suspect, some of those same folks who had accompanied our tour barely a year and a half earlier. The production was chilling as the NPR team aired reconstructions of the horrific crimes the Nazis perpetrated on the local Jews in the early days of the war... There was no real reaction on the part of my dad. By that time his cognitive faculties were largely gone.

If you know anything about the pathology of Alzheimer's you're aware that speech and coherent expression go pretty early on. For multi-lingual persons the last language learned is the first forgotten. So, his English was gone. He and I largely communicated in Yiddish and Polish by that time. And I noticed that when the correspondent interviews began in the feature, the first 5-10 seconds of the interview are heard in the local language (Polish). That was when Dad's ears perked up. But it was hopeless after that. Once the piece finished, I got carried away, I suppose, and began to tell him what the significance of the day was, the topic of the piece....... all to the same wan smile and blank stare. I grew sad.

That evening I pulled out the Pickauski VHS tape because.... I guess it just seemed like the right place and time to view it again. Dad was still sitting in his chair, largely silent as the film ran. I deliberately paused the tape at the spot where Pickauski had focused in on an extended view of the mill, the one that dad loved so much. I kept it on hold for a few minutes while he stared intently. And suddenly he pointed at it once and then again, several times in slow succession. And I detected a glint and, unless I am clouded in forgetfulness, I detected a tear in his eye....

What I am sure about is that he viewed that scene intently, implacably, as long as I had it on pause. It's a memory that will stay with me forever.

Regrets, Reflections, Research (1990's-early 2000's)

Szulim passed in '94 and I never went back to Makow again. Nor did I feel any need to do so. But during the traditional period of mourning after dad's death, I felt an impulsive and immediate urge to make sense of his life. And I was drawn back to Makow in a deeper, almost spiritual way. I faulted myself for not having read the original volume after its publication. But my biggest regret was not making a concerted effort to quiz dad about his youth and his background in systematic fashion when he still had his faculties. That rash of impulses and immediacy highlighted the reality…. that a golden opportunity was forever gone. That the living record of Makow, the Holocaust, its aftermath, the D.P. rehab of 7 years, our move to the US, and my most direct ties to the Old Country were now history. That the organic connection was effectively gone. No one, or nearly no one, left to ask……or to provide eyewitness recall.

Yes, isolated images remained. With the exception of the mill, the river and Cywiner's narrative there was little to resuscitate this once thriving place that Szulim had described lovingly, frequently but ultimately in fragmentary fashion. Quite the contrary. The visit placed it all in a negative light. I could not overlay dad's colorful recollections of his childhood years to this run-down place that never (at that time) recovered from the war. If nothing else I needed to gain perspective on dad's early life, and mine more generally, chronological gaps and discontinuities notwithstanding.

From what I understand in discussions with other 2G's my attempts to develop a holistic perspective on my parents' childhood lives and bygone settings was not unique. Not by a long shot. What was this feeling really? The only clarity, I concluded, was a lack of closure, as one generation tries to bridge to its successor a continuity…… of heritage and personality, corresponding to cultural and personal identity respectively. I was haunted by that thought, the year after dad died, when the finality of loss is most impactful.

So, I pointedly asked my 2G contemporaries if and how they experienced similar identity voids. And nearly all did. Were my contemporaries more diligent than me in quizzing their families about their pasts? Was I simply either too lazy or otherwise uncomfortable about going about that gruesome task, forcing parents to dig up horrific memories when they were alive? And then kicking themselves for having let the opportunities slip away?

Not remarkably, I found that most 2G's shared the same doubts about marching down the uncomfortable road of inquiry. We all tried to procure information from parents and relatives with varying degrees of success. The 2G's relative success in extracting oral histories ranged from detailed (few) to fragmentary (most) to non-existent (rare). In dad's case his stories were a series of isolated vignettes that provided the vaguest of glimpses to his past. No thread of continuity. And the reasons are now well documented by historians and psychologists who study these things. The idyllic past was truncated by trauma that produced a disconnect of inestimable pain and permanence. Call them (very unclinically) "post-mortem" recall. Holocaust studies have shown this to be true or, more scientifically, a hypothesis worth testing. Selective recall is the norm. The term "compartmentalization" is part of the explanatory currency amongst Holocaust researchers. You remember the good, shun the bad.

And the range of variability is enormous. My mother was very good at it. For Nina the Warsaw Ghetto, Majdanek, Auschwitz…. that was then. America was now. Move on. For Szulim, Makow, ah Makow, what a place to grow up in…… the rest, you don't need to know. I always thought that there was a simple elegance in their concrete and contrasting assessments. Was there a sub-text to all of this… how could there not be? But these were superficial explanations of a coping mechanism, and it helped them push through life.

But I simply needed to know, to get chronologies and events of the past straight. If nothing else, the Makow trip forced my hand to research it, despite the loss of, yes, the primary sources. For me as a scientist, no amount of detail from secondary accounts was excessive. In the '90's, prior to the Internet, I filled out forms for emerging international survivor networks that facilitated connections to groups focused on genealogies or linking families to long-lost relatives. I networked with my paternal first cousins who were similarly motivated.

In time, I was able to piece together a working timeline from a variety of sources. First and foremost was the DP card, tattered and worn in a drawer along with other relevant documents. Next detailed archives from the Yad Vashem center in Jerusalem. Third, Martin Gilbert's supremely detailed *Atlas of the Holocaust* (published in 1989 and revisions). And perhaps most significant the Internet, whose vast data base expands almost exponentially and on a daily basis, it seems. Kudos to the USHMM for their continued efforts to synthesize these data bases systematically and with algorithms that challenge even computer geek capabilities.

Finally, there were isolated facts that I obtained from the very few family survivors (mainly on the Frenkel side) that outlived dad and whom I interviewed in Israel and in the U.S. They are all gone now.

I had known, even from dad, that our ties to Makow did not really extend further back than the second decade of the 20th century. Szulim was born in Breslau, Germany, formerly Prussia (now Wroclaw, Poland) before the family moved to Makow from Warsaw. The DP records list his date and place of birth on 3 April 1914. However, the chronology and circumstances of the move are as uncertain as they are puzzling. The Schuldenreins were a prominent Warsaw family and owned one of the largest, if not the signature kosher wine and spirits distributorship in Poland and across much of Eastern Europe. The extended family belonged to the Gerer Hasidic sect. In fact, the Schuldenrein family roots trace back to the Peshischa Hasidim that gave rise to the Gerer (through the Gerer Rebbe's lineage). Dad's oldest brother was named Simcha Bunim in honor of the founder of the antecedent Peshischa Rov. You could not have more "Yichus" than that!

Circumstances leading to the move to Makow and related to family developments between the World Wars remain speculative. I inferred that my paternal grandfather left Warsaw to move south because he married into the Frenkel clan. Moreover, the likelihood of his succeeding economically was bolstered by that connection where he opened his business near the aforementioned Rynek. "Yichus" yet again.

I am indebted to the Makow town elder that I met in the Rynek for providing geographic context to our place of business. Paternal grandfather Yitchak Shloime Schuldenrein remained a devout Gerer Hasid, but his wife, Chaya Frenkel was more of a progressive. According to Dad she secretly funded his engineering studies at a time when Dad was ostensibly studying for the Rabbinate at the prominent Lomzhe Yeshiva some 80 km northeast of Makow. Yitchak Shloime had considered Szulim the most capable and appropriate of his four sons to follow in the footsteps of the Gerer Rebbe. This turned out be a notorious miscalculation. Szulim's first love was technology and engineering. I recall that on more than one occasion he claimed to have repaired one of the few privately owned vehicles in Makow. Instead of completing his Talmud studies at Lomzhe Yeshiva, Dad, rebel, and iconoclast that he was, matriculated at the esteemed Warsaw Technical University (then known as Wawelberg). At the same time, probably 1936, his older brother Pinchus, an artistic prodigy, had matriculated at the Warsaw Academy of Fine Arts. I don't know if they lived together or not. Szulim's (and Pinchas') movements between '39 and '43 are shrouded in mystery. It is unclear whether they moved back and forth from Warsaw to Makow during those critical years, when ghettos were constructed, transports to death camps became the norm, and the hell of Jewish life in Poland entered its most destructive phases.

Thereafter there is considerable documentation listing Szulim as having been dispatched to Majdanek Concentration camp on 15 May 1943 from Warsaw, the day the Ghetto was liquidated.

The DP card lists "Majdanek, Scaszycycko, Czestochowa" as his places of interment during those years. When I examined the card, I was stunned. For one thing, I could not, and actually refused to believe the Majdanek connection and the fact that both parents, Szulim and Nina were transported there on the same day. How did I not know this? Maybe they didn't realize this gruesome overlap either. Another fact I cannot confirm!

For the balance of Szulim's odyssey in the later war years, I checked the Martin Gilbert book which chronicles the precise dates of the Majdanek evacuation. The next mention of his whereabouts is in September 1943 when he was transported from Majdanek to the forced labor camp at Sakzysko-Kamienna where fully 90% of inmates perished. The camp was liquidated on 1 August 1944 but by then he had already arrived in Czestochowa (July). Szulim's name appears on the roster of the liberated on the historic day of 16 January 1945, when a one-day battle between the advancing Russians and retreating German resistance marked a turning point in the victorious Allied campaign. 1946 found him in Berlin briefly.

In January 1946 the DP camp at Eschwege opened and temporary refugee resettlement was in full force by March of that year. On May 15, 1946, there was a double wedding. Szulim Schuldenrein and Nina Schiffer as well as his brother Pinchas and Jenia Weinberg were married. Shortly thereafter Pinchas and Jenia immigrated to the U.S. The Schuldenreins remained in Germany for another five years. Dad was a machinist and engineering instructor in the DP rehabilitation program at Eschwege. We stayed on until the closure of Eschwege on April 26, 1949 and I was apparently conceived there, but born in Bad Nauheim on 12 November 1949. We immigrated to NYC subsequently arriving in Ellis Island in April of 1952.

I remain wondering as to what happened to the rest of Schuldenrein and Frenkel clans before, during and after the war. Amongst the (native) born Makower Frenkels, those with foresight and Zionistic aspirations dispersed, mainly to Israel and America, prior to 1939. The remaining majority met their fates in the regional (Warsaw Gubernia) extermination centers at Auschwitz-Birkenau, Treblinka, and Gross Rosen. The only Schuldenreins were my grandparents, relocated from Warsaw. Dad's cousin Fela (Frenkel) mentioned that they died in the bombing of Warsaw, but that remains conjecture. After the war the remaining Frenkel survivors scattered most widely to Israel in the '50's and '60's. For whatever reason, many of Dad's maternal cousins remained in Poland until the post-war purge of 1968, ultimately setting up new lives in Israel.

My fervent hope is that the grandparents avoided the Makow evacuation chaos that is so precisely narrated in the three accounts of the invasion by M-H Ciechanower, M. Rubin, and M Chiechanower. Perhaps they left in one of the truck convoys as described by Chichanover. Alternatively, they may have gotten swept up in the "pack and run" migrations to Warsaw in the first five days of the evacuation.

For the life of me I will never know how, in addition to Szulim and Pinchus, the two remaining brothers made it out. I have a post-card from the oldest brother, Symcha Bunim, stamped Stalingrad and pre-dating the famous siege. He noted that he was bracing for the cruel winter. Youngest brother Yechiel ended up in Israel on the famed illegal Altalena ship in 1948.

Whether or not I will ever find out any more details is anyone's guess, but I suspect that the odds nowadays are reasonably good.

The Book: Organization and Translations (2020-2022)

It's easy to overlook that this book, the Makower Yiskor volume, is more than just a diary of a memorialized people. The Jewish community of Makow evolved over centuries. It experienced cycles of prosperity as well as pain and oppression. In that sense, The Jewish history of Makow was ubiquitous, no different from that of thousands of European towns and villages which can now be considered "Judenrein" (Yiddish and German for "devoid of Jews"). Theologians and ethnographers often emphasize the need to highlight the positive elements of a community's history as a "sustaining legacy", especially when the history's darker side is often cast in the forefront.

In that sense the organization of the Makow volume is balanced. It highlights the broader perspective that must accompany readings of the town's heritage. The historic background that opens the presentations is succeeded by a detailed discussion of pre-Holocaust lifeways, as well as its economic, political, and social organization. It ends with tributes to historic figures and persons whose contributions to both Jewish culture and world progress made a difference. Over a third of the volume's narratives document collective community and individual achievements.

That said, the volume is centered on a past and a history. And it is clear the timeline ends with destruction and devastation. The reality is that more than three quarters of a century has passed so that this little town's present and future…well, these latter phases of the timeline point to finality. They impart little or no meaning for and to our people other than a universal need to remember or to "Never Forget"… The question remains is this yet another cycle or is it an end?

Against this backdrop, there is nothing……absolutely nothing that prepares one for the bracing first-hand accounts of the Shoah, Churban ("decimation" in Hebrew and Yiddish), Holocaust or whatever term one assigns to the Genocide that forms the bulk of the Yizkor text.

In translating the longer, individualized Holocaust accounts, I was struck by the parallels amongst them, pieces that were authored by "shtetlach yidn" (loosely, "Jewish townsfolk"). I refer here to cheder-educated (Orthodox elementary school trained), working class Jews. Their remarkably descriptive prose is unlike any Yiddish texts I had ever read. No resemblance to the prosaic narratives of Sholom Aleichem, Peretz, or Bashevis Singer, the giants of secular Yiddish literature. Just simple, stark, and poignant recounting of the most horrific tragedies that blind-sided the populace of a once typical, oft dominantly Jewish small town in Poland.

The most riveting accounts were of the initial days of the invasion, between September 1 and 5, 1939. Descriptions recount a whirlwind of confusion, chaos, that ultimately manifest as a transformative collective depression. The reality of the occupation began to sink in within hours. It began as the deafening air assaults were accompanied by the non-stop incursions of ground forces, Gestapo police, and wanton devastation of community infra-structures. Within days and weeks, the citizenry experienced a town-wide stupor as the citizens could not digest not only what was happening around them but also the speed at which these changes took place.

That message is initially conveyed in the most shocking of terms by the three main authors, M. Chiekanover, M.H. Chiekanover, and M. Rubin. Each described separate incidents, depending on where the author was at a given point in time. But the theme of shock, panic, terror, and confusion, pervaded throughout. Those first few days totally overturned the prevailing community Zeitgeist. Forever.

In those early days, before the Gestapo established order, chaos reigned, as families packed up and ran away, without plans, running largely, almost aimlessly east and south. It amounted to a human herd mentality. Images of corpses, destroyed buildings and dead horses in the streets. That was the face of mass shock in response to wanton destruction, and it permeated every aspect of human behavior. Yes, there were pockets of hope, organized escape plans, accounts of group prayers in isolated community houses, but by and large…fear, terror, and mass hysteria.

Within weeks the Makow Judenrat (Jewish community Magistrate and Police) was established fully under control of the Gestapo Commandant Herr Steinmetz. By all accounts this man was the most brutal of sadists who took charge of operations and clinically implemented the Nazi process of wearing down the human spirit of Jewish Makow. It began to take hold almost immediately.

Holocaust historians and academicians have since detailed, even diagnosed, the systematic logistics, precision, planning and sequential process of the Gestapo war on mass populations. But nowhere is that message more accurately and soulfully conveyed than in the eyewitness accounts of the Makower "shtetl yiden".

By October 1940 the Makow Ghetto was officially set up. And the Gestapo organizational structure was in full force. Jewish pedestrians were no longer permitted to walk in groups, nor on sidewalks. Men were not allowed to wear beards, had to remove their hats when German officers approached, and women's heads were shaved or shorn to permissible lengths. By that time work camps with daily dispatches of Jewish laborers (scheduled and unscheduled) were routine. In short order, public hangings and isolated mass beatings and shootings in the street were commonplace.

There were incidents of resistance (ie. "The Skap affair") and very occasional escapes from Makow to the hinterlands. All such acts of defiance were punished brutally by public hangings and executions of innocent Jews and possible collaborators. Poles and ethnic Ukrainians were often recruited by the Germans to perform much of the dirty work.

As the war continued systematic transports to concentration camps, replaced the daily dispatches to "labor camps". Ultimately, the death camp transports accelerated in frequency and volume to the point where they almost choked the rail lines. By the early winter of 1942 the Makow Ghetto was liquidated, and the remaining Jews evacuated to the nearby town of Mlawa from which the final transports departed to the larger concentration camps, Auschwitz-Birkenau and Treblinka. Trains ran nearly round the clock. And everyone knew what that meant. The clock was running out. And fast.

The post-transport survivor accounts in the volume are almost uniformly sketchy, lacking in detail, and detached, almost perfunctory. Yes, the recounting of the final stages of survival in Auschwitz-Birkenau up to and including liberation unmistakably convey the despair in the hearts and souls of the inmates. We know now that many of the liberated did not even know what was happening when they were finally freed. They were too numbed to even care.

In the reading of these accounts, it almost feels that the 3 authors, all of whom experienced these events, were drained. I got the impression that each writer, consciously or sub-consciously, was sapped, exhausted, and immune.... That the cumulative effect of a 6 years period of unimaginable suffering and privation left the soul vapid, the tongue mute, the eyes blind. That the survivor authors may have been as functionally compromised now (that is, when writing the final section) as they were then (wandering about in the soon to be liberated camps).

I could not help but ask myself whether they were mentally drained because of the challenge of experiential recall, the act of writing, or both?

As a point of reference, I recalled my mother's response at the close of her interview for USHMM. When the young interviewer posed a final question about her condition at the liberation Nina replied simply "Well that's it for me. I think I have said enough". The interviewer seemed puzzled by the response. Days later I asked mom about the response, and she stared at me, with a wry look "What's the word? 'Dazed' in English?" And that said it all.

Makow Post-script (January, 2023)

November 18, 1942. Modkhe Ciechanower, the author of "Along Blood-Drenched Roads", recalled that day as the one "where it all ended". ...when the last Jew left the Makow Ghetto en route to the train station at nearby Mlawa. Auschwitz-Birkenau or Treblinka were the next and final destinations for all but a few. As I write these words it has been almost exactly 80 years since Makow became "Judenrein". To my knowledge no Jews have returned to revive this once thriving community that gave rise and housed such prominent individuals as Nahum Sokolow, Hyman Rickover, David Azrieli and any number of prominent business, philanthropic and religious leaders of our faith.

As I read these piercing, tragic accounts of Makow's last days I flashed back to that decrepit factory on Centre Street. Visions of the peculiar group of Makower refugees. I recalled especially the ones who pinched me on the cheeks and smiled, joyfully at a little kid whose curiosity and enthusiasm took them out of their labors, their thoughts, their pain, during what must have been a most difficult period of adjustment in the New World. I don't know what became of most of them. But I am sure that some were able to make the adjustments, others not so much. I do know that in my own way I brought some joy to that place. And Szulim was happy about that.

Several months ago, as I was finishing up one of the translations, I paused to watch a showing of Peter Bogdanovitch's signature film "The Last Picture Show" (1971) about Paris, Texas. If you have not seen this film, it is a post-script for a changing America where the old cowboy way of life is in decline. Paris served a rural dying community whose death knell was the closing of the last movie house. The old, grizzled actor Ben Johnson waxed poetic about "being a sucker for the way things used to be and how they had changed so fast." The cinematography is haunting as if to emphasize the passage of time. Howling winds, blowing sagebrush, boarded up windows, dogs barking in the distance. All previewing a dying community and pre-saging a ghost town. It reminded me of my own impressions of Makow the day I visited, some 35 years ago.

My mind hearkened back to my dad's transfixed gaze at the Pukarski film. And I re-read Modkhe Cywiner's closing words when he left Makow forever.

> It was a gray dawn, in December 1939, a backpack drawn across my shoulders. I stand on the hilltop that leads to (the towns of) Ruzhan and Krasnochelz. At that hour my block was exposed in all its solitude; even the tall synagogue seemed somehow diminished, and a distant longing came over me. Far-off visions of my street flash before my eyes, images I've absorbed since birth and up through that very morning when I left home. My last look back made me wonder: would I ever see any and all of this again?

DP card of Szulim Schuldenrein

DP camp at Eschwege. Szulim Schuldenrein circled in red

DP camp in Eschwege. Szulim Schuldenrein circled in red.

Dr. Joseph Schuldenrein

*The original Makow Yiskor Book cover was designed by Pinchas Sharon (Schuldenrein) as seen in libraries across the world. See NYPL edition.

Geopolitical Information

Maków Mazowiecki, Poland is located at 52°52' N 21°06' E and 43 miles N of Warszaw

	Town	District	Province	Country
Before WWI (c. 1900):	Maków	Maków	Łomża	Russian Empire
Between the wars (c. 1930):	Maków	Maków	Warszawa	Poland
After WWII (c. 1950):	Maków Mazowiecki			Poland
Today (c. 2000):	Maków Mazowiecki			Poland

Alternate Names for the Town:

Maków Mazowiecki **[Pol]**, Makov **[Yid]**, Makuv-Mazovyetzki **[Rus]**, Makov Mazovyetsk, Makova, Makovi, Maków nad Orzycem

Nearby Jewish Communities:

Pułtusk 10 miles S
Krasnosielc 12 miles NNE
Różan 13 miles E
Przasnysz 15 miles NW
Goworowo 20 miles E
Ciechanów 20 miles W
Długosiodło 22 miles ESE
Nasielsk 23 miles SSW
Baranowo 23 miles NNE
Wąsewo 24 miles E
Wyszków 24 miles SE
Serock 24 miles S

Ostrołęka 25 miles NE
Nowe Miasto 25 miles SW
Kamieńczyk 26 miles SE
Brańszczyk 26 miles SE
Poręba-Kocęby 27 miles ESE
Czerwin 28 miles ENE
Poręba Średnia 28 miles ESE
Kuchary Żydowskie 29 miles SW
Chorzele 29 miles NNW
Sochocin 29 miles WSW
Kadzidło 30 miles NNE

Jewish Population: 4,448 (in 1897), 3,683 (in 1931)

Map of Poland showing the location of **Maków Mazowiecki**

Table of Contents

Personalities and Images

Memorial Book of the Community of (Maków Mazowiecki, Poland)

52°52' / 21°06'

Translation of
Sefer zikaron le-kehilat Maków-Mazowiecki

Edited by: J. Brat

Published in Tel Aviv, 1969

Acknowledgments

Project Coordinator:

Anita Frishman Gabbay

Our sincere appreciation to Yad Vashem
for the submission of this material for placement on the JewishGen web site
and to Sondra Ettlinger for extracting the pictures from the original book,
enabling their addition to the project.

This is a translation from: *Sefer zikaron le-kehilat Maków-Mazowiecki* (Memorial book of the community of Maków-Mazowiecki),
Editors: J. Bram, Tel Aviv, the former residents of Maków-Mazowiecki in Israel, 1969 (Hebrew, Yiddish, 505 pages).

Note: The original book can be seen online at the NY Public Library site: Makow-Mazowiecki

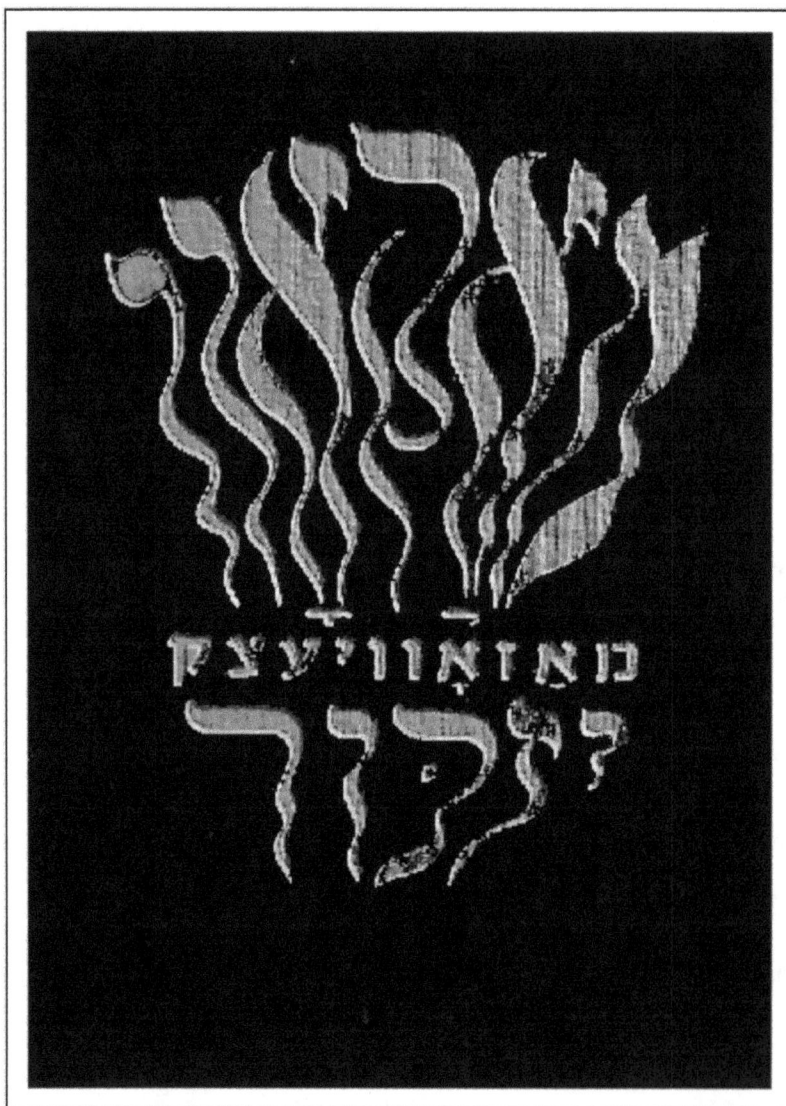

[Page 7]

Introduction

by Yakov M. Skornik (Kibbutz Shoval)

Translated by Naomi Gal

"Let the living remember his dead for
Behold they are here,
Behold their eyes cast around and about.
So let us not rest
May our lives be worthy of their memory".

(Abba Kovner from Yizkor at Yom HaShoah v'Hazikaron–Remembrance Day of the Holocaust)

This Yizkor Book is not written to satisfy a *certain need* of the readers. It is one of hundreds of Yizkor Books of Jewish Communities that were ruined and destroyed by the Nazi beasts and their henchmen.

The book is the first for all of us, for the remainders of our city's citizens in Israel and in other countries around the world; an expression of mourning and grief, for the sorrow and fury of the loss of our parents, brothers, sisters, our relatives and friends, men and women, old and young – who were murdered together with the other six million Jews in strange deaths, despite their innocence.

So that we will know and remember till the end of time what the murderers did to us – the few who miraculously saved themselves from the crematoriums and had written down the horrors, the abuses of body and soul and deadly terror that was their daily life; the horrific and cruel extermination they saw with their own eyes since the day the Germans conquered the city until they were released at the end of the war, broken and depressed. Their testimonies are printed in this book as they were written without beautifying anything.

At first people refused to remember and recall these bloody times whether in writing or orally. Not thinking about it was the only way to transition from madness to normal human lives again. But after many deliberations they recognized the importance of their testimonies so that they would be engraved for eternal memory till the end of time.

When we began reading the Shoah narratives they wrote, we were shocked and were too heartbroken and pained and had to postpone the reading to the next day. But also, on the second and third time some of us broke down crying hysterically while reading – and had to stop.

[Page 8]

I have read and heard a lot about the Shoah, still I had a difficult time sleeping at night while I was reading this terrible chronical of heartbreak. Not just because the horrible sights and nightmares when I witnessed how my mother, sisters, brother and their children perished, I was sleepless also because of my contained rage and impotence confronting the disturbing question: why and wherefore did the Germans inflict such destruction and Holocaust on the Jewish People?!

I am about seventy years old now, and I hereby testify and bear witness for the next generations: everything described in this book about torture, abuse and murderous acts – is the truth and nothing but the truth! It was all written according to the remaining witnesses of Maków.

"Behold their eyes cast around and about. So let us not rest, may our lives be worthy of their memory!"

The history chapters, the memories and the poems about the city's Jews, about their lives, traditions, way of life – were written by our city's citizens, most of them simple people who tell things the way they happened about their perished dearest and nearest, nestling lovingly within the landscape of the town where they were born and raised, and their accounts – like writings on tombs, we are engraving with this book on the unknown graves of our sacred…

so that our sons and grandsons after us would know what the Nazi murderers did to rip us apart, not because we were the worst people ever, but because we were the best and weakest among them.

[Page 9]

Forward

by Yitzhak Brat, Tel Aviv, Adar, 5769

Translated by Anita Frishman Gabbay

With fear and trepidation, I undertook the Holy task – to edit this Yiskor Book.

I was never in Maków Mazowiecki. I didn't know its Jews that lived there, its institutions they established, and the schools and Beis–Midrashim they built over the course of time.

MM was an old, deeply rooted and established community with its unique Jewish lifestyle, with her traditions, with her suffering and her joy… a branch of a larger tree: Polish Jewry.

Then suddenly came the bloody Hitler–era; both the large tree and its branches were cut down and destroyed. Maków shared the same fate as all the Jewish communities in Poland, they were exterminated by the German occupation. Like I said, the Maków community was unfamiliar to me. But when I started to read and review the preserved material, reviewed the witness accounts, MM , each day, became more familiar to me, closer, like I also came from Maków. It seemed to me, I walked alongside the youth of Maków in the "pine–forest", reflected in the waters of the Ozycz, attended their assemblies, marched with the children through the Makover streets on the days of Lag B'Omer celebrations, participated in the Zionist manifestations, flower–day, bazaars. I was in awe of the devoted Jewish members of philanthropic institutions and its members, from magistrates to employees, who worked with devotion for a common goal without seeking personal reward.

I became acquainted with the history of Maków since the 16th century, with her Torah scholars, Rabbis and Gaonim, educated ones, yeshivahs, teachers, tutors, writers and poets. I loitered in the market–square, sat in the "potchekalnye"[station], greeted the children at the kindergarten, cheder, folk–schul, Jewish gymnasia: I watched Jewish merchants, shopkeepers, craftsmen, wagon– drivers, fur–tradesmen, Tzizot–makers[religious undergarment]! I saw the righteous women of the city, who, every Erev Shabbat and Erev Yom–Tov[holiday], distributed challas [bread] for the needy Jews, visited the sick and elderly in hospitals.

[Page 10]

I saw the Jews, bedecked in their finest garments, going to synagogue to pray so the Almighty will wash away their sins, which generally they did not commit.

This is why my hand trembled and my heart ached, when I had to edit [bear witness] the cruel descriptions of the destruction of this community.

Who can endure, who can explain this hellish torment of these victims.

Those that survived the Hitlerite executioners and their killing–machines, who endured long hours of suffering at the hands of the Germans, endless days and nights, in concentration camps, ghettos– the refined Nazi tortures and killing methods of the sadistic beasts. Gruesome pictures began to enfold before my eyes: here they chase a group of Jews, old ones, women and children into the train cars Whoever remains behind, is either beaten or shot. Everywhere– death, death and death…selections, gas chambers, crematoriums–factories of death. The officers and S.S. personnel, with great enthusiasm, carry out Hitler's order for his *valid solution*" to the Jewish Question".

This is all from the first source that was written and described–also about the Makover heroes in the death camps and in other places. These pages will serve as historical evidence –documents to provide witness to the largest mass murder in human history, which the Germans and their henchmen carried out in the years of the second World War. This will be our memorial, not only for us, but for future generations, to REMEMBER, NEVER FORGET! What the German *Amelak* did to the Jewish people.

The organization, *Yotzei Maków*, in Israel and the Makover Landsleit [brothers] in America , on the occasion of the printing of this Yiskor Book, created an everlasting monument to their destroyed community.

This book shall serve as a memorial to the victims of Maków Mazowiecki, who were so brutally cut down, just because they were Jews.

Blessed be their memory!

[Page 11]

The Blood Chronicles

by Yekhezkel Itzcovitch / Tel Aviv

Translated by Janie Respitz

With a trembling hand and a sense of sanctity and respect, we bring to you, dear brothers and sisters this memorial book, the blood chronicles of our tragically exterminated Jewish community.

We the survivors have the obligation to describe for you and future generations the tragic fate of this shocking period when our town was exterminated by the Nazi murderers – a period, when the greatest crimes in human history were perpetrated against the Jews, before the eyes of the whole world.

May this memorial book serve as a dignified monument for the thousands of fathers, mothers, sisters and brothers, sons and daughters who tragically suffered a martyr's death, whose bones and ashes are strewn over deserted fields and forests in Europe.

It was not easy for us to gather and assemble the material for this book. All the Maków historical sources and archives were destroyed with the town. It was through great will and stubbornness that we succeeded in producing this sanctified work. We collected material from various sources. It was with immense effort that we were able to build this monument brick by brick.

We tried as best we could to reflect our town in this book from all sides of light and shadow, beginning with the history of its establishment until its tragic destruction. This book contains descriptions, accounts and memories of the various institutions, political parties, cultural societies, personalities, rabbis, community workers, folk types etc…

A large part of this book is about the period of destruction and heroism. Those from our town who experienced hell and miraculously were saved made a huge and painful effort to relive their horrific memories from extermination camps, ghettos and put it on paper. They also described the uprising in Auschwitz concentration camp in which many Maków Jews took part and died a hero's death.

[Page 12]

Our hearts bleed when we see, through reading, the scenes of those dark days, when thousands of Maków Jewish lives squirmed in fear and suffering, cold and hunger, in the abyss of horrifying death, and the world remained silent;

Our hearts bleed for the murdered children, who had no conception of what was wanted from them and what was going on. They were torn from their mother's arms, from their mother's breasts, and killed.

In this book we can hear the cries of all the Maków martyrs and heroes who were so cruelly exterminated.

Our hearts ace and bleed when we read the history of our annihilated home where we grew up together with our family nests of fathers, mothers, sisters, brothers, children and friends;

Our hearts ache for our dear town, all the Maków holy men, the scholars, the ignorant and common folk, all the heroes of Maków that fell under all kinds of circumstances rising up to the murderers;

Our hearts ache for all the exterminated lives, for all those who died in the worst destruction of our history.

May their memories serve as a blessing!

[Page 13]

The History of the Memorial Book

by Mordkhai Ciechanower

Translated by Janie Respitz

It all began at the memorial on the 3rd of Tevet, 1945. The first survivors arrived with the illegal immigration to the Land of Israel. The wounds in their hearts were still fresh and their bodies were still not totally healed. After the cantor finished singing the memorial prayer, one of the survivors told me in his simple Maków accent, how Maków Jews were exterminated. He spent two hours describing the horrific end, which began with the Nazi occupation until the last days of the Maków martyrs. Those gathered were shocked. Everyone cried: some out loud, others in silence. Everyone felt they were standing in front of the open graves of relatives. That evening, everyone felt in their hearts that we must never forget. Already then peopled made a vow to erect a monument for the unknown graves. It was decided to plant a Martyr's Forest. Others suggested we publish a memorial book.

Years passed and nothing was done about the book.

Due to the initiative of Yad Vashem and diligent workers from the American "Relief", the Organization of Jews from Maków in Israel succeeded in erecting a monument in the Martyr's Forest in Jerusalem. Later two more monuments were erected, one in the Chamber of the Holocaust and the other on Mt. Zion.

This however did not please many of the survivors. They could not rest. They wanted to publish a memorial book. At every opportunity, either at a meeting or memorial evening they brought up the plan of a memorial book. Many of the people from Maków doubted this was possible. They argued that it would be difficult to carry out this plan with the poor amount of Maków strength. Many were passive and did not react at all. They emphasized they if we could find a few "crazy" people to deal with this matter, it may be possible to think about writing a memorial book.

[Page 14]

Finally, a few "crazy" people were found. They argued, such a book must be published. They did not forge the last will of people going to their deaths that we should remember, recount and describe this great destruction, so the future generations could know, remember and take revenge.

There were many difficulties and disruptions on the path to realize the plan to publish the book. We had to overcome everything.

After the War of Independence, Yisroel Frenkel approached me a few times, and others as well, with the suggestion of starting to work on a memorial book. When hearing about the horrible past, Yisroel Frenkel would always say: "why isn't this all recorded? Memoirs must be collected to be the foundation of the memorial book". Yisroel Frenkel said this to everyone whom he met from Maków, especially those who remembered and could tell their story. His ability to persuade helped with the first steps as well the later activity in connection to the publication of this book.

A meeting was called on February 22nd 1964 dedicated solely to this book. Those participating that evening were: Yisroel Frenkel, Yekhezkel Itzcovitch, Natan Shachar, Khaim Vilenberg, Dovid Bukhner, Nisn Zilberberg, Rokhl Makover (Goldvaser), Dvoyre Heller (Goldvaser) and Mordkhai Ciechanower. There were others at that meeting who were skeptical. Thanks to the persuasive power of 3–4 participants the majority decided to publish a book. The following were elected to the book committee at this meeting:

1. Yakov Moishe Skurnik – chairman of the committee.
2. Yekhezkel Itzcovitch – external secretary, concentrating on material.
3. Yisroel Frenkel – vice – chairman.
4. Natan Shachar – treasurer.
5. Mordkhai Ciechanower – secretary.

Each of these 5 members devoted themselves to the work with heart and soul. Besides the functions of each of these members the following was decided at a meeting on March 7th 1964:

A. Yakov Moishe Skrunik would establish contact with the library of the Hebrew University of Jerusalem and other archives to search for material about Jewish life in Maków, and later edit the material.

[Page 15]

B. Natan Shachar will write to the Jewish Historical Institute in Warsaw and request historical material about Maków Jewry.
C. Yekhezkel Itzcovitch had to contact Mr. Tzinovitz (researcher of Jewish life in Poland) and at the same time look for an appropriate editor.

After we began our activity in Israel the Americans also created a book committee. Close contact exited between these two committees. The correspondence from Israel was led by Yekhezkel Itzcovitch and from America, Yakov Khaim Sobol. The committees worked together each informing the other of their activities.

In 1964 a circular was once again sent to everyone from Maków. They were asked to submit descriptions, documents, photographs and other material for the book. We also turned to Maków city hall, to the secretary, for material as well as a map of Maków. Unfortunately we did not receive anything from them.

The first amount of 1000 Israeli ponds was loaned to us from the Maków Society.

Until October 1964, Yekhezkel Itzcovitch met with a few editors. One of them was our present editor Mr. Yitzkhak Brat. After everyone on the book committee met Mr. Brat it was decided he would be our editor. One important condition was that Mr. Brat meet with people form Maków who remember a lot, especially about the holocaust. They will recount, and he will write. At the same time, we reached out to everyone from Maków asking everyone who wanted to tell or send to something to the editor, to send it through the committee. This is how are first descriptions came to be.

Thanks to the written contact made by Natan Shachar to Professor Ber Mark of blessed memory (former director of the Jewish Historical Institute in Warsaw) we received a few very important documents.

The correspondence between our committee and Yakov Khaim Sobol (secretary of the American book committee) was intensive. The warm letters and encouragement our committee received from Yakov Khaim Sobol influenced us greatly in achieving our goal. Yakov Khaim wrote the following in one of his letters: "We are walking with you hand in hand toward the publication of this memorial book, which will remain a monument for generations to come.

[Page 16]

ŻYDOWSKI INSTYTUT HISTORYCZNY

ייִדישער היסטאָרישער אינסטיטוט

WARSZAWA, AL. GEN. ŚWIERCZEWSKIEGO 79

Telefony: 628·30·826·12　　　　　　　　　W-wa. dn. 26. V. 196 4 r.

L.dz.789/64 /64 S.G.

Do

Zarządu Związku Makowiar

ul. Aleksander Janai 23

Tel Aviv

I_s_r_a_e_l

W związku z prośbą Sz.PP. w załączeniu przesyłamy odpisy ·
czterech dokumentów pochodzących z akc "Jointu" /nr 135/ ,
znajdujących się w naszym Archiwum :

    1. Pismo gminy żydowskiej w Makowie do Jointu z 22.III.40

    2. Zaświadczenie burmistrza m.Makowa z 22.IV.1940 r.

    3. Pismo Jointu do gminy żydowskiej w Makowie z 2 maja
                                     1940 r.

    4. Pismo gminy żydowskiej w Makowie do Jointu z 19.XII.
                                       1940 r.

Kierownik Archiwum

/mgr T.Berenstein/

A letter from Professor Berl Mark, in Polish from the Jewish Historical Institute in
Warsaw, dated May 26, 1964

[Page 17]

We would like to help you spiritually, technically and financially in everything you desire".

This is how the American book committee accompanied us from the beginning until the book was published.

A few years ago our friend Hillel Raytchik, one of the most energetic workers on the American committee doubted the realization of our plan. He thought our possibilities were very limited. A while later, when he saw our dreams were being realized he really devoted himself and did everything to help us in every respect.

In 1966 our friends from America, Ida and Avreyml Garfinkel moved to Israel. As active members of the American committee they provided us with an exact account of the activity there. In December 1966 the first descriptions and photos arrived from America. We also began to receive more material from Maków Jews in Israel. We decided to invite Ida and

Avreyml Garfinkel to join our committee. They diligently worked and participated in our committee meetings which took place every Wednesday at the Garfinkel's home.

In time the work broadened. We had to review the material sent to us, improve, rewrite, match appropriate photos with texts trying as hard as possible to leave anything out. Although we had received some names from America, we sat until late at night and did a "walk" through Maków, from street to street, from house to house. Thanks to the intensive work of searching for names, we prepared a maximal list of all the Maków martyrs.

Seeing how the material was growing from day to day, our friend Yakov Moishe Sobol began to work intensively. For a long period of time, he left his kibbutz Shoval and sat in the libraries in Jerusalem and Tal Aviv. He took notes, collected material, and improved his work until we received the interesting historical descriptions of Jewish life in Maków.

I cannot begin to imagine what the book would have looked like, or if it would have been published altogether without the intensive work and devotion of Yekhezkel Itzcovitch. He carried out the correspondence with our friends abroad, maintained regular contact with the editor and was the living spirit of the book committee.

[Page 18]

Having full trust in the American book committee that they would help financially and with collecting material for the memorial book, in December 1967 we were ready to realize our plan. We signed a contract with a publisher and finally regulated matters with our editor. The book committee in Israel committed to submit the material while at the same time guaranteed the sum owed according to the contract. The publisher and editor both committed to carry out the agreed upon terms.

Our committee faced one problem, the drawing of a map of Maków. Luckily, we found an architect who came from Maków. This is: Novomaysky – Shelsky. He took this task upon himself, and with the help of Moishe Katz, Yitzkhak Shlomivitch, Shmuel Taub, Dovid Gromb and others, the map was drawn from memory. Our thanks go out to these friends for this important work.

We would also like to thank our friend Pinchas Shuldenrein* from America who drew the cover page. The flaming letters express the content of this book.

To everyone, who helped bring about this memorial book, some editing material, others registering and sending the names of our martyrs and others with material help and encouragement, a heartfelt thank you!

And lastly, I am obliged in the name of the committee in Israel and America, and also in the name of all Jews who come from Maków, to thank the editor, Mr. Yitzkhak Brat who accompanied us on this journey, from the first day until the day this book was published.

*Pinchas Schuldenrein, later known by the name Paul Sharon, studied in the Warsaw Academy of Arts, (1912–1998). He taught art to the children in the displaced persons' camp in Zeilsheim, where he created his famous works–"Yiskor". He immigrated to the U.S. and he became an independent graphic artist and worked for the Schlesinger Brothers.

[Page 19]

Organization of Former Residents of Maków in Israel

by Yisroel Frankl, Givatayim

Translated by Naomi Gal

In preparation for the publication of the "Yizkor" Book to memorialize the Maków Community I was instructed to give a review on the organization of the "Association of Maków Residents in Israel", about its "birth" and its operation to this day.

Contrary to what is considered among our city residents as the beginning of the organization when the Charity Fund was created – in my opinion, I believe the founding of the Charity Fund in 1951 was only one of the organization's activities, as we will see below; the Fund had existed since 1945.

Unfortunately, I could not find in the archives any data from this early period of time, but as far as my memory goes, the founding of the organization was a subject of discussion among its members as early as the early thirties. The few Aliyah pioneers from our city [Maków] were dispersed all over Israel, sometimes they got together by chance and then the conversation shifted to discussing the need to establish an organization of "Maków Landsleit" [former residents]. There were disagreements and those who were opposed to establishing an organization underlined the point that they needed to *"burn all bridges"* and terminate the *"small minded shtetl"*. This was the belief among those early pioneers who wanted to get established in this country, build a new society and forge a new "type" of Jew.

I was one of those who was for it – *"Let's establish"*. Of course, I could not fathom what was going to happen to the Jewish People but I learned from the few survivors of Maków who arrived in Israel after the war, how deep the need was for a "help society" to address these needs. I remember when the late Berko Hendel arriving in Israel and his difficult absorption, the problem of a melting–pot existed back then as well. The reality in Israel was different from the training and the training–camps of Hashomer–Hatzair (to which he belonged). He debated a lot about the social problems and was delighted to find my home open to him. (He stayed with me for some time). Here he was able to meet people, acquaintances, he learned the country's customs and explored all the possibilities of working in his profession – he was good at drawing. There were other Maków residents who sought out our help. Among them were Yehiel–Meir Plato, Yaakov Haim Goldstein; they sought advise how to put down roots in Israel.

I was hoping for more such applications, and I did not want my response to be an individual one. Some arrived as *"tourists"* and were willing to lose their return ticket, in case they were unable to find their *place* [opportunities for employment] here, they needed encouragement and which they received with the close, welcoming, friendly reception and sometimes also: *"Where we sleep – you will sleep too, we will add a tomato to the salad and there will be enough for all of us..."*

I had felt this "new immigrant" insecurity first hand. Although my brother was already a veteran of nearly two years in Israel, he and other relatives helped me with my first steps of absorption in the new country. I had a deep wish to meet with Maków residents who preceded me in making Aliyah, to talk to them about their experiences, transitioning from life in a village to a more meaningful life towards fulfilling the[Zionist] ideals, at the same time drawing from the *source* [Maków] of our previous lives[in the shtetl]. I felt all this again when I was asked to give my opinion about the need to establish an "Organization of Former Residents of Maków", and despite the fond memories I carry in my heart of these good–deeds, what individuals did for each other, and which I personally enjoyed, for instance: the house of Sara Nesher–Orlik, where I met for the first time our city residents who were members of the Zionist movement, the family – Duba and Itzhak Sheinberg, old veterans of Maków; despite their warm welcome in their home – I knew these were rare and random occurrences. The general need was absolutely justified for the founding of a public address[building] for all the needy could use.

[Page 20]

As said: we were only talking among friends, and it didn't come to fruition. A new reality (and not so new) was taking place in Israel. The Arabs were conducting riots that spread all over Israel. The roads became insecure. Israel entered a period of new events. Similar to the numerous fires [pogroms, etc.] in Maków, that marked different periods of the lives of Jews in our town – so were the bloody events in Israel, the time of the riots of 1936–1939, which lasted until World War II. All the inhabitants were busy after working hours guarding and training and did not think about *"less important issues"*. And if the organization was founded despite this and an address was created for whomever needed it – one should see it as the fulfillment of a vision that its members had in previous years.

A group of pioneers with Moshe Kliner preparing for his Aliyah in 1930

[Page 21]

I mentioned before that there is no official date for the establishment of the organization, but according to receipts that were given to different doners in 1945 you can see that the organization already existed in the beginning of 1945 and maybe even before, we find from that year a list of people who donated 330 Israeli Lira, collected by members Devora Heller–Goldwasser, Epstein–Vilenberg, Sara and David Bochner.

Unfortunately, the committee did not engage in activities like the ones the previous idealists had in mind but were busy with current affairs: things they had to deal with– the extermination that the twentieth century "Haman" descended upon us.

In a letter from Hiam (Leibel) Vilenberg from 9/13/1945 at the end of World War Two, sent from Maków, he lists the names of the survivors he knows: Azrielevitz, Dobres, Goldwasser, Plotke, Students, Rachel Bloom, Raychik (in Estonia) and the late Ingberman (who later died on his way from New York to Israel on board on El–Al airplane over Bulgaria). He expresses his gratitude for the food–packages that were sent to Maków. According to receipts of that year such packages were also sent to refugees of our city living in Russia.

That year's letters began to arrive (not always from Maków residents) asking to get news about the fate of their relatives who were driven away from their villages to the Maków ghetto. These letters, written in a style of heart–wrenching pleas, arrived most of the time to the late Yahushua Makover's address. (Who knows what their effect was on his weak heart…?)

In 1946 the first letter from Etta Segal arrived from New York, in which she describes their hard work, striving to connect survivors with their relatives in America. In that letter Etta asks about our possibilities to help those who are in Poland or Germany and wish to make Aliyah [to Israel]. They were willing to fund–raise money for this purpose, in addition to the 200 dollars they had sent to assist the needy. She goes on to detail the horrific descriptions the first survivor – Yaakov Sheinberg made on them when he arrived in New York. He personally recounted all the sufferings and tortures, that our city residents experienced under the regime of Hitler, may his name be forever erased.

A connection was established between the committee of the organization [Israel] and the "Hilfes–Camitata") (The Help Committee) in New York and in one of the letters Chil Raychik (the secretary of Maków residents in the US) asks about the additional 200 dollars that was sent to the committee which did not get official approval – although they found out the money did reach its destination. He goes on to ask that we send "a request"[visa] for Rabbi Newman to visit Israel and when he arrives to make sure he has a place to stay.

Meanwhile refugees from Maków arrived in Israel, and the committee assisted them. Since they had meagre means the committee asked all Maków people wherever they are to help as much as possible. To our chagrin, only Maków people in New York enlisted to help. They increased the packages: sending food and clothes, sometimes money, keeping the principal "giving in secret". That help from Maków residents in New York was very helpful back then but with time it was not enough for the growing needs.

[Page 22]

That kind of help did not please the people here and although they saw themselves as messengers of Mitzvah, they claimed that it wasn't the adequate way to handle things. They believed that the assistance has to be a constructive help: to assist workmen to buy work tools, to find a livelihood, lodgings etc.... Hence, they thought that creating a special Charity Fund would be the best tool to achieve these goals. The committee people here explained in length this idea to the committee members in the US, detailing the benefits changing the distribution money as gifts not to be returned – to lending money with no interest [rate] and getting it back in small installments.

As a result of this explanation the members in the US increased their support but added a list of the people who needed help, a principal common with Americans but was very much against the concepts of people in Israel.

In January 1950 a letter arrived from Mr. Sobol – a member of the committee in the US. He expressed his gratitude for the detailed letter and for the activities the committee was performing and announced the sum of a thousand dollars they intend to send as a token of appreciation and that would assist with our sacred work.

The news strengthened the spirits of the committee members who had to operate with such dire means, they felt better seeing hope in continuing to work with our friends in the US. But soon enough the tedious exchange of letters resumed. Procrastination increased alongside the disappointment. The impatient members reacted by resigning or by being completely indifferent. How distressed was the committee member Eliezer Shahar (Montshkovsky) when a new immigrant asked him to approve a loan for financing her first steps in Israel – and he had to refuse because the fund's worth, that was around 60 liras, was given to borrowers who could not pay back.

There were members who were not discouraged and saw the procrastination as a mere misunderstanding that would eventually disappear and believed in the good will of the people in America who were performing a Mitzvah.

Meanwhile the committee was busy with activities that did not demand a great deal of money. They were in touch with establishments that wanted to raise a "monument" to commemorate the exterminated communities. They continued to try and clarify the reason that the money promised by Mr. Sobol has not yet arrived, they had faith in the members in America. We saw in this promise the base for establishing the Charity Fund. In the general assembly in 1951 it was decided to establish the fund with the hope that the committee in America would help. It was also decided to continue with the initiative of commemorating the community by publishing a Yizkor Book.

In 1952–1953 they began fund–raising by planting a grove in the name of the sacred Maków people in the Holy–Grove and again an exhausting endeavor began to enlist the members in the US.

[Page 23]

בס״ד, כ״ג אדר שני, תש״ו.

26סטער מערץ, 1946.

ליבע ברידער

אברהם נאהרי'נקל

יצחק גראנ'עמ'ץ,

יעקב ש־מ־בערג

און אלע אונדזערע פארעלי'גענע מאכ־ער ברידער:

א־ער בריה ה־ס דער רש״ה פון די י׳בערגעבלי׳בענע צה״ און פערציק
מאכ־אוער ־דן, ה־ע ט לעבע א־ר ח־ם. ה־אבן מ־ר דער־אלט. מ־ר ה־אבן א־בערגע־
גע־בן דער ־ר'ש־ער ־ערעם די רש־מ־ה 'ס גע־מ צום פארע־פ־נט ־לעכב און ה־וו־ ג־ן
ה־ מ־ר ־ע־לן ה־אבן אל ־ו / ־ערערא′מע רעזולטאטן פון די מש־חות ־ ־על
מ־ר א״ר א־נ ע־א־נ־מ־ר־ל.

שר־גם אונדז נעני אונ ו־ספ־ר־לעך א־ן האסע א־ר נ־ט־חם ז־ך אמ־
ערסטן: ה־ און מ־ס ה־אם מ־ר חעני ל־נדערן א־ערע ג־סערע ל־אנ ב. ג־ס א־בער
א הארעמען און א־ך הארעצ־קן מ־ספ־לעו־ד נ־ום אונדזערע א־מל־׳קל־עכע געבארעפ־ע
ברידער, ־ע ום ז־ ־־ ־או א מ־ספ־ל־ד ־ארץ פון ־ער ל־אנדסמא־שאמ ברוכב ה־גו
ז־, ח־ל און ה־ע מ־א־ה ז־ מ־נה־לם, ז־ם נ־שם ג־פ־אלן׳ מ־םעח ז־ך־ ס־א־ם
א פ־א־קם׳ נ־מם א־ן דעם מ־אקם מ־ס ־־א קי ־לו ק־ראזש און ס־ל־ק־מ־ פ־ר פון אונדזער
ז־ם ה־ען ־על־פ ־ די לעבע־־קע

רי מ־א־ק־א־ער ל־אנדסמא־נש־אמ ה־אם א־גע־ה־אלמ ס־ם א ק־רצער צ־־ מ צ־ר־ק,
א מ־אסט־מ־נ־ע ל־פוב ־די מ־א־עלי־־עני ־ די פ־ר־א־מע־לע ה־אן ־ר־־סנע־ה־־ין א מ־פ־ן
און ה־ארעמען א־־נ־ערע פ־ר א־ך.

מ־ס ע־מל־עכ־ע טע־ן צור־ק רגן מ־ר ־ע־ק־ס גע־־פ־ס א ק־ל־עראגראם צו ד־ 10
־דן א־ן מ־א־קא־ א־נ־פ־ר־עו־נ־ר־יק א־ן אה־ ז־ נ־ס־ק־ן ז־ך אמ־טעמם. מ־ר ה־אבן
ב־אצצ־לם פ־אר־ן ע־ל־פס־ר א־ן פ־אר־א־י־ס א־פ־ער מ־ר ה־אבן נ־אכ־ל־ש־ ג־ה־ר־אנ־ן ק־ן
ע־נ־ס־פ־ר. א־וו־ ז־ ־ מ־ע־ל־ע־ך ס־ר־בם ה־אס ה־אם א־טער. ג־ם אן ג־־מ־ן ה־על־עכע א־ר ג־פ־נ־ס
אוו־ס. א־וו־ ־ס ע־ג־ ל ־ ך ד ד־ערמ־אנ־ס ־ ע־ר־ער, אז ז־ נ־ע־פ־נ־ען ז־ן.

מ־ר ל־נ גנ בי ־ ע־מל־עכע א־נ ר־נ־צ־אנ־א־לע ס־אר־ק,

ז־ם אלע ה־ארצ־ק נ־ענר־ס

מ־ם ו־ארמ־ע ה־ארצ־קע גר־ס

ס־א־ר־א־ינ־קס־ער מ־א־מ־מ־ר מ־א־קא־אוער ר־על־ץ ק־א־מ־ס,

דויך כ.ר.ק

אדרעס פ־אר גר":

Mr. Hilel Raichek

956 - 51st St.,

Brooklyn , N.Y.

*A letter of encouragement from the Maków "Relief" in the United–States
to the remains of Maków people in Germany*

[Page 24]

In 1954 Mr. Chiechanower, an active member in the New York organization visited Israel. We met him and explained the committee member's opinion about the need to change the way of assisting, replacing simple "distributing" with offering loans. Mr. Chiechanower was convinced by our argument and promised that once he will be back in the US he will promote the idea in order to get support among the members of his committee.

In 1955 a letter from New York committee was received, written by Mr. David Hersh Hendel (the son of Yitzhak Avrahamtaches) and Mr. Chiechanower: In their letter they demanded to know who are the members of Israel's committee. They described in the letter the difficulties they encountered concerning the new terms of using the money they intended to send. They expressed their hope to be able to convince the members to agree to the suggested changes and its benefits.

A few days after this letter we again heard from Mr. Chiechanower relating that at Purim the committee met at the home of Yehezkel Mendel Segal, where it was decided to give 700 dollars to be transferred to the Charity Fund – despite the objection of some members who demanded to send instead 70 "*Scripps*" to the needy. He added that he is delaying sending the money because he does not know to whom to send it. Meanwhile, with the holidays approaching, he asks us to contribute to the needy using the money the committee here promised to collect for the fund – these monies in addition to the 700 dollars will be sent once he will find out the names of the approved members. Finally, the 700 dollars were received in the name of Eliezer Shahar and Haim Willenberg and shortly afterwards an additional 300 dollars were received by the member Shraga Cohen, who visited Israel.

This achievement, which was mainly accomplished with the help of Mr. Chiechanower's intervention, and was reported in the general assembly that was held on May 3rd 1955– it was decided to join the central charity for funds in Israel. On December 7th that year an approval was granted by Mr. Cooperman, the county's head, to nominate the organization: "Charity Fund in the name of Maków–Mazowiecki, Tel Aviv".

The members elected to manage the fund were: Eliezer Shahar (Montshkovsky), David Buchner, Haim Willenberg and Sara Epstein–Willenberg. To the general committee elected were the members: Israel Frankl, Mordechai Ciechanower, Sima Vishinski–Perlberg and Katz, Moshe. To the audit committee elected were: Yahushua Katz from Haifa, Ben–Zion Hendel from Rishon–Lezion and S. Galant from Tel Aviv.

At the first meeting of the committee the members discussed mainly the "Yizkor" Book and they agreed that the publishing of the book entails a lot of work so they decided to elect a sub–committee. The elected members were: Mordechai Ciechanower, Sara Epstein–Willenberg, David Buchner and Moshe Katz.

I elaborated about the labor invested in reaching a unanimous policy between us and our American colleagues about supporting the Charity Fund and the way it should function. This is the time to express gratitude to Sara Epstein who labored tirelessly and patiently staying continuously in touch with our Maków townspeople in America as well as with Mr. Chiechanower from the New York organization who lobbied for this idea among the committee members – till the goal was achieved. Also, it should be mentioned that a big effort was made to finish the endeavor of planting trees in the Forest of the Martyrs, its success is due mainly to the Garfinkel family from the US, to Sara Epstein and Yehezkel Itskowitcz from the Israeli organization.

[Page 25]

In the general assembly that took place on the eve of the yearly memorial in 1957, those elected to the committee: Frankl, Itsikovitch, Zilberberg, Shahar, Epstein, Hendel, Buchner, Vishinski, Willenberg, Ciechnower and Katz. Once this committee was elected there was a considerable improvement in the managing of the cashier ledgers. The contact between the committee and the borrowers was Mr. Zilberberg, the secretary was Itskowitcz who was involved in all the committee's activities, besides being the secretary.

That same year we visited the grave of Mr. Berko Hendel in Ein–Shemer Kibbutz, where he fell while fighting.

On December 22nd 1958 we held a yearly memorial for our city's martyrs and later held the general yearly meeting where the following members were elected to the committee: Frankl, Itskowicz, Willenberg, Zilberberg, Hendel (from Rishon–Lezion) and Gromb (from Haifa).

To the Audit Committee elected were: Eliezer Shahar and Levinson (from Rehovot).

We were highly satisfied to read the letter of Mr. Hillel Raichik from the committee of "The Maków Relief" about the successful ball they had in New York with the participation of multitudes from the "Landsmanshaft". They enjoyed meeting each other and the revenue was good.

According to his letter it was due to the detailed report our committee sent from here and thus, they saw themselves united with their city citizens who are in Israel. This was a great satisfaction after being used to read about the many difficulties they encountered due to the public's indifference. Mr. Itskowicz especially saw gratification in nourishing mutual trust between us [Israel] and Maków people in America.

From the money collected at this ball they sent the fund 800 dollars and this helped to increase the fund's activities. We were delighted to hear that the Cohen family (Shraga's parents) are very active, with their son Shraga, in the American Maków Organization – are about to visit Israel. We are already making preparations to make their stay enjoyable.

On May 5th 1959, the day of Holocaust Remembrance we held a general assembly in the Forest of the Martyrs and afterwards we commemorated next to the memorial stone in the Maków Grove (that is listed on "The Forest of the Martyrs of Poland" map number 5, plot 105). This date represents the end of planting the grove and will now remain a memorial forever and ever.

That same year the families Borstein and Maruzky from Australia visited Israel and since the committee was unsuccessful in establishing contacts with Maków people on that continent and as they were very active, especially in the "Bond" Party in Maków – we had high expectations that their visit would create this desired contact. Mainly, we wanted to get material for the book from Mr. Borstein, who is a journalist to this day. Hence, we met with him at the hall of Korsky's Library. They were interested in the organization's activities and in the fund's balance and reprimanded us for not doing enough for Yiddish, but they did promise to stay in touch with us to write articles for the book and to support us with money, but nothing came out of these promises.

[Page 26]

By the end of 1959 the deliberations about the establishing of the organization and the performing of different activities came to end. The administration was functioning smoothly with a considerable capital in the Charity Fund that grew since the sixties, due to the support of the Maków people in the US and the devotion of the committee in New York – the amount available was over twenty thousand liras.

The dream about publishing the book was starting to become a reality, too. Slowly–slowly material for the book arrived, especially from the "War of Hitler"[Holocaust], may his name be erased; the Holocaust's wounds healed slowly, allowing the survivors to tell their very painful memories. With shock they began to read their writings, concentrate, and turn them into reading material. The worry of getting historical material from previous periods evaporated when the Skornik family made Aliyah. We trusted this man's capacity, who was involved with every public affair in Maków, to contribute to this end his views, and he did not disappoint!

As mentioned, the handling of the book passed to the sub–committee especially elected so that the general committee was able to continue their work in matters like loans, help to the needy, meeting with Maków visitors from overseas etc., etc.

Other problems, mainly technical, were not solved to this day. For instance: yearly global contributions of Maków people in Israel for the organization, changing the tenure of the committee members and dealing with Haifa's people suspicions about being discriminated in the organization's activities (by the way: the attempts to include them in the committee failed). With the initiation of the Book's Committee a council was created in Haifa headed by Mr. Moshe Katz and a general meeting was held in "Beitenu" Hall in Haifa. The members from Tel Aviv who participated were: Ciechanower, Garfinkel, Itzkowitz and Frankl. The subject of the "Yizkor Book" was most the important item on the agenda and yielded positive results like: more material [information] about the Maków Ghetto and the role Maków residents played in the rebellions which took place in the extermination camps, also we got, in Haifa, names of unknown Maków residents[survivors] and the city's map.

In that meeting we spoke about general organizational problems and many complaints were voiced, especially old ones, it was decided that the committee will discuss all these issues and together with Haifa's people [former Maków residents] try to find solutions.

Finally, I expressed my hope: the same way we overcame many obstacles in establishing the organization, we shall in the future overcome existing and new problems and so that the organization will continue functioning as a liason for Maków landsleit all over the world and will serve the needs of its people as well as promoting the memory of this glorious community that existed for so many years in Maków.

[Page 27]

<u>HISTORY</u>

[Page 28] Blank

[Page 29]

Makow

by Yacov M. Skornik-Kibbutz Shuval

Translated by Dr. Joseph Schuldenrein and Janie Respitz

A History of a Decimated Community

In the northeast of Mazovia, once Greater-Poland, the town of Makow-Mazowiecki, county seat of Powiat, is set on the banks of the River Orzysz The town is nestled in the dense forests and deep sands of the regional terrain. It was also referred to as "Makow on the Orzysz", surrounded by the neighboring towns of Pultusk, Tchechianov, and Pruznitz (Pshasnish). The villages of Ruzhan and Krasnow-Sielcz were part of the county as well.

The first known mention of Makow is in a Latin document dated to AD 1065 wherein reference is made to a location on the trade-route and communication center along the Orzysz. Makow served as node for the wood trade and general barter center along the steppe country of the River Narew and the main drainage-way of the Vistula which empties into the Baltic Sea.

In 1421, Duke Januscz Mazowiecki granted Makow the status of a self-governing and independent city. Mazowshe remained an independent principality under the sovereignty of the Polish Crown and King Sigmund August until 1527.

While it is not clear when the Jews originally settled in Makow, we can infer from the pure Polish surnames, such as Arendasz, and Drindasz, as well as other long-standing surnames in the town, that these initial settlers were not from the early forced migrations from Germany to Poland because of the persecutions in the 1400's; that reference is to the age of Casimir the Great when the suffix surnames were "stein", berg", "krantz" and so on.

After the unification of Mazovia and Crown Poland, we start to see mentions of Jewish merchants, as well as artisans and craftsmen, especially tailors. A document dated to 1731 notes that the Mayor added an annual tax of 10 zlotys to benefit the city. The tax was levied to (non-Native) "others", amongst them Jews, who were then granted the right to work at designated and approved trades. A case is cited wherein a Jew, by the name of "Yossel" was granted a license from the City Council to build a brewery on Bridge Street. Jews also received permits to trade in salt and Nafta.

[Page 30]

The Community

The first mention of an organized Jewish community dates to the second half of the 16th century when that community started to come together. As far as population growth, trade emergence, citizens' rights and protections are concerned we know next to nothing. The first community records as well as documents from the Jewish Burial society (Chevra Kadisha) were destroyed in a great fire that overtook the town in 1787. There is written documentation that the Church leased out acreage to the Jewish Community at an annual cost of 86 zlotys and 18 groschen (Polish currency) irrespective of land use and product yield. Subsequently the Commissar raised the annual rates (effectively taxes) to 128 zlotys and 15 groschen.

Jewish properties were located along the riverbank, subsequently called "The Green Market". There is a record of a Beis-Midrash that was built there, as well as a Mikvah, and a home for the elderly and infirm. The Jewish cemetery was on the opposite bank of the River. There are no longer any traces of it. The Makow community, along with neighboring communities in Mlawa, Plonsk, Januschitzeh and smaller villages, fell under the regional administrative domain based in Chiechanow until the latter half of the 18th century. Many of the smaller communities were involved in conflicts centered on the tax base that was assessed for the Jewish minority.

[Page 31]

Makow and the "Four Districts"

At the meeting of the "Four Districts Council" in Jaroslav in 1726, reference is made to Makow along with other tax paying communities. "The Jews of Makow", it was noted, were supported with payments on the order of 200 zlotys. However, the basis or reason for this support was not mentioned. History tells us that at the time those communities was greatly impoverished because of the excessive taxes imposed or extorted from the Jews, along with other fees. In addition costly bribes were paid for redemptive purposes based on unjust decrees, bloody pogroms, and classic "blood libels" which the Jews of Poland had long paid, especially the communities from Mazovia.

When the Four District Council met in Jaroslav on September 18, 1753, under the watchful eyes of Government officials, the chief representative of the Chiechanover region, Avrahan Ben-Leizer, proposed that the Jews no longer pay taxes (he represented the towns of Makow, Mlawa, Plonsk, and Janushitze). He argued for disengagement from the Chiechanover community (to which they were formerly belonged) and proposed that the Jews make their decisions internally and levy their own taxes.

Makow is mentioned, again in association with the surrounding communities, at the special meeting of the "Financial Commission" that proposed how to pay off the debts of the "Four Districts Council as well as its smaller district committees. After resigning from the Council, by decree of the Sejm in 1764, the debts of the committees amounted to the huge sum of 3 million zlotys for a population of 550,000 Jews in Crown-Poland (inclusive of children). The largest component of the debt was the governmental tax, with the balance covering the clerics and the magnates in fulfillment of loan and interest charges. The Commission met on March 21, 1767; under pressure from the government and debtors a decision was taken to levy a special per-person tax of 3 zlotys for every Jew. The purpose was to free the Jewish population from future debt obligations.

[Page 32]

Persecutions against Jews in the City

The bloody events in Poland in 1648, known by the fearful name of The Cossack Massacres of 1648- 49, and the later attacks by the Haydamaks on Jewish communities did not reach Mazovie. However, our region was not spared the attacks and excesses perpetrated on the Jews by the city population in the 18th century.[6]

In a document from 1747 it is written that elected members of the Jewish community submitted a "Protestation" to the mayor and municipal government against the attacks and violence of the Poles against the Jews on the roads. The "Protestation" was signed in Yiddish by the following elected members of the Jewish community: Abramovitch, Lepek, Tchekhanovsky and Notkevitch. According to the documents, the mayor promised the Jews protection against the attacks.[7]

The Polish Legions defeated the Swedes under the leadership of the great anti -Semite and monster Stefan Tchernitsky (1755-56). The Legionnaires attacked Jews in the cities, robbing and murdering them. They burned Study Houses and synagogues and destroyed many Jewish communities.[8] The war -storm, with the bloody consequences for Jews did not evade the Jewish community of Makov.

In the book "The History of the Jews in Poland" by Dr. Rafael Mahler, this important writer writes on page 36: "From historic songs in Yiddish one can add to the bloody list more names of those who were tortured and killed at that time as a result of Blood Libels. Among those accounted for one can find the martyr Nakhman ben Nosn from Makov.

Rabbis

According to correspondence from Makov, published in "Hatzfira" in 1900, which is included in this book, our town was known for its renowned great rabbis, Talmudic geniuses. Many of these rabbis have left behind sacred books about Jewish law, biblical interpretation, questions and answers on sacred matters and Kabbalah (Jewish mysticism). The well-known rabbi from Warsaw, Reb Arye Leyb Tzuntz, author of many books, was a rabbi in Makov for some time. In his Book "The Face of Arye" it is written:

[Page 33]

"When we taught question under Talmudic study in the holy city of Makov in the year 5587 (1826-27)."

The rabbis taught Torah to boys from near and far. In those years Makov was renown as a city of Torah and learning. The rabbi, Reb Moishe Zvi Zinger wrote in his book "Chidushei Maharm Zvi", part 2, page 54: "The largest part of my sermon was held in the holy city of Makov on the weekly portion Vayigash (Then he Drew Near) when I was appointed as Rabbi there. Since this was my first sermon there I thought it should be an important interpretation well suited to the importance of a Jewish community which is accustomed to great Jewish minds.

According to the correspondence in "Hatzfira" the first rabbi in town was Reb Avrom Avish of blessed memory. He passed away in the year 5514 (around 1757). Translators' note: the Jewish year 5514 corresponds to 1753-1754.

Reb Dovid Magid

In the year 1774, the rabbi Reb Dovid Magid, the one who decides rabbinical law, founded the Mishna Society where he himself taught every evening between Mincha and Ma'ariv evening prayers and on the Sabbath before Mincha.

The society was popular, existed until recently and had its own quorum on the first floor of the Old House of Study which burned down in 1930. A few events in town were written in the register of the society, including the great fire which broke out in 1787 in which half the town burned down, as well as the Cholera epidemic which raged in 1866-67 and took the lives of many Jews. "In one day" recounts the chronicler, "there were 17 funerals". They also tell about Jews who risked their lives to care for the sick and saved many from death. The Burial Society also deserves praise for helping the sick and burying the dead which was dangerous.

The register of the Mishna Society was either lost or burned in the second (or third) fire in 1898.

Reb Dovid Magid was a well-known personality in the history of the Jews of Poland at that time due to his scholarship, communal activity and most of all his fanatic opposition to the Hasidim and their Rebbes who he fought against in his sermons and writings. His name is mentioned with the greatest respect by the greats of his time to whom he would turn with questions on matters of Jewish law. In the book "Chemdat Shlomo" by Reb Shloime – Zalman, the rabbi in Poznan, we find a response to a question of Reb Dovid Magid's, about a woman who had an affair with a soldier and her husband wanted to remarry without divorcing his first wife.

[Page 34]

In his response the rabbi from Poznan addresses Reb Dovid Magid with the most distinguished and honorific title.

Scholars and historians of the great conflict between Misnagdim and Hasidim refer to Reb Dovid as the classic, fanatic opponent of Hasidism and its Rebbes, as can be found in the book "Zamir Aritizim" which is written in rhyme and other sacred books which have remained in manuscript. Here are a few characteristic quotes from the book "Zamir Aritizim": "The Rebbes are fat and have double chins". "They have become rich and famous from other people's money, they redeem souls, which they take from the misfortunate poor". "The Hasidim are like the Freemasons". In another place in the book we read: "Hasidim worship portraits and idols". "The Hasidic courts are altars for pagan god Baal". "They celebrate with feasts and meals and smoke pipes". "They are occupied with healing the sick and barren". "They pursue you for payment". "They fill their homes with money of distressed poor people", and so on and so forth.

A second book by Reb Dovid Magid called "Shever Poshim", a document of the history of the conflict between Misnagdin and Hasidim, was never published but widely distributed in hand written copies. According to what Reb Dovid said in his first book, the Preacher from Kozhitz sent a messenger to the wealthy Jews of Warsaw to stop them from publishing more anti – Hasidic books.[9]

In the book "Kriya Neamna", the author writes he has obtained a treatise by Reb Dovid Magid called "Zameret in Ha'Aretz". In the library at Oxford there is a manuscript by Reb Dovid Magid called: "Sefer Zot Torah Haknaim".[10]

Reb Dovid Magid passed away in 1815. All of Polish Jewry eulogized him. The preacher from Bialystok, Reb Moishe Zev gave a great eulogy which was later published in his book "Agudat Azov", 1824, fifth sermon, page 88. A tent was placed at his grave in the old cemetery. People came from near and far to visit his grave, especially on the anniversary of his death, to pray and leave notes.

[Page 35]

Tens of years after the passing of Magid conflicts erupted in town between Misnagdim and Hasidim, whose numbers were increasing especially at the time when the rabbi was appointed. These were conflicts that on more than one occasion ended in beatings as well as fights between fathers in law and sons in law that often resulted in divorce for the young couple. In the end the Hasidim were victorious and many descendants of Magid were Ger and Amshinov Hasidim.

After the Partition of Poland

In a span of twenty years Poland was partitioned three times, after wars and internal turmoil between Prussia, Russia and Austria. The political and legal situation of Jews in Poland did not improve in the first years after partition. Despite this, the Jewish population of our city continued to grow. In 1775 the Jewish community received a permanent lease from the church for 5 lots near Prushnitz Street with permission from the government and the bishop as well as a loan of one thousand zlotys at an annual rate of 5 percent. The loan was signed by: Hersh Notkevitch, Gedaliye Gershonovitch and Akiva Nakhmanovitch.[11]

According to a story from 1810 the Jewish community numbered 2,007 comprising 72% of the general population of the city.[12] The community buildings were too old and small for the growing Jewish population. On the leased lots they slowly built a House of Study, a ritual bath with a bath house, and a Talmud Torah, a religious school for poor children. The Jewish community together with its leaders planned to build a large synagogue.

The Synagogue

It is difficult to understand how the Jews of our city dared and how they found the means to build such a large, tall building with thick walls which together with the women's section on both sides took up a practically the entire neighbourhood of what was later called Shul Gas (Synagogue Street); at a time when Jewish communities in Poland were impoverished by edicts, high taxes, war and inner conflicts.

[Page 36]

The synagogues, Houses of Study, Yeshivas, Talmud Torahs as well as other communal institutions which Jews established with their few groschens in Poland and other places in exile, at all times and under all conditions, show the vitality of the Jewish people, with self sacrifice, stubbornness and confidence always making sure the light of the Jews and the Jews themselves would not be extinguished wherever they wandered.

My grandfather, Hershk Katz, who in his old age was the manager of the synagogue, told me, among other things, that Jewish bricklayers volunteered to lay the bricks of these thick walls. Jewish builders and carpenters worked for a long time without pay, laying the many thick boards and beams of the complicated roof in a Byzantium style, which was covered the first time with shingles and then zinc metal.

The artistic oil paintings on the walls and ceiling and the ornaments on the high pillars on the four sides of the bimah which held up the ceiling, were painted by a local artist, a pious very talented Jew. A large bronze candelabra hung from the ceiling. Experts were amazed by the candelabra which was given the synagogue as a gift by Yitzkhak and Khane Goldshtyen from Danzig in 1837. The candelabra hung between the bimah and the Holy Ark, under a drawing on the ceiling of a sky with light bluish clouds on the horizon and a sun, which shone by day and by night. When the candelabra burned, a half moon shone and stars sparkled. The large Holy Ark which could be reached from both sides of the lectern by wide steps, was decorated on both sides with wood carvings of musical instruments painted gold on a white background. The instruments looked like they were made of metal and always sparkled.

Above the Holy Ark were the traditional two lions in their natural colour holding the ten commandments. Above the tablets was a golden crown and up high, an inscription: "Keter Torah" (Crown of the Torah).

The Holy Ark was covered with a curtain made of satin, velvet and plush, in colours to suit the Sabbath and High Holidays, purple, white and blue, with flowers and trees stitched with gold thread, as well as deer, lions and passages from the Torah, by delicate, gentle fingers of modest young brides and God-fearing mothers, who wove their dreams and hopes, sorrows and joy, anxieties and longing into the curtain.

[Page 37]

A celebration in the large synagogue marking the opening of the Jerusalem University, April, 1925

[Page 38]

There were about two dozen Torah scrolls in the Holy Ark, old and new, big and small, with artistic works of the Tree of Life made of wood and ivory, adorned with coats of satin and silk. Silver pointers hung on some of the Torah scrolls to guide the readers, and fringes with engraved names of childless couples, who with their hard-earned savings sponsored the writing of a Torah, to ensure the memory of their names after they die. When the Torah scrolls were ceremoniously brought to the synagogue, under a wedding canopy with music and dancing and with the participation of the entire Jewish community and guests from other towns, the childless husband and wife felt the joy of parents leading their child to the wedding canopy.

On both sides of the large anteroom, under and over the first, second and third stories, were the so- called "little prayer houses". This is where the Psalm Society and Eyn Yakov prayed as well as artisans according to their professions. Each society had a Rebbe who would teach, especially on Saturday afternoons.

The extraordinary, large, beautiful synagogue, one of the few in Poland, was pilfered by the Nazis, may their names be wiped out. They desecrated the Torah scrolls and destroyed it down to the foundation together with the Jewish community. May God avenge their blood.

Makov During the Time of Napoleon and the Uprisings Against Russia

During the years 1806-1809 Napoleon's army conquered the part of Poland from Prussia to Austria and created under its protectorate the Duchy of Poland with Warsaw as its capitol. The Napoleonic constitution proclaimed religious freedom and equal rights for all citizens of Poland, which, concerning the Jews, was never realized. Edicts against the Jews continued. They were forbidden to buy land from the nobility, there were limitations in business, expulsion of the Jewish artisans and lease holders from villages and numerous cities. Other cities forced Jews into ghettos. In accordance with the demands of the Poles in the city, there was a designated area where Jews had to live in Makov. (A law dated January 29th 1813).[13]

In the chronicle from a church in town from 1827 it is written that in the years 1806-07 the French military garrison installed a military bakery in the church, with three baking ovens, taking apart fences, stalls, warehouses and cells for wood to bake bread for the military, with requisitioned grain and flour. There was great hunger and suffering in town. The soldiers emptied and impoverished the town. It took years to restore the situation.[14]

[Page 39]

After the defeat of Napoleon's army outside Moscow, practically the entire Duchy of Poland fell under the rule of the Russia. The constitution of October 27th 1815 which the Russian Tsar gave Poland, in fact legalized the Jew's lack of rights. Therefore, it is understandable, that when Poles rebelled against Russia, the Jews participated, hoping they would receive the same rights as all other citizens of Poland.[15]

In the rebellion of 1863 the were battles in forests and villages around our city. In a confrontation with 156 Cossacks near the village of Karniova, a few rebels from our town fell, among them, a Jew, Ignacy Goldshteyn. He died from his wounds in captivity. The Russian gendarmes and the Cossacks would openly beat up unarmed citizens, for the smallest suspicion that they were helping the rebellion. Many Jews in town and in the surrounding villages were beaten.

This chronicle from a Polish source is characteristic: "The head of a division of rebels in our region that supplied provisions and eliminated spies was a young Jewish woman Carolina Mikhelson, born in Kalisz".

"On a white horse" the source continues to recount, "armed from head to foot, leading the patriots, she raced through fields and forests, from town to town, from village to village, calling on peopled to rebel, speaking and agitating, collecting money, weapons, horses and recruiting." The forest merchant, Reb Feyvl Blum, subsidized the rebels with money and weapons. One of the Blums fought in the ranks of the rebels in the Plotzk region. After the rebellion was repressed, he escaped to France. The former Prime Minister of France, Leon Blum stems from this family".[16]

[Page 40]

Still standing today in town is a three storied large house, once the largest in the city, which belonged to the Blum family. Kahane the watch maker and a relative of the Blums lived there and managed the property.

The Rabbi Reb Efraim – Fishl Salomon of blessed memory

He was appointed rabbi in 1855. Because of his intelligence, kindness and love of the masses he was loved in town, even by non-Jews. He was a renowned scholar and a jurist. In the book "Mincha Chadasha" he is referred to with title: "The light of Torah and vision, the famous, righteous scholar Efraim Fishl from Lithuania, Av Bet Din (Father of the Jewish Court) in Makow.[17] At his initiative, and mainly with his own money, the new House of Study was built in 1857-58 next to the synagogue. The rabbi lived upstairs and would teach young men every day. He was active in organizing the societies of the Jewish community. For 25 years Reb Efraim – Fishl of blessed memory served as head rabbi of Makov and was a devoted leader of the community.

Reb Efraim – Fishl, referred to with love and respect as Reb Fishele, passed away on the 20th of Shevat, 1881. A tent was erected over his grave. On the anniversary of his death, candles were lit in the Houses of Study and people would study Mishna to uplift their souls and go to his grave and recite psalms. His wife Rivka of blessed memory also passed away that same year. Righteous women would refer to her as: Rivkele the Rebbetzin or Rivkele the Righteous.

On a list of people from our town who donated money to help Jews who suffered in pogroms in southern Russia, published in "Hatzfira" in June 1881 you can find the names of Reb Efraim – Fishl and his wife, a widow by that time. They donated 50 kopeks.

The correspondence from Makow was signed by their grandson, later a contributor to "Hatzfira", knowledgeable in many languages and well educated, Eliezer – Dovid Finkel son of Rabbi Mordkhai, may his light shine upon us, who organized this campaign and contributed 2 rubles. Rabbi Mordkhai Nayman of blessed memory, Efraim Fishele's daughter Miriam's son in law, was the Righteous Teacher and jurist in town. He was called: Reb Motele the Judge. He lived above the new House of Study, in his grandfather's apartment.

Reb Motele passed away on the 25th of Kislev, 1914 and was buried beside Reb Efraim – Fishl of blessed memory. Reb Motele's son, named after his grandfather Reb Efraim – Fishl, was the rabbi in the Makow synagogue in New York.

[Page 41]

Nokhem Sokolov

In the second half of the 19th century there was a small group of wealthy Jews who were forest and wheat dealers, leasers of water and wind mills. Reb Yitzkhak – Hersh Segal was a landowner, owner of a water mill in the village Podesh, had a large one-story house in the marketplace where he lived with his wife Dobeh who was called Dobele, and children, sons and daughters. The girls were well educated for those times. They were able to read and write Yiddish, Polish and Russian. Their home was religious, but not fanatic. Yitzkhak – Hersh Segal was a Misnagid, prayed at the new House of Study where they tolerated the two Jews in short jackets, Shatzky, the Russian teacher from the public school for Jewish children and Kahane the watchmaker who would come there to pray every Sabbath.

Wealthy Jews looked for well educated sons-in-law promising them dowries, a few years of room and board and later help with finding a profession to earn a living. This was not easy. Besides being wealthy, Reb Yitzkhak – Hersh Segal claimed good pedigree. He was a descendent of Reb Dovid Magid and was looking for a match for his eldest daughter Rivkele (Rebecca). Nokhem Sokolov's parents who lived in Plotzk were distant relatives of the Segals. Nokhem – Tuvye was a student of the well-known rabbi from Kutne, Reb Yisroel Yehoshua Trunk, known as Reb Yehoshuale Kutner. Already at a young age Nokhem was considered to be a genius. Reb Yitzkhak – Hersh Segal sent his friend, Reb Rafael Hirsh of blessed memory, a scholar, advisor and arbitrator in town, to Nokhem's parents to discuss a match as well as examine Nokhem who was then 14 years old. Reb Rafael Hirsh gave his high approval of the 14-year-old boy, Nokhem – Tuvye, and advised to proceed with the match. Reb Hersh Segal together with his wife Dobele, left immediately for Plotzk for further negotiations with Nokhem's parents about the dowry, room and board and other matters which both sides at that time discussed before closing the deal. With good fortune the prenuptials were drawn up and in 1876. When Nokhem was 17 there was a great wedding celebration in town. The young couple, Rivkele and Nokem lived on the first floor of his in – law's house.

Freed from the burden of having to earn a living, Nokhem Sokolov began to study history, geography, literature, languages and wrote. His mother in law would tell her neighbours: "My son in law sits upstairs all day and night and studies". No one in the house disturbed his studying or writing. His wife Rivkele and his father - in- law recognized his talents and were pleased with his learning, even secular subjects. Nokhem found a few Jews in town to befriend. His closest friend was Reb Avrom – Yosef Rozental, a grandson of Reb Dovid Magid, was an exceptional man with many great qualities: Torah, intellect, good habits and a deep analytical mind. Even though he was much older than Nokhem a strong friendship developed. They understood one another. In an article written after Reb Avrom – Yosef Rozental died, published in "Hatzfira" and later in book form, Nokhem Sokolov wrote: "Like grapes in the desert, I found this this distinguished man, this outstanding knowledgeable man, in the city where I lived for a few years. I was attached to him with heart and soul. It was hard for me part from him when I left that town".

[Page 42]

Another friend from Makow about whom N.Sokolov published grieving words of comfort after his passing was the rabbi Reb Mordkhai Finkel of blessed memory. He was a great Talmudic scholar and an enlightened Jew, charitable and the son of Reb Efraim Fishele of blessed memory.

Nokhem tried to be a business man. Three years after their wedding he travelled to Germany on business. He was no businessman, but his first trip abroad opened the path to his later journeys and important national missions as a leader to various countries and continents. The five years that N. Sokolov lived with his in – laws were, according to him, the best years of his life: "they were good healthy ears of corn for me. I acquired many books and thoroughly learned 8 languages, old and new, besides natural science and history which were my chosen subjects of study. In 1880 Nokhem Sokolov became the chief editor of the daily newspaper "Hatzfira". He quickly became popular and loved by Hebrew readers, especially Yeshiva boys, whose mentality he knew well. With his refined Hebrew which he drew from many sources, old and new, he knew how to talk to the hearts and minds of his Jews. His work as editor of "Hatzfira" led Sokolov down the path of being a writer, diplomat, and world-renowned leader.

[Page 43]

For 48 years Rivka -Rebecca accompanied her important husband on his successful yet difficult life journey. When she died in 1924 in London, Nokhem Sokolov wrote to his friend Dr. Klatzkin: "Since I've been alive I have not felt such profound sadness which torments body and soul as I felt on that bitter day when the wife of my youth was taken from me".

Prof. Chaim Weizmann of blessed memory said in his eulogy: "She was the symbol of a Jewish woman, a devoted wife of an intellectual who understood how to value her husband and help him in his life's work, in times of suffering and times of joy". In his book about Spinoza which was published later, Nokhem Sokolov wrote the following dedication: "In memory of the soul of the wife of my youth and my lifelong friend".[18]

Nokhem Sokolov's death in London in 1936 saddened Jews around the world as well as leading personalities who knew and respected him. The newly established State of Israel brought the remains of the great Nokhem Sokolov and laid him down for eternal rest on Mt. Herzl in Jerusalem.

Fear of Pogroms in our City

The wave of pogroms and slaughter of Jews in southern Russia in 1881 reached Warsaw and threw the Jews of Poland into a state of fear. In a letter published in "Hatzfira" in January 1881 we read: "We have been informed of the following from the city of Makov: After hearing about the excesses in Warsaw, the Jews were afraid that the masses there would also carry out a pogrom. They turned to the honest Christians, enlightened men, to talk to the ignorant, and tell them not to allow secret instigations which would bring tragedy to our city. To our delight, the commander of the fire fighter's society, which had been established a year before, gave a command that all fire fighters, dressed in uniform, with their apprentices and workers, should gather in the theatre. When everyone was gathered, the educated Christian, Dr. Krakh, gave a speech and explained that "the task of the firefighters is not only to fight fires which can leave a town in ashes but also to fight every destructive instrument that could bring tragedy to all".

[Page 44]

With harsh words he explained that the mob in Warsaw committed a sin against God in what they did against the Jews. He told them to assess all the virtues and good traits of the People of Israel. "It is a lie" he said, "what they try to tell you, that every Jew sleeps on a sack of money. They often call me to care for their sick and I see so much poverty and destitution in their homes, it could make your hair stand up. Yet in my life I have never seen such strong love from a hardworking toiling father toward his wife and child as in these poor dwellings".

"The doctor predicated for two hours and one felt his words were achieving their goal. Some of the Christians gathered were moved to tears. After he finished speaking there was applause and our distinguished friend, the lawyer Yezhersky, the teacher Shatzky and a few other Jews went up on the stage and thanked the doctor in the name of the entire Jewish community".

The correspondence ends with the following:

"It is just and worthy that his name be fondly remembered in this newspaper".

Thanks to this the Jews in town only suffered from fear and collected money for victims of pogroms in other cities. In the edition of "Hatzfira" from June 12th 1881 a list of those who donated was published. The campaign was organized by Eliezer Finkel and his friend Nosn Avigdor Rozenberg. In total they collected 29 rubles.

The Rabbi Reb Yehuda – Leyb Groybard [Graubart] of blessed memory

The rabbi Reb Yehuda – Leyb Groybard of blessed memory, a young man of 27 years, captured the town "which was accustomed to great rabbis", with his first sermon, and quickly gained the praise of scholars and simple folk with his knowledge and sharpness. Due to the initiative of Reb Yehuda - Leyb Groybard, a Yeshiva was established in town. The famous Makov Yeshiva under the direction of Reb Notele Khilinovitch [Chilinovitch] from Lomza who was also the head of the Yeshiva. More than 300 students studied in the three classes of the Yeshiva, the majority from out of town. The Yeshiva boys ate a meal every day with another family. Tuesdays and Fridays were market days in town. Most of the business was run by women who were too busy on those days to prepare meals even for their own children. The Yeshiva boys were often hungry on those two days, and had to subsist on black bread and water. However, they accepted it as "This was the way of the Torah: You should eat bread and salt, drink a lot of water and sleep on the ground" etc... This is what Jews learned every summer on the Sabbath in Ethics of our Fathers. It was therefore self – explanatory.

[Page 45]

Cover page of a book by Rabbi Yehuda – Leyb Groybard

The rabbi and the head of the Yeshiva Reb Notele instituted the learning of Gemara with explanations. This meant they learned without the subtle argumentation of fine points know as Pilpul. They did not study Musar (moralizing based on moral introspection) but once a week, at the third Sabbath meal, listened to Reb Notele. Rabbis, scholars, writers and intellectual emerged from this Yeshiva. It existed (most recently under the direction of Reb Shimon Khilinovitch may his light shine upon us) until the First World War.

[Page 46]

The first book "Chavalim B' Neimim" from Rabbi Yehuda – Leyb Groybard's large collection in 5 volumes, was published while he was chief rabbi of Makow.

In 1900 Rabbi Yehuda – Leyb Groybard left our town and was given the great honour of being Rabbi and chief judge of the Jewish court in Stashov, in the Kielce region. From then on, he was known as the "Stashov Rabbi".

Elderly Jews from Makow spoke a lot about the rabbi's accomplishments in the 17 years in was in town and complained to members of the Jewish communal council for allowing such a great rabbi to leave for, according to what they said, a few extra rubles a month.

He passed away in Toronto, Canada on October 6th 1937.

In accordance to his last book "Yevia Omer", written in Yiddish and published in 1936, which dealt with timely topics and with filled with deep thoughts and quotes from Greek philosophers, this can be said about Rabbi Yehuda – Leyb Groybard of blessed memory: "As scholars age, their wisdom increases".

Honour his memory![19]

The Great Fire

In "Hatzfira" from August 9th 1898 we read:

"A very sad announcement arrived to us from Makow, in the Lomza region from Rabbi Mordkhai Finkel.

This week, on Monday, God's hand brought tragedy to our city which burned from a blaze. The fire broke out in three places and the same moment and a storm carried the flames which were ablaze everywhere and could not be extinguished. Sadly, this occurred on a Christian holiday when the entire Christina population went the villages to celebrate, including the firefighters. Only the Jewish inhabitants were in town. The fire became so big, within minutes, streets were transformed into rivers of fire. Our brothers were helpless and people were stunned. They did not save their possessions and barely saved their lives.

[Page 47]

In addition to this they were lacking water. They could not do a thing until firefighters arrived from two nearby villages and slowly began to put out the fire.

Meanwhile a few hundred homes were lost and three thousand families were left bare naked, without bread or a roof.

The firefighters worked all night until morning, extinguishing embers which are still smoking. The appearance of burnt houses, the ruins of collapsed buildings leave a terrible impression when we remember just a few days ago people were sitting comfortably, some wealthy, and overnight they became impoverished, poor people who have to beg for alms from other good people. This old town nourished 300 Yeshiva boys, learning Torah. The benevolent townsfolk are now asking for mercy and pity at this time of trouble and shortages. The catastrophe is enormous. Who can bear it?! A committee was founded to support the victims of the fire. The writer of these lines was also chosen to sit on this committee, to collect donations that were sent for our unfortunate brothers at a time when the rabbi was not in town. The aid is extremely necessary and we must hurry to collect it now as summer is passing and winter is around the corner. We must protect the unfortunate victims of the fire from frost and cold".

It must be said that the houses were built from wood and covered with shingled roofs, one on top of the other. The streets were narrow. Even the smallest fire endangered the whole city.

The year of the fire became a reference date in people's lives. My mother would day to me: "You were born one year before the fire and your sister Shaindl, one year after the fire". Weddings and large and small events in the family were referenced by how many years before or after the fire they took place.

After the fire a law was passed saying that every house built must have a brick wall on the right side of the building, the so-called fire-wall.

Slowly, the Jews began to rebuild the burnt houses. Some built nicer and larger homes than before. Some with their own strength and means and some with the help of the committee, led by our energetic rabbi, Rabbi Yehuda – Lyeb Groybard of blessed memory, and the well -known scholar and philanthropist Reb Mordkhai Finkel of blessed memory. Life in town normalized to the extent that in June 1903, 5 years after the fire, a list was published in "Hatzfira" of 100 families in town who donated lesser and greater sums of money for the victims of the pogrom in Kishinev, one of the bloodiest pogroms not only in Russia, but in the whole world. 76 rubles and 80 kopeks were collected. There were donations of 3 and 2 rubles, and 16 who gave a ruble each. This was a sign that once again there were wealthy Jews in town.

[Page 48]

Industry, Trade and Business

There were no Jewish clerks in the government nor city hall. The town never had large industry. There was a sugar factory owned by a Polish magnate, 9 kilometres from town that operated in the winter months. Jews did not receive work there except one Jewish family, a father and son who specialized in copper. There were two small leather factories built by the Jews Mates Raytchik (Mates the tanner) and Zalmen Orlik (Zalmen the tanner). By the end of the 19th century they were doing handiwork with hard leather and cowhide. Later, they were partially mechanized and hired 80 workers, mainly Poles. There were three buckwheat hand mills, three small undertakings to press oil, which only operated in the winter when the farmers came with their kernels to be pressed into oil. There were two spinning wheels to make ritual fringes (Tsitsis) a factory for soda water and kvass, two rope makers and 2 soap boilers.

The artisans were mainly tailors, more than 50 families were tailors for men and women, manufacturing cheap, poor quality clothes for the village and selling their goods on market days and at fairs in our town and neighbouring cities. The tailors bought their fabric from larger merchants in town who would bring them from Lodz and Warsaw. Later, the wealthier tailors travelled on their own to buy fabric. All the tailors in town were Jews. Some tailors sold old used clothes brought from Germany. They repaired them and sold them to farmers. We would see them wearing dress coats and checkered pants, or three- quarter length coats with long slits, wide lapels with many pockets, big and small and other strange pieces of clothing which were cheap and affordable for poor farmers.

[Page 49]

There were approximately 30 shoemaker families who made boots for farmers. Women's shoes were made by Polish shoemakers and sold on market days and fairs. There were a few shoemaker workshops that only made shoes to order. There were hat makers and furriers who also sold pelts in the winter. The hat makers who were also furriers travelled once a year to Loyvitch to the fair for furs and sometimes bought ready made pelts. They would prepare and sew everything on time for the winter season. Sales took place in the markets on fair days.

There were also Jewish carpenters, tinsmiths, blacksmiths who would make wagons, wheel makers, lathe operators, one locksmith, bricklayers, painters, bakers, butchers, cake and candy makers, saddle makers, a watchmaker and goldsmiths, barbers and shavers, one medic, one dentist, later two dentists, sometimes a Jewish doctor, a midwife and two large mangles for laundry.

In those years people worked in the workshops from early in the morning until late at night. The apprentices, mainly unmarried boys (after their wedding each apprentice would go out on his own and become a master), would eat at his boss's, usually at the machine or work table. Wages were small, the master himself was poor. Due to a lot of competition at the market they could not offer better working conditions (See Peretz: "Once There Was a King"). However, you heard singing, cantorial pieces and later folk songs as you passed the house of a tailor or shoemaker. They worked where they lived.

There were never any vocational schools in town. When a poor Jew wanted his son to become an artisan, he had to send him, at age 13-14 to be apprenticed. This lasted one year, without pay. The apprentice had to sweep the house, bring water, wood, light the oven, hold the child until the woman of the house finished cooking and simply obey. Later, he would be allowed to sew a button on a pair of pants or hammer in a peg. After a few years of suffering he would learn the trade, receive a bit of food and later a bit of money as well. Trades were passed down from fathers to their children. There were artisans who permitted their sons to study and found good matches for them. Some became merchants while other even became ordained rabbis.

There were all kinds of merchants in town. Until the anti – Jewish boycott in 1905, they were all Jewish. There were small merchants who did not have their own shops but sold their goods: fabric, haberdashery, tablecloths and seat covers

[Page 50]

on market days at fairs. Tuesday and Friday were market days and every sixth Wednesday there was a fair (later every Wednesday after the first of the month). After the harvest and before Christian holidays market days and fairs were bigger. There was not enough place in the four cornered market for all the peasant's wagons, because most of the market place was taken up by local merchants and artisans as well as those who came from surrounding towns. Many merchants and tailors set up stalls in advance, covered and hid the walls with thick canvas and laid out their wares to sell.

The streets around the market were filled with peasant's wagons who arrived late and could not find place for their horses and wagons in the marketplace. Police or officials from city hall kept order by placing the wagons and trying to prevent fights that would break out among merchants and artisans arriving from out of town to set up or sell their goods.

Jewish grain dealers walked among the peasant's wagons where there were open bags of rye, wheat, barley, oats and other grains, but mostly rye. They examined the grains, bargained with the farmer, and if he bought something, paid half the money and asked them to bring the gain in the evening to the granary. There they weighed it, did a calculation and paid. There were cases when unknown farmers took money from one and sold the grain to another and ran away. Smaller grain merchants who did not have their own granaries would buy and immediately sell the goods to larger merchants or the owner of the large steam mill, Reb Bezalel Vilenberg, take the money and return to the marketplace. There were Jews who did not even have enough money to buy a small bag of grain. Before the fair they received money from bigger merchants to buy for them.

Beggars and cripples came to the fairs. They sat on sidewalks and sang monotonous church songs accompanied by old hoarse accordions. When people gave them alms they whispered something to them and the beggars mumbled a prayer, crossed themselves and continued to sing and play.

Organ grinders also came to the fairs, bizarre, sun tanned, mainly Jews. They churned out old Russian melodies from the organs which stood on one foot. A parrot would sit on top in a bird cage. They were able to pull out from a box, small white envelopes with cheap rings, earrings, brooches and the like.

[Page 51]

Young peasant girls paid to hear the songs and were excited when the parrot or a mouse withdrew something from the box.

All types of thieves came to the fairs as well. Pickpockets, grain thieves and regular swindlers who fooled naïve peasants and Jews too.

If a market day or fair fell on a Jewish holiday it would not take place. The peasants knew not to come to town when a Jewish holiday fell on a Tuesday or Friday. If a Jewish holiday fell on a Wednesday that was supposed have a fair, it was postponed for a week. The municipal drummer, with a large drum, stood at the corners of the marketplace and on the streets on the two market days before the fair, and Sunday, when the peasants came out of church, banged the drum loudly and shouted out loudly until a lot of people gathered. Then, in a loud voice he would shout that the fair was postponed due to a Jewish holiday.

There were cases when peasants from far away did not know and came with wagons of grain or wood to the market or the fair on a day that was a Jewish holiday. Such a peasant would be confused when he arrived at the market to finds all the shops, except for the non -kosher butcher shops and government alcohol shops locked. It was quiet at the marketplace, you did not see a living soul. He did not understand what was going on. "Is today Tuesday or Wednesday?" he would ask surprised. "What happened to the market and the fair?" Poles and Jews would have fun with the confused peasant. He would either have to sell his products for cheap to the Poles or take them home with him.

There are two episodes from those times I cannot forget. They should be written down for future generations in order to remember the spiritual fortitude of the pious Jews which was not seen among other people.

Short Fridays occur in Poland before the Christian New Year. There were large markets as big as fairs in town of Fridays. On these short days it is light at 8 o'clock in the morning. By the time the peasants arrive at the marketplace and go to the tavern or tea house to have something to eat or drink it is already noon. The stalls fill with peasant men and women buying whatever they need. The tables of the tailors and shoemakers are surrounded by customers from the villages. It is impossible to answer everyone and sell at the same time. And then, at 3 o'clock, three people appear in the marketplace, the rabbinic judge with two other Jews, dressed for the Sabbath and telling Jews to close their shops, pack up their goods and prepare for the Sabbath. The shopkeepers close their doors quickly and send away their village customers who were buying necessities. The market pilots throw the goods into baskets sending them home quickly on small sleighs. Apprentice tailors grab parcels of pants and short jackets on their backs and run home quickly over the trampled snow. After them, the stall owners; the shoemakers left their customers, took the racks and boots which hung on them, and ran home.

[Page 52]

We had a shop for women's fabric and kerchiefs. My mother Perl, may God avenge her blood, was a widow with 5 small children. My father, Yekhiel – Alter of blessed memory left this world at the age of 36. I was the eldest child. I remember on Friday evening when there were few customers remaining in the shop I closed one door and wanted to sell the goods quickly before closing the store. Mother went into the house to prepare the candles for the Sabbath. She soon came to me and said: "For God's sake Yakov -Moishe, what are you doing? Send everyone away and close the shop. I must make the blessing and light the Sabbath candles". Whether I wanted to or not, this is what I had to do. The 10 rubles that I and other merchants could have earned had we worked until night could have been useful, not only for our livelihood but also to be able to pay off the promissory note right after the Sabbath and not have to go to the bank asking them to wait another day without protest. But when it is five minutes before candle lighting the shops must close and the marketplace must be emptied of its merchants. Jews celebrate the Sabbath at all cost.

Wednesday, the eve of Yom Kippur, there was a fair in town. Merchants and artisans from further places did not come this time. They would not make it home on time for the meal before the fast. However, merchants came from towns that were less than three quarters of an hour away, set up their stalls, hung up their wares, clothes and boots. The season: end of summer, after reaping and threshing. The farmers are selling new grain, their wives, young chickens, eggs, cheese and butter. They walk around examining, trying things on and bargaining for a better price. It is noisy in the marketplace. At 3 o'clock in the afternoon, in the midst of this noise, three unfamiliar merchants began to hurriedly pack their goods, clothes and boots into their wagons. Peasants who were haggling earlier looking for cheaper prices now wanted to buy the coats or boots at the previous price. They had already tried things on earlier, they were just hoping to bring down the price. The peasants did not consider the fact that the Jews would suddenly pack up their stuff and leave. How could the Jews not leave in a hurry, its was Erev Yom Kippur. One had to arrive at evening prayers on time. The peasants who watched the Jews pack their wares and leave in such a hurry in the middle of the day were frightened and could not imagine what was happening. They too grabbed their horses and wagons and ran home.

[Page 53]

This is how our fathers and grandfathers conducted themselves, those who the Nazis, may their memories be blotted out, exterminated so brutally in order to build "The Thousand Year Reich" with their blood for the "Higher Aryan Race".

Jew and Peasant

The relationship between Jews and Christians in our region was peaceful and friendly from the time the peasants were liberated in Poland until the rise of the Nazis. Jews went from village to village buying various good from the peasants. Others carried packs of fabric and haberdashery from village to village selling and sometimes buying. Some Jews lived in the larger villages around Makow, in all, just a few families. They had shops there. Others were tenant farmers who bought milk from the nobility and peasants and brought it to town to sell and make cheese and butter. It should be mentioned that pious Jews, due to Jewish dietary laws, did not buy milk butter or cheese from non- Jews, however they did buy from the Jewish tenant farmers who were present at the milking of the cows and made sure it was kosher. Because of this, the milk- Jew was no less useful to the nobleman and peasant than the city Jew. There was in town a special ritual slaughterer for the villages who during the week would ride or walk from village to village where Jews lived and slaughter chickens and the occasional cow for the Sabbath and holidays. On Rosh Hashana and Yom Kippur, the village Jews would come with their families to town. The larger villages which were not far from each other organized their own quorums for prayer and brought a Torah reader from the city for Rosh Hashana who brought home all kinds of good things for his wife and children. In order to come to pray on the Sabbath and walk home, the Jews made a wired border to indicate an area where things can be carried on the Sabbath. This was often made under the supervision of the cantor. Erev Yom Kippur and after the fast they ate at the home of a village Jew where they prayed and remained until after the holiday.

[Page 54]

There were a few families called "Kremers" (shopkeepers), brothers or fathers and sons who went to nearby villages with horse and wagon selling fabric, kerchiefs, underwear and other items. They would leave home on Sunday and return Thursday evening, summer and winter. The slept and ate at peasant homes. The peasant women knew what they could and could not eat; they knew to ask in the morning if they already prayed. They were all pious Jews and often prayed wrapped in prayer shawls and phylacteries in the peasant's home or barn. When these peasants came to town they would stay in the homes of these "Kremers". Until recently it was rare that Jews in the neighbouring villages would be insulted or treated poorly. There was one sad incident from that time. A Jew who travelled from village to village whose name was Robek, went to a village to do business and did not return. The Russian police and gendarmes searched and investigated but until today we do not know where he disappeared. He left orphans and a young wife, an Agunah who could not remarry as she had no proof of death.

Transport

The city was situated 35 kilometres from a train station and in those days, there were few paved roads. The means of transport was a carriage drawn by 2 horses. This is how people travelled to far away cities like Plotzk, and later to Lomza and Warsaw. They would travel with horse and wagon to nearby towns and later with droshkies (horse drawn carriages). All the teamsters were Jews and when they hired Polish coachmen, they spoke Yiddish like the Jews. The pioneers of the transport system from Makow to Warsaw were the Khunovitchs. Khone Khunovitch and later his sons, good honest Jews. Later on, another family joined the line; Notke Kashtan, a typical teamster, a character like Sholem Aleichem's Tevye, always throwing around biblical quotes, not fully understanding them. Two of Khone Khunovitch's grandsons are rabbi today in America. Another teamster, Avrom Vonskolaser, who had a droshky to rent, was apparently a close relative (an uncle) of the owners of the famous film company "Warner Brothers". They came from Pultusk. They were the children of Avrom Vonskolaser's brother who lived in Pultusk.

To travel to Warsaw which was 85 kilometres away, they would ride in stage coaches for16 to 18 hours stopping in every city to allow the horses to graze. In the winter, after the snow fell they would travel in coaches however on sleighs. Besides passengers, these coaches would also transport calves, chicken cages, raw hides and other materials. Magnificent wagons, sometimes pulled by 3 or 4 horses would transport cargo such as: finished leather, flour from the water mills etc.... and they would return from Warsaw with merchandise which Jewish merchants would sell. Later, the teamster would drive buses, pulled by 4 horses to Warsaw. The stage coaches, magnificent wagons and buses were parked in a large yard at 17 Bonifrat Street. There were also wagons from other towns. Chickens and eggs were sold from this same yard by women who came from the province. It was always noisy there early in the morning. The small synagogue was packed with Jews who came to Warsaw to shop but would pray first thing in the morning. This yard also did not lack thieves, the famous Warsaw "pickpockets" who would steal anything they possibly could.

[Page 55]

Shkoles and Heders

"Shkoles" is a Slavic word used in Polish Yiddish for government schools where they taught the language of the land and secular subjects. Religious Jews feared the "Shkoles" and gymnasia (high schools) as students emerged from there as Maskilim (enlightened Jews), who ran away from Judaism and piety, became heretics, if not worse, which was occurring among Jewish youth in Western Europe and central and southern Russia. When Bialik published his poem "On the Threshold of the House of Study" in 1893, pouring out his heart about the devasted Houses of Study, the ark without Torah, boys still sweetly studied in our town at Houses of Study and small Hasidic synagogues.

After the last failed Polish uprising, two Russian elementary schools opened in our city, one for Christian children and the other for Jewish children. It had the same poor program and was closed on Saturdays.

The schools had 4 classes: a preparatory class and first, second and third. The pedagogic level of the schools was low. The school only had two rooms, two classes in each room and only one teacher. The children in the third class had to learn with the lower classes. There was a Jewish teacher who worked in the Jewish school, who, in the early years had to go from house to house asking people to send their children to this school. Religious Jews, as mentioned earlier, were afraid to send their children to the "Shkole", in fear they would be "ruined". Small groups of boys and girls attended the school, only from certain families, they were mainly children who did not want to go to Heder (religious school), or ordinary children who had learning difficulties. It was not suitable for an artisan to send them away. The founders of libraries and leaders of organizations in our city would emerge from this school.

[Page 56]

All Jewish children, poor and rich, learned in "Heder" beginning at the age of four. Those who could not pay tuition sent their children to the Talmud Torah. There were also teachers of young children who taught them Hebrew and how to pray: Khumash (Pentateuch) and Rashi and Gemara (commentary on the Talmud) as well as translations and explanations. The Torah portion of the week was taught in Heder every Friday. They also studied Prophets and Writings. It was rare if a Jew could not correctly read or quote a passage from the Bible or Talmud. From Heder they went on to Yeshiva, the Beys Medresh (House of Study) or learned a trade after becoming a Bar Mitzvah. The Beys Medresh was filled with people studying. One had to arrive early in order to find a place to sit. If not, you had to stand at a lectern and study. We cannot not say that every young man studied Torah for the sake of learning. There were those who knew, if they studied hard they would have a better chance at finding a bride with a rich father in law, a good dowry and many years of room and board. Every Jew strove to find a Talmudic scholar to marry his daughter. In later years, when scholarship lost its former prestige, young girls who were engaged, even educated ones, would brag to their friend: "My bridegroom is an intellectual and a Talmudic scholar".

A class from the Folk – Shul in Makow, 1924

[Page 57]

In our town girls did not go to "Heder". Special Rebbetzins, (Rabbi's wives) would teach the girls to read prayers in Hebrew and read the bible in Yiddish translation. A girl, who was able to pray and write a Yiddish letter with a Russian address was considered in those years to be well educated. Every Jew in town knew how to pray, and the majority could write a Yiddish letter. Not everyone could write the Russian address. Jews were also able to calculate, at least addition, subtraction and multiplication. Hasidic and pious Jews, are depicted as "obscurantists" who are all swindlers, hypocrites and evil, by some Maskilic (enlightened) writers, or ordinary fools and idiots like the Jews in Mendele's "Travels of Benjamin the Third". In any event, not in our town of Makow. And our rabbis were certainly not the ones like in Peretz's "Shtreiml". Under the Shtreimls (fur hats) of Makow's rabbis were clever heads with sharp minds, proficient in worldly matters. The last two rabbis in town, Rabbi Mordkhai – Dov Eydelberg and Rabbi Yitzkhak Zvi Adelberg, may God avenge their deaths, were great Talmudic scholars with some secular education. They knew languages and often lectured students and non – Jews in correct Polish.

Of course, there were pious Jews, zealots, who fought hard for piety and a religious way of life according to the Code of Jewish Law. This was not because of self – interest, influence or honour, but because of their firm belief that this was the only way Jews could live. Where could you find those naïve, honest, Kosher Jews with their honest, modest daughters and sons?

New Times

The Russo – Japanese war of 1904-1905, even though it was thousands of kilometres away, brought prosperity to our town. The peasants in the village sold a lot of their produce. Shoemakers, tailors and other artisans had a lot of work. The two leather factories increased their production and hired 80 workers, Jews and Poles. However, the situation of workers and apprentices did not improve. Working 12-14 hours a day, for example, a leather worker barely earned a living.

[Page 58]

The worker was subject to the mercy of his employer, his boss. The Russian government did not permit workers to organize or strike. The Revolutionary movement at that time in Russia and worker's strikes had reached our town. On one hand, the Polish bourgeois, wearing four cornered national caps, prepared for a resistance against Russia. On the other hand, the workers were preparing to strike in order to improve their economic situation. The first to go on strike were the leather workers, led by the worker Avrom Baumgarten. Soon after the shoemakers and tailors went on strike, organized by Aron Gutman, whose nickname was "Head", Yakov Gerlitz, Leybl Beylis and the private tutor Hershl Katz. Their declared demands were: higher pay, shorter 10-hour work days, and to ensure apprentices should not have to do housework.

The secret and clandestine meetings took place in small groups in the nearby forest. In town there were three Russian policemen to keep order and two gendarmes to supress every national or social movement. When the nationalist rebellion movement and strikes became increased, the gendarmes called upon 10 Cossacks, and together they began to make "order". They arrested the leader of the rebellion, the landowner Podchasky. A combat group broke into the jailhouse, took the arrestee and hid him in the pharmacy. A larger group of Poles, with the firefighters and their orchestra, demonstrated in the marketplace with the national flag. The Cossacks arrived on their horses, shot in the air. There was an uproar in town. The shops closed and everyone ran. Arrests took place. Avrom Baumgarten was also arrested and sent with other Poles to Siberia. He escaped from there to Paris. The National Polish Revolutionary Movement was supressed and the strikes were broken by terror and Cossack's "whips". However, slowly the worker's conditions in town began to improve. The improvements could be seen in small wage increases as well as a shorter work day.

The revolution and strikes of 1905, the Zionist congresses, the spread of political Zionism of Among Jews in Poland and the death of Dr. Theodore Herzl began to impact the students in the Yeshivas and Houses of Study in our town.

[Page 59]

Besides the fact that Makow was known as a town of Hasidim and pious Jews, there was always a small number of Maskilim (Enlightened Jews), open and hidden. Maskilim like Reb Yosef Rozental, born in 1811, Nokhem [Nahum] Sokolov, an older member, Reb Mordkhai Finkel, born in 1833, whose well – written correspondence from town were published in "Hatzfira" in the 1880s. Sokolov dedicated articles to both in "Hatzfira" after they died. There were other older Maskilim for whom enlightenment and religion, a page of Talmud and an article in "Ha Shachar" about improvement of religion could live peacefully together. Cases of Jewish boys who ran away from the House of Study, their parent's homes, became heretics, activist atheists and assimilationists almost never happened here until the revolution of 1905. At the end of the 19th century there was a case when a Jewish girl from a prestigious wealthy family allowed herself to be persuaded by a young Christian man, an activist. She ran away with him, converted to Christianly and got married in a church. This was considered a tragedy not only by her family who did everything to try and save her, but by the entire Jewish population who mourned her and recounted this episode with pain and shame for many years.

The attack on religious Jewish life of Jewish youth and students in town came from two directions simultaneously: The Worker's Movement and the National Movement. After the successful strikes, terror and arrests, a secret Worker's Party was founded called the "Bund". It was founded in Vilna in 1897 and quickly became popular among Jewish workers in Russia and Poland.

The founders were Yakov Gerlitz (who lives in the United States today), Leybl Beylis (moved to London), and the private tutor Hershl Katz. At the same time a group of young people tried to obtain permission from the Russian authorities to open a library called "Lovers of Reading". Since they did not receive permission the library was opened secretly and was situated in the private home of Marcus Vilenberg who also ran the library with Yekhiel Meir Pliato and Soreh Segal.

There were a few Zionists, Lovers of Zion and shekel purchasers in town earlier. In 1910 a youth organization was founded called "Tzeirei Tzion" ("Young Zionists"). The founders were: Yekhezkl Joloshinsky, his sister Feygele, Yosef Titonovitch, Moishe Bzhoza and his sister Esther, Shloymeh Abludziner, Esther Mokover (today in Israel), Yekhezkl – Mendl Degal, Yosef Hendel, Meir Ostri, Yuta Rekhtman, Shimon Rozental and others. Shimon Rozental was elected president and the secretary was Moishe Bzhoza, a son from a wealthy family who graduated from the Russian school, knew Hebrew and Yiddish and until his departure in 1917 was the leader and living spirit of the Zionist movement in town. We lived in his parent's house. I studied at the Yeshiva. One day he took me up to the attic and showed me, in a corner, behind a small wall, on a table, Herzl's picture, a blue and white box from the Jewish National Fund (Keren Kayemet), a few Zionist brochures and a pamphlet stating the protocols of the activities of the "Young Zionists". He warned me not to tell anyone what I saw. The boys at the House of Study began secretly to read books, learn Russian and became members of the "Young Zionists" and the "Bund". On these grounds, conflicts developed between fathers and children. Young men left for bigger cities, and some to America. Ben – Tzion Khilinovitch, the son of the head of the Yeshiva, Reb Noteleh, who was preparing to become a rabbi, left the Yeshiva and his home and went to Bialystok. There he studied secular subjects and later became a contributor to the Warsaw daily newspaper "Moment" and other newspapers in Poland.

[Page 60]

The Houses of Study slowly emptied of students. A few boys remained in the small Hasidic synagogues of Ger, Amshinov and Alexander.

Great disagreements broke out between parents and children when the youth began to organize a literary – musical evenings under the leadership of Yekhiel – Meir Pliato who had a beautiful tenor voice and could sing. The parents of the children who participated in this event were called to the rabbi, Rabbi Yisroel – Nisn Kupershtokh, who according to his behaviour was more of a Hasidic Rebbe than a rabbi. The parents were warned not to allow their children to participate in this evening. Despite everything, the evening took place in the private home of Hershl Feldsher. The hall was too small for everyone who came to get in. The street was filled with youth as well as older people who were able to listen to the choir sing through the open window on the first floor. They performed Sholem Aleichem's one act play "Only a Doctor". For a long time after, the youth in town sang the songs sung by the choir that evening; "Feel Brothers Feel", "May is Here Again". "The Sun Sets in Flames", "Great God, We Are Singing Songs".

[Page 61]

Reforms in the Heder

Neither the intercession by the religious teachers nor bribing Gromnim, the highest police official in town helped him not to force the teachers to carry out their "edicts" to teach the children in a separate room. The children were not permitted to sit around a table, rather they had to sit at special long, narrow tables with attached benches which were called "planks". These "planks" were placed either one behind the other or in the shape of a horseshoe. The children had to study Russian and arithmetic two hours every day in the state-run elementary school.

At this time the teacher in the Russian elementary school was Khaykl Gutman. A nice Jewish man from Lithuania, a religious man who would pray every Sabbath in the new House of Study. Most fathers were already pleased their children were going to "Shkole", Russian school as it was time for them to learn a bit of Russian and arithmetic. But why should they sit with bare heads? Jewish children must keep their heads covered.

A delegation went to Khaykl the teacher to try to prevail upon him to allow his pupils to wear caps. Khaykl the teacher showed them a picture of the Czar and the Russian flag that were in the school. He explained, that according to the law, one must remove his hat when entering a place which has a picture of the Czar and a Russian flag. He offered this advice: they should bring a certified Jewish teacher to teach Russian to the children in Heder. Then they would not have to go to the "Shkole" and obey the law of removing hats. Religious Jewish fathers accepted this advice. They brought a religious teacher who wore a Jewish cap, had a beard and sidelocks and wore a long black caftan. His name was Grossman. He would spend his day going from one Heder to another giving lessons, smoking cigars and telling stories in Yiddish, no less, mainly to the Rebbe. And us kids eavesdropped. When the school inspector came from Lomza to inspect the government school and the Heders, Gromnim, the police chief, informed the teachers early that morning. There was a panic. Grossman the teacher began to speak very quickly: "We must remove the cobwebs from the corners; clean the room, wash the floor, we must…we must…", and he ran off. When the inspector finally arrived with the teacher and Gromnim the policeman, all the boys removed their caps. Even the Rebbe who wore his skullcap stood until the inspector told him to be seated.

[Page 62]

After examining the pupils in Russian and arithmetic the inspector turned to the Grossman and began to speak loudly and in anger. The teacher turned pale and shook with fear. We did not understand what the inspector said to our teacher nor did we understand what he shouted to the Rebbe who was totally confused. The next morning the Rebbe asked Grossman why the inspector was so angry with him. It turns out he was angry that he walls and floor had not been whitewashed for a long time. A few days after the inspection, Grossman told the Rebbe a few stories about inspections in other Heders and the inspector asked forgiveness for his anger.

During the time of Khaykl Gutman, parents wanted their children to study at the government school, especially girls. However, there was only enough place for one child per family. Khaykl's wife, who knew languages opened evening classes in the school where anyone could learn for 1 ruble a month, Yiddish, Russian, Polish and also German. May Jewish children in our town, thanks to this intelligent woman learned to read and write Yiddish, Russian and Polish. There was also a private tutor, Dovid Refalkes, whose surname was Rozental, taught Jewish children to write letters from a sample book and how to write their address in Russian. Before the First World War all Jewish children could read and write Yiddish and many also knew Hebrew, Polish and Russian.

Berish Viseberg of blessed memory, arrived in town. He was the son in law of Rabbi of Prushnitz. He was a learned man and was an ordained rabbi. He was enlightened, knew bible and grammar. His son Yisakhar lives with his family today in Natanya. (Yisakhar Viseberg's son died fighting in the Six Day War). Berish Viseberg opened a printing shop in Makow. He also gave Hebrew lessons. Many young people learned the fundamentals of Hebrew from him and were able to read Hebrew literature and newspapers. Thanks to Berish Viseberg, the youth in town, myself included, began to learn Hebrew language and grammar. He was killed during the holocaust together with his entire family. May their blood be avenged.

Memorial Evenings

On the 20th of Tamuz 1911, in a lone house among the thick pine trees where people would come spend summer, the first illegal memorial evening for Herzl took place.

[Page 63]

Around thirty people participated. My neighbour, the leader of the illegal "Young Zionists", Moishe Bzhoza, took me to the evening which left a great impression on me. In a large dark room with closed shutters there was a table with a picture of Dr. Theodore Herzl, veiled in black crepe. Two black eyes peered out of a pale face, framed with dark eyebrows and a rabbinical beard. Two candlesticks with white lit candles were tied together with black ribbon. Under the candlesticks there was a sign with large letters which read: "If you will it, it is not a dream". People did not speak to one another. When Yekhiel – Meir Pliato, quietly, in his soft tenor voice began to sing the mourner's prayer, everyone had tears in their eyes.

Moishe Bzhoza and Yosef Titonovitch spoke about Dr. Herzl. Titonovitch was an educated young man and a good speaker. (He died of Tuberculosis in 1914. In the edition of "Hatzfira" dated February 10th 1914 an obituary was published, signed by "Young Zionists" from Makow, and they planted a tree in The Herzl Forest in his memory).

Boycott of the Jews

As a result of the revolution, Russia received a parliament from the Czar in 1906, called the Duma in Russian, which brought trouble and tragedy for the Jews including mass pogroms in many towns. In Poland, the dominating party was a national chauvinistic party of the nobility, city bourgeois and petty bourgeois called "Naradova Demokratia" (Naitonal Democrats), in short: "Endeks". Their representative at the Duma, Domovsky a fanatical anti – Semite and Jew hater joined the Russian Reactionary Party promoting edicts against the Jews. In Warsaw, in the years 1909 – 1910, with the help of Jewish votes, a Polish Social Democrat Jagello was elected to the Duma, against the will of the "Endeks" who demanded Jews vote for their candidate Kukhozhevsky, a well-known anti – Semite. As revenge, they proclaimed a boycott against the Jews. The Polish newspapers which always encouraged anti– Jewish agitation told the Poles not to buy from Jews. There were signs in public places and in newspapers which read "Buy from Your Own". As mentioned, the Polish population in our region lived well with Jews. There were few Polish shops in our town. A peasant knew he had to buy from Jews as well as sell to Jews.

The "Endeks" in our town opened a cooperative for food articles, encouraged and helped by loans from Poles so they could open shops in town and in the villages, deliver propaganda with the help of the church and stop people from buying from Jews. Jewish merchants were anxious. This boycott did not feel good. Slowly, the peasants began to buy from Jews again, where they did not have to stand in line and felt freer and more at home than at the large stores of the cooperative. Due to the boycott and increased anti -Semitism, many Jewish merchants and artisans lost their livelihood and had to wander off to America, where there were already Jews from Makow. They sent dollars to their families in the old home and wrote that in America you really have to work hard, but you can earn a living and they don't bother Jews. About ten years earlier, Jews who needed dowries for their daughters went to America. They would spend a year and return with a few hundred dollars and marry off their daughters. They remaining money was soon "eaten up" and he would return the "Golden Land". A few men went back and forth but some took their families to America. There were many women in town called "Amerikankes" who remained with their children and for years would receive money from across the ocean to live, until they were reunited.

[Page 64]

Mendl Beylis

The arrest of Mendl Beylis in Kiev in 1911 and the accusation that he murdered a Christian boy Yutchinsky for ritual purposes scared the Jews. The anti – Semites in town as in the rest of Poland used this shameful blood libel in their plots against the Jews. Even after Beylis' release in 1913, Poles in town, particularly the youth would still cry out "Jews are all like Beylis", often accompanied by rock throwing. After the priest Matzoch was sentenced to many years in jail for murder and for stealing the diamond eyes from the statue of Mary, the mother of God in the city of Tchenstochov, Jewish adults and children responded to the Poles who shouted "Jews are all like Beylis" with: "Matzokh is languishing and Beylis lives".

[Page 65]

The War of 1914

Our town is situated 40 kilometres from the border of eastern Germany. When the war broke out between Russia and Germany Jews came to our town from the border towns Khorzhel and Yanov, chased out by the military power. Among them were families whose main bread winners had been mobilized in the war. These Jews, who were now called "homeless" settled into the Houses of Study, women's synagogues, small synagogues and cellars in private homes, 4-5 families per dwelling. A committee was established to help the poor homeless. Due to a lack of means the committee could barely help the large amount of needy. We began to feel the war in our town. Masses of military from all formations marched and rode through toward the front. The soldiers, with small exceptions, behaved nicely and asked if it was still far to Berlin. Often, soldiers would sleep in private homes. The commandant mobilized men, Jews and Poles to guard the telegraph poles at night which were 7 kilometres from town. The Russian army entered eastern Germany, captured German cities and prepared to march on Berlin. After a strong counter offensive from the German military, the Russian front was surrounded and broken. A portion of the Russian army was taken prisoner and the rest ran back, in disarray. The retreating soldiers robbed Jewish shops and homes, insulted and beat up Jews and accused them of spying for Germany. Two Jews, Furmansky and Orlik were shot by Cossacks and robbed when they were travelling by horse and wagon to the village to sell their goods. The horrible double murder and the dramatic funeral, accompanied by lamenting and crying by the entire Jewish population, cast a feeling of dread, sadness and despair on the Jews who suddenly saw their lives were turned upside down. Large numbers of refugees arrived from the neighbouring town of Prushnitz and told us that the Germans bombed their town which had passed a few times from hand to hand and then was completely destroyed. Hundreds of wounded Russian soldiers, brought by wagon from the front, lay on sacks of straw beside the sidewalks of the marketplace and streets. Jewish women brought them food and drink. Jewish boys and girls walked around with tea pots, bread and fruit, giving to anyone who could eat or drink. Tens of soldiers died without receiving any medical help. They lay there for a few days until they were taken away. A typhus epidemic broke out. Mortality was high. Nine well respected men from town received an order from the military authority saying they must, in order to keep safe, leave town and go to Vitebsk in White Russia.

[Page 66]

Help from Jews in Russia

In June 1915 representatives from the "Moscow Jewish Community", Mr. Shteynberg and his wife, came to our town to organize help for the homeless. They sent 600 men who could work to Homel where a division of the "Moscow Committee" organized work for them. Families which lived in crowded and poor sanitary conditions received larger and better temporary apartments, rebuilt from various buildings. A special women's committee helped them to get organized, visited and gave whatever help possible. A store was opened where 300 registered poor families received food for free. Mrs. Shteynberg set up a dormitory for the children of the homeless. There they received a proper education from a female teacher as well as meals. A committee comprised of women and girls helped the teacher to wash and comb the children and take them on walks. The youth organized to help the homeless and ease their situation. Mr. Shteynberg rented a house which stood in the middle of the forest and set up an isolated place for typhus patients under the supervision of a doctor and a nurse.[20]

The Russians Leave Town

The front was nearing. One could hear the thunder of canons day and night. At night the sky was red from fires. The government institutions, city hall and command centre left town. A civil militia with Jews and Poles was created to keep order. Intelligence patrols in small groups, cavalry, mainly Cossacks, visited our town often terrorizing the Jewish population. A few bombs from German airplanes fell on our town. During the difficult days of war, on the 20th of Tamuz, the Young Zionist Organization organized a memorial evening for Dr. Theodore Herzl in the home of Mendl Dzhershgovsky. This was done secretly at great risk. In the large reception hall, without Herzl's picture or candles, those gathered sat and listened to Yekhiel Meir Pliato sing the memorial prayer. Moishe Bzhoza gave a short speech and quoted from Herzl's "Alt -Neu Land". The streets were filled with military and military wagons. Quietly, one by one, the members gathered and quietly, one by one they snuck home around 10 o'clock at night.

[Page 67]

In the month of Av, 1915 battles ensued in town. Jews hid in their cellars. One Russian soldier entered the home of Leybish Rebak and grabbed his watch. As he ran out he was hit by a piece of shrapnel and died on the spot.

The Russians retreated, setting the wooden bridge on fire as well as the eastern section of town near the river and a portion of the marketplace. The Germans entered that evening. The Jews wished each other "Mazel Tov" as they were now rid of the Cossacks and the fear of death. It appeared, that from the shooting and bombing, one woman, Rivka Freshberg was killed, and a few Jews, lightly wounded. Firefighters, with help from the youth, began to extinguish the fires. Some were slightly wounded on their feet from bullets of the retreating Russians. The entire residential area near the river was burned. They tried to prevent the fire from spreading throughout the town.

In the war year of 1914- 1915, during the terror and fear of death, Jewish merchants and artisans, street sellers of baked goods, lemonade and fruit, did good business. The masses of marching soldiers bought everything. There were some who grabbed food and ran away. Contractors sold everything they received from the army in town. Russian officers bought the best fabrics, underwear, kerchiefs, perfumes, chocolate and delicacies to send home or to give as gifts to girls who were with them. Soldiers who served behind the front bought boots, cigarettes, haberdashery and food. After the Germans captured our city store owners were left with little merchandise and with many thousands of rubles and Russian bonds. Jews who were sure "the Russians would not go bankrupt" held on to their thousands of paper rubles and bonds until they lost all their value.

Under German Occupation (During the First World War)

Jews in town felt freer and more secure under German occupation than under Russian rule. The Yiddish language made it easier to understand the Germans. For the first time on Polish soil, Jewish clerks could get jobs in the district, city hall and other government and municipal institutions. Larger schools were opened with Polish and German as the language of instruction, one for Polish children and the other for Jewish children where Jewish teachers taught every day except Saturday. With the permission of the authorities a cultural society was create under the former illegal name "Lovers of Reading". The society which previously had its own library, rented a locale with a theatre hall which had been the Polish "Lutnia" society that stopped its activity when the Germans arrived. The "Lovers of Reading", later called "Community Centre" concentrated on cultural activities for the youth in town disregarding party affiliations. At the time there was not yet a cinema or radio. Every evening the hall was filled with people, especially Friday nights, when they organized the so-called "Box Evenings" and literary trials, or simply readings. From time to time the drama club would perform one act plays, monologues or dramas, such as "The Jewish King Lear" by Gordon. Literary figures came from Warsaw, writers and party leaders, to give talks and lectures. They also organized a Purim party with dancing.

[Page 68]

In time, political groups and organizations were organized which later formed the Jewish political – social life in Poland, like the Zionist organization, the orthodox "Shlomi Emunei Yisroel", "The Bund", "Mizrachi", "Poalei Zion", "Young Mizrachi", a Zionist youth organization "Prachei Zion" (Flowers of Zion) etc.…

Lag Ba'Omer celebrations of "Pirchei Zion", Makow, 1918

[Page 69]

A Visit by Hillel Zeitlin – May God Avenge his Death

In May 1916 we received the sad news of the death of Sholem Aleichem in New York. Sholem Aleichem was very popular among Yiddish readers, young and old. It was decided to organize a memorial evening with the participation of well – known writers. At that time, Reb Hillel Zeitlin was the most famous writer and journalist. The daily newspaper "Der Moment", in which Hillel Zeitlin was a contributor, was the most widely read newspaper in town, due to its polemics and other articles. For this reason, Hillel Zeitlin was invited to our memorial evening as the speaker. A reception committee was elected and they decided our important guest would stay at the house of the wealthy man Reb Velvl Bzhoza. Hillel Zeitlin left Warsaw on the Nadvishlansk train and disembarked at the small train station in Poshetzky, 35 kilometres from town. A coach pulled by two horses waited there with a few committee members to bring our guest to town. A delegation went to the edge of town to welcome him. The girls carried flowers and with pounding hearts awaited the arrival of Hillel Zeitlin. Finally, the coach arrived. The teamster stopped the sweaty panting horses. When Hillel Zeitlin and his companions came out of the coach, one of them introduced the welcome committee. The girls gave him the flowers. Hillel Zeitlin, with his long beard, soft eyes,

Hillel Zeitlin's visit to Makow in 1918

[Page 70]

fedora and three – quarter overcoat made an impression not as a writer like Peretz and Sholem Aleichem, but as a Rebbe. This was also the respect shown to him by the youth who received him and treated him like he was their Rebbe and they were his Hasidim. This was the first time many of the youth in town came face to face with a writer. As his coach rode through the streets and marketplace they were filled with people, as was the courtyard of the home where he was staying.

Other writers and journalists who visited our town were: Yosef Heftman, Yisroel Shtern, Z. Segalovitch. Later, Peretz Markish, Orzhekh, Erlikh, Yakov Pat (invited by the "Bund") and others. Also, actors, like Yosele Kolodny and ordinary wandering troupes, good and bad, came to perform for packed halls.

Yisroel Shtern of blessed memory

There was a young man who lived in our town, a son in law, Kalman Shtern from Ostrolenke. He was a Torah scholar, a Hasid who also had knowledge in secular subjects. He was a scribe and also sold prayer shawls. Yisroel Shtern was his brother and often came to visit.

As he would come to visit his brother sometimes on Passover we asked him to speak at a memorial for Y.L. Peretz whose Yortzeyt (anniversary of death) falls during Passover. When we went to his brother's house to discuss it with him we found dire poverty. And even more indigence appeared on Yisroel Shtern's face, clothing and shoes. We were ashamed: A Jewish poet looking like this! We listened to his interesting, original, beautiful speech about Peretz. Yisroel Shtern of blessed memory presented an analogy between Peretz's "The Golden Chain" and Ibsen's "Brand". Between the rabbi Reb Shloime who wants to bring and eternal Sabbath which the Jews won't allow and the priest Brand, who want s to lead his followers to a poor fishing village, near the Norwegian fjords, to a more beautiful and higher life and they abandon him when they hear the sea is calm and filled with fish.

During his speech, Yisroel Shtern paced the stage with half – closed eyes, and with his poetic language and winged words carried his listeners off to another world. At that moment, the poet Yisroel Shtern himself looked like a spiritual prince emitting a glow. At the banquet which took place at a member's home he read one of his poems which some of us did not understand. He taught us songs: "Yesterday is no Longer", and"Pairs of Doves Standing on and Under the Mountain" with his own interpretation of sadness, longing and prayer.

[Page 71]

The "Bund" Leaves the Community Centre

The growth of the "Bund" in Poland and its fight with the Zionists, aggravated the relations between the Bundists and the nationalist section of youth at the community centre. They took down Dr. Herzl's picture which hung in one of the rooms; they interrupted Zionist speakers. This created scandals and fights.

In February 1918 a memorial evening was planned for Dr. Yekhiel Khlonev who had recently died. The Bundists who were present interrupted the speaker, poked fun and disturbed the memorial ceremony. A fight broke out. They were barely able to calm everyone down and continue with the program. The Zionists paid back the Bundists at their events. It became impossible to work together under one roof. The Zionists were the majority at the community centre. It was the Bundists who had to find another place for their activities.

The "Bund" rented their own space, founded a library and carried out a wide range of cultural work among their members. The drama club successfully performed a few Yiddish plays, among them, Sholem Asch's "Motke the Thief". One of their members, Leybl Gogol, a fanatic theatre lover, excelled in the role of Motke. He died recently in Israel. His son Shmuel Gogol is a well-known harmonica player in Tel Aviv.

The debates between Bundists and Zionists in town did not stop. Sharp polemics ensued. After a speaker came from the Bund in Warsaw or the Zionist central office, the Zionists, with their sharp tongues would make comments after the Bundist speaker and the Bundists would do the same after a Zionist lecture. This occurred in all the cities and towns in Poland. It brought life, interest and warmth and chased away the boredom in the poor Jewish streets.

After the Bundists left, the community centre belonged to the Zionist organization and their intensive cultural and educational activities took place there.

[Page 72]

The Economic Situation Under German Occupation in 1915

The German occupiers did not particularly persecute Jews. The soldiers hardly stole Jewish possessions. However, the German occupying power robbed the land through confiscations and requisitions of raw materials, metals, grains and manufactured products. The German word "Bashlogt" applied to everyone. When the Germans arrived, there was an order that all brass and copper dishes and items in your home, even candlesticks, must be given to the German authority, even brass doorknobs on doors. This all had to be brought to a specific place and if you did not obey you were severely punished. The Germans even took the large copper soda water canisters from the soda factory. They even tried to take the three large brass bells from the church tower, however the town's Christians protested strongly. The Germans took only two and left the third in the tower. Merchants had to provide lists of all their merchandise, beginning with food as well as textiles, leather and soap. Everything bought and sold had to be written down. In order to receive permission to bring a certain quantity of textiles from Warsaw, the merchant had to present a 10-ruble gold piece to the regional office. Peasants could not freely sell their grain. They had to sell it at a specific place in town at an official government price. All the mills in the region were closed except for one large mill in town which belonged to Reb Bezalel Vilenberg, which milled only for the Germans and was under their control. All the bakeries and baking ovens in town were also sealed, except one bakery, which baked bread that was divided by bread cards. The bread was black, baked from flour mixed with ersatz, which had no taste and burned the stomach. There were also cards for sugar. There was no soap, no kerosene. There was no electricity in town at that time. The houses were lit with carbide lamps which infected the air, especially in winter when the doors and windows were closed. It was forbidden to sew new clothes. Instead of throwing away old clothes, they were patched, repurposed, made from big to small and used. At that time the folk song "I Have an Old Shawl" was popular. Instead of leather shoes, people wore wooden shoes and sandals of various styles. There was great poverty and destitution in town. Jews worked at public jobs, on highways and chopping down forests, which the Germans organized to alleviated some of the unemployment. The few that had the talent and luck to know the German person in power in town was able to receive, through various paths, food products and therefore did good business.

[Page 73]

The destitution and unemployment among Jews and the lack of essential articles, led to a class of merchants called: "Smugglers". Older, experienced merchants were helpless due to the German draconian laws, requisitions and "Bashlangnamen". Audacious boys would go out at night and through back roads and bring from villages and nearby towns essential items such as, fat, kerosene. They would buy wheat from the peasants, milled in some abandoned area in a small watermill, bring the flour to town and sell it secretly to those who had unsealed ovens. The women would bake Challah for the Sabbath or rolls. The Germans created a municipal militia comprised of Jews and Poles to keep order and help the gendarmes combat smuggling.

When the militia captured a smuggler, he could not bribe them. They took everything away: flour, white baked goods from the unlucky bakers, meat from the illegal butchers. Sometimes, they would bring the smuggler to the gendarmes, who would confiscate the merchandise together with the horse and wagon and beat him up. The Germans gave beatings for every small thing to old and young alike.

In April 1917 the regional chief ordered elections to a city council and city hall according to the Kurien system. Three Kuries had to choose 9 councilmen. Jews comprised more than 75% of the population in town. The Poles demanded that the Jews give them an absolute majority on city council. The Jews renounced their right as the majority and gave the Poles 50 % councilmen. The Poles did not agree and boycotted the election. All 9 councilmen elected were Jews. A few Poles were elected to city hall. The Jewish merchant Yakov Meir Segal was elected mayor, and the Pole, Stash Artipikevitch, vice- mayor. One other Pole was a member of the administration of city hall. At one of the meetings of city council it was decided, against the votes of the orthodox, to introduce Jewish subjects for Jewish children in the municipal elementary school. The orthodox councilmen believed Jewish subjects must be taught in Heder.

[Page 74]

Thanks to the initiative of Yishaye Rekant of blessed memory, a passionate enlightened Jew who knew Hebrew, a kindergarten was founded with the help of the Zionist organization, headed by the certified teacher Mrs. L. Asherovsky from Warsaw. It was decided to open a Hebrew school and create a parent committee chaired by Yishaye Rekant. They brought the teacher Anshl Kotziak, a scholar and a good pedagogue to run the school which helped spread the Hebrew language and Jewish knowledge in town. The Zionist organization opened evening Hebrew courses where tens of boys and girls learned Hebrew, bible and Jewish history.

In order to help the large amount of needy people a free kitchen was opened which distributed three hundred hot meals daily. One of the most active who gave his heart and soul to this matter was the communal activist Meir Ostri. He was crowned with the nickname "Cooking Spoon". At the same time a dormitory was opened for poor children where besides education they received food and some clothing. Young people volunteered to work in the kitchen and dormitory.

In general, one can say, on one hand, the German occupation brought a business crisis, unemployment and poverty. However, on the other hand it gave the youth and Jewish society the opportunity to organize, and allow the Jewish political parties and cultural institutions to become active. They continued and broadened their work also after Poland was liberated, until the arrival of the Nazis, may their names be blotted out, who murdered the Jews together with their religious, cultural and social institutions, which were built over the course of one thousand years of Jewish history in Poland.

In Independent Poland

The poverty in our town during the last year of German occupation was great. Artisans did not have work and merchants did not earn a livelihood. Women and children whose husbands and fathers were in America, England or other places overseas were starving because men could not send money to their dearest in a country ruled by Germans who were at war with America and England. The organized Jewish community as well as other social institutions were impoverished and did not have the ability to help the destitute. The majority of Jews in town were pleased with the departure of the Germans who let them live but took the bread from their mouths.

[Page 75]

The authority of the city was taken over by the P.O.W (Polska Organizacja Wojskowa), which was illegal under German occupation. Jews were frightened seeing young Poles armed with guns. The Poles and Polish newspapers wanted revenge when the Germans left. On November 10th 1918 the Poles in town created a civil committee which called a meeting and a patriotic demonstration in the marketplace. The speakers did not even mention Jews.

However, the last ones in town were anxious and filled with fear from the news in the Yiddish newspapers about attacks on Jews in Warsaw and many other places which began right after the liberation of Poland. The pinnacle was the terrible pogrom, murders and burning of Jewish homes and a synagogue in Lemberg at the end of 1918. Most of the Polish press, with the exception of the worker's paper "Rabotnik", together with patriotic articles in honour of the liberation of Poland, openly lampooned and made up scandalous blood libels against the Jews.

The city administration with the Jewish mayor Yakov Meir Segal during the German
occupation in the First World War

[Page 76]

Soldiers arrived in town wearing black uniforms with brass buttons and black caps with shiny visors. They were called "Ludovtzi". Jews were even more frightened: "Who knows what type of guys these are?" This was the military of the Socialist People's Government which was founded in Lublin, led by the worker's leader Dashinsky. The soldiers behaved politely and correctly the short time they were in our town.

On December 14th 1919 an election took place in city council. Of the 23 councilmen elected 14 were Jews, 9 from the National Bloc and 5 from the "Bund". Heading the Polish councilmen was the priest Theodore Mateushevitch. At the first meeting of city council he called upon the Jews to help him maintain good relations between Poles and Jews by electing a city council made up only of Poles. Other Polish councilmen declared that if the Jews did not accept the suggestion of the priest, the Poles would leave council.

Due to terror perpetrated on Jews in the country and the oppressive mood in town, the Jewish councilmen, after long deliberation, gave into the pressure of the Poles. At the second meeting of city council a mayor, vice – mayor and a councilman were elected, all Poles. To the contrary, the second councilman was a Jew, a Mizrachist, Hillel Sheynberg. Later it turned out this was a political mistake because with that a precedent for the future was created. A Jew was never elected mayor in our town again although Jews comprised 60 -70 percent of the total population.

In order to increase the number of Poles elected to city council, the Starosta (community elder) coopted two nearby villages to the town increasing the number of Polish councilmen.

At the time of elections to city council as well as the Sejm there were struggles between Jewish parties and groups who presented separate lists. Meetings were organized in Houses of Study, party offices as well as the marketplace. Speakers and functionaries would come to these meeting from Warsaw. At these meeting there were discussions, arguments and sometimes, fist fights. For every election campaign the Bundists brought the popular journalist and writer Yakov Pat, of blessed memory, from Vilna. His sharp and clever preacher – like speeches, intertwined with biblical quotes and exegesis always brought out the masses to hear him.

[Page 77]

One of the many curiosities in connection to elections in town is worthwhile mentioning:

During the elections to the second city council which took place in the month of Elul 1927, the "Bund" put forth an election proclamation against the candidates from the United National list, reproaching the Zionist candidate for offering a cigarette to the rabbi on a Friday night, when he and other religious Jews came to the Zionist locale to scold the Zionists for desecrating the Sabbath in public. In the same Bundist lampoon it was indicated that another Zionist candidate took a group of Jewish kids to a nearby town on Yom Kippur and organized a party. This calling out ended with these words: "Whoever wants to be signed in the Book of Life should vote for the Bundist list".

The newspaper of the left – wing "Poalei Zion" in Poland published a facsimile of those pointing out to show how far the "Bund" galloped down the road of election propaganda for the city councils in order to win votes from religious voters.

The Poalei – Zion movement in Makow, 1919

[Page 78]

They called out Zionist candidates, accused the writer in municipal court after he refused to go to an honour court. A special representative came from the "Bund" in Warsaw reprimanded the members for causing shame to the Bundist party. The writer of the proclamation apologized publicly, withdrew his accusations against the Zionists, paid a fine and peace was restored between the two parties.

In the first elected city council there was harmony and understanding between Jews and Poles. Everyone had good intentions and looked for common ways to rebuild and develop the town for the good of both Jews and Poles. They succeeded in getting a loan from the government for one hundred thousand marks for public works and to ease the unemployment in town. In accordance with the suggestions and initiative of the Jewish councilmen, the council turned to the government and received permission to take wood from surrounding government forests for poor people to cook and heat their ovens during winter, buy flour and potatoes without consignment in order to distribute among the needy in town. The city administration also founded and maintained two kindergartens for poor children, Jewish and Polish. The Jewish kindergarten was placed under the supervision of a special Jewish committee which was elected for this purpose.

The Polish – Bolshevik War

The war which broke out in 1920 jolted the already ruined economy, which had remained after the German occupation, and brought price fixing of all articles and inflation and increased the poverty throughout the country, especially in cities and towns.

In addition, the Jews suffered from greater persecution, excesses, murders and robberies by armed Polish soldiers.

The Polish press blamed the Jews for all the problems, even the war, accusing the Jews of being "Bolsheviks, speculators and enemies of the land".

At that time the Jews in our town "only" suffered shameful actions by the "Halerchikes" who distinguished themselves with scissors or plucking Jewish beards and throwing Jews off moving trains. The first victim was an elderly Jew, Reb Moishe Rekhtman who had a lovely long half – grey beard. The "Halerchikes" found him in the marketplace and cut half of it off. Reb Moishe walked around for a long time bandaged until his cut beard grew back.

[Page 79]

In 1920 the Bundist party in Poland was banned. The following activists and councilmen were arrested: Yisroel Shikora (today in Israel), Yehonasn Nayman, Aron Yosef Aronovitch (Kirtchekov), Dovid Minoga (Dovid "Torah"), Avrom Malakh and Leybl Gogol of blessed memory, the father of the popular harmonic player in Israel Shmuel Gogol. They were supposed to be sent to the unfortunately famous concentration camp Kartuz [Kartuska] Bereza but in the meantime the area was captured by the Bolsheviks.

For 9 months these Bundist activists wallowed and were tortured in various prisons. Right after the Bolshevik invasion they were freed and came home broken and dejected. It took them a long time to recover and return to normal life.

Not only was the civilian population terrorized by Polish soldiers, Jewish recruits were persecuted and tortured by Polish soldiers as well.

Recruits from Makow in 1927

[Page 80]

When a Jewish recruit arrived in a military camp everything he had was taken from him, even his clothes and shoes, and were never returned. The Jewish recruits suffered especially from instructors, soldiers of a lower military rank. During military exercises they tortured and ridiculed helpless Jewish recruits. They received beatings from all directions, even while standing in line for food. They were woken up at night for various tasks or simply chased, half naked and barefoot outdoors. When I arrived the first day at military camp in Mokotov, Warsaw, I was slapped in the face with a herring while standing in line for food. When I ran to pick up the slung herring and bent down to pick it up, a bucket of cold water was poured on me. I did not remain in that camp for more than a day. That same evening, at a cost, I left with the help of a note which permitted me to stay in a hotel.

City boys, who could not bear the torment, escaped from the army. Others, from the beginning did not appear before the military commission and recruitment offices. By illegal means, they left for Germany, Belgium and France. Some went to America.

There were Jewish soldiers from our town that excelled in the war. Some fell in battle, like Leyb Kersh, Dovid Vaysman, Aron Botshan and others. Their names are mentioned in a report by the P.O.W in our region.[*]

The Bolsheviks in Town

At the beginning of August 1920, the Bolsheviks entered our town. We did not have an organized communist party. Heading the city committee, which was created by the Bolshevik commissar were: an old Pole who worked at a press machine on the highway and a young Jewish man, Feyvl Blum, who arrived recently and was known in town as Zionist activist and speaker, a member of the "Young Zionists", co-founder of "Prachei Zion", the youth organization where he was active. After the revolution in Russia he left the Zionist movement. He also escaped from the Polish army and was hidden until the arrival of the Bolsheviks. The Pole and Feyvl Blum would deliver sharp communist speeches at meetings which took place in the marketplace in Yiddish, Russian and Polish. The Pole Artipikevitch was chosen as mayor of our town. The city council was manned by the father, sister and brother of Feyvl Blum. They did not receive any salary but they did receive a loaf of black bread and a bit of food.

[Page 81]

The Bolsheviks arrested the priest right away. Jews tried to get him released. We tried to explain to Feyvl Blum, the head of the municipal committee who remained our friend even after he left the Zionist organization that arresting the priest can only bring tragedy for the Jews. The priest was released and Jews breathed freely.

The poorly dressed Russian soldiers bought everything they could and paid with paper money, small bills, torn or cut from long sheets, like large postage stamps.

An order was given by the city commissioner saying that merchants must receive and register their goods in the presence of a communist functionary.

My friend and comrade Feyvl Blum came to our dry goods store to receive the merchandise. He stood in our shop and paid attention to how I measured the fabric., counted the kerchiefs and calculated everything. He explained to me that this must be done for the sake of the revolution and for the sake of the poor and the workers who are being exploited by the bourgeois. He then calmed me down and told me we will not be the first to have our merchandise confiscated because my mother was a widow and he did not think we were bourgeois, only petty bourgeois who they have to win over for the revolution.

Meanwhile, the Russian front was broken near Warsaw. The Bolsheviks chased by the Polish military ran back in a disorganized way, and did not succeed in taking the already registered merchandise from our town. However, they did manage, in a short time, to practically empty our shops, buying everything with their worthless paper rubles, while grabbing clothes and boots from poor tailors and shoemakers.

Many soldiers who had escaped left with the Bolsheviks. Only a small number managed to slip through the Polish border.

[Page 82]

The majority could not run after the fast retreating Bolsheviks and were captured by the Polish military, sent to prison and beaten. The parents of sons who had been arrested were very nervous about the fate of the arrestees. According the law one could receive a death sentence for desertion. There were many cases where Jewish and Polish deserters were sentenced to death. The Jewish National Council at the Sejm, headed by Yitzkhak Grinboym, intervened with the Polish military authority in the government for amnesty due to victory over the Bolsheviks. An amnesty that would also include deserters, of which the majority were Poles. On September 20th, 1920 an amnesty was proclaimed, sign by Yuzef Pilsudsky, chief of the Polish army. The majority of those arrested were freed, and the rest, a short time later.

Feyvl Blum – Communist Functionary and Writer

Feyvl Blum left town with the last Bolshevik soldiers. On a warm night at the end of August he came to us, his childhood friends, to say goodbye. His face which was always pale was white and his black eyes burned with the fire of tuberculosis. The knapsack on his back was made from his father's prayer shawl bag; he was carrying a gun. The girls did not want to say goodbye to him, they didn't even want to talk to him because at meetings, with contempt, he spoke about "the gentle female hands, that do not work and remain empty all day". Then he warned "these hands will be chopped off if they are lifted up against the Bolshevik authority". Quietly, practically without any words, we shook hands. We understood it was hard for him to leave town and the friends he had spent so many years with. We were also sad. It was a pity to lose such a joyful and clever friend. No one was able to read Sholem Aleichem stories and monologues aloud as masterfully as he did; and certainly not Reisen's poem which he read with such emotion. Feyvl even wrote his own poetry.

In a letter I received from him a while later from Minsk he wrote he was a contributor to a newspaper, active in the communist party and was writing a book where he was describing Jewish characters in Makow.

[Page 83]

One day I received a letter from him from Vilna, where according to the address I saw he was there using a false pass, on a party mission. He wrote articles and feuilletons for the Vilna "Tog". His humorous short letters from Vilna, which were published every Friday in the newspaper were very successful and loved by the readers. He wrote under the pseudonym "Feyvele". He got married in Vilna and his son, who was born here was named "October". Knowing the secret police had an eye on him, he returned to Russia, got sick with his family illness of Tuberculosis, travelled to Crimea on the Black Sea for treatment. I received a few happy letters from him from the spa. He died at the age of 32-33. He left behind a small book called "Samum" by F. Blum, stories about the lives of plantation workers in Sumara, published by "School and Book", Moscow, 1928. (From the cover page).

When you find the name Blum, F. in "The Lexicon of Modern Yiddish Literature", author of the book "Samum", without details of his life or death, you should know, he was the son from a poor family in Makow, born in 1896.

When the Bolsheviks ran away so did Feyvl's younger brother Velvl Blum, founder and leader of the left wing Poalei Zion in our town.

At the meetings and demonstrations organized by the Bolsheviks in the marketplace, the Russian who led the meeting would announce, just as Feyvl was finishing his speech: "Soon Comrade Blum the second will speak". Velvel, a short, cross- eyed guy, would go up onto the podium and make people laugh. He spoke quickly and in one breath would quote Marx, Lenin and…Borochov.

In the early years his friends received letters from him. He was a teacher in the Yiddish school. During the mass arrests in Russia he was arrested and never heard from again.

The Fight Against Speculation and Jews

The lack of goods during the Polish – Bolshevik war and after led to price fixing, inflation and the fall in value of Polish currency. In all towns and cities the government created a bureau to fight speculation and usury, which focused first and foremost on the small Jewish merchants and shopkeepers. The set prices on goods had to be hung up and visible in all stalls and shops. There were large fines and arrests for those who charged more than the official price. The set prices were often unrealistic. If they were appropriate one day, the next day they were not, as prices went up daily. Peasants and shop owners took what they wanted for their products. The dry goods merchants and fabric importers did not consider going to the bureau to fight the price hikes. The agents of the bureau who were against speculation actually bankrupted the Jewish merchants who were always being punished with large fines for taking a groshn or two above the official price, or had to bribe the agent to leave him alone. Because of this there was a lack of salt, kerosene, sugar and other items in town.

[Page 84]

With the fall in value of the Polish mark and because of the quick rise in prices of goods, the few successful merchants in town, that had large credit, became even richer. Some poor also became rich with thousands and millions of marks but their stock shrank from day to day.

There was a wealthy Jew in town, Motl Hurvitz. He was jealous of the large dry goods merchants who were "making millions". He sold his watermill and began to deal in dry goods and candy. He bought and sold and made volumes of business, millions until…he remained with a few dozen cheap pairs of pants which cost tens of millions of marks. However, with these millions he could not buy back one stone from his mill. Merchants borrowed from "Americans" (women whose husbands were in America), hundreds of dollars with interest; They borrowed dollars or English pounds from girls who had collected this money for their dowries. The price for dollars or pounds increased ten times and there was less merchandise in the shops. If the merchant sold everything, the millions of Polish marks would not be enough to pay for the dollars he borrowed. Because of this, fights broke out in town, people cried. Jews, arbitrators and community workers meddled until the conflicts were solved. Those who borrowed were obligated to pay back their loans. However, Hitler's murderous soldiers, may their names be obliterated, tortured and burned the lenders and the borrowers in the crematoria, with the rest of the Jews from our town.

[Page 85]

In Makow there were 7 shops with concessions to sell alcohol, 5 Jewish and 2 Polish. When the law was passed at the Sejm to limit the consumption of alcohol, the government took away the 5 Jewish concessions in town. Two Polish merchants remained with permission to sell hard drinks. This happened in many other towns. Jewish deputies demanded interpolation at the Sejm.

A Sejm Deputy Speaks and Poles Cry

In the Warsaw newspaper "Haynt" from September 22nd 1921, in the section called "What the Post Brings Us", Mr. K from Makow recounts: It was a non – Jewish holiday and a Sejm deputy from Makow stood on the street in front of the church and began to speak.

Instead of giving a report about his own activities, he read a eulogy for the government. He cursed the laws concerning 8-hour work days and the Jews. The Jews are guilty of everything he said. Jews create inflation Jews squandered Upper Silesia etc. And then the deputy told a story about the cross in the Sejm: "The Jews united with the socialists and prevailed to have the cross hang outside the Sejm in the corridor and not inside. The entire Sejm looks like a Jewish synagogue".

Hearing these words, the crowd burst into tears. People began to shout: "Death to the Jews!" "Down with the Sejm!" After the deputy spoke, a secretary from some small town took his place and also spoke against the Jews. He said it was forbidden to beat up Jews, it was inappropriate, but the boycott must be applied. You should not do business with Jews. "In general," this "clever" anti -Semite preached, "it is not worthwhile to sell because the marks the Jews give us are worthless…"

The police stood to the side and guarded this untouchable anti – Semitic deputy who supported the boycott.

The notice ended with these words: "Our folk jokester, Reb Elye Makover, lies there in his grave and listens to the anti - Semitic nonsense from the Sejm deputy. He rolls over in his grave laughing and listening to the Makow crowds cry".

[Page 86]

Communal and Cultural Activities

The communal and cultural activities in town did not stop, even during the war with the Bolsheviks. The rooms of the community centre where all the communal activities of the nationalist youth took place, and the library had to be given to the Polish organization "Lutniya", which renewed its work. It was impossible to find a suitable location in town. The Jewish community centre move to an old wooden storied house with creaking stairs, near the new House of Study. This did not interrupt the development of the Zionist and cultural work.

A large crowd came to the first meeting in their new location to discuss the issues, which were on the agenda for the fourth Zionist Conference in Warsaw, August 17, 1919. Nosn Montsahkovsky (today Shachar in Israel) was elected as a delegate for the conference.

Goodbye evening in honour of Reb Moishe Bzhoza when he left for Lodz in 1918

[Page 87]

Leafing through the newspaper "Hatzfira" from 1920 I found lists of names of those who donated to The Jewish National Fund and collectors from many cities and towns in Poland, including Makow. I am providing here 2 of the lists in their Hebrew original. They have historical value because of the weddings, engagements and celebrations that took place during this year of crisis and are mentioned in connection with collections for the Jewish National Fund (Keren Kayemet).

"Hatzfira" March 6, 1920
Makow, "Young Zionists"
Invitees to the ball at Hendl Fishberg's planted 2 trees in her name.

Invitees to the ball for the groom Reb Gliksberg and the bride Sh. Lilentl	20 marks
Two trees in honour if the bride and groom	20 marks
Moshe Fridman, one tree	15 marks
Simcha Tzentua, one tree	10 marks

"Hatzfira" March 23, 1920
Makow "Young Zionists"

Mindl Bramzon and Brayna Lifson, one tree	10 marks
Moshe Rozenberg in honour of David Miner, one tree	10 marks
Members: Rivka Rebak, Sara Blum and Ester Sara Hertzberg	
In honour of the bride Mindl Blum and M. Skurnik, one tree	10 marks
Gitl Segal planted 4 trees	40 marks
Leah Khilinovitch in honour of Mindl Blum and M. Skurnik's wedding. One tree	10 marks
In honour of Z. Shamovitch and Leah Khilinovitch	
In honour of Mindl Vilenberg and Yakov Fishl Munkrash's wedding, 13 trees	134,50 marks
In honour of the members of the "Young Zionists"	157 marks
In honour of the "Young Zionists' in the Golden Book	129.55 marks

On the list of donations and collectors from "Keren Kayemet" in the newspapers in those years we find tens of names of Jews from Makow, familiar names of dear, innocent young people with whom we did community work together, studied, discussed, dreamed and sang and believed in a better tomorrow which the revolutions in Russia and Germany were supposed to bring. Only a few of them were saved from the German Nazi hell. The majority are no longer with us. We don't even know where their remains lie.

[Page 88]

In May 1920, we celebrated with all Jews the great victory of the Zionist movement after we entered the peace agreement with Turkey, in San Remo. The Balfour declaration that gave Jews the right to build their home in Palestine. A large meeting took place in the new House of Study, which was filled with Jews, young and old. A passionate speech was given by the Hebrew teacher, the talented speaker and Zionist activist, Shmuel Berenholtz of blessed memory, from Ostrov – Mazovietzk. At the celebrations and gatherings, a telegram was read with greetings from London to the worker's committee in Warsaw. It was published in the newspaper and signed by Rivka Sokolov, the wife of Nokhem Sokolov and the daughter of Yitzkhak Hersh Segal from Makow. This greeting, signed by someone from Makow made us feel like relatives at the wedding. Moreover, we believed, that with the acceptance of the Balfour declaration and an agreement with Turkey, the Turkish government would open the doors and gates of the Land of Israel and call on Jews to come and settle. Just as we naively believed that when Poland signed the peace agreement, the rights of all national minorities would be secured and a new chapter would begin for Jews in Poland without discrimination and without persecution.

A Visit from Alexander Olshvanger and Moishe Gordon

On a cold snowy winter night, the lawyer Olshvanger and the student Moishe Gordon arrived at the train station in Pasheky, 35 kilometres away. They were representatives from the central office in Warsaw. Olshvanger, the lawyer, had a small beard, a hunched back, wore glassed and was dressed like a Polish officer, with a back pack on his back. They soon felt at home with us.

At this urgent member consultation which was called that same night in the home of Yekhiel Meir Pliato, may his blood be avenged, the president of the Zionist Organization, member of the Jewish Community Council and city councillor, Olshvanger announced that he came, according to the circular we received, as a messenger from the Zionist central committee in Warsaw to re-organize the Zionist activity in our town. He wanted to unite our organization with the central office in Warsaw as well as handle a few political problems connected to the struggle with the temporary Jewish National Council for the rights of Jews in Poland. A matter that could not be dealt with in writing.

[Page 89]

Moishe Gordon told us he was sent to create a youth – scouting organization which would also be involved with nationalist education of the youth. He presented a plan for the work over the first few months and shared copies of the periodical "Ha Shomer" in Polish as well as a brochure about youth scouts by Badn Paul in Polish.

The scout organization was soon created by members of "Young Zion". It was comprised mainly of school children. The scout stick, blouse, necktie, hat and short pants, together with walks, games and songs, attracted the youth of our town from all social classes, even religious homes. The youth movement, which was later called "Shomer Hatzair" had a big influence in town. They took part in all national work and collection of money for Zionist funds. During those year, Yehuda Gothelf, today the editor of "Davar", was head of the "Main Leadership" in Poland. They were the best and most successful in planning activities for "Hashomer Hatzair" in our town in all fields of education and scouting. We always received well collected instructional material from the "Main Leadership" about cultural and educational programs in all the groups. The leaders' manuals which were edited and put together by Yehuda Gotholf, were very helpful for group leaders in their devoted work. They themselves learned as they inspired others to read and learn. Children, boys and girls from fanatic religious families suffered at home. They fought with their parents. Sometimes, fathers would drag their daughters out of their shops by their braids. They could not tolerate the fact that their daughters were going to a place that taught them the song by David Shimoni that advises the youth not to listen to their parents. This song was very popular in "Hashomer".

A group of scouts called "Reuven" in Makow in 1918

[Page 90]

The children did not give into the pressure by their parents and continued to go to the club where happiness ruled and they sang and danced. When we meet these members of "Hashomer" today, now grandparents themselves, they remember their romantic young years with love and nostalgia. They remember the campfires in the fields on clear summer nights, organized hikes in the thick forests near our town and nearby small towns and villages, the summer colonies and the club houses in the region, the songs and dancing the Hora which gave them so much joy and chased away the daily worries of the Jewish home in our town. Many of them went to Zionist training camps and today are living in Israel. Some on Kibbutzim and others spread out through various countries and continents. They carry with them the instructions and national education they received from "Hashomer Hatzair" and in Hebrew evening courses where besides Hebrew they learned bible, Jewish history and literature.

The heart breaks and the soul is wrapped in sadness when we remember the hundreds of idealistic youth from Makow who were killed by the Nazi murderers, may their names be blotted out. They were dragged to death camps together with their parents and other Jews from our town.

Thanks to the initiative of the pharmacist Yishayahu Rekant, may his blood be avenged, and others, a branch of "Tarbut" was founded at the same time. They were given permission to open a Hebrew learning institution, library and sports club. The "Tarbut" opened a kindergarten, headed by the certified teacher Golde (Zahava) Dzinekevitch. By the way, Zahava grew up in "Hashomer Hatzair", took the evening Hebrew courses and today is a teacher on Kibbutz Bet – Alfa.

[Page 91]

"Agudas Shlomi Emunei Yisroel"

The orthodox party in Poland "Shlomi Emunei Yisroel" had a branch in Makow. The leaders of this party in our town, Reb Velvl Feyntzeyg and Kalmen Shtern, a scribe, were smart, activist orthodox Jews with whom we would quarrel during elections to the Sejm and city council. Once, on a Friday night in winter, they brought the rabbi from our town, Reb Yisroel – Nisn

Kupershtokh of blessed memory (who passed away in Israel), to the hall of the Zionist organization which was filled with members who had come to hear a lecture about literature. We were surprised by the sudden visit by the rabbi who came with a few other men. A few of those present who were from religious homes hid under the tables. The speaker, who was standing beside a table near the entrance did not become flustered, he politely welcomed the uninvited guests and asked what they desired. The rabbi, who was a nice man and behaved like a Rebbe, was never a great speaker. In choppy sentences he said:

"I came because they told me that the Zionists desecrate the Sabbath in public. They sit with bear heads, boys and girls together and this is a great sin".

The speaker replied: "If these boys and girls would not be here, they would be walking together in the dark city park where they would probably desecrate the Sabbath even more. So, it is better that they sit here together and learn something Jewish."

Kalmen Soyfer said a few moralizing words and began to leave. Then one of the men with him noticed there was no mezuzah when he exited. The rabbi returned and asked them, in the Name of God, to hang a mezuzah on the doorpost, wished them a good Sabbath and left.

In 1924, the "Shlomei Emunei Yisroel", with the help of a wealthy man Reb Bezalel Vilnberg of blessed memory, built a large wooden building for a Heder called "Foundations of the Torah". The principal, who taught 240 boys was Reb Velvl Feyntzveyg. Polish and general studies were taught in the Heder following the government program for private elementary school, under the leadership of Shmuel Pianko, principal of the government elementary school for Jewish children in town. Children paid tuition but poor children learned for free. The deficit was covered mainly by Reb Bezalel Vilenberg, owner of a mill and member of the Jewish community council.

[Page 92]

We are providing a letter from our town which was published in the daily newspaper "Hayom" ("Today") in 1926, not to provoke anger, God forbid, as the majority of the Jews we argued with are no longer among the living. All were brutally killed during the attacks by "the honourable nation" of Europe. We are republishing he correspondence as a reminder of the disagreements that existed, only to tell the historical truth.

[Letter in Hebrew translated by Jerrold Landau]

Today, Warsaw, February 17, 1926

On Tuesday, 28 Shvat, the Rabbi and Gaon Hager, renowned in the Zionist world as a spokesman and activist for the Keren Kayemet [Jewish National Fund] arrived in Maków.

When the people of the Agudah found out about his arrival, they attempted to discredit him in the eyes of the masses through various disparagements. However, despite all this, he delivered his speech that day in the Mizrachi Hall in the presence of the members of Mizrachi and the Zionists.

His lecture was full of meaningful content and enchanted all those gathered. They unanimously accepted a decision that the lecture be repeated the next day, that is on Wednesday, in the *Beis Midrash*.

Information about the lecture in the *Beis Midrash* spread very quickly among all the strata of the crowd, and by dusk, the *Beis Midrash* was already filled to the brim. The rabbi began his lecture at 5:00 p.m. It enchanted the hearts of the entire audience.

However, the Agudah did not slumber or sleep, and they "led their trained men"[1] and their rabblerousers to raise a tumult and disrupt the lecturing rabbi in his national work. These deeds aroused great resentment amongst those gathered in the *Beis Midrash*, and they girded themselves to protect the honor of the rabbi with calls for revenge. They removed the rabblerousers from the *Beis Midrash*. The rabbi interrupted his lecture to prevent the dispute that broke out between the masses and the Aguda from igniting.

The city was frothing and boiling like a cauldron: It was impossible to quiet and calm the anger and ire of the masses. As a sign of protest against the brazenness of the Agudah, they girded themselves strongly for the benefit of the Keren Kayemet LeYisrael.

Thus, the bad intentions of the Agudah turned out for the good, for this incident brought great benefit to the Keren Kayemet LeYisrael. The charity boxes that had been tossed out by the Agudah people before the rabbi arrived were brought back in. They hoped that the income of the Keren Kayemet would grow greatly from what it had been to that point.

Y. L.

[Page 93]

The truth must be noted: there were in town members of the "Agudah" who contributed to the Jewish National Fund for certain projects and not all religious Jews were members of the "Agudah" which fundamentally was a political party run by the court of the Ger Rebbe.

Pauperization of Jews in Town

With the encouragement of the government and the help of Polish financial institutions, Polis businesses opened in town. The food cooperative, which existed before the war, grew. New Polish business emerged for manufacturing, haberdashery, iron, building material and more.

The amount of food shops as well as other stores increased the villages as well. Until the First World War in 1914 many Jewish families lived in the large villages around out town, owned shops and did business and earned a nice living.

With the outbreak of the First World War they had to leave the villages and they never returned. At that time many left for America. The small farmers in our region, the majority of which were calm and good to the Jews, were influenced by the constant anti – Semitic and boycott agitations and began slowly to avoid Jewish businesses.

The greatest cause of impoverishment in town were the heavy taxes.

The merchants and shopkeepers, mainly trade in small measure, did not keep business books. The clerk of the tax bureau in town decided on the tax rate. Formally, there was a tax commission made up of merchants and artisan representatives. however, the clerk rarely took their opinions into account, raising taxes, the first being the "Danino", which was added to the population right after the Polish – Bolshevik war. Until the taxes on business volume and income, Jewish merchants in town had to pay almost double than the Poles in the same line of business who sold and earned much more than a Jewish merchant.

For many years there was a clerk in Makow for business and income tax who was a young Pole, a cynical anti -Semite and simply, a bad person. His name alone caused fear among the Jews. Men would come to him with complaints and women would come crying due the high taxes which they had to pay, often more than the value of their shops. The Pole listened to them with a harden face and watery eyes and did not reply. Jews groaned, protested, sent delegations with memoranda to the "Provisional Jewish National Council" at the Sejm, but nothing helped. Jews cried and paid. If they did not, the tax bureau too everything from their shops and homes, even things he did not own...

[Page 94]

Merchants became poor people. They did not have any business capital but nevertheless had to continue doing business to earn a living. There were merchants in town who ran their businesses without their own money. They took loans from other Jews in town. They would borrow one hundred zlotys from one and fifty from another and would travel to Warsaw to bur merchandise, sold at fairs in marks. They would pay back their debts, and then, borrow again, buy and sell, and toil to bring home enough to provide for the Sabbath, holidays and make weddings for their children. As we sing in this sad folk song:

"I possess in my shop two groshn worth of goods, I drag around my poverty and bless the Creator..."

Many small tailor and shoemaker workshops had to liquidate. The tradesmen had to go work for someone else for starvation wages. Others took home work from more successful tailors and shoemakers. When these artisans would take work home the husband, wife and older children would all work to barely have enough for a poor existence, and only in the summer and winter seasons which lasted only 6 months a year.

Merchants, shopkeepers and artisans could only continue to work thanks to the credit from the Jewish Cooperative Bank and the Free Loan Society.

The Cooperative Bank was founded with the help of the "Joint" in June 1926. By the end of the year it had 227 members and a capital of 3,605 zlotys, with 611 zlotys deposited in the bank.

In 1937 the bank had 345 members and a capital of 32,652 zlotys; they gave out loans totaling 384,784 zlotys; deposits – 50, 345 zlotys.

Among the 345 members there were 2 farmers, 155 artisans, 141 small merchants and businessmen, 13 larger merchants and manufacturers (mill owners, leather factories), 34 employees and others. The served a small number of Poles.

[Page 95]

A cell of the "Hashomer Hatzair" movement in Malkw, 1930

[Page 96]

Activists in "Hashomer Hatzair", 1929

A branch of "Hechalutz" in Makow, 1926

[Page 97]

The transportation between towns was from the start in Jewish hands. At first, they travelled in covered wagons and later in horse drawn carriages, coaches and buses. In independent Poland they created an association with the teamsters and placed buses on the roads from Makow to Warsaw and later, Makow to Mlave, through Prushnitz, as well as the towns Ruzhan and Krasnosheltz. The transportation slowly developed and became comfortable and punctual. It provided a livelihood for 10 Jewish families.

In 1932 the government took Jewish concessions on these routes away from the Jews and placed government buses where no Jew could get a job as a driver or conductor. The government only allowed the proprietor of the bus line from Makow to the train station in Pasheky to keep his job because he was a Pole. One of the partners in the bus association, Hersh – Ber Orlik, of blessed memory, who was a driver and was left without an income, immigrated to the Land of Israel, served in the Haganah and fought in the War of Independence. He died two years ago, having had a good reputation among friends and acquaintances.

Many Jews who lost their livelihoods at that time would have gladly emigrated overseas, however they did not have money to cover expenses.

Jewish youth who had absolutely nothing to do in town struggled to go to the Land of Israel. However, during the most difficult years for Jews in independent Poland the English authorities in Mandate Palestine did not permit Jewish immigration. Of the thousands of certificates given by the Jewish Agency, over ten thousand pioneers and members of "Hashomer Hatzair" in Poland, completed the Zionist training camps and were ready to immigrate. In Makow, there were more than 100 young people who wanted to go the Land of Israel. However, only a few lucky ones received certificates and immigrated.

Here are some numbers of Jewish emigration from Makow in the 1930s:

In 1932	10	Jews emigrated	1	To the Land of Israel
In 1933	17	- " -	14	- " -
In 1934	2	- " -	1	- " -
In 1936	59	- " -	29	- " -
1935	20	- " -	13	- " -
1937	29	- " -	18	- " -

[Page 98]

During the same period only 12 Poles emigrated from our town where they comprised barely 40 percent of the population.

Together with the poverty in mortality increased in our town which can be seen in the numbers below and pertain only to Jews[*]

Year	Deaths	
	Male	Female
1932	3	1
1933	7	10
1934	8	6
1935	15	8
1936	21	12
1937	28	25

After the agreement between Poland and Hitler's Germany in 1934 and the death of Pilsudsky in May 1935, persecutions against the Jews increased in Poland and reached our calm town.

Truth be told, in order to carry out unrest in town the anti -Semites had to bring in students from Warsaw to incite violence on market days and at fairs, encouraging the peasants to attack the Jews by pouring kerosene on the products they bought in Jewish stores and stood in front of Jewish shops and did not allow Poles to enter. But even this was not entirely successful. Thanks to the clerk of public security and the vice – commander of the police who were both fine, honest Poles, serious unrest never befell our town. Let them, at this time be remembered fondly.

This is how life passed in our town, until of Hitler's murderers, may their names be blotted out, arrived and began to torture the Jews, imprison them in ghettos, murdered some on the spot. The remaining thousands of men, women, elderly and children, tormented, sick and dejected, were dragged to death camps and killed by various means, only because they were Jews. Why? What for?

May God avenge their blood!

Kibbutz Shoval, Tammuz, 1968.

Original footnotes:
* I. Wesolek: Monograph Makow, Zarzad, 1938.

6.   Graetz: Divrei Yamei Yisrael, translated by Sh. P. Rabinovitch, vol. 7, pp. 332,348.
7.   Versalek: A Monograph of the City of Makov
8.   Graetz as above, vol. 8, p. 151; Dobnow, vol. 7, pp. 19-20: R. Mahler, pp. 348, 352.
9.   Prof. Mahler: Divrei Yemei Yisrael, The last Generations, Vol 1, third book, pp. 260, 303, 306.
10.   Prof. Graetz: Divrei Yemei Yisrael, the last section, translated by Y.A. Trivsh, Vilna 1908, note 2, p. 11.
11.   Y.Vesolek: A Monograph of the City of Makov
12.   Rafael Mahler: Divrei Yemei Yisrael – The Last Generations, Vol. 1 chapter iii, p. 64.
13.   Rafael Mahler: Divrei Yemei Yisrael, The Last Gerations, first volume, their book, page 74.
14.   Y. Vesolek: Monograph from the City Makov.
15.   Efraim Kupfer: Legal and Actual Situation of Jews in Poland, Pages from History, Vol. V.
16.   Y. Vesolek: Monograph form the City Makov.
17.   Efraim Fishl Nayman: Bet Efraim, New York, 1923, p. 31.
18.   Sefer Sokolov, edited by Shimon Ravidovitch, Jerusalem, "Personalities of a Nation", published by the Zionist Library, 1962.
19.   A larger biography of Rabbi Yehuda – Leyb Groybard of blessed memory was written with love and respect to the great deceased by the writer N. Shemen and can be found in the Book of Stashov published in January 1962 in Israel.
20.   Moishe Bzhoza: "Hatzfira", June 17th 1915.

Translator's Footnote:
1.   Based on Genesis 14: 14

[Page 99]

Sing!

From the poem "Song of the Murdered Jewish People"

by Yitzhak Katznelson (1885-1944)

Translated by Anita Frishman Gabbay

Sing! Take your harp in hand, hollow, stripped, and despised
On its fine strings set your fingers, heavy
Like hearts filled with pain, sing the song, the last song,
Sing of the last Jews on Europe's soil.

How can I sing? How can I open my mouth?
When only I am left alone, alone in the ruins-
And my wife and our two helpless children? - Oh! Horror!
A horror appalls me…I weep! And in the distance I hear weeping.

Sing! Sing! Raise your voice, your pained and broken voice,
Search! Search for Him above, whether He is even still there-
And sing to Him…sing to Him the last song of the last Jews
To have lived, but who are now dead, unburied- gone.

-How can I sing? How can I raise my head?
My wife led away, and my dearest little Benji and, then, Yomele-only a child-
I do not have them here with me, but they do not leave me alone!
O dark shadows of my most radiant beloved ones, o shadows so cold and blind!

Sing! Sing the last time while still on this Earth, throw
Your head back, plant your eyes firmly on Him,
And sing to Him for one last time, play to Him on your harp:
Now there are no more Jews! Slaughtered off, gone forever!

[Page 100]

How can I sing? How can I raise eyes frozen
In my head? A frozen tear has…
Blurred my eyes…a tear wells up, welling up
From my eye, but it cannot fall- oh God, My God!

"Sing, Sing, raise your glance to the high and blind Heavens,
As though there were a God there in the Heavens…wave to Him, wave-
As though some great good fortune might still appear there and illuminate us!
Sit on the ruins of the slaughtered people and sing!

How can I sing when only a dismal world is left to me?
How can I play with broken hands?
Where are my dead? I search for the dead-my dead, God? -in

every dunghill,
In every small and little heap of ashes - Oh! tell me where you are?

Cry out from every patch of sand, from under every stone,
From all the dust, cry out from all the flames, from every puff of smoke-
It is your blood, your lifeblood, it is your bone and marrow,
It is your body and life! Shout, cry out loud!

[Page 101]

Show yourself to me, my people, appear, stretch your hands
Out of deep graves, miles-long, and crammed full,
Level upon level, drenched with lime and charred,
Rise up! Rise up! Climb out from the lowest, from the deepest level!

Come out, all of you, from Treblinka, from Sobibor, from Aushwitz,
From Belzec come, from Ponar, and from elsewhere! Yes, from
all the other places,
With eyes torn open, frozen in a shout, a cry for help, and with a
single voice-
Come from the swamps, from the depths sunk in blood, from the rotting muck.

Come all of you, dried up, crushed, and ground up, come and
show yourselves
In a circle, in a great circle around me, a great ring-
Dearest grandfathers, grandmothers, fathers, mothers with little
children on your laps,
Come, Jewish bones, come from the piles of dust, from the little pieces of soap.

Appear to me, show yourselves all to me, come all, come,
I want to see you all, I want to look at you, I want
To cast a glance at my People, my slaughtered off, silent, silenced people,
And I want to sing…Yes…give me my harp- and I will play!

5-10-43

[Page 102]

I Play

I play. I sit down low on the ground
I play and mournfully sing: Oh, my people!
Millions of Jewish people stood around me, and heard,
Millions slaughtered were standing, listened-a great success!

A great success, a great camp Ezekiel Valley-
Full of bones can hide in a corner-
He alone, Ezekiel, could not hide, could not believe,
The exterminated people, he would break his hands like me.

Like me, like I would lift my head with disbelief,
Disturbing the sky, grey, white and a wasteland,

And again he descends with difficulty, down, down,
A petrified stone buried in the ground, deep and silent.

Ezekiel! Jew, you Jew in Babylon, you saw
The dried up bones of your people, you saw
And allowed this, Ezekiel...confused like a statue
From the upper part of the valley and allowed those to be lead.

And allowed themselves to be led: Ezekiel! Say, do you want
To receive more bones? You know no yes or no-
Do what you want, Ezekiel, what shall I say! Alas! A disaster!
No bones from my slaughtered people are left!

There is no place to put a *lion[symbol of a Jewish grave]*, not a body to bury,
In which a spirit can enter-
See, see, my entire slaughtered nation, dead
A nation killed, without anyone looking, without anyone caring.

[Page 103]

See, see, millions of heads and hands stretched out to us-count!
See their faces and lips-a prayer and a cry!
Go to them, touch them-there is no trace-a grave!
I have invented a Jewish nation! I invented them!

Not them! And they will no longer be here on earth!
I invented them. Yes, I sit here and devise-
Only torment can be seen, the pain, the pain,
Their slaughter is true and obvious.

See, see, they are standing all around me far and wide,
And all of them-a shock goes through me-through my body,
They look with Ben-Zion's, with Yomke's lonely eyes yearning,
They look at me with sorrowful eyes of my wife.

With my brother Berel's big blue eyes, yes!
How does his glance come to them? Here he is! He alone!
He looks for his children, not knowing they are here
Among the millions here-I don't tell him, no...

My Khanele was taken together with my two sons!
My Khane knows, she took them with her-
She doesn't know where Tzvi is, she doesn't know about me-
She doesn't know about my disaster, she doesn't know, that I live...

[Page 104]

Come, silent ones, with so much to tell, come Khane, come
Pay attention, listen to my voice and recognize me!

Listen, my Benzik'l[Ben-Zion], my young one, my genius, you understand,
Lamentations, I sing, the last of my last, of the last Jew-

And you, my Yomele, my light, my heart,
Where is your smile, YomOh smile, don't smile…

I fear for him, my Yomele, like is necessary
For me to smile, not to frighten…listen to my song…
I threw my hand like my heart on a harp
And let us ?!…Woe is me, woe is me!

Eziekiel? Not him; Jeremiah…No, he is also superfluous to me,
I cried out to them: Help me, give me a hand!
But no more will I wait for them with my song-the last one to be sung
Because they are one with their prophecy, but I am one with my grief.

15.10. 1943

Additional verses:

I am the one who saw it all up close
Children, wives and husbands, and
Those hoary-headed old men of mine
Like stones and slivers tossed on carts by an executioner
Who flogged them without a shade of pity,
Abused them with inhumane words.

I looked at all this through the window
And saw bands of killers-
Oh God, I saw those who were beaten
Marching to their death…

I wrought my hands in shame…
Shame and disgrace-
Through Jewish hands the death
Came upon the Jews-the
Defenseless Jews!

Traitors, those in shining bootlegs
Who ran in empty streets
Like a swastika on their caps-it
was with David's shield that they
Marched full of ire.

With their mouths that wounded
those words foreign to them,
Arrogant and ferocious,
Who threw us down the stairs and
dragged us from our homes.

Who tore doors open only to burst
in with violence, those bastards,
With a club raised high and ready to hit-
Into the homes overwhelmed with terror.

They pounded on us, hustling the
Elders and shoving the youngest
Somewhere into the streets overflowing with fear.
And they spat straight into God's face.
They found us in the closets and
Pulled us from under the beds,
And foul-mouthedly yelled: "Press
On, to Hell, to umschlag, where it is
That you belong"

They dragged us all from our homes,
Only to hunt inside them a bit longer.
To take the last piece of cloth, a
Bite of bread and groats.

And once in the street-they went
Mad! Look and cringe, for
This dead street came to be a single cry of terror-

From one end to another so empty
And yet as never before-
Lorries! Heavy with so much
Despair and screaming...

Inside them sit the Jews! Pulling
Their hair and wringing their hands.
Some remain silent-their silence
Screams even louder.

They stare...their gaze...is it for real?
Or maybe it's no more but a horrible dream?
Next to them are standing the Jewish police-
Atrocious and savage scoundrels!

Nearby-a German with a slight smile,
Keeps an eye on them.
The German stands at a distance and observes-
He doesn't need to meddle in,
For he kills my Jews with the Jewish hands!

*

Woe is unto me, nobody is left!
There was a people and it is no more.
There was a people and it is...Gone...
What a tale. It began in the Bible and lasted till now...A very sad tale.
A tale that began with Amelek and concluded with the far crueller Germans...
O distant sky, wide earth, vast seas,
Do not crush and don't destroy the wicked.
Let them destroy themselves!

* * *

Itzhak Katznelson, born in 1886 in Karelichy near Minsk, Belarus:

To recall the circumstances in which this lament was written: between October 3, 1943 and January 18, 1944, during his interment in the Vittel concentration camp, while awaiting deportation to Auschwitz, Katznelson composed this gripping poem.

He had been deliberately smuggled out of the Warsaw Ghetto with his son Zvi so that he could tell the story of the murder of the Jews. On August 14, 1942, his wife Hannah, and two young sons, Ben-Zion and Benjamin, had already been deported and murdered in Treblinka.

While in the French Vittel concentration camp, Katznelson buried one copy of the poem in glass milk bottles on the grounds and smuggled another copy sewn into a suitcase handle. At the end of April 1944, Katznelson and his son were deported to Auschwitz and murdered on May 1, 1944.

[Page 105]

Maków Before the First World War

by Rafael–Zvi Baharav, Haifa

Translated by Naomi Gal

My hometown Maków–Mazowiecki was situated next to the Orzyc River that runs into Narew River. It was the provincial town and its jurisdiction included the neighboring villages: Różan and Krasnosielc and many other surrounding villages. The city had beautiful views, large meadows, vegetables–gardens and gorgeous orchards, clean air and sweet–river water. In addition to these treasures there was an old forest, healing and refreshing, filled with good air. Because of these qualities the forest served as a destination for excursions, entertainment and fun and during the summer vacation, it was a place for convalescence and tourists. Every ball or public celebration, including the annual parties of the local fire–department, which included Jews and Poles, lasted for several days; all were held in the forest.

The Jews were the majority of the Maków population. In 1897 the population of the city was 7,206 people, 4,448 of them Jews. And although their livelihood was not easy, they lacked for nothing[met their needs]. Mostly they were small merchants or craftworkers and they were content with a quiet and modest life, without great ambitions.

The laborers in town, mostly tailors and cobblers, excelled in their work and there was a large demand for their products in the fairs that took place in our city and its neighboring villages.

The sugar factory, that belonged to the Polish landowners in nearby Jusczyna, the two factories of leather processing belonging to R' Zalman Orlik and R' Matisyahu Raichik, the flour–mills of R' Bezalel Willenberg were important sources of income and these establishments employed quite a few Jews in labor, commerce and mediation.

Maków was famous and well–known in all of Poland and beyond, due to the products it produced, which reached faraway places and even across the ocean. It had a good reputation as a Torah city in which our Yeshiva was located.

The founder was the late R' The Genius Neta from Lomza, the father of Ben–Zion Hilonovitch [Chilinovitch], may he rest in peace, who was a member of the daily Warsaw newspaper "The Moment" and who perished in the Holocaust.

The Jews of Maków loved the Torah and were blessed by their Yeshiva and its students who came from near and far, and they maintained her as much as possible with contributions, paying for its students' lodgings and food. There was not a house in which a Yeshiva student did not get a meal.

The Yeshiva building had two stories and stood proudly downtown, close to the market square, which was surrounded by big houses. Nearby there were several Beit Midrashim for Torah and prayers as well as the "Shtiebel" of the Gur, Alexander and Amshinov [Mszczonów] Hassidim as well as buildings of other assistance and charity establishments. In their midst stood proudly the big magnificent synagogue, which inspired all with its beautiful design and its interior paintings, done by a famous artist.

[Page 106]

The synagogues were full of praying people all day long as well as students and teachers of Mikra, Mishna, Halacha and Agada, that took place each dawn before the morning prayer and at sunset too, between Mincha and Maariv.

The city was often frequented by speakers and preachers who discussed and lectured about morals and Torah up–dates in the evenings. And if the speaker was famous many men and women flocked from all corners of the city to hear his Godly Words. They used to fill the Beit Midrash to capacity and after a mesmerizing speech, he was generously compensated.

After Maariv Prayers in the Beit Midrash, the studies began of Talmud, especially by Yeshiva students who lived at their father–in–laws and by youngsters who graduated from Cheder in GPT[1] They were beginners and studied independently, in pairs, assisted by the older students who were fluent in explaining and guiding.

Indeed, the voice of Torah that came out of the Yeshiva and the Beit Midrash was heard as pleasant music all over town until the late hours of the night.

These Torah establishments infused the citizens with love for Torah and tradition and their blessed influence was reflected in their every–day life and mannerisms.

The main worry of Maków Orthodox Jews was the education of their sons in the spirit and devotion to the Torah, but this goal was not always achieved despite their many efforts, since many of the teachers were inadequate as teachers, not knowing the profession or for lack of pedagogical aptitude. They often had to use a stick, lash or other forceful means to let the Torah penetrate their students' minds, but they achieved the opposite result: by terrorizing them, they made their students hate them and the Cheder, where the students were held all day long, except an hour or two for lunch; this became the *yoke* and a painful burden for some. And if the children persisted, despite the harsh conditions, to carry the *yoke*, it was only due to their extreme dedication.

The exception was the Cheder of my Rabbi and teacher R' Mendel Warsawer, may his memory be blessed. He was a distinguished, well–mannered man and loved clarity and order, he transferred his wisdom to his students who excelled in their knowledge and behavior.

Although there were enough Cheders for sacred studies, there was only one municipal school for the Jewish children to study secular studies, which were taught in Russian.

This school excelled because of its multi–talented teacher–principal, my teacher R' Haykel Gutman, may his memory be blessed. He was an educated and knowledgeable man, honest and respected by all, except some ultra–orthodox who could not forgive the fact that his students were studying with no cover on their heads and girls and boys studied together. After this teacher–principial left Maków in order to become a county inspector of the schools, he was replaced by his student and mentor (who went to school with him) Shmuel Pianko, who perished in the Holocaust, may his memory be blessed.

[Page 107]

In addition to this school there were also private lessons for Yiddish, Polish and Calculus which were taught to individuals and to groups by Mrs. Gutman, the aforementioned teacher's wife, and by R' David Rosenthal. The students in these classes came mostly from circles that avoided the municipal school for religious reasons.

Maków was proud of the great rabbis who served her. And, indeed, in the old cemetery there were many *tents* on the graves of the greatest rabbis and righteous, among them the famous Magid R' David Makower, may his memory be blessed, who was admired by everybody while he was alive. The elders of his generation praised him and described him as an outstanding man.

Because of its historical importance I will copy here an expert from the Russian–Jewish encyclopedia in my free translation:" Makower David Magid–Speaker was one of the first objectors to the Hassidic movement. He wrote a book called

"The Song of the Populist". He lived in the last quarter of the 18th century in Maków–Mazowiecki, fought the Hassidim by denouncing their way of life and beliefs and the behavior of their followers. He finished writing this book in 1798 but did not publish it in his lifetime fearing the revenge and persecution of the Hassidim. The hand–written book was distributed only after his death and it is an important source for researching Hassidic history."

The members of "Haskalah" in Maków, 1912

[Page 108]

According to the hypothesis of the great historian S. Dubnow, David Makower is the writer of the book challenging the Hassidic "Zamir Arizim" ("Tyrant's Mockingbird"). The late Dr. S. A. Hordeski shares this opinion in his book "The Hassidim and the Hassid".

The Maków families Jerozolimski and Gorlitz (my mother's family, may her memory be blessed) are its descendants.

Due to his energetic war on the Hassidic Movement, his followers saw in him as a distinct student of the Vilna Gaon, may his memory be blessed.

During his time in Maków Rabbi Yehuda Leib Graubart, may his memory be blessed, served as the great Head of Judges. He wrote and published in Maków his book "Havalim Baneimim", Torah novelties about Shas dilemmas. He was famous as a wise and brilliant Torah scholar and was elected to become the Rabbi of Staszów. When the First World War broke the evil regime expelled him to Russia as a hostage. While in Russia for more than three years, he was very active in the educational and cultural arena and helped other exiled rabbis. After the war he wrote and published a book called "A Memory Book" where he depicted Jewish lives and their hardships during those years.

When he returned to his city of Staszów he found her destroyed and in rubble. Shortly after, he was invited to become a Rabbi in Toronto. He served there with respect and dignity until his last day and worked with faith and dedication for local public charities and general Jewish issues. He succeeded in founding institutions of Torah and charity. He died there accomplishing many endeavors with an excellent reputation. May his memory be blessed. `

When this Rabbi left Maków he was replaced in 1903 by Rabbi Israel Nissan Cooperstock, may his memory be blessed. He was one of the most prominent followers of Alexander and was a great sage in Torah and faith. The local Alexander followers admired him. But the Gur Hassidim treated him very differently since he was appointed without their will and consent. They wanted their own candidate, a Gur Hassid. But their candidate lost the election for lack of votes. The Gur Hassid did not accept his loss.

The settlement of the Land–of–Israel was very important to Rabbi Cooperstock and he waited impatiently for the time when he would be able to fulfill this Mitzvah. When the fourth Aliyah came, he saw a window of opportunity to fulfill his life–long dream and without hesitation, he left the city and his rabbinical position, which he served for twenty years; he and his wife, the Rebbetzin, Haya Zipporah, their daughter Yehudit, her husband and their household all made Aliyah.

This bold step made a great impression on all. He was admired by all.

[Page 109]

People gathered and his departure was celebrated with great veneration and joy. Merchants closed their businesses, workers left their work and almost the whole city came to say goodbye to their Rabbi and his family, and wish them good–luck on their journey to the Holy–Land.

The Rabbi's farewell was emotional and touching, and his parting words to his congregation were moving. His many admirers danced and sang accompanying the Rabbi and his family to Pułtusk, the nearby city.

The Rabbi earned his respect with this daring step. Many Rabbis, who until then were indifferent and distanced from themselves from Zionism and settling in the Land–of–Israel; many were affected by what the rabbi did and changed their minds and some of them eventually followed him and made Aliyah.

Healthy and happy, the Rabbi and his family reached their destination in Holy Jerusalem. A short time after his Aliyah the Rabbi published a book called "The Love of Zion and Jerusalem" in which he discussed the four parts of the "Shulchan Aruch".

Unfortunately, he arrived in Israel during a financial crisis and this, like other factors, prevented him from achieving the place he deserved. He had many deliberations in his struggles for his livelihood and status. Unfortunately, he got involved in an attempt to establish a separate slaughter–house, despite the objections of the local Rabbinate and to the dismay of the inhabitants.

This unfortunate affair, in which he failed miserably, caused him much sorrow, suffering and disappointment. The suffering and the pain took a toll on his frail health, he became ill and after a prolonged disease died, after many years of hardships. On 2/2/1840, at the age of 72, he was led to his burial on the Olive Mount. He rests among the righteous, may his Memory be Blessed, for his " Love of Zion and Jerusalem" and his just ways inspired a generation of faithful people.

The Jews in Maków were proud that Nahum Sokolow lived in their city after his marriage to the local honorable and businessman R' Yitzhak Zvi Segal's daughter, may his memory be blessed, who hosted him for several years. During this time, Sokolow studied Torah and general studies and also wrote his geographical book, one of his firsts, "Mezukay Eretz". After a few years he moved to Warsaw where he found a larger audience for his talents and became the president of the Zionist Histadrut.

By the way, I have heard that my uncle, the great scholar, the late Rabbi Rafael Hirsh Gorlitz (I am named after him) reviewed Nahum Sokolow and studied him before signing him up, as was the custom back then – he was deeply impressed by the young man's brilliance and found him very gifted. He also predicted him to have a great future in Israel in Torah, wisdom and science. When the businessman heard the examiner's praises, he *grabbed* the youngster as a groom for his daughter.

In the summer of 1898, a large fire broke out in the city and the local fire department was unable to contain it until firemen from other cities came to their aid, more than half the city burned down.

Assets and generations of hard work were gone in one night. Horrible and shocking were the sufferings of the burned people who remained without shelter and means. It took many years till they were able to bounce back, rebuild from the rubble and make a new life.

[Page 110]

After a few years our Maków citizens endured more hardships: the Russian–Japanese war broke out and afterwards the Russian Revolution in 1904–1905, which decimated the economy and sacrificed the safety of Poland's Jews, especially in small places like Maków where the situation was far worse.

In those years of confusion and hardship, the Poles found an opportunity to renew their struggle for independence and at the same time to get rid of the Jews, which they hated, and so they used pressure to push the Jews away from their sources of livelihood. They declared an economic boycott and a total war, forbidding Poles from maintaining any commercial contacts with Jews. They led a vicious and relentless propaganda against the Jews, their labor and their commerce.

Antisemitism increased and the relationships between Jews and Poles deteriorated, to the point that it became intolerable. The livelihood of many Jews was destroyed and some had to leave their homes they inhabited for many generations and immigrate – mainly to the United Sates.

As *God's will*, in this case, they were lucky. The distress and sufferings of these brothers brought them advantages. And we now see that they escaped the *Holocaust*, which followed and they found refuge and safety in America.

The sons' of Maków were well organized in the US; they prospered and helped our people and our country[Israel] and like loyal brothers– they continued assisting their needy brothers. "The Organization of Maków Descendants" and the "Charity Fund" were sustained successfully in Israel due to their constant help and support.

The economic situation in Poland, prepared the groundwork for the Zionist ideology, which began to grow roots in Maków as well. Especially the youth who organized their Zionist groups– the first steps were cultural while preparing for the future.

At the initiation of Moshe Brjoza, Fishel Segal, his sister Sara, Yosef Hendel, Yehiel Meir Plato, Yosef Titonovitz, Shlomo Abelodeziner, Yitzhak Dobra and Israel Meir Menchikovsky, Israel Yosef Rosenman and the writer of this narrative, a library was created (the first in Makow), where Hebrew and other classes were given. We also held meetings, lectures, etc. For a while we had to manage the library and do everything in secret because of objectors from the right and the left. The committee was a convenient way to mange our activities. Under duress we fought the objectors and finally, after many efforts we managed to overcome the obstacles and with the money we received from the authorities we got a license to found the library and a club. We breathed a sigh of relief and energetically continued our work.

Our devoted work proved the objectors and the disrupters the importance of our activities.

[Page 111]

We even managed to convince the extremists, the deniers of our Zionist ideals and majestic dreams, not to ignore the importance of our activities and give us their blessing,[believing it was intended as an act for assimilation], which were dangerous and destructive against Jews[many Chasidic groups were anti–Israel and there was also inter–sect fighting– if they did not adhere to the same beliefs and principles].

Our activities, which were essential and important, helped the youth gain National self–esteem, while still adhering to "old–generation traditions". They realized that there was no future for Jews in antisemitic Poland. They got rid of the *idle* and *decaying* way of life and trained themselves [also physical training] to adapt to the new reality of Hebrew lives in a Jewish Homeland, those who were fortunate to make Aliyah before the Holocaust (I, who made Aliya in 1925, am one of the lucky ones) were able to be part of the country and contribute to its building and statehood.

Kiryat Motzkin, 1962

"The fourth "Hagalil" Conference in Maków, 1930

Translator's footnote:

1.   Gemara, Rashi, additions

[Page 112] Blank

[Page 113]

<u>Ways of Life</u>

[Page 114] Blank

[Page 115]

Once There Was a City Called Makow...

by Yakov – Khaim Sobel / New York

Translated by Janie Respitz

"For they have devoured Jacob and laid waste his habitation". (Psalms 79:7)

"Tell your children of it, and let your children tell their children, and their children another generation" (Joel 1:3)

The horrific destruction of European Jewry had and will continue to have in the future a far reaching effect not only on survivors, who miraculously were saved, but on all Jews in the diaspora, because European Jewry – the largest amount from Poland – were the spiritual centre from where all other Jewish communities in the world were nourished.

The Jews of Poland over centuries formed an exemplary life style: every Jewish community had its own cultural society and religious and charitable institutions. Makow also had its establishments, institutions, and organizations. Schools, Houses of Study, small Hasidic synagogues, and the "Respectable" synagogue where for generations people inherited their seats.

Seventh grade graduates from the Folk Shule (elementary school), Makow, 1937

[Page 116]

This was all annihilated by the Nazi murderers. Jewish Makow was torn from its roots, gone.

All those who were born and raised in Makow: all those who are alive will never forget their city. The Makow Jews that were so pitilessly murdered stand as if they were still alive before our eyes. I would like to describe for the next generation a bit of the way of life in Makow, something from the spiritual treasure which it possessed: the Jewish people who lived and produced: all the institutions and organizations: the activists and leaders of communal life.

We have sworn never to forget, to remember eternally. While remembering the past life and activities we will eternalize the memory of the martyrs. Let the whole world know what occurred during this terrifying time in order for it not to happen again in human history.

As far as my memory will serve me, I will try to do this so we will have a living monument for generations to come.

Worrying About the New Generation

After the First World War when Poland was freed, Makow began to get back on its feet and slowly organize its Jewish life.

The first task was to take care of the children after the war, providing religious and secular schools to educate the young.

Thanks to the effort of a few important people like: Hillel Sheynberg, Yishayahu Rekant, Abba Birnboym, Yishayahu Sobel and others, a modern religious school called The Hebrew School "Toshiya" (Initiative) was founded where they taught bible, biblical commentaries and Hebrew in Hebrew.

The established members of the community understood that the old religious schools and their teachers were a thing of the past. Because of this, Reb Hillel Sheynberg and Reb Yishayahu Rekant, both learned men, engaged their friend Anshl Kotzyak (from Grayeve), who with the help of his son Alter and Henekh Shultz ran the new school. They called him "Moreh" (the Hebrew word for teacher) and not Rebbbe as in the past, because Mr. Kotzyak was really a guide and educator of the new generation in the spirit of nationalism and "Hibat Zion" (Lovers of Zion).

[Page 117]

For the first time they held "exams" in the school, every Purim. Fathers were happy to hear their children recite a chapter form the bible. The school published its own Hebrew monthly newspaper called "The Little Hebrew" which was written by the children and distributed to the benefactors.

There was another similar religious school called "The Modern Religious School" which was run by Reb Yekhezkl Levkovitch and his sons Yudl and Moishe.

There did remain a few old fashioned traditional religious schools with old styled teachers. Many of the younger generation that later got involved with Zionist work in town should be grateful to these schools: "Toshiya School" and the "Modern Religious School" for the Jewish national education they received.

Also open schools were opened by the government, with a separate school for Jewish children, with Jewish male and female teachers under the leadership of Mr. Shmuel Pianko, a Jewish intellectual, well educated and a devoted communal activist, which thanks to his effort and work, new departments opened in the school every year, until there were seven departments. When a student finished this school he was able to enter the fourth class in high school, without exams.

A class from the "Yavneh" school in Makow,
1935

[Page 118]

In those schools all subjects were taught in the Polish language, even Jewish religion and Jewish history.

When the children attending the new religious schools grew up the parents looked for an institute of higher learning for them, and later a Jewish high school was actually founded thanks to the initiative of: Yekhiel – Meir Plata, Shloimeh Granievitch, Hillel Sheynberg, Abba Birnboym, Meir Ostri, Yishayahu Rekant, Yishayahu Sobol, Hershl Blum, Mrs. Khaya Shuldenrayn, Mrs. Gitl Vilenberg and others. Besides secular studies, they also taught Hebrew. The teacher was Mr. Shmuel Bernholtz, a great Hebraist and a devoted Zionist. By the way, he survived the war, came to America and died in New York in 1966.

Unfortunately the Jewish high school did not exist for long due to its difficult financial situation. However many of the students continued their education in the Polish high school in Makow and others left to study in Pultusk, Mlave and Warsaw.

Among the first to graduate from the Polish high school were: Avrom Rozental and his wife Rayzl Montshkovsky, Moishe Bzhoza, Avrom – Borukh Segal, Khaim – Borukh Segal, Yakov Likhtenshteyn and others. Many of these students continued their education in Warsaw.

The desire to study began to rise among the youth that were now growing up. Many of the students who graduated from the General Government Schools left to study in Warsaw, at "Takhmoni" and Poznansky's seminar. Leybl Vilenberg (now in Israel), Simkha Shuldnreyn (now a rabbi in America), Pinkhas Zgal and Mordkhai Veysgarber all graduated from Poznansky's seminar.

Time did not stand still. A new generation grew up and we had to worry about them. A new religious school called "Yavneh" was founded, a new educational institution from the "Mizrachi" (religious Zionists) movement. The founders were: Yishayahu Rekant, Yekhiel Perkal, Mendl Klayner, Yishayahu Sobol, Hershl Khunovitch and Mrs. Yetta Segal (today in America).

Besides the Pentateuch, Rashi, the Prophets and biblical commentaries the also taught Hebrew. Many of the pupils were children of poor parents and the committee had a difficult task covering the budget. The Jewish community offered partial subsidies. They also received periodic support from fellow townsmen living in America.

Later another religious school was founded called "Foundations of the Torah" thanks to the philanthropist Reb Betzalel Vilenberg, may he rest in peace, under the supervision of "Agudah". This religious school took in the students from the former ones.

[Page 119]

Some of the orthodox youth left to study in Yeshivas where they received rabbinic ordination. They were: Shmuel Hilert (the son of my teacher Reb Henekh Hilert), Boylman and Figa. (All three survived and live in Brooklyn, New York).

Just as general life was beginning to normalize, there was the Bolshevik invasion. Again war, shootings and casualties. The invasion did not last long. Thanks to the so called "Miracle on the Vistula", Marshal Pilsudsky pushed back the Red Army. Jewish life was reinstated more or less and began to pulsate once again.

The Economic Situation

The general economic situation was not too good. The Jews of Makow once again began to concern themselves with earning a living, business and handwork like: tailoring, shoe making, carpentry, baking, hat making etc…

People travelled to fairs in nearby cities and waited for the two market days in the week (Tuesday and Friday) to sell their goods and manufactured clothing and shoes etc…

A class from the Jewish high school in Makow, 1920

[Page 120]

After the Bolshevik invasion in the early 1920s, tourists began to arrive in town, former townsmen from America who came to visit their relatives, a brother, sister, or those who came to visit graves, inspecting the old and new cemeteries, the tombstones of parents or other relatives.

Right after the First World War Makow Jews in America organized a Relief Fund. Their task was to send support to Makow.

The founders of the aid committee were: the rabbi Reb Fishl Nayman, the Makow rabbi (a son of Reb Motele Dayan) who died on a ship on his way to settle in the Land of Israel: Yakov Sobol, Khantshe Hamer, Fishl Solomon, Hirsh Moishe Kohen, (Yakov – Meir Segal's son in law), Herman Goldman, the Stavisky brothers, Khane – Khave Gold, Grodovitch and others. At he same time, they were the first contributors to the aid fund.

In America they nominated a committee of Jews in Makow that would manage the work of distributing the aid to the needy, like the necessary provisions for Passover, aid for the High Holidays, wood and potatoes for the winter and subsidies for the following intuitions: The Society to Spend the Night with the Sick, the religious school "Yavneh" and others.

The committee was comprised of the following householders: Shmuel Pianko, Shmuel Vayntryob, Hershl Losher, Moishe Efraim Grinberg, Yishayahu Sobol, Khaim Yitzkhak Glogaver, Elkoneh Khvitayko, Leybke Zgrizek.

These were honest, sincere Jews filled with the desire to help the poor. These were Jews who understood the situation of a poor artisan, an ordinary person in town who required help.

Later the Ladies Auxiliary took over the relief work. A group of kind hearted women with Mrs. Berkovitch (Yekhezkihu's daughter) as chairperson. These important women were: Khane Karp, Rokhl – Leah Rubin, Basah Ostri, Esther Kantor, Khane Makover, Malke Fridman (Tirtza's Malke), Esther Kohen, Mrs. Khshanover and others.

The women gave time and energy and worked hard to collect money to achieve this goal. Malke Fridman, Esther Kantor, Esther Kohen and Mrs. Khshanover organized receptions in their homes, card parties and looked for ways to raise money to support the poor in Makow. The sending of financial aid from America lasted a few years. Later the work was restricted to the sending of necessary provisions for Passover which continued until the outbreak of the Second World War.

[Page 121]

The Religious, Economic and Communal Life

The street where the synagogue, both Houses of Study, a few small houses and the rabbi's house were situated was called Synagogue Street. You had to go up a small hill as if you were ascending to a holy place. My hands start to tremble, tears begin to form, and my heart grieves when I remember the Makow synagogue, the magnificent Holy Ark which was known throughout Poland.

A group of "Mizrachi" youth in Makow, 1920

When you entered the synagogue, you couldn't help but feel respect just for the beauty. The German murderers, may their names be blotted out, destroyed it right down to its foundation.

Let us remember those who prayed there: Borukh Rizika (Butche), Yankl Katz (Yankl the tailor), Itzl Shamovitch, Itche – Meir Likhtenshteyn, Mordkhai Ezrilevitch, his sons Rafael Hirsh and Ezriel Ezrilevitch, Shayma Pekartchik, Fishl Unger, Alter Shmulevitch, Moishe Segal, (Moishe the wholesaler) and the beadle who always walked around making sure that no one, God forbid, would cough loudly, or a little boy would not be mischievous during the reading of the Torah.

[Page 122]

During the High Holidays the synagogue was packed. From the women's section on the balcony, looking down on their husbands and children, the compassionate Makow mothers derived great pleasure. The sweet voices of the cantor Malkhiel, cantor Alter Ribka and Yitzkhak Zilberberg with his choirboys or Berl Gonteh rang through the synagogue. Many tears were shed in this synagogue with prayers for a better tomorrow.

In the synagogue, upstairs and downstairs there were smaller places of worship.

The tailors, shoemakers, wagon drivers, furriers and ordinary Jews each had their own little synagogue where they prayed all year.

The common folk, the artisans, small businessmen, the simple Jews, went to the House of Study after along difficult work day to pray, listen to a preacher and hear the latest news from town and around the world.

It was mainly the simple folk who congregated in the old House of Study, the simple everyday Jew. The House of Study was like a second home. There was a warm atmosphere, not only from the heated ceramic oven but from the surroundings. The Jews themselves were warm and kind to each other.

The Respected Men

Let us remember the respected well established men in the old House of Study: Reb Shmuel – Yosl Kit, Yekhiel Rebak (Avrom Itche's son), Yishayahu Sobol, Moishe Efraim Grinberg, Meir Ovadia (the beadle) with his hoarse voice. After him, Manes Ingberman (Manes the broker), who was the beadle and the rabbi's assistant, and who prayed beautifully at the podium. Reb Sender Freshberg, a sincere Jew who's singing of the prayers during the Days of Awe still rings in my ears. Yakov – Meir Freshberg was a Jew who worked in a village and came home Thursday for the Sabbath. However he knew the entire Book of Psalms by heart. He would walk around with his arms folded listening to others pray and when he heard someone reciting the Kaddish (memorial prayer), he was there to say Amen. He tried to do the holy act of saying as many Amens as possible. (He was actually called "Yakov Meir Amen"), and the well known psalm reciter Mendl Kirshnboym.

[Page 123]

Every Saturday morning, before prayers, Jews sat around the long table in the House of Study dressed in their Sabbath clothes. Reb Shmuel Oppenheim (Shmuel the little rabbi) taught them the Torah portion of the week.

Reb Shmuel was a small man with a beautiful white silvery beard and deep eyes. A man with a stately appearance.

After Reb Shmuel died this role was taken over by Reb Yakov Zgal (Yankl Bliakhazh). My father used to take me along to these lessons. Even later when I grew up I continued to go as I loved it very much. When Reb Yakov Zgal took over it was Shabbat Bereishit (Genesis Sabbath). Until today I remember his interpretation of the word Bereishit and what each letter stood for, using a mystical technique by which the letters of a Hebrew word are interpreted as initials of other words. Reb Yakov Zgal with his black beard and clever eyes was a great scholar and a wise man. He had a special way of explaining the weekly portion, appropriate for his audience. The rabbis did not get paid for their teaching except for a piece of meat the butcher would bring them for the Sabbath.

The Committee to Spend the Night with the sick. Makow. 1930

[Page 124]

The Committee to rebuild the old House of Study in Makow, 1929

[Page 125]

The manager of the "Ein Yakov" society was Reb Yakov Shliazer, an honest man, a butcher by profession, with a good heart. He would provide meat for many poor families on the Sabbath. In our town he was the so called "diplomat" and "strategist". During the First World War and the Bolshevik invasion he understood all the strategies. After the evening prayers he would stand beside the ceramic oven and explain to the Jews how the war was unfolding, where the Germans were and where the Russians were. Everyone enjoyed this very much.

Seated at another table were men who learned psalms every Saturday morning with Reb Khaim Dovidl (my teacher) – a small thin man with a pointed little beard. He explained the psalms so people would understand what they were saying. The manager of the Psalm Society was Reb Velvl Kirshenboym, who would pray at the podium and could also read from the Torah.

In our town there was also: The Ger Hasisdic small synagogue with its distinguished Jews like: Reb Tzalel Vilemberg, Yisroel Segal, Mendl Student, Itch Meir Mashgiakh, Yehoshua Montshkovsky, Yekhiel Meir Ber, Itche Meir Frenkl, Pintche Tazman, Dovid Hendl (who later became a rabbi in Warsaw), Khone Binem Vengerke, and many others. The Amshinov Hasisdim had their small synagogue and gained a fine reputation with these dear Jews: Reb Moishe Yosef Garfinkl, Velvel Feyntzyeg, and Kalman Sofer – Shtern, Khaim Dovidl the teacher Govarchik, the ritual slaughterer Alter Ribka, Pinkhas Lifshitz, Meir Ostri, Abba Bernboym, Yankl Dovid Hendl and many others. The Alexander little synagogue had the following respected members: Reb Moishe Nisl Rubin, Sender Grinshpan, Alter Moishe Tziviner, Eliyahu Katz, Pinkhas Katz, Avrom Skaleh, Itche Chiml, Shaykeh Makover, Manes Ingberman, and many others. The Mishana Society was located upstairs in the old House of Study. Among its distinguished members were: Shmuel Rozengerg, Khaim Leyb Lilental, Shmuel Yablonke and many others.

In our town we had a Society to Spend the Night with the Sick, an Interest Free Loan Society, and a Society to Visit the Sick. These were all organized and run by Jews to help other Jews in need. Those involved in the Society to Spend the Night with the Sick were: Itche Meir Likhtenshteyn, Yitzkhak Paskovitch, Yishayahu Sobol, the cantor Reb Alter Ribka, Yitzkhak Vesolek, Alter Epshteyn, Avrom Garfinkl, Yitzkhak Shuldenreyn, Noyakh Visoker, and Shimen – Khaim Khilianovitch.

The Society to Visit the Sick had a women's committee. These women visited the sick, spent the night, arranged for medication and provided preserves to delight the soul, and whatever other help was needed. The women involved were: Khaye Shuldenreyn, Perl Skurnik, Yakhet Sheynberg, Zviya Plata, Khane – Blimeh Perlberg, Esther – Leah Vonsiak, Rivka Blum, Fraidele Bernboym, under the leadership of the beloved Sheva Khilinovitch.

[Page 126]

The new House of Study was not far from the synagogue. This is where the more progressive Jews were concentrated – members of "Mizrachi", the religious Zionist movement, and the younger up and coming householders. The new House of Study was smaller than the old one and a bit more intimate. Some of these people were:

Yekhiel – Meir Pliyato with his stately appearance, Reb Hillel Shaynberg, a tall handsome man, a Talmudic scholar who was also knowledgeable in secular studies. I still remember how he prayed at the podium. When Yekhiel – Meir Pliyato was assisted by his deep baritone voice, you felt it in your heart because he knew what he was saying. His reading from the Torah sounded like beautiful music. This will continue to ring in my ears forever, especially when he read on Simkhas Torah. Other important men in town were: Yitzkhak Dobres, Yakov Moishe Dobres (now in America), and Reb Feyvl Blum, the rabbi's assistant who made sure the House of Study was kept clean and tidy. Hershl Blum (Feyvl's son), Yekhiel Perkal, Yekhezkl Kantor, Fishl Glagover, Dovid – Leyb Goldshteyn, Khaim Leyzer Segal, Yitzkhak Kaber, and many many others.

The Committee To Spend the Night With the Sick in Makow,
chairman Yitzkhak Vesolek, of blessed memory, 1928

[Page 127]

We must remember Reb Yishayahu Rekant (the pharmacist) – a learned Jew, an enlightened Jew, a great Hebraist, a good Zionist, who devoted a lot of time and energy to "Tarbut" and the "Yavneh" religious school in town. He possessed a warm Jewish heart helping many poor people with advice and medicine. He was able to make a diagnosis just like a doctor. He always liked to discuss Talmud and bible. Even the Hasidim considered him a scholar. Reb Kalman Sofer loved talking with him about Torah. When the Jewish Agency began to collect money in town the largest donations came from the distinguished members of the new House of Study.

In 1926 Dr. Shoshkes and Dr. Shulman arrived in Makow to organize a Jewish cooperative bank. The main goal of this bank was to provide artisans and small businesses an opportunity to borrow money at a low interest. The founders were Shloimeh Granievitch, Henekh Viseman, Yishayahu Sobol, Shmuel Veyntroyb, Meir Ostri, Yishayahu Montshkovsky, and others. The first meeting took place in my father's house. The bank developed nicely and later became a dominating factor in the economic life of our town and a great help to the common man. One could receive a loan of 600 zloty which was a lot of money at the time. This was very helpful to the artisans and small business owners.

A Jewish Majority on City Council

Municipal life in town was getting organized. There were elections for city council as well as elections in the Jewish community. The second city council election made a great impression. Jews always comprised the majority of the population of Makow. This time, Jewish community activists felt they must be represented on city council and at city hall. A meeting took place at the home of Yekhiel Meir Pliyato (chairman of the Zionist organization). The meeting was attended by representatives of all organizations and movements except the Bund. It was decided to create a national bloc which would even include the "Agudah". Included in this bloc were: the Zionist organizations: Mizrachi religious Zionists) and the left wing Poalei Zion (Labour Zionists), the Artisan Union and Merchant Union. One list was presented in order to obtain more Jewish representatives on the city council so that all Jewish organizations and institutions would be able to enjoy subsidies proportionately.

[Page 128]

Farewell evening for Yisroel Frenkel when he left for Eretz Yisrael in 1931

[Page 129]

The election process began. A fight broke out between the Bund and the "National Bloc". The actions of the National Bloc were mostly run by the members of the Zionist organizations, from "HeChalutz" and the "Shomer Hatzair". Mass meetings and gatherings took place. The younger elements of the Zionist groups were led by Moishe Rezenberg (Rivka Mensashe's son in law), Yakov Moishe Skurnik, Yisroel Frenkel, Litman Montshkovsky and Khaim Sobol.

Moishe Rozenberg was a dynamic Jew, very energetic and devoted. He had great organizational skills.

Yakov Moishe Skurnik (now in Israel with his wife Mindl and their daughter Mala), was the leader of "Tarbut" and the "Shomer Hatzair". Everyone in town loved him. He was everyone's friend. Even the leaders of the Bund held him in high esteem and respected his sense of justice and devotion. He dedicated a lot of time and energy to the election process. Yakov Khaim Sobol (now in America) was one of the main speakers at all the mass gatherings and meetings. Litman Montshkovsky (now in Israel) worked hard and devoted a lot of energy to this cause.

The Frenkel brothers, Yisroel – Gershon and Shmuel Dovid actively worked on the election committee as well as many others from young Zionist groups.

The results of the election were successful. It brought great victory to the Jewish population in town. The National Bloc won. For the first time in the history of Makow there was a Jewish majority on city council and at city hall, where among the councilmen we had two Jewish representatives, Moishe Rozenberg and Yishayahu Montshkovsky. The last one was a Ger Hasid who was a very smart man. He endured and even progressed a bit. He spoke Polish fluently which was rare among the older Jews. The Jewish councilmen fought honourably to defend Jewish interests and demanded equal rights and support for Jewish institutions. When the mayor was on leave, he was replaced by Moishe Rozenberg.

Later, Yehoshua Montshkovsky and Borukh Riziko also became councilmen.

[Page 130]

Purim Ball organized by the Jewish National Fund, Makow, 1936

[Page 131]

For the first time in our town's history Jews were employed as clerks in city hall:

Itzl Sahmovitch, who was Yosl Shamovitch's son, Moishe Rozenberg and Yakov Khaim Sobol.

A kindergarten was founded in town for poor Jewish children. The teacher was Yente Shniderman. Her assistant was her sister Brontche.

Yente Shniderman had been a student of the great martyr Janus Korczak. She ran the school with immense devotion and love. She was blessed with a beautiful voice. She studied music with her uncle Avrom Modrikamien. The children loved to listen to her sing and teach.

Thanks to the Jewish aldermen and councilmen the Jewish school received a subsidy from city hall. Moishe Rozenberg showed a special interest in this children's school as well as other councilmen, Dovid Minoga, Yakov Moishe Skrunik and Avigdor Tchimiel.

Zionist Activity

The Zionist movement expanded greatly after the proclamation of the Balfour Declaration. People believed that the long waited dream to return to Zion and finally become a reality.

The General Zionist Organization had already existed in our town for many years. The leaders were: Yekhiel Meir Pliyato – chairman, Moishe Rozenberg – secretary, Yekhezkl Segal (now in America), Yekhezkl Kantor, Yosef Kantor, Fishl Glogover, Mordkhai Blum, Yakov Segal (now in America), Khaim Montlak, Binyomin Yustman, Moishe Yehuda Freshberg, Yakov – Moishe Skrunik, Yisroel Gershon Frenkel, Litman Montshkovsky and others. Women also took part in this work: Gitl Segal, Zviya Pliyato, Shaindl Rekant, Golde Vilenberg, Yetta Segal, and from the younger generation: Soreh – Etta Skurnik, Rokhl Likhtenshteyn, Tzirl Skurnik, Raizl Montshkovsky and others.

There was also a youth organization in Makow called "Flowers of Zion". The younger element belonged to this group. Many of them were former Yeshiva students. In general, the Zionist ideal captured the youth. The "Flowers of Zion" later dissolved because its leaders, the active members immigrated, some to America and some to Latin America like: Hillel Raitchik, Yedidia Raitchik and others.

[Page 132]

The older youth organized the "Shomer Hatzair", "Hechalutz" and Hachalutz Hatazir". These young people began to run diversified intensive programs. The General Zionist Organization was devoted to collecting money for The Jewish Agency and The Jewish National Fund, selling shekels and spreading the Zionist idea. Thanks to Mr. Yeshayahu Rekant and Yakov – Moishe Skurnik the "Tarbut" organization was founded. Its task was to teach and spread the Hebrew language. They organized Hebrew evening courses.

The "Tarbut" also was involved in cultural work. They held lectures, discussions, and checkers evenings Friday nights. The Zionist Organization, "Tarbut" and the youth organizations brought in prominent speakers and writers from Warsaw, as well as appearances of Jewish actors, performances and recitations. It is worthwhile to stress that the following personalities visited Makow: Reb Hillel Zeitlin, Rabbi Milaylkovsky, Dr. Shiffer, Yosef Heftman, Dr. Iserovitch, Yehuda Gothelf, Yitzkhak Funt, Mordkhai Yafeh, Shloimeh Mintz, Shefner, Zerubavel, Ben – Tzion Hilinovitch and others. The Zionist Organization had a Sholem Aleichem Library with a large collection of Hebrew, Yiddish and Polish books – and the people read. Those involved with the library were: Khaya Itteh Perlberg, Yakov Yedvabnik, Yakov Segal, Yisroel – Gershon Frenkel and others. They dedicated time and energy to enrich the library with books and to properly serve the reader.

The committee of the Sholem Aleichem Library of the Zionist Organization in Makow, 1929

[Page 133]

Flower Day in Honour of the The Jewish National Fund 1933

A Bazaar for the Jewish National Fund Makow 1933

[Page 134]

The work for The Jewish National Fund was based on fund raising. They distributed collection boxes to the houses, organized "Flower Days", a Purim ball and a bazaar almost every year. It is worthwhile mentioning the JNF bazaars in Makow were very successful. The day of the bazaar was a Zionist holiday in town. The distinguished women were: Zviya Pliyato, Khave Ribak, Mindl Skurnik, Golde Vilenberg, Khaya Soreh Lesman, Yetta Segal, Sortche Blum (Feyvl's daughter in law). Among the younger ones: Khaya – Itte Perlberg, Esther Piekartchik, Soreh Vilenberg (now in Israel), Rokhl Blum (now in Sweden), Alta Hendel, Khaya – Sorcheh Raitchik, Feyge – Rivka Raitchik and others. These were the devoted workers at the bazaars.

Mordkhai Blum (Shimshon's son) donated a new house he had built to the bazaar without any reward. Only a Makow Jew totally devoted to Zionism would do this.

The women prepared a delicious buffet which was served the evenings of the bazaar. The central committee of the JNF in Warsaw placed the Makow bazaars in first place among all the surrounding towns.

We must mention the devoted work of Hershl Vaysberg, Berko Hendl, may he rest in peace, who enriched the Makow JNF bazaars with decorations. The members: Litman Montshkovsky, Yakov – Moishe Skurnik, Yakov – Khaim Goldshteyn, and Yakov – Khaim Sobol organized the cultural component and Khaim – Leyzer Rogoza took care of the technical part.

We also had a religious Zionist organization in town, "Mizrachi". Most of its members were older religious Jews from the small synagogues, the old and new Houses of Study, the synagogue as well as simple ordinary common folk. Their work was dedicated to the Jewish Agency and the "Yavneh" school. Those active were: Meir Ostri, Hillel Sheynberg, Abba Birnboym, Yishayahu Rekant, Yishayahu Sobol, Alter Moishe Tziviner, (a great scholar and a kind man who died young). "Mizrachi" also had a youth wing called "Young Mizrachi", which did its own work. The active members were: Mordkhai Tziviner (now in America), Yakov Goldvaser of blessed memory (survived the war, lived in America and died young), Eliyahu Levinzon, Leybl Montshkovsky, Meir Skala, Yakov Levkovitch, Moishe Rozenblum, Mordkhai Yedvabnik. Some of them participated in a pioneer training program "Hachshara" and immigrated to Eretz Yisrael, like: Leybl Montshkovsky, Yakov Levkovitch, Eliyahu Levinzon, Meir Skakla (now a sailor on an Israeli ship).

[Page 135]

The "Young Pioneer" movement in Makow 1926

[Page 136]

"Hechalutz" Movement

In 1925, thanks to the initiative of the two Yakov –Khaims, Yakov – Khaim Goldshteyn and Yakov– Khaim Sobol, the "Hechalutz" (Pioneer) organization was founded. They invited their friends from Pultusk: Yitzkhak Dan (now in Israel, principal of "Amidar" in Beersheva), Hertzke Burshtin and Yehuda Leyb Piekazh to help found the "Hechalutz" organization in Makow. They had experience since this organization already exited in Pultusk. The first meeting took place in the home of Yakov –Khaim Sobol and the participants were: Shmuel Yitzkhak Kleynhoyz, Khaim Leyzer Freshberg, Khaim Yosef Hendel (now in Israel), Hershl Vaysberg, Meir Fishl Likhtenshteyn, Yitzkhak Segal and both Yakov – Khaims.

The first chairman of "Hechalutz" was Binyomin Shniadovsky (died in Havana, Cuba), an old member of "Flowers of Zion". Yakov – Khaim Sobol and Yakov –Khaim Goldshteyn were elected as secretaries, treasurer was Meir Fishl Likhtenshteyn and his assistant was Nakhman Zukerman (now in Brazil).

The organization began to recruit members. It did not take long until membership reached 40 people.

The ideal of "Hechalutz", "Hachshara" and "Aliya" greatly influenced the youth, especially those from middle class families. The work began and its activity was soon felt throughout the town. The leadership roles were taken by: Yakov – Khaim Goldshteyn and Yakov –Khaim Sobol together with a committee of active members: Yitzkhak Kleynhoyz (now in America), Khaim Yosef Hendel, Moishe Makover (now in America), Meir Fishl Likhtenshteyn, Yitzkhak Segal, Tsima Perlberg, Khaya Gitl Freshberg (the last two now in Israel), Hershl Vaysberg and Moishe Kleyner (now in Israel). The membership began to grow among the younger element. Due to them they founded "Hechalutz Hatzair" (The Young Pioneer). The most active members were: Yehoshua Makover (recently died in Israel), a very intelligent an knowledgeable young man, Yisakhar Vaysberg, Yoel –Dovid Bukhner (both now in Israel), Nosn Kleynhoyz, Avrom Ezrielevitch (both now in America), Shepsl Zaklitzever (now in Israel), Yosef Ingberman, Dr. Kurnik and a few others.

[Page 137]

A branch of "Hechalutz Hatzair" 1933

The committee of "Hechalutz Hatzair" 1928

[Page 138]

The work of "Hechalutz Hatzair" was overseen by older members.

This group carried out its work in groups. The leaders of the groups were older members from "Hechalutz": Khaya Gitl Freshberg, Tzima Perlberg, Khaim Yosef Hendel, Khaya – Bluma Vonsiak, Khaim Leyzer Freshberg, Dvoyre Levenzon (now in Israel), and Hershl Vaysberg. Both organizations did intensive work. A while later the members of "Hechalutz" left for "Hachshara" (pioneer training) in various places, wherever the central organization decided. After six months a member was eligible to receive a certificate to immigrate to the Land of Israel. Fruits of this labour were soon evident, with the accomplishments of the pioneer ideal at the moment when the first boys and girls from our town, members of "Hechalutz" received their certificates to immigrate.

Among the first to immigrate were: Dovid Hendel (died recently in Israel), Yehoshua Kanarke, Khaim, Yosef Hendel, Dvoyre Levenzon, Moishe Klayner, Shmuel Dovid Bukhner, Tzima Perlberg, Isakhar Vaysberg, Yehoshua Makover, Avrom Student, Berele Kurnik, Yosef Ingberman, Perl Inkovsky, Fishl Novodvorsky, Soreh Kleynhoyz, Shepsl Zaklitzever, Leybl Piasetzky, Dvoyre Bukner and others.

The organization "HaShomer Hatzair" was founded before "Hechalutz" which existed previously. Their membership was comprised of the same youth element as "Hechalutz", but the amount of members was greater. Their leader or battalion head as they called him was Shmuel Zelig Hendel, of blessed memory, a knowledgeable Zionist and a kind young man (immigrated to America, died young). After him the leadership was taken over by Dov Hendel, known as "Berkeh". He had the honour to immigrate to the Land of Israel and realize his ideal. He was killed in battle in Israel. May his memory serve as a blessing. He possessed exceptional talents and was a very good organizer. He dedicated time and energy, practically his whole life the "Hashomer Hatzair". He was loved by all.

The news of his death caused great sadness in town. A commemorative gathering was organized in his memory.

Groups were organized in Hashomer Hatzair according to the age of the members. The cultural work was done by gifted, conscientious, energetic members: Menkhem Kotsiak (Dr. Menakhem Gur today in Israel), who was then a student, very conscientious with a deep national Jewish education, Freda Vengerka, who came from a fanatic – orthodox home, very conscientious and secretly led one of the groups.

[Page 139]

Yosef Krukover, smart and very precise, was the treasurer. Alteh Hendel (Berke's sister) knew Hebrew very well, understood nature and knew how to educate the children in the spirit of nationalism. Esther Piekarchik, Soreh Vilenberg, Khaya – Sortcheh Raitchik, Rokhl Blum, Yente Shnayderman, Rashiniak and others were active in the organization.

Prior to the immigration members of Hashomer Hatzair to the Land of Israel,
Soreh Orlik and Baylcheh Skurnik, 1926

The head of Hashomer Hatzair and Hechalutz in town was Yakov – Moishe Skurnik, who was devoted with heart and soul to the organization. He understood the importance of educating the youth, the avant garde, in the spirit of the pioneers with love of our people and love for the Land of Israel.

A short while later, according to instructions from the central office, both organizations were united: "Hechalutz" and "Hashomer Hatzair". The members of "Hashomer Hatzair" also went to the pioneer training program and later immigrated to the Land of Israel.

The following were among the first to immigrate:

Yakov – Hirsh Orlik, Baylcheh Skurnik (today in Canada), Soreh Orlik, Shmuel –Dovid Frenkel, Dvoyre – Leah Goldvaser, Rokhl Orlik (today in America) and others.

[Page 140]

Political Party Life in Town

The youth organizations were a dominating factor in the Zionist and communal life in town. We also took over a portion of the work from the older Zionists. When the university in Jerusalem was opened a great parade was organized by all the Zionist organizations. Everyone marched into the synagogue where the celebration took place. The synagogue was packed and the strength of the Zionist movement was felt in town.

Every year on the holiday of Lag Ba Omer a parade was organized through the streets with the participation of all the Zionist organizations. The scene was very impressive: the children from the "Yavneh" school and from the kindergarten, held blue and white flags in their hands and sang Hebrew songs as they marched. Who knows how many important devoted Jews would had emerged from this group of children had they not been killed.

The sports organization "Maccabi" also existed in town with a soccer team. They organized games at the bazaar. From time to time the team went to play games in neighbouring towns. The founder and leader of Maccabi was Litman Montshkovsky. Those who excelled in soccer were: Vevkeh Klaynhoyz, Yitzkhak Grinberg, Avrom Grinberg, Yosef Shmulevitch. Later the organization was dissolved.

The left wing Poalei Zion party existed in Makow. The main leaders were: Avigdor Tchmiel (a councilman at city hall), Sholem Stonitz, Yosef Furmansky, Yekhzkl Segal and others.

The left Poalei Zion ran their activities in a smaller format as they had fewer members. When the professional unions were organized in town, the party actively participated. We must mention from among the leaders: Khone Stolnitz, a boot maker. He was endowed with talent. He wrote poetry. His book can be found at YIVO (Institute of Yiddish Research). Yakov Berman was also a boot maker. He was a very intelligent young man, quiet, modest, he was one of the most active in the Poalei Zion. It is worthwhile to mention Yitzkhak Skala, one of the main leaders of the party. He was an intelligent young man, and a good speaker. Later he worked in Warsaw as an employee. He died in the Warsaw ghetto.

[Page 141]

The Bund had existed in Makow for a few years already. Until the strengthening of the Zionist movement the Bund was held in high esteem. Thanks to the Bund the professional Tailor Union was founded. The Bund had a representative in the State Health Insurance Fund. The membership was comprised of the following workers: tailors, shoemakers, carpenters etc…the Bund ran the Y.L. Peretz Library with a large collection of Yiddish books. The main leaders of the Bund were: Dovid Minogo, Avrom Malakh, Henekh Vaysman, Yitzkhak Domb, Aron Erlikh, Zalmen Shlomovitch, Yehuda –Meir Riatchik, and Sender Burshteyn (now in Australia). These were all people who were devoted with all their heart to improve the situation of the working class. Some of these leaders were councilmen on the city council. The Bund also had a representative on the Jewish community council. In general, when there was discussion on a Jewish issue or about subsidies to Jewish institutions at city council, these representatives honourably fought for and defended Jewish interests.

The Bund's youth wing "Di Tzukunft" (The Future) ran their own cultural activities which included readings and lectures. They would invited prominent speakers and representatives from the Bund central office in Warsaw.

Makow Kindergarten under the direction of Yente Shanyderman, 1924

[Page 142]

May 1st demonstration in Makow, 1917

[Page 143]

The Bund also had a drama club led by Leybl Gogol (now in Israel). One of the plays they performed was "Motke the Thief".

Despite their political differences, the members of the Bund were kind hearted devoted community workers. Members of the Bund and the left wing Poalei Zion played and active role in ORT and TOZ.

The "Agudah" also existed in our town. This party was comprised of orthodox Jews, mainly Ger Hasidim. They did their work in their spirit and style, in a religious orthodox manner.

The youth in town did their utmost to expand cultural activity. A group made up of Zionists and others created a branch of the YIVO institute and a People's University. The leaders of this branch were: Sender Hertzberg, Menakhem Kotziak, Yakov Berman, Yakov – Khaim Goldshteyn and Yakov – Khaim Sobol. They devoted their work to collecting Yiddish folklore and put together questionnaires about the Jewish lifestyle in town. At YIVO in New York you can find the questionnaire about Shabbes Shira (the Sabbath of Song) as described by the Jews of Makow.

The People's University under the direction of Simkha Tzentura and Sender Hertzberg, from time to time organized lectures on literary themes and invited prominent speakers from Warsaw to give the lectures.

The Marketplace in Town

The marketplace in town was a large four cornered space, paved with stones with asphalt sidewalks all around. The marketplace served as a central meeting point. A large part of Jewish life was reflected there. On market days Jewish shopkeepers and businessmen set up shop. Jews wandered around looking for an interest free loan, a regular loan, or sometimes just to chat. On Sundays, Jews waited for the gentiles to come out of church so they could hire a coachman to take them to the fair. Reb Feyvl Blum set up a waiting room in the middle of the marketplace. This is where the Jews waited for the bus from Warsaw, grabbed a cold drink and met with merchants. The simple Jews walked through the marketplace, they did not allow themselves to walk on the sidewalks.

[Page 144]

Only the youngsters walked on the sidewalks around the marketplace. The majority of Jewish shops were situated there. On Saturday when the Jewish shops were closed the marketplace spirit of the Sabbath could be felt.

Sunday in the Makow marketplace

Makow, like every other Jewish town had its town fool and some crazy people. They did not, God forbid, harm anyone. They were sick people. Victims of hunger and suffering. Let us remember them as well. There was crazy Ruven who would bang his chest saying "Bread", and crazy Beyleh who would steal an apple from a street stall, and Basheh (the daughter of Leybl Bayger the teacher), and Avrom Ribak who would walk up and down Prashnitzer Street and not say a word, and Kalmen Kopl.

The sinister year of 1933 arrived when Hitler, may his name be blotted out, the sadistic murderer rose to power in Germany. Other winds began to blow. Anti Semitism was rampant. The economic situation of the Jews worsened from day to day. Everyone was afraid and feared what tomorrow would bring. A black cloud hovered over all of Jewish life. Hooligans arrived in our town impeding Jewish business, tearing away customers from Jewish street stalls on market days. It is worthwhile to mention the following fact: once, before a monthly fair, a rumour suddenly spread that a gang of hooligans would be coming to the fair to beat up Jews and steal their goods.

[Page 145]

The leaders of our town, from all the different parties consulted on how to avoid this.

The Bund informed the P.P.S of the hooligan's plans of picketing, headed by a landowner. Two committees were quickly created: one – the P.P.S and the Bund with Dovid Minogo and Avrom Domb representing the Bund. The second, civic, was comprised of Yudl Rozenboym, Abba Bernboym, Yehoshua Montshkovsky, Avrom Garfinkel and Mendl Student. The two committees worked in great secrecy. Those working with the P.P.S took it upon themselves to intervene and influence the landowner to call off the planned picketing of Jewish shops, but without success.

At that time in Makow, security matters in town were handled by Henrik Lange. The vice – commandant was Stanislav Voytchekhovsky. They were both considered friends of the Jews.

Seeing that the Hooligan's actions were inevitable, the civic committee delegated a representative who was very friendly with Lange and Voytchekhovsky to inform them of the situation. He invited them to the house of Rabbi Adelberg the rabbi of Makow and informed them of the impending situation and asked them to take the appropriate steps. They both promised and assured they would do everything in their power to ensure the fair would pass peacefully.

An appropriated resistance action of the P.P.S was prepared in the event of an attack against the picketers of the Jewish shops in the marketplace.

Wednesday, the day of the fair, all the Jewish merchants and the shopkeepers in the marketplace opened their shops as usual. We did however notice a large swell of gentile boys from the surrounding villages.

At noon, when the fair was in full swing, two picketers that were standing beside Abba Berenboym's shop and did not allow customers to enter. They began to shout incendiary words against the Jews. The P.P.S stood on guard and saw how the hooligans were not allowing Christian customers to enter Jewish shops which resulted in a fight between the picketers and the P.P.S.

[Page 146]

The market vendors began to pack up their goods and close their shops.

Soon Lange arrived the police. Both gentile guys were brought to the police station. Things calmed down. The Jewish stores reopened. The shopkeepers unpacked their goods and returned to business.

Avreymele the water carrier in Makow

Lange and Voytchekhovsky called in extra police from the surrounding villages on that day. Thanks to them, rioting was avoided at that fair.

[Page 147]

Edicts and Acts of Violence

The Nazi government in Germany came out with edicts and acts violence against Jews. From day to day we began to feel the anti Semitism more and more.

What could we, in our town do? We went out with our old weapon: shouting, protesting and appealing to the conscience of the world. The Jews organized a large meeting on a Thursday night between afternoon and evening prayers under the open sky. The meeting took place on Synagogue Street, beside the house of Rozenshteyn (the leather dealer). The street was filled with people. Practically all of the Jewish population attended this protest meeting. The main speakers were: the rabbi, Rabbi Zvi Adelberg, Meir Ostri, Yonatan Nayman, Yakov – Khaim Sobol and others. They called for justice in the world and equality as people and as citizens of the country. We hoped that somewhere our protest would be heard. Unfortunately, it was like a voice lost in the desert. The whole world remained silent. Jewish property became worthless. However none of us anticipated the frightful catastrophe looming where one third of our people would be exterminated by the German murderers.

Once upon a time there was a town called Makow. A town with a large Jewish population. Fine, well established men and their families who derived great pleasure from their modest lifestyle. Once there were young people in Makow who lived, dreamed, worked and ran a cultural and social life. Once…it was and is no longer.

Makow is now clean of Jews. There is not even a remnant of a tombstone at the Jewish cemetery. The cemeteries were plowed and flattened.

Those of us who survived, no matter where we are in the world must never forget our beloved parents, brothers, sisters, relatives and friends who were brutally murdered.

May their souls be bound up in the bond of everlasting life. Makow and its Jews will remain in our hearts eternally.

[Page 148]

The Market

by Avraham Shilah (Rybak), Haifa

Translated by Janie Respitz

Our town Makow was actually no different from other small Jewish towns in Eastern Poland. They were all built according to the same system: small wooden houses with slanted roofs with red shingles, which emanated a certain charm when you looked down from the hills onto the town as you walked to the forest through the "Bazaar". The tall roofs of the church and town clock look majestic in comparison to the large synagogue, whose greatness was in its holiness.

The Market in town was different. There were two storied brick houses surrounded by shops, which for the most part belonged to Jews who earned their living on the two market days, Tuesdays and Fridays, when peasants from the surrounding region came to buy products for their personal use, or at fairs which took place on Wednesdays, but only the first Wednesday of the month. Then it was really a holiday. Everything awaited that day. Jews, grain merchants, would walk among the wagons, touch the sacks and wait for their price. Finally they would buy the goods. Every market day went like this: they did business, wandered around and earned a living. Jewish women bought chickens from the female non Jewish farmers, as well as eggs and butter, sticking their small finger in the butter to taste for freshness.

Shoemakers, tailors and other merchants would come from nearby towns in large open sided wagons and grab a spot. Using tarps and poles they laid out their merchandise and impatiently awaited customers.

The market also served as a dating place for young couples. They would do the circuit a few times, especially in the evening. The market was the safest place. If someone wanted to go out walking in the dark alleys of "Skerke Volnoshchi" or past the turbine, they could have returned with smashed ribs and a bloodied face from the gentile boys who felt free and confident in their "territory".

[Page 149]

Walking around for hours and getting very tired, the youth would rest in the late evening hours on the thresholds of the closed shops, and talked loudly disturbing the sleep of the residents. They would more often than not get sprayed with ink by Feyvl Hiber or a visit from the two policemen, Ferdinand and Tomoshevsky, with the same refrain: "Blood hounds, what's going on?" We would quickly run away.

Talking about the market, how can I not mention the pump, which satisfied so many residents with its sweet water and provided a livelihood for the water carriers who filled barrels at Jewish homes with water, especially water for tea…

The marketplace was a central point for all idlers who would walk around with their hands on their backsides, or have political discussions, waited for newspapers which would arrive on the bus from Warsaw…

Membership card of Abram Rybak for "HaShomer HaTzair" Makow 1927

[Page 150]

The marketplace took on another look when Makow became the central traffic point for buses from Mlawa to Warsaw. They built a station which became the business centre of town. They built two gas stations like in other cities. This was an omen of the changes that would be coming in transportation: cars would be replacing horses…

Until this time, I lived in the town and participated in communal life. I was fortunate to immigrate to Israel, and thus saved from what my nearest and dearest did not survive.

I will always see the people before my eyes who I left behind in the town where I lived for twenty years.

Makow – A Town With Desires

by Nosn (Natan) Shachar (Montshkovsky)

Dedicated to my unforgettable wife Grunia Segal (Montshkovsky)

Translated by Janie Respitz

Makow. This name awakens many associations. Therefore it is twice as hard to write impressions and offer details about the cultural and communal life of Jews in Makow. It is difficult, very difficult, to free myself from feelings of sadness and pain due to friends and those close to me who were brutally murdered, those who honourably partook in the national revival movement in Makow. It is, for example, impossible to write memories and not mention the names of my closest friends Y.M Platau, Moishe Bzhoza, Sh. Rekant; and those involved with the school: Sh. Pianka, Avrom and Rayzl Rozental and the Hebrew teachers – Vogmeister and Kotziak.

As I am writing Sholem Aleichem's "Motl Peysy the Cantor's Son" pops into my head, when he tells about his impressions of London where there is a fair every day, and he asks: Where did all these people come from?

[Page 151]

There was not a fair every day in Makow. However despite the small amount of Jews that numbered around 4500 souls, the small Makow had big desires and ambitions and awakened in its youth a national and social liberation.

The town is situated on a flat valley near the Orzhitz River. When you arrive from the hilly market side, you saw the Gothic top of the church tower and it seemed the residents live a calm life. However precisely this calmness was bubbling with a social and cultural life. For example, in March 1917, thanks to the initiative of those already mentioned, together with the help of Young Zionist organization in Makow, the first Hebrew kindergarten school was founded under the direction of Mrs. Osherovsky who was sent to Makow from the central Tarbut office in Warsaw.

The success of the kindergarten inspired the members of the Zionist Organization to establish a high school in Makow under the direction of Mrs. Perlman and Yuzepovitch.

Economically the Jews of Makow did not hold any important positions. The exceptions were the two tanneries belonging to the Orliks and Raytchiks which supplied leather products to their buyers in Warsaw: the two steam mills which belonged to Bezalel Vilenberg and the firm "Raylikht".

*The Board of Directors of the first Hebrew kindergarten in Makow,
under the direction of Mrs. Osherovsky in 1916*

[Page 152]

In earlier years the production of religious fringed garments (Tzitzit) developed in Makow and were shipped in large quantities around the world. The brilliant N. Sokolov defined this production and asked: "What is the difference between Makow, Berlin and Madrid?" and he answered: "Berlin is famous for its culture, Madrid for its bulls and Makow for its fringed garments"…

While writing my impressions of Makow it is worthwhile to mention the name Yekhiel Smolozh who at the time was one of the first Zionist propaganda pioneers in Makow. For example, he had himself photographed as if walking to the Land of Israel, had the photographer frame it with the caption "Yekhiel Smolozh Walks to the Land of Israel" and hang it on an abandoned advertisement board in the marketplace on the wall of Reshilevsky's delicatessen.

After the First World War, Jews in Makow, just as Jews from other small Jewish towns in Poland looked for an opportunity to emigrate in order to improve their economic situation. Individuals as well as entire families left Makow, some for larger cities in Poland such as Warsaw and Lodz and others immigrated to the Land of Israel. The majority went to America. When the Second World War broke out we were in Warsaw and as a result were forced into the tragic struggle of the Warsaw ghetto and feel the pain and suffering of the cruel deaths of our closest. This same pain and suffering however called upon us to do something and strengthened our desire to seek revenge for the innocent victims. Thanks to the help of some friends who were connected to the Polish anti- Hitler movement, my brother and I succeeded, actually during the ghetto uprising in April 1943, to free ourselves from the fighting in the ghetto and join the Jewish partisan group of Captain Yekhiel Grinshpan which was operating in the region of Partchev – Lublin.

Our escape from the ghetto and our joining the above mentioned partisan group demanded three important conditions: a) time, b) affirmation and c) tact.

We must also thank the Polish family Markovsky for helping is escape from the ghetto. They permitted us to hide for four weeks in their garage which was situated on the Aryan side on 46 Karolkova Street next to the tramway in the Volkser area. This place also served for a time as a workplace at night for guards. Hiding in the garage put both sides in danger. Therefore our friends helped us get organized in a clandestine dwelling of a Polish family in the neighbourhood of Mokotov at 25 Vishniyova Street.

[Page 153]

We hid in this place until December 25th 1943. The entire time we were locked away from the rest of the world because on the outside of the door there was a bolt. From time to time we would receive a small amount of food. Already living at this place were the wife and children of Mr. Feld, the secretary of the TOZ organization in Warsaw, who during the Polish uprising in the capital were killed despite the fact that the house on Vishniyova Street remained in tact and undamaged.

The Connection

After two unsuccessful attempts to connect to a partisan group which was operating in the area near Vishkov, we managed miraculously to return to the clandestine dwelling in Warsaw. On the 25th of December 1943 we were finally delegated through the central office of G.L, the authorized Mrs. X who gave us the secret partisan password and ordered us to meet in the building of the main train station of Warsaw where we had to buy train tickets to Lublin.

That same night, mid – journey, according to instructions, we disembarked in the region of Partchev. We arrived in the large village of Rikhevo (Ozhekhuv). However, that night there was a raid by German gendarmes in the same village. Miraculously, we were saved hiding deep in a snow covered bunker which was not far from the house where we were staying.

We wandered from village to village for three weeks until finally we had the opportunity to join the ranks of the Captain Grinshpan's group which consisted of seventy young fighters.

January 1944 was a difficult month. There were heavy snow falls and it was very cold.

[Page 154]

We consequently received our first instructions how to survive the snowy cold winter nights. We actually slept on hot coals covered with a thick layer of snow. The heat from the coals warmed our bodies and battled the cold which often fell below thirty   degrees.
During this period Captain Grinshpan's group carried out important acts of sabotage, destroying train bridges as well as tens of kilometres of telegraph and telephone connections on the lines connecting Partchev – Vlodava – Brest.

We actively participated in the fight against the Nazi murderers and as a result helped to liberate Poland.

We were helped through this difficult time by the Zionist spirit of Makow which we absorbed during our childhood.

My Town Makow

by Dobeh Gudes Kalina, Costa Rica

Translated by Janie Respitz

Our town Makow, on the outskirts of Warsaw was a lively town. Summer and winter it was very lively. The surrounding nature bestowed on Makow helped. The mountains, the wide quiet river, the magnificent forest all added to the special flavour! Even during the coldest days of winter we had fun, sliding on the river, throwing snow balls, making a snowman with a broom in his hand.

We would ride on sleighs and enjoy the ringing of the bells. The town was comprised of merchants who held an honourable place; retailers who sold their merchandise at the marketplace.

It was lively in town Friday evenings, when we led a bride to the wedding canopy, to the synagogue where we had to make a considerable path. Men on one side, women on the other, making a chain.

[Page 155]

The musicians played a happy tune accompanied by Zalmen Fandl on his bass. The bride was more dragged than led by the her mother and mother in law, pathetic, crying as the Badkhn (master of ceremonies) tugged at her soul singing "cry little bride, cry!" – and did not have the courage to adjust her veil which during all the pushing was moved. And this is how with luck she arrived at the synagogue where her betrothed was already waiting for her under the wedding canopy.

A celebration among the youth in Makow, accompanied by local musicians Shloimeh Modrikamien and Zalmen Podl[1] 1919

Saturday morning the whole town went to synagogue. Women in particular could barely wait for the holy day, where Khaya – Ite sat in her fine gold hat singing supplications in a heartfelt melody. Women, who did not know Hebrew, gladly gathered around her repeating her every word while crying bitter tears. Khayteh had a talent of tugging at your soul! The women forgot about everything. One day a goat entered the synagogue. Khayteh said: "and God said to Abraham" and without changing her supplication melody continued: - "Have mercy children, chase out the goat". When the women heard the name of our forefather Abraham, they wailed and repeated: "and God said to Abraham. Have mercy children and chase out the goat!" later, they laughed about this in town.

[Page 156]

Coming home from synagogue the tables were filled with chopped fish, cholent (Sabbath stew) and noodle pudding. When your stomach is full, your soul is happy…everyone sang Sabbath melodies which rang through the town.

My father did not leave out one song, especially when he learned a new one when he spent the Sabbath at the Radzimer Rebbe's, of blessed memory. In the evening when the sun set and reflected in the river like a red burning flame, and a cool breeze blew, everyone in town went for a walk in the forest. All strata of society met there, even the poorest of the poor – Naftali and his wife whose entire fortune lay in her jewellery: a watch hanging on a chain, which even in my grandmother's day did not tell time…

When Naftali would see a poor man from a distance he would say to his wife: "Shprintze, put it inside!" so no one would be jealous or cast an evil omen. She would put it in her bosom. When he the wealthiest man in town, the leader of the Zionist organization Yekhiel Meir Plateh, or the director of the Yiddish school Shmilke Piankeh appeared, he would order: "Shprintze, take it out!"…

For us, the kids, it was a pity the Sabbath ended so quickly because we had to go back to our school work, and who had the desire when the street was calling with its charm.

In school, Yudisl, the Rabbi's daughter sat beside me. She was a calm, pale dreamer with a kind Jewish heart. She never forgot to give the buttered bagel her mother gave her everyday to the town's blind cripple Shayne Rozhe, who sat and sang heart wrenching love songs to her Itche Binyominl…secretly, I would see the room where the Rabbi sat and studied Torah. The Divine Presence rested in every corner.

When Purim came around the Rabbi's wife asked us to wash our hands, put on aprons and kerchiefs and sat us down to pick through the wheat for matzah made under the strictest supervision starting with the harvest of the grain. We spread the wheat head to head in long rows and when the table was full, the Rabbi came in, inspected our work and put it in a snow white bag.

When our beloved Rabbi decided he did not want to die in the diaspora, and wanted to immigrate to our holy land, the entire town was on guard and prepared themselves not to miss out, God forbid, on saying goodbye. His wife, Khaya Beyle, pitifully went around for eight days applying vinegar to head kerchiefs. When the day arrived, shopkeepers closed their stores, artisans put down their work and everyone came out to the marketplace. Remarkably: That same day, Yisroel the water carrier threw down buckets and the pump stood orphaned. The Rabbi's wife and Yudisl sat on the horse drawn carriage smiling and happy that they lived to realize their dream of walking on the soil of our holy land.

[Page 157]

Slowly, Hershke the wagon driver drove the horses and was happy he had the privilege of carrying out this important mission. Musicians played and the Hasidim danced and clapped their hands: you could barely see the Rabbi in the crowd. Their exaltation was so great it felt as if the whole world was dancing with them.

When we left town and stood on the hill, Zalmen Pandel (Translator's note: previously spelled Fandl) tugged at our souls when he sang the song: "Oy, oy, oy the Rabbi is leaving, let us say goodbye, the Rabbi is leaving!" The women's wailing could have torn your heart out. The Rabbi began to say his goodbyes, his wife and Yudisl as well. The Hasidim asked of him, for the sake of God, not to forget to put some earth from the Land of Israel into his letters. The Rabbi climbed onto the horse drawn carriage saying the blessing: "Next year in Jerusalem", and left town. Hershke whipped the horses and shouted: "Giddyup horses, giddyup!" they left the town soon after.

Everyone returned home with their heads down and in bad moods: the Rabbi and his wife were both dear to us.

Oh, our beloved town Makow!

Translator's footnote:

1.   Previously spelled Fandl

[Page 158]

From My Town[1]

by Khone Stolnitz

Translated by Janie Respitz

*Khone Stolnitz, of blessed memory,
the proletariat poet from Makow*

In the corners of my town destitution cries in the streets:
Machines are silenced as if they are broken.
The wheels covered by the leather straps are not making noise.
It is a holiday in town on a regular weekday…

Surrounded by fear we run from our town, like from a hovel which is collapsing.

The destitution is chasing us onto trains and ships, which are going out into the world;
Mothers remain, lonely and shattered like trees sawed down in the forest,
Tortured with such pain that could be found in an empty field…

The sadness is being chased away although there is already cinema and radio.
Young broad shouldered men with hands thick as iron,
Measure the streets and finding no place to harness:
To find some bread to feed a wife and child…

[Page 159]

The days drag on slowly and pass quietly, like clouds of smoke,
Hunger burns like a fire in the houses, bent to the ground,
Those satisfied are smiling in brick walls with levels, tearing up high.
The youth want to dunk the town in red, - the mold is not swept up…
In the corners of my town destitution cries in the streets:
Machines are silenced as if they are broken,
The wheels covered by leather straps are not making noise,
It is a holiday in town on a regular weekday…

Cover of the booklet "Light in the Night" by Khone Stolnitz,
Makow, 1934
In memory of the poet of "Light in the Night"

[Page 160]

The Cries of Old Fathers

Where should we go with our difficult suffering?
Where should we go with our wounds?
No one wants to hear us out,
We walk lost, we are disappearing…

Our youth has strayed away,
They have thrown away the small prayer house and the lecterns,
They left to carry bricks
To transform lands…

We, the fathers, the elderly, are leaving this world,
As they are leaving piety and God's wonders.
The loneliness is chasing us from God's dwelling, the Shul,
We have lost our own children…

Where should we go with this difficult pain?
Where shall we go with our wounds?
No one is ready to listen to us,
We are walking lost, we are disappearing.

Jews of Makow digging trenches in 1939

[Page 161]

The bridge on the road to the forest

In the Black of Night

In the black of night with darkness mute and blind,
When father with pain struggles with death, -
And mother depressed cried like a child:
That's when my little sisters asked for: A piece of bread!...

In the darkness a flame flickered from the lamp in the kitchen.
Mother saw how father was passing away,
And my brothers on their beds were dreaming:
That they were holding a piece of bread and bowls of food on their
laps…

Dawn broke cutting the stillness of the night,
Father was already dead…
We, the small children cried and thought:
Who will feed us and bring us bread?...

Original footnote:

1.   From the book "Light in the Night", Poems, Makow, 1934. The author wrote in the introduction: in these chaotic time, when such a juicy fruit like poetry calls out a weak quiet echo, I am even afraid to reveal with song, but the silence awakens the silent cry of my children – the poems, the want to enter this phase of life and torture me to show the world am now taking the first steps to attempt to begin. "The author" This booklet contains 30 pages and 26 poems. We are presenting a few here.

[Page 162]

A Day in Makow
(A memoir)

by Dr. M. Gur (Kotsiak), Haifa

Translated by Janie Respitz

Spring 1932. The bus from Orlik, which goes from Warsaw to Makow is approaching town. We can see the forests of Gzhanke. The Pultusker highway leads to town. The bus passes by the chestnut trees that line both sides of the highway. It groans up the wooden bridge which lies on the Orshitz River and panting, pulls into the marketplace. The marketplace is large, four cornered, built up with fenced two storied houses. All around are businesses, shops and stores.

Yakov – Moishe Skurnik's kiosk stands in the middle of the marketplace. There you can buy soda water, sweets and ice cream. The bus stops beside this hut where a large crowd is awaiting guests from Warsaw. They have come to greet friends and relatives and to hear news from the big city.

Menakhem, a young student who studied at Makow High School and is now a student at Warsaw University steps down with assured steps and heads to the home of Reb Dovidl Hertzberg. His son, Sender is a childhood friend. Walking through the market you must say hello to friends and acquaintances.

Reb Abba Berenboym is standing beside his store. He is a handsome honourable Jew. His wife Fraydele, daughter Shorusia and son Motke are inside running the business. Reb Abba himself is busy with communal work, mainly with the township. He is standing and discussing this with two good friends, also community workers, Ostri and Rekant, both left – the first his tavern and wine business, and the second – his pharmacy warehouse. When they see the student they welcome him warmly. Is that Abba's son Khaim, Menakhem's childhood friend? This same Ostri's daughter, married the young journalist from "Haynt", Bernholtz (Selim). Rekant's children were students of Reb Menakhem's father Reb Anshl, who used to be a teacher and school director in Makow. Meanwhile, Menakhem was going from one shop to the next.

[Page 163]

First to Montshkovsky, a little further on to Sheynberg, and then Kleynhoyz – that was one part of the marketplace. Further on was the Christian section: Adamsky's book shop, Yazhvinsky's sausage shop, Shultz' pharmacy and other Christian businesses. The third section – Goldwasser, Student, as well as other Jewish businesses. The fourth section ended at Segal's warehouse and the last section was Blum's store, Tzukerman's store and other businesses. "Segal the Mayor" – this name dates back to the German occupation in 1915 when he was the mayor of the town.

Menakhem runs quickly through the marketplace and enters Tchekhanover Street. Every house is familiar to him. At the end – Platoy's residence, and in the courtyard – Hendel's house. Here he must stop to say good morning to Itche Hendel and his wife, and ask about his friends Berko, Alte and Khaim. There are shops tugging from both sides of Tchekhanover Street – Katz', Pinake's book store, the director of the Povshekhner School and other shops. He turned into Prushnitzer Street and entered the house of Reb Dovidl Hertzberg. Reb Dovid is seated on his small cobbler's bench. He stands up, wipes his hands on his leather apron and gives a heartfelt welcome to the young student. He was like a son coming in over the course of many years to his cobbler workshop – a friend of his eldest son, Sender.

Cinema "Shviatovid" in Makow

[Page 164]

Soon after Sender comes in. He is already married and lives upstairs – in a room that was added on. Soon the table is set: fresh black bread, butter, cheese, tomatoes and onion, milk and coffee. Menakhem is already sitting at the table surrounded by Reb Dovid's family, and everyone is asking, recounting and listening to news form the big city and telling the news of the town.

Menakhem observes the room. It seems to him it has become smaller. Under the beds are large pieces of leather from which Reb Dovid cuts out soles for nice boots which he makes for the peasants in the surrounding villages. Reb Dovid's boots have a great reputation. Even the young officers, Menakhem's friends from high school order their boots from Reb Dovid. The apprentices sit all around the workshop hammering wooden nails into the soles or sewing the borders with thick waxed thread.

Menakhem remembered how every day running home from school he would drop in to read the newspaper, the "Folks Tzeitung". This was the organ of the Bund. Reb Dovid's apprentices belonged to the Bund. They often had discussions with Menakhem who was active in the Zionist movement. The words and slogans "Eretz Yisroel", "Hebrew", Yiddish", "Significance of Exile", "Fight to Remain" would echo in Dovid's workshop. Seated at the long low work table, Menakhem began to write his first poems and then read them to his friend Sender who was enraptured by them. He encouraged Menakhem to continue writing. "If the editors in Warsaw were as delighted with my poems as Sender, I would've been a great poet long ago" thought Menakhem. But he could not sit and think for long.

After breakfast Sender took his friend to see the town, to meet acquaintances, friends and comrades. Menakhem wants to be left alone in his small town, its streets and alleys, whereas a little boy he ran around barefoot. He wants to remain alone with his past childhood which he enjoyed in this town.

Finding an excuse, Menakhem remains alone. He walks until the end of Tchekhanover Street, to the large houses. These are wooden buildings where his father, Reb Anshl's school was situated. This is where his family lived. He approached the house. Now strangers are living there. He goes into the courtyard, looks at the well they had dug, greets the neighbours, who remember him from his childhood. The old policeman Zbishensky approaches.

[Page 165]

The Scout Organization in Makow, 1916

[Page 166]

Beyond the houses lie the estates of Grokhovsky, Kishelevsky and others. It is mainly Grokhovsky's estate that attracts him. There used to be a well there with pure water. Menakhem used to go there often with buckets to draw water. The road and the path were very familiar to him. They run through the fields. The old peasants greet the young student and ask about his parents, sisters and brothers whom they knew and invite him in to their homes: however Menakhem continues on the Sloniyover Road. There stands a cross and a "holy" picture, surrounded by an iron fence. It is the same as all the other crosses and pictures on the roads which run through the Polish villages.

This is where Menakhem and his friends would run to during their long recess at school. This is where they would play, dream, lie in the soft grass, build and destroy worlds. Once again Manakhem lies on the grass, snuggles up to the ground and it seems to him he is a barefoot little boy again looking with his childlike eyes at the world. He is delighted by every flower, the blueness of the sky, with the bird's song. It is here that he jotted down these verses:

> "Where is the beginning,
> And where is the end
> Of a humane day?
> He comes from infinity
> And departs with it…

Who wrote this? An older experienced person who understands life? No, this was written by a fifteen year old boy, a pupil in his final year of public school in Makow.

Menakhem felt intoxicated by the scents and fresh greenery which spurted out from the black fields. A spring wind caresses his hair, kisses his hot forehead. It seems to him he wrote this poem just yesterday:

> "A human hand did not want to caresses me,
> I went to the winds…"

He returns to the road dreamily and heads back to town. He finds himself at Zygmuntovitch's garden. This is where he used to buy fruit: apples and pears. This is where he would walk on Saturday with his friends, and later on, in Friedman's garden. They would call Friedman "Reb Motiye the gardener".

[Page 167]

He leased a garden from Christians and sold his fruits and vegetables in the market. His garden was near the large houses. Menakhem and his friends would occasionally steal an apple or pear from his garden. Later, when Menakhem joined Ha Shomer Ha Tzair and became friends with Reb Motiye's daughter Hadassah he would be invited to their house. It was then that he told Reb Motiye about the stolen fruit. Reb Motiye laughed and place a plate filled with fruit on the table. Menakhem claimed this fruit did not taste good as the stolen green and sour apples of his childhood…

Menakhem snuck through the marketplace to avoid meeting all the Jews he knew and would have to stop to chat with. He spent most of the day in the village and still wanted to visit a few places connected to his childhood. He walked through the meadows to the nearby forest. He was familiar with every corner, every tree. This is where he would go for walks and dream. This is where the groups of Ha Shomer HaTzair would meet. This is where they would sit until late at night singing Hebrew and Yiddish songs. This was a Jewish forest. You rarely saw a young or old gentile. Once in a while peasant women came to pick black and red berries. Menakhem can still sense the sour –sweet taste of the black and red berries which shine through the green grass. He returns from the forest to the water mill, and from there to the garden. This is where the former high school once stood where he studied from 1925 – 1928; he spent four years within those walls. Days of joy and sadness, sorrow and happiness. He goes to the paths of the garden where he would run during recess. He meets the old guard who used to ring the big bell during the breaks. He is already grey and bent over, old Antoni. He recognizes Menakhem and is happy to see him. "The good days are gone" he says, "the silence is a sign of looming death". He presses Menakhem's hand and tears well up in the eyes of the old guard who has remained the only sign of the past.

His feet take him to the Orshitz River which twists through the meadows. This is where Menakhem and his friends swam in the summer and rowed boats. He finds himself at the turbine which had once been a sensation in town and was now the road from town into the forest. As he leaves this place the sun starts to set in the west. The sky turns red. Black clouds cover the sun as if with a black shawl and swaddle the sun before it goes to sleep.

[Page 168]

A branch of Ha Shomer Ha Tzair in Makow, 1928

[Page 169]

Everything in town has changed: the houses are now lower, the people, smaller. Only the sky remained the same. It is now sparkling with stars; darkness is slowly falling on the ground. Menakhem senses the taste of dusk, from the twilight which caresses and calms with its stillness. He recalls these verses from the past.

> "I waited until deep in the night,
> You did not come yesterday,
> And I brought you from the street
> Black bread and red flowers…"

Yes, then the bread was black and the flowers had to be red.

When Menakhem returns to town the houses are lit. Tired merchants stand in their shops awaiting their last sale. The youth are out walking. A new generation has grown up. Not all remember Menakhem. After supper he meets many friends. That sit around like in old times on the steps of the shops and talk about everything that has transpired in town: who got married, who immigrated. What news have we heard from friends who are living in Eretz Yisrael. There is a mixture of talk, laughter, jokes, serious discussion and everything gets swallowed into the darkness of the night. It's late. They have to go to sleep. Tomorrow morning he will be returning to Warsaw. Menakhem wants to absorb as much of the town as possible. He feels connected by thousands of threads. He friends cling to him asking advice: some want to go to Eretz Yisrael, some want to move to the big city. The town has gotten smaller and the youth want to leave; there is no work in town, no future. However a new youth has emerged which is dreaming in town, walking through the alleys and going to the forests. "A generation leaves and a new one comes" – thought Menakhem. They said their good byes, shook hands, slapped each other on the back. At night it was difficult to fall asleep. Thousands of thoughts all mixed together, pictures and dreams. He fell asleep just before dawn. But soon after they woke him up. He wakes up quickly. He believes he will be late for school and would have to run there before eating breakfast. Then he's fully awake and realizes he must catch the bus that leaves at daybreak from Makow to Warsaw.

Menakhem says a warm goodbye to Reb Dovidl and his family and leaves for the bus. The bus departs from town. It is already on the Pultusker highway. When the last trees of the Makow forest have disappeared, Menakhem feels a big part of him has remained behind in town. The landscape of fields and forests is not longer familiar, this is no longer part of Makow. He closes his eyes wanting to keep the picture of Makow. Who knows when he will return, he thinks. He is overtaken by sorrow. Perhaps, already then he had the premonition that this would be his last visit to Jewish Makow. He turned his head wanting one more glance of the town – but it had already disappeared, disappeared forever.

[Page 170]

Memories of My Birthplace Makow

by Eliezer Shakhar (Montshkovsky), Tel Aviv

Translated by Janie Respitz

In memory of my father Yehushua Khaim Ha Kohen (Montshkovsky),
former member of the city board of directors and his family.

36 years have past since I left my birthplace. However, with the publication of this memorial book I feel it necessary to provide short lines, memories of friends with whom I spent a large portion of my youth, and they, unfortunately were not privileged to see the fruits of their devotion to the Zionist movement, the establishment of the State of Israel, where we have the privilege to live.

Let these lines serve as a memorial for all our friends who were tragically murdered by Hitler's criminals (with active collaboration of our former Polish neighbours).

My childhood in Makow was no different that the other cities and towns in Poland. We studied in Heder (religious school) from early morning until late in the evening, summer and winter, rain or snow. More than once we wanted to enjoy the beautiful nature surrounding our town, the Ozshitz River, the nearby forest, but our Rebbe did not let. The fear was great. We sat with Leybl Bayger, Mendl Varshever and other teachers and learned the Torah portion of the week so that on the Sabbath, when father would test us, we knew it well.

[Page 171]

Who among us does not remember the dark nights when we returned home from Heder and, trembling with fear, accompanied each other home with a lantern.

When we compare our childhood and the conditions in which we lived to the great opportunities and freedom of our Israeli children, it seems many generations have passed, not the short time in which radical changes have occurred since our youth.

Pilsudsky Street – on the right: the post office

In my opinion, a new period began in Makow with the opening of Reb Anshl Kotziak's, of blessed memory, first modern school (Heder Metukan) in 1916. Despite the opposition of "Agudas Yisroel" (Orthodox religious movement), who under no circumstances would agree to any small progress the schools offered, and applied all sorts of measures to close them – the school managed to exist for a few years.

After the Jewish high school closed, some students switched to the Polish gymnasia (high school) and continued their studies.

The city, and especially the youth, lost a lot with the closing of the Hebrew school.

In 1919 a large group of youngsters like: Notteh Vilenberg, Gedalyahu Raytshik, Puleh Perelberg, Grunia Segal and others, decide to become farmers in preparation to emigrate to the Eretz Yisrael (the Land of Israel). I remember the great impression they made when they returned to town after a day's work with their tools. Unfortunately, only a small portion of them emigrated.

[Page 172]

At the same time the following organizations were founded in town: "Ha Shomer HaTzair", (The Young Guard), "Prakhei Zion" (Flowers of Zion), and "Maccabi". All of these youth movements held literary evenings, performances and discussions.

"Maccabi" formed a football (soccer) team which played matches against teams from the Polish gymnasia and the military in Ruzhan. At that time, in 1921, this was revolutionary in Makow. When we returned from our matches wearing our sports clothes we had big fights with our parents who did not understand us. On the other hand, we showed our Polish neighbours we were also capable of competing in sports which raised our national honour.

The water turbine for electrical power

In 1925 the Hebrew University opened in Jerusalem. We celebrated this event with a commemorative gathering in the big synagogue, organized by all the Zionist organizations.

[Page 173]

For the first time in the history of Zhetl a co–ed choir sang in the synagogue and Shoshana Kotziak of blessed memory, read a chapter from the bible.

We had many disruptions from opponents however, the well organized Zionist youth kept order and the commemoration was very successful. The participants were: Moishe – Yehuda Freshberg, Yosef Kantor, Yakov Yedvabnik of blessed memory, and others who contributed to this success.

In 1929 when we received news of attacks on Jewish colonies we organized a large portion of our youth, especially reservists from the Polish army. We sent a telegram to the Palestine Office in Warsaw to allow these members to go to Eretz Yisrael to fight the Arabs, however the gates of the country were locked.

Although the youth in town were in fact unemployed and the perspective of a future was unfavourable, emigration from Makow was negligible. Only a small group of members from "HeChalutz" (The Pioneer) and "HaSHomer HaTzair" made the effort to leave their old home and begin a new life in Eretz Yisrael. One of those who emigrated was Berko Hendel of blessed memory. Soon after he arrived he fell in battle on Kibbutz Ein – Shemer.

I remember my meetings with Berko, the joy in his work on the Kibbutz and his constant worry about all those who remained in Makow due to the difficulties of emigration.

After the great destruction that befell our people, after the downfall of Jewish youth in Poland and together with our townsfolk, we feel the great loss even more.

Those miraculously saved from Hitler's hell, who arrived here in Israel were helped with financial support, thanks to the interest free loan society which we created.

[Page 174]

The Mill

by Nechama Sela–Lewkowicz, Tel Aviv

Translated by Naomi Gal

In our city Maków, there was a magical mill,
Jews and Goyim all flocked there,
Since it had prominent merit:
The flour grinded there was the kind no one ever saw,
The best *quality* and *beauty* that was not to be found
In any major cities or its surroundings.
*

Admirers abundant, from all over Poland,
Whoever tasted it came back by all means
Our mother, too, arrived punctually,
Singing its praises time and again.
Its beauty and brilliance, like the midday sun
And its taste, like manna from heaven.
Kneading the dough– in awe,
How it rose, puffed up, up and up,
Blessings came from within – she said:
Using a bit, reaping plenty.
Her lips whispered a warm prayer to God:
There is no flour like Bezalel Flour in the whole wide world.

*

Finally, a legend was weaved around the mill,
That Elijah the prophet visited at will.
Since no one knew whose blessing this was,
That made the flour so tasty and scrumptious.

*

And as pure as the flour, were Bezalel's deeds,
Helping every needy and distressed person,
Wagons full with sacks of flour were driven

[Page 175]

To every corner where Torah words were heard;
To Ostrava and Łomża and back again –
From Warsaw to Bialystok, to each community.
Due to its support rabbis were ordained,

Geniuses were raised, scholars proliferated,
Their faces glowing with radiance,
Since flour and Torah go hand in hand.

*

Each Shabbat evening the gate opened:
Bezalel did not discriminate between old and young,
He gave generously flour to all:
All hungry and needy were welcome.
Their backs bent under the burden,
Lines and lines of paupers formed
And across their shabby clothes –
Glowed the white sack of flour.

*

And when a whip descended on the city's Jews,
When Grabski inflicted heavy taxes;
Squeezing their blood and *peeling* their skin,
Emptying their cupboards and leaving them naked.
The number of bankrupts grew and grew
And beggars too – since hunger sprouted:
The hand of evil reached the magical mill as well
But to no avail – it was stronger.
Despite the taxes cast upon it
It never stopped working, its wheels turning on and on
And Bezalel did not decrease the quotas he allocated,
He gave even more and more.

*

And at midnight, during the second shift,
The mill's sound broke the silence,
And together with the voices of the Torah learners
Became one great and beautiful harmony…

[Page 176]

A Street In Makow

by Mordechai Cywiner

Translated by Dr. Joseph Schuldenrein

*To the memory of parents, Sarah and Alter Moshe Cywiner,
my brother Meir Rotblatt, and my grandparents Dreyzl and Fayvel Kurnik*

Was there a soul in Makow who was unfamiliar with my little street, "Zhiloni Rynek" (Green Market)? It wasn't a major street; it began at a dead end and ended at the river.

Ours was a poor block. No wealthy or prosperous folks lived here. Plain and simple Jews, tailors, shoemakers populated the single story, ramshackle cottages. Here, from my childhood on, it seemed as if my block was the center of town. Every occasion, sad or joyous, eventually worked its way through my street.

There's a wedding in town with the bride and groom surrounded by well wishers at the Chupah by the synagogue. On wintry evenings, my street is covered in deep snow. Outside the ice cracks. Two long rows of women with lanterns in hand accompany the bride. Shloyme Klezmer with his sons, Zalman Fogel and his large bass play wedding songs outside. A bunch of kids run after the party with snowballs and heave them at the bride. I stand outside and a warm feeling overcomes me. Somehow my block is so radiant and joyful, as if all of us spectators are the proud in-laws.

And then there's a funeral procession moving down my street right by the synagogue. Beryl the Assistant Shamas (Synagogue Caretaker) follows the coffin, rhythmically shaking the pushke (charity box) and shouting "Charity wards off death". Grieving relatives wail and a sea of stooped heads crosses the street. Doors fly open from every house on the block as folks run out quickly, lest they be left behind and not fulfill the mitzvah of escorting the dead.

I stand prepared with a litre of water by the window sill. When my mother returns, she washes her hands and lets out a deep groan, a sad look in her eyes.

Every Saturday morning, I get up and pray. The local streets are blanketed by snow. Everything is still. But (the snows) on our street are already criss- crossed with narrow trails like a chessboard. They all lead to the Beis Hamidrash

[Page 177]

(study house), to the Alexanderer shtibel (small orthodox synagogue), and then to the (main) synagogue and to the "new" Beis Hamidrash. Folks stream in from all sides, from Reb Bezalel Willenburg's mill, to Meshulem Reitchik's mill, from the market and from all the side streets. All of them, resplendent in their Sabbath clothes, making their way through, big and small. A calming, Sabbath peace emanates along the block.

From all sides the melodious Sabbath tunes (negunim) resonate. In the middle of the (Sabbath) day my block is packed with kids from all parts of town. At Yudel's, the Shamas's house, there is a knoll that winds up to the synagogue. The knoll is capped with snow that turns to lustrous ice. The kids slide down from the crest of the knoll: standing, sitting, crouching, knees bent. And when they finally make it down they land in sooty snow.

Liberty Avenue

Sabbath evening. A red sun sets on the Sloniver Road, a precursor to a major overnight frost. People reappear on our block, plodding heavily, recently awakened from their Sabbath naps. They are off to Mincha (afternoon prayer), as I head into the Alexanderer shtibl, where my father and grandfather always dahvened. A warm haze envelops me. The outside air seems dense, as all the windows are shuttered and sealed for the winter. The shtibl is dark--night falls fast. Hasidim are seated around the long table. Pieces of Challah and small chunks of herring are spread out. One can barely see a thing. Blue, shady silhouettes sway and sing a haunting niggun, from "Bnei Hayichleh D'chseyphun" (prayer).

[Page 178]

I've heard many different tunes and musical pieces in my day, but none as awe inspiring and resonant as the "triple feast" (Sabbath prayer) zmiros (festive songs).

We children, sit in the dark regaling each other with silly tales of spirits, ghosts and clowns under the little bridge as folks wend their way to the synagogue on through the night, heeding the call of the Torah.

My heart pounding, I sidle up to the wall where the winter coats hang. I find a well-worn fur. I wrap myself up in the warm coat, shut my eyes anxiously, finally overhearing the familiar banging on the posts and then the familiar strains of "And the all merciful will forgive us our sins" (prayer).

It is the evening of Passover ("Erev Paysech"). The last of the winter snow has melted beneath the spring sun. On our block the ice still freezes over the gutters. Isolated sewerage and discharge impart different colors to the ice; blue from the laundry; reddish from dyes; and gray from plain dirt. From the Mikveh (ritual bath), the waters cascade onto the Canal Street and empty into the river; it's as if all the gutters and drainage lines agreed to converge on Canal Street. We (kids) keep on playing games and running around in the square near the Beis Hamidrash. From Moishe Babel's house our senses warm to the intoxicating aroma of the freshly baked matzohs, our mouths fairly drooling.

Summer days on the block. It's hot. At the dead-end street wagons pull out, stacked high with freshly cut bales of rye and wheat. Cows with swollen udders wander in from the pasture and fields near the bazaar. Doors and windows wide open. From Freidel Ashenmill's house you can hear the whir of the engraver's machine at work. In our courtyard Hirsh-Ber Glicksberg stands engraving stylized letters on stone blocks for grave monuments. At Shepsel Chaptko's and Eliezer Mechanik's you can hear the whirring of new machinery. The block is empty, the stillness occasionally broken up by a lone passerby on his way to the Beis Hamidrash for Mincha.

The women sit on the little benches gossiping amongst themselves. There goes Chaya-Etta walking slowly and deliberately in her black shawl draped across her shoulders, the kerchief on her head ringed with various crystals and gemstones looking like diamonds, her hand holding a rumpled handkerchief. She stops by each and every house to collect a few groshen (small change) for Tzedakah.

[Page 179]

The High Holy Days are upon us. Yom Kippur Eve on my block. Grandmother and mother have just said the blessing over the candles and had a good cry. We are off to prayer. The block is jammed with activity. Men and women converge from all sides. They move deliberately, very somber.

There's Avram Skahla, dressed in his kittel (Hasidic holiday frock) covered by his tallis (prayer shawl). Now Tuvia Skahla, Nottke Kasten, Yechiel Rybbak, Dovid-Beryl Kurnik, Avram Gershon the Shamas. And up there--Arkeh Lichtenshtayn--in his tall boots. They glisten from the freshly applied boot polish. And then the rest of the townsfolk, all stopping and wishing

grandmother and aunt Rochelle Lilienthal a Happy New Year. Later on, the street will empty--everyone is in shul. I'm off to the "Great Synagogue". Its huge center doors are wide open. I linger in amazement. I'll never forget that sight, just beyond the open portals; the synagogue all lit up and the congregants wrapped in their prayer shawls. My childish fantasies acting out. I'm certain that this is what Yom Kippur night was like in the Temple ("Beis Midrash") in its heyday.

I'd just like to reflect about one particular house on our block.

[Page 180]

On one side of the river there stood a large granary and on the other side a house that belonged to Shmuel Hufnagel. It was called the "Hufnagel house". The building is ingrained in my memory; that where everyone congregated for major occasions. Just as the Orthodox Jews used to pass through our block on their way to all the Beis Midrashim and shtibels, that's how all the young people were drawn to the Hufnagel house. It's where the Zionist organization held meetings. There was a large library that became the home for (such organizations as) the Hashomer Hatzair (Young Guard), the Chalutz (Pioneer), the Young Chalutz, and the Mizrachi (Religious) Chalutz. A perpetual echo of young people's laughter and singing resounded through the windows of that house.

I grew older. In our town it was common to take evening strolls down to the central market and square. Often I overheard young people poke fun and deride our block, sarcastically calling it the "green market". And then an inexplicable resentment came over me, as if my block had been stripped of its crown.

It was a gray dawn, in December, 1939, a back-pack drawn across my shoulders. I stand on the hilltop that leads to (the towns of) Ruzhan and Krasnochelz. At that hour the block was exposed in all its solitude; even the tall synagogue seemed somehow diminished, and a distant longing came over me. Far-off visions of my street flash before my eyes, images I've absorbed since birth and up through that very morning when I left home. My last look back made me wonder: would I ever see any and all of this again?

My home town Makow! Do you, can you still shed a tear for your decimated Jewish people?

A Youth Group, 1923

[Page 181]

What Used to be Said About the Makow Synagogue

by Rabbi Shmuel Hilert, New York

Translated by Janie Respitz

I heard this from old men 50 years ago. Not only old people told this story. Almost everyone from town knew about it. When we would meet fellow Jews from other towns, all of us from Makow felt proud when they asked us about the mystery connected to the building of our large, beautiful synagogue.

Makow was the oldest Jewish settlement of the surrounding communities. Old people said, according to legend, Makow belonged to Vengrov when it was still active in the Council of Four Lands.

When the old House of Study burned down in 1927, they claimed it had existed for 216 years. At the time when they began to build the synagogue there was no other prayer house other than the House of Study. Makow was inhabited almost exclusively by orthodox well–established Jews. They prayed in the Ashkenazi style. At the time the well–known preacher Reb Dovid of blessed memory lived in Makow. He was a great opponent of Hasidism. I saw with my own eyes in the record books of the Bible Society, which was founded by the preacher in 1769 his opening sermon, in his own handwriting. His grandchildren remembered a lot. I heard a lot from them. They were: Reb Dovid Refalkes, a teacher and Reb Yitzhak, a religious fringed garment maker, of blessed memory. The Magid's home was across from the House of Study, where in later years Reb Moishe Blum lived who was called Moishe Potatoes.

There was already the in our town the first sprouts of Hasidism. The genius scholar, the holy Reb Khaim Hamdurer of blessed memory, one of the great students of the preacher from Mezeritch, of blessed memory, was in Makow and this is where his son in law settled, Reb Nosn Notte Hiler, of blessed memory, one of the students of the Visionary of Lublin of blessed memory. Also living in Makow at the time was Reb Avrom Abli of blessed memory, a student of Khiam Khyake Hamdurer, the author of the book "The Blessing of Abraham". There was also a certain Reb Akiva Altshuler who was a student of the Visionary of Lublin. According to legend, these were the first Hasidim in Makow. They began to pray in the Sephardic style and prayed apart from the others.

[Page 182]

This was on the corner of Synagogue Street, on Kanalov Lane where Reb Yudl Khever Shamash of blessed memory lived.

In those times an important guest arrived in Makow. This was Reb Levi Yitzkhak of Berdichev, of blessed memory. The Hasidim were triumphant with their guest. The Rebbe from Berdichev gave a passionate sermon in his holy fashion. The Magid and his students were not impressed. Seeing that people were being influenced and carried away by the holy passion of the Berdichever, his students decided, when the Berdichever will pray on the Sabbath according to the Sephardic style they will not allow anyone to go as this would be a big victory for the Hasidim. And that is exactly was happened. As soon as the Berdichever began his prayers there was such a commotion, the Berdichever had to escape through the window. They pointed out this was the window to the right of the Holy Ark.

The place where the synagogue was built had been an empty lot which ran from Synagogue Street until Grobave to the east and from Zelyoni Rynek until Franciscan Street to the north. The empty lot belonged to two gentiles. A cross stood on the lot which the gentiles erected as a memorial and "remedy" of an epidemic which broke out in olden times.

Looking out of the window from the House of Study you can see the cross. Of course this was very distressing. The Berdichever Rebbe told his audience: "This spot is appropriate for a Holy Place".

It has been told that suddenly a storm wind broke out. It tore out the cross and slung it far, up to the river. It was also told the river did not flow then as it did in our day, but close to the sandy shores near the highway which they travelled on to

Krasnosheltz. Recently, there have been swamps there. The gentiles called it "Stara Zheka". The gentiles brought the cross back and planted it in the old spot and secured it with stones. A couple of days later there was another storm which ripped out the cross and again slung it to the river. When our ancestors saw this they felt the holiness of the Rebbe from Berdichev. Everyone, without exception, the Hasidim and the Orthodox, got together and began to think how to convince the gentiles to remove the cross and place it somewhere else. The owners of the property were no longer alive, but there were many inheritors, some of whom still lived in Makow, and others who had left. It cost a lot but they were convinced to move the cross to the other side of the river where they would travel to Ruzhan [Rozan] and Krasnosielc.

[Page 183]

They began to dig the large foundation in order to build a luxurious building. It was to be built on the entire square which had been previously designated. However they had to withstand great difficulties brought upon by the anti -Semites. They incited the inheritors telling them not to allow the synagogue to be built on their land. As much as they gave them, was not sufficient. They tore down at night what was built during the day. Obviously, the excitement of the Jews was so great, none of these disturbances weakened them. Everyone who went to the House of Study to pray, stopped to help build. Some handed bricks to the masons while others helped mix the lime. Reb Avrom Gershon of blessed memory told me his grandmother organized the women to carry sand in their aprons every day from river to the building site where they mixed it with building materials. Everyone participated in the work. Everyone who had their own materials such as lumber, stones or bricks, donated it to the building. The synagogue was the largest building in town. When people arrived from neighbouring cities the first thing they saw was the Star of David on the top of the Makow synagogue which was built with devotion and exceptional effort from all segments of Makow's Jews. The great Rabbis of Makow bragged about praying there like Reb Leybish Kharif, Reb Feyvele Gritzer, Reb Elazar Sokhachover, Reb Fishele Salomon the Rabbi from Zagrov, Reb Yehuda Leyb Graubart, the Stachover Rabbi, Reb Yisroel Nisn Kupershtokh, my Rabbi Reb Mordkhai Dovid Eidelberg, the Rabbi from Plotzk, and the last Rabbi, Rabbi Adelberg, may all their memories be blessed. The holy places were destroyed. The holy people were murdered. May God seek revenge for their blood.

[Page 184] Blank

[Page 185]

Page 186] Blank

In the New World

[Page 187]

The Jews of Makow in the New World

by Yakov Khaim Sobel / New York

Translated by Janie Respitz

In memory of Rokhele Zgal – Sobel, three years old, the only child of Beylche and Pinkhas Zgal, killed by the Nazi's murderous hands and did not have the privilege to begin her life in this world. And in memory of all the other Rokheles, the young children of Makow's parents, who were killed in a horrifying way.

In 1965–66 YIVO (the Institute of Yiddish Research) in New York held an exhibit called "100 Years of Jewish Immigration".

An entire century had passed since the first Jewish immigrants from Europe took wandering sticks in hand, left their cities and towns and began their journey to the "New World". The old slogans "Lech Lecha – Leave" and "Veyetzei Veyavo – Leave and Arrive" made a large impression on them for various important reasons and incited them to leave the "old home". These reasons were: the strong anti –Semitism which raged at the time, the difficult material situation, hunger, destitution and no prospects for the future.

The desire for a better tomorrow, the drive to travel to the new world, America, where a new life could be created, with the possibility to live as free people, dominated the Jews of Makow. Makow Jews first arrived in America in the 80s of the previous century.

The Jewish population of Makow was poor. Until today it is a riddle, how they managed to make ends meet? The suffering and the fight for existence is what brought them to the shores of America.

At first only men left. They left their wives and children under God's protection and crossed the ocean. Some because of their financial situations and others because they did not want to serve in the Czar.

[Page 188]

My father, may God avenge his death, told me there was an expression around town: "he left to close the shutters (most of the houses were low), and went to America". This was in fact true. There were many such cases. The first mode of transport was with Lomen Noske (a well known wagon driver at the time) to Khazhel and from there, they crossed the border illegally into Germany.

With great honour we remember the first Makow emigrants who arrived in America. The were: Nosn Feyvl Kit, Zerakh Kirzhner, Shloime Salomon, Gedalye Kirzhner Goldman (my maternal grandfather), Moishe Shmuel Sobel (16 years old), Yakov Sobel, Ruven Hirsh Rubin, Shtutzka, Borukh Moishe Goldman, Feyvl Sobel, Avrom Moishe Unger, Harry Zusman, Yisroel Gold, Meir – Leyb Morison (Liasek), the Lis brothers, Yitzkhak Goldman, Mordkhai Sobel, the brothers Mendl and Fishl Stavisky, Philip Hirsh, Khantche Hamer and a few more.

At the beginning of the 20th century, on the eve of the First World War the emigration from Makow grew a bit. These were not mass numbers, only a few individuals tore themselves away. Some of them were: Jack Goldberg, the brothers: Berish, Yitzkhak and Moishe Rizer, Avigdor Friedman, Dovid Hendel, Rabbi Fishl Newman, Avrom Khzhannover, Avrom Kohen, Jack Galina, Hirsh Moishe Kohen, Sholem Potcheba, Bertche Ludvinovitz, Leybl Rozenberg, Herman Goldman, Abie Grodovitz, Khaim Shloime Blum, Moishe Khunovitz, Velvl Palukh, ("Green Velvl"), Itche Rogoza ("Yellow Itche").

Interestingly, the same Itche Rogoza brought over the Amshinov Rabbi of blessed memory to America. He travelled from city to city collecting money in order to save the rabbi. This showed, a Makow Jew was as Amshinov Hasid.

The first immigrants could not acclimatize. They found it difficult adjusting to their new home. A few even returned to Makow and others went back and forth. Having saved a few dollars they began to do business or set up a small workshops in Makow, then they would lose money and return to America.

After the First World War when Poland was an independent state in the 1920s, families began to emigrate, uniting wives and children with their husbands and fathers. Whole families arrived: Yudis Blum, Esther Kohen, Khane Makover, Ena Blime Kleshevski, Moishe Khunovtz' family, Khaya Rokhl Batzian, Hirsh Ber Kolender's family, Malke Friedman (Malke Tirtza's) Eta Gast, Rivka Krimkevitz, Brayne Makovsky, Esther Kantor and other families.

[Page 189]

At the same time some of the grown youth began to emigrate, some legally and some illegally, – to a brother, a sister, an uncle, an aunt or to any relative. A few of them were: Moishe Biala, Yekhekl and Ite Segal, Hillel and Rokhl Raytchik, Max Brown, Moishe and Dvoyre Shelsky, Moishe Rogoza, Shmuel Langleyb, Velvl Krukover (Goodman), Shmuel Zelig Hendel, Yudl Rozenman, Isidore Kahn, Gedalye and Gitl Raytchik, Hershl Zhutkov, Nokhem Hendel, Esther Kleynhoyz, the Gliksberg sisters, Velvl Tzentner, Simkha and Soreh Markus and others.

Due the "quota", the newly emerged law which greatly restricted emigration, the wandering to America practically stopped, except for a few exceptions. However, this did not stop people from Makow from heading out into the world.

When it was difficult to go to the United States the stream of emigrants began to look for other routes to get to Latin America and other parts of the world like: Cuba, Uruguay, Colombia, Brazil, Argentina, Costa Rica, Mexico, Canada and even Australia.

Makow can boast and say that there is practically no place in the world where Makow Jews do not live or have not lived.

Among those who immigrated to Latin America were:

Cuba – Yosl Sobol, Binyomin Shniadovsky, Moishe Shniadovsky, Yisroel Godlshteyn, Soreh Eta Skurnik, Elke Segal, Leybl Gogol, Yosef Furmansky, Mikhla Likhtenshteyn, Shmuel (Itchke) Kleynhoyz, Soreh Segal, Simlha Botzian, the Vonskolaser sisters, Yakov Moishe and Mindl Skurnik with their family (today in Israel) and others.

Uruguay – Avrom Tzion who later brought over his parents and brothers, Yerakhmiel Kotziak, Zaklitzever, Khaim Borenshteyn and Feyge Blum.

Colombia – Shloime Glogover.

Bolivia – Mendl Piasetzly.

Costa Rica – Zelig Gudes who later brought over his wife and children.

Mexico – Fishl Sobol and his family and Hershl Kubaba and his family.

[Page 190]

Brazil – Nakhman Tzukerman, Efraim Katz and family.

Argentina – Hershl Orlik, Yedida Raytchik, Tzima Vilenberg, Leybish Segal, Yakov and his wife Yeta Shelsky (today in America).

Australia – Sender Burshtyn, the Borshtch sisiters, Dovid Mrotzky and his wife Esther Feyge and his sister, Aron Gutleyzer.

Canada – Fishl Zaks and his family, Notte Vilenberg, Yitzkhak Pas, the brothers Smulko and Khaim Leyzer Rogoza (today in America), the Goldshten sisters (Yitzkhak Menahse's children), Moishe Veltshevsky and his wife (Karpman) and Beyltze Skurnik (today Morgnshtern).

Many Jews from Makow married people from Zhetl, townsmen. This proved to be successful in saving more people as they emigrated to prospective grooms or brides. Those who were among the last to immigrate to America before the outbreak of the Second World War were: Masha Tziviner and Yakov Khaim Sobol, and to Canada, Khaim Leyzer Rogoza.

In the late 1920s,and early 1930s immigration began to the Land of Israel (then Palestine), thanks to the activities and educational work of the Zionist Organizations such as: "HeChalutz" (the Pioneer), "HeChalutz Hatzair" (the Young Pioneer), "Hashomer Hatzair" (the Young Guard), "Mizrachi" (religious Zionists) and "Hapoel Hamizrachi". Many Jews from Makow eventually made their home in the State of Israel.

The Social and Communal Life in America.
The Makow Synagogue, the "Society" and the Makow "Relief".

The first immigrants that arrived in America faced great difficulties settling in. First of all it was difficult to find work, an apartment and in general the labour pains of arriving in a new country. It was not easy. It was a miracle they did not earn a lot as many would have surly returned to Makow. Longing for wife and child, for the quiet life of the small town, the old home: longing for the religious life – the House of Study, the small synagogue, tormented them.

Jews from Makow were always friendly to one another and their relationships were warm. Also on new soil, in the new country, they continued this tradition. They lived together as "Borders" and helped each other out. They found work in factories (shops), mainly in the clothing industry and in time worked their way up. Until recently, the familiar east side of New York was where most immigrants lived, including those from Makow.

[Page 191]

Important Jews and important people emerged from the east side. In order to ease the homesickness and loneliness the Jews from Makow founded a society where townspeople could meet often and most important, have their won holy place. The first Makow Society was founded in 1898 called "Chevra Midrash Anshei Makow" and a few years later built their own synagogue, the well known Makow synagogue at 23 Henry Street, which still exists today.

The finest of the immigrants from Makow belonged to the society. The society purchased its own cemetery so after reaching the age of 120 everyone would have their own plot, observing the old tradition of "You shall lie with your fathers".

The synagogue served as a true gathering place for our townsmen. After a difficult work week, people waited for the Sabbath to meet one another in the synagogue, meet friends and go to someone's house for Kiddush after prayers.

The main founders and builders of the synagogue were: Nosn Feyvl Kit, Feyvl Sobel, Mr. Lis, Yitzkhak Goldman and a few more. A lot of time, effort, work and money were given by Jews to the synagogue and the society.

When Rabbi Fishl Nayman of blessed memory (Reb Motele the rabbinic judge's son, and the grandson of Reb Fishele of blessed memory) came to America he was immediately hired as the rabbi of the Makow synagogue. He was loved and held in high esteem by all.

Hirsh – Moishe Kohen (who died two years ago) was president of the synagogue and the society for a long time. The present officials are:

Mr. David Roys – President
Mr. Harry Zusman (Dovid Refalkes' relative) – secretary
Mr. Avrom Khshanover – Trustee

Unfortunately the Society is not very active today. Many of the members died and we have no new members from the second generation.

In July 1907 another Makow society was founded called "Independent Young Men's Benevolent Association".

The organizers were: Sam Greenberg, Charlie Hamer, Sam Shlamovitch, Sam Kohen, Abe Bromberg, Hymie Rakover, Mendl Broder, Harry Zusman and the Botshan brothers.

[Page 192]

The membership of this society was comprised of a younger group. At first the amount of members was small, but in time, when more Makow Jews arrived, the amount increased.

Today there are 300 members. It is the largest Makow society in New York.

The society holds a meeting once a month where a variety of issues and problems relating to the welfare of members are discussed such as: financial aid, sick benefits, visiting sick members etc... besides helping its members, the Society financially supports Jewish institutions with yearly dues like: The United Jewish Appeal, The Histadrut (Jewish Agency) Campaign, HIAS, and from time to time buys Israeli Bonds.

The present officials are:

Louis Goldberg – president.
Jack Galina – vide president.
Dovid Hendel – secretary.
Milton S. Goldberg – finance secretary.
Nathan Deutch – Trustee.

Not many members attend meetings. This year they are planning a banquet to celebrate their 60th anniversary.

The active members are: the president Mr. Louis Goldberg, Avrom Khshanover and Dovid Hendel (Yitkhak Abramche's son). These members take an interest in all endeavours organized by their townsmen.

At the same time, June 1907 another society of Makow townsmen was founded called: "Makow Young Men's Aid Society". The founders of this society were: Frank Kohen, Hirsh Moishe Kohen, Jake Goldberg, Avrom Gilbert, Max Gilbert, Abe Nashek and a few others.

This society was comprised of unmarried men who came to America with their families and were looking for a way to derive pleasure in their own way.

[Page 193]

At first the amount of members was small. Later, when more young people arrived the amount of members increased thanks to the active members like: the Gilbert brothers, Y. Levin Y. Hendler, Jake Goldberg, Abe Grodovitz, Nathan Appleboym, Charlie Granat, Dovid Moscovitz, Morris Rizer, Frank Kohen, Hymie Goldman, Sam Friedman and others.

In the early years the society met once a week in order for the members to see each other often. Over the years the membership grew. The following new members were active: Max Brown, Sam Friedman, Herman Goldman, Sam Potcheba, Hyman Rozenman and others, and later Hillel Raytchik, Yudl Rozenman, Moishe Shlsky, Sam Markus and others.

This society also purchased their own cemetery and provided their members with plots.

The society created a loan society to help members with loans. The leaders were: Philip Kohen, Herman Goldman, William Lenes and Sam Potcheba.

Today the society had 90 members. They periodically organize events such as: banquets, and anniversary celebrations etc... a few years ago there was a banquet in honour of Mr. Y. Hendler (secretary of the society) and this year they are planning a great celebration marking 60 years of the existence of the society.

The society is active enough. There are meetings once a month. Unfortunately – as in the other society – not to many people attend the meetings. Problems facing our townsmen are discussed at the meetings.

Max Brown, who died recently, was president for many years. He was devoted to and very active in the society. Moishe Shelsky who also died recently, was vice president for a long time and very active and devoted as well. Honour their memory.

The present officials are:

Irwin Rizer (son of Moishe Rizer) – president.
Jake Goldberg – vice president.
Isidore Hendler – finance secretary.
Morris Kaminsky – secretary.
Herman Goldman – treasurer and chairman of the cemetery.
Hillel Raytchik, Sam Friedman, Morris Rizer – trustees.

[Page 194]

The present officials are very active in all aspects. They display a great interest and dedicate time and work for the existence and development of the society.

Within a few years the Jews from Makow began to leave the east side and moved to other regions of New York like: Brooklyn and The Bronx. They began to spread out and live in different areas.

Our townsmen in Brooklyn also founded societies, "Chevra Acim" and "Chevra Anshei Yosef". These societies did not play an important role it the lives of Makow Jews and today they no longer exist.

The amount of Makow townspeople in New York is much larger than the amount of members in the societies as many to not belong to the societies, especially the very young, the children, the new generation which was born in America. They have joined various general fraternal organizations or clubs.

After the First World War, due to the initiative of active members of all Makow societies the United Makow Relief Fund was created, under the leadership of very important hard working townsmen, representatives from all the societies. They were:

Mr. and Mrs. Yakov Sobel, Shloime Salomon, Hirsh Moishe Kohen, Herman Goldman, Khane and Khave Gold, Dovid Hendel, Sam Greenberg, Abe Grodovitz, Sam Levin, Khantche Hamer, the Stavisky brothers, Mrs. Bercovitz and others.

The "Relief" helped provide financial support for Jews in Makow. The "Relief" collected large sums of money by organizing various events such as: theatre benefits, yearly balls and individual contributions. The "Relief" carried out active and intensive work. Financial aid was sent to Makow to a committee of Makow's respected men who were chosen by the "Relief" in New York.

This work continued for a few years. Later it was taken over by a women's committee, the "Ladies Auxiliary" run by these respected women: Rokhl Rotenberg, Dora Shalesky, Mrs. Bercovitz, Khane Karp, Khane Makower, Malke Friedman, Ester Kantor, Esther Kohen, Rokhl Leah Rubin, Yetta Segal, Rokhl Raytchik, Gitl Raytchik and others. The support from the women's committee was later limited to only sending necessities for Passover and helping certain institutions like: the hospice for the poor and the interest free loan society.

[Page 195]

By the early 30s a few townsmen founded the "Tarbut" organization. The task of this organization was to collect funds to support Zionist institutions in Makow such as: the "Yavne" school, the Zionist library named for Sholem Aleichem, and most important, providing financial aid to young pioneers who wanted to immigrate to the Land of Israel. Those active were: the brothers Yisroel Yosef and Yudl Rozenman, Pauline Gold, Yehushua and Mindl Friedman, Hillel and Ruthie Raytchik, Yekhezkl and Yetta Segal, the brothers Khaim Leyb and Moishe Makover, Gedalye and Gitl Raytchik, and Shmuel Zelig Hendel.

The idea to establish this organization came from Yehoshua and Mindl Friedman (Raytchik), who arrived in America in 1932. Mindl, a new comer really knew the situation and understood the importance of helping these specific institutions.

This work continued for along time and the money sent helped many young people emigrate.

After the Second World War, at the end of 1945, we received news of survivors from Makow. Those who survived the Holocaust were now in different countries including: Poland, Sweden with the majority, in Germany.

Due to the initiative of these well known active townsmen: Mr. And Mrs. Hillel Raytchik, Mr. and Mrs. Yekhezkl Segal, Mishe Shelsky, Dovid Hendel, Herman Goldman, Mr. and Mrs. Gedalye Raytchik, Mr. and Mrs. Avrom Khshanover, a new Relief was organized under the name "The United Makow Relief", supported by all Makow societies. The first founding meeting took place at the home of Mr. and Mrs. Hillel Raytchik who were known for their devotion and hard work for Makow's townsmen, and their warm home is still today a meeting place for work for the benefit of all.

At the end of 1945 Yakov Khaim Sobel returned from Europe. He had been freed from service in the American army. He immediately became involved with the Relief which made contact with survivors everywhere, where ever they were, and collected funds. To achieve this goal different events were organized, such as: theatre benefits, a Purim ball and collections. They sent packages of food, clothing and money to the townsmen in various countries.

[Page 196]

The active members of the relief committee were: Max Brown of blessed memory, Moishe Shelsky, of blessed memory, Hillel Raytchik, Gedalye Raytchik, Avrom Khshanover, Yekhezkl Segal, Herman Goldman, Yekhezkl Kohen, Yakov Khaim Sobel, and others. They gave up their Sundays, their rest day to pack packages in Moishe Friedman's grocery store, where they sorted, packed and addressed parcels. Rabbi Fishl Newman of blessed memory, played an active role in the relief work. The first chairman was Mr. Philip Krasner, a devoted worker. Later, Sam Greenberg, an active society member in relief work. After him the chairmanship was taken over by Avrom Khshanover a devoted worker of the Makow societies in general, and specifically relief work and holds this position until today.

In time, survivors from Makow began to arrive in America and The Land of Israel. The new arrivals quickly engaged in relief work. Those active were: Avrom and Yetta Garfinkel, Avrom Lesman, Leybl Goldvaser, Mordkhai Tziviner and others. The Relief worked together with the Society of Makow Jews in Israel and increased the funds for the interest free loan society in Israel. Besides supporting the fund the Relief sent money to Israel on a yearly basis for Passover necessities. The United Makow Relief organizes a ceremony every year in memory of Makow Jews who died a martyr's death during the Holocaust.

Survivors Around the World

Unfortunately, not many survived from our beautiful Jewish community in Makow, who before the Second World War amounted to almost 5000. Only a small number were saved and they are spread out across the world. They came to the United States, Canada, Latin America, Australia, Sweden and a distinguished amount to Israel.

The first of the survivors to arrive in America (New York) was Yakov Sheynberg. Those who greeted him upon his arrival were: Rokhl Raytchik, Yetta Segal, Mindl Friedman, Yakov Khaim Sobel and his cousin.

With tears in our eyes and great sorrow in our hearts we received the first news and heart wrenching reports of what happened and who survived. The loss is horrible and the destruction of the Makow Jewish community was cruel. He, Yakov Sheynberg, the first survivor to walk on American soil, did not talk much at first as he was a broken bitter man. One thing he did share right away was the anniversary of the death of Makow's martyrs. We will all remember the date, the 3rd day of Tevet, for generations to come.

[Page 197]

Who Are Makow's Jews in the World

Jews from Makow all over the world can be proud of their townspeople. Without exaggeration, wherever they are, we hear about them, we know about them because they have held or still hold important positions in the community, in cultural, economic, scientific and social areas.

The importance of the former Makow Jewish community, of which we are proud, is very old. In the rabbinic world Makow had great scholars and rabbis who stood at the helm of religious and general Jewish life. On cultural and social levels we take pride in some great personalities who are world famous.

Let us mention a few:

Nokhem Sokolov, a great Jew, a Zionist leader and a leader of our people. He was a son in law of Makow's Dobe Segal of blessed memory.

Leon Blum of blessed memory, a socialist leader and simultaneously the long serving premier of France, descended from a Makow family, the Kahans. Yisroel Shtern, may God avenge his murder, was a poet and the brother of Reb Kalmen Sofer.

Ben –Zion Khilinovitch, may God avenge his murder, journalist and writer, contributor to the Warsaw Yiddish newspaper "The Moment". He was the brother of Reb Shimon – Khaim, Feygl and Laytche Dobres.

Khone Stolnitz, may God avenge his murder, the talented, young poet who was killed in the Holocaust, was a young man from Makow, and many others who are mentioned in this book. As difficult as the times were, even some of the early immigrants managed to reach high levels in America.

We will mention a few:

Philip Hirsh of blessed memory, was, years ago, the director of HIAS (Hebrew Immigrant Aid Society) in New York. This institution played a large role in bringing over relatives and helped many Jewish immigrants get settled.

[Page 198]

Admiral Hyman Rikover, the so called father of the atomic submarine is a great personality in America. Although he has distanced himself from Jews and Judaism, he in fact stems from Makow, Dovid Rikover's (Dovid the carpenter's) nephew.

Dr. Menakhem Merlub – Sobel, PhD in chemical engineering, was a professor at the Polytechnic in Haifa, and now serves as an advisor to the Israeli government in the field of chemistry and lives in Israel. He is the son of Moishe Shmuel Sobel (my uncle) of blessed memory. One of the first emigrants from Makow.

Dr. Max Pianka, known as "Moniek", lives in London. He is a great scholar, known throughout the world. The following countries: America, Belgium, Poland and France have invited him to guest lecture at their universities and colleges. He is the son of Khaye and Shmuel Pianka, the beloved community worker in Makow and director of the state school.

The later immigrants who arrived in America in the 1920s made every effort to provide their children with higher education, both secular and Jewish.

Yehoshua Friedman and Yonatan Kleshevsky (the second died young a few years ago) were the first children of Makow immigrants to graduate from the Hebrew college "Herzliya" in New York. In America, Israel and other countries there are many doctors, professors, engineers, lawyers, dentists, accountants and teachers who are immigrants or of the children of immigrants from Makow.

There are also our townsmen among the rabbis in America, some of which are heads of their communities. They are involved with the Talmud Torah Schools and are very active in the education department of the "Mizrachi" movement. They are among the spiritual leaders of Jewish American life.

Rabbi Y. Khunovitch is a rabbi in the Bronx. His brother, Rabbi Harold Khunivitch is chief rabbi in San Juan, Puerto Rico. They both graduated from Yeshiva Elkhanan. They are the children of Moishe and Rokhl Khunovitch of blessed memory, immigrants from Makow. There are also rabbis among the more recent arrivals. Rabbi Simkha – Binem Shuldenreyn, is the rabbi in Dorchester (near Boston).

[Page 199]

Rabbi Shmuel Hilert is a rabbi and ritual slaughterer in Brooklyn, New York. Rabbi Ben – Zion Rozental (son in law of Reb Motl Yismakh) is a rabbi in Chicago. Rabbi Figa, is head of a Yeshiva in Brooklyn, New York.

We also want to mention Rabbi Pinkhas Ingberman of blessed memory, (son of Manes and Brayndl Pakter) survivors from Makow who came to America through China after the war. Pinkhas Ingberman was a very gifted young man, a great scholar and very knowledgeable. He was a good speaker. He studied at Yeshiva University and received a doctorate. He was hired as rabbi in one of the largest synagogues in Brooklyn.

Unfortunately he did not live to see his career develop. In 1955, flying to Israel to visit his brother Yosef, he was killed when his plane was shot down over Bulgaria, taken from this world too young. Let us honour his memory. We all lost a dear devoted member of our town.

A few of our townsmen were active in Jewish communal life in America, particularly in the Zionist "Mizrachi" movement, Israel Bonds, the Labour Zionist Movement and others. It is worthwhile to mention, the children of those who arrived after the Holocaust all study in colleges and want to become doctors, engineers or scientists. Some of them are teaching in Yeshivas and Hebrew schools. They will hopefully occupy fitting positions in society as personalities, leaders, good citizens and good Jews.

History has imposed a great responsibility on the survivors from the former exterminated Makow Jewish community. In the future they must continue to follow the slogan "The actions of fathers are carried by their children". They must continue to forge the golden chain as Jews, in the spirit of the martyrs whose memories will eternally remain in our hearts.

[Page 200]

Help from Far Off Shanghai

by M.Z.

Translated by Janie Respitz

The community activists in Makow also concerned themselves with professional training for the youth. A branch of ORT was founded in the 1930s. However, the financial support from the head office of ORT was small. Therefore, the administration of ORT in Makow turned to a few institutions around the world for help. In an appeal dated November 9th, 1938 to Mrs. Esther – Rivka Piasetzka in Shanghai, the following, among other things, were said:

> "We would like our young people not to have to receive gifts from their brothers, rather we would like them to be able to earn enough to live off. If we teach our youth a trade we will turn them into useful, productive people in society. With the spreading of professional education among the Jewish population we hope to see the Jewish craftsman at the same level as the non–Jew and not be pushed out of his economic position."

In a second letter to Mrs. Piasetzky dated June 1938, the administration if ORT in Makow wrote: "as long as the older generation still holds onto the factions of the sinking Jewish economic ship, the youth will remain totally without any prospects of obtaining economic possibilities".

The administration therefore decided to found a trade school. To achieve this goal they required 50 thousand zlotys, that is to say, ten thousand dollars. In connection to this they appealed to Mrs. Piasetzky in Shanghai for help in this regard.

Mrs. Piasetzky responded. She did not forget her townspeople despite the fact she left our city long ago and lives in the Far East.

In Makow there was a "TOZ" society (The Society for Safeguarding the Health of Jewish Children) which concerned itself with children's health sending them to respite colonies etc…

[Page 201]

This is to certify that Mrs. Reveccah Piasetzkaia is requested by the organization " O R T " of the town Makovie - Mazovietzky (Poland) to collect donations for the above organization. Your assistance in the noble work of Mrs. Piasetzkaia for the worthy Institution will be much appreciated.

Separate receipts for the donations collected will be issued by our Association

SHANGHAI ASHKENAZI JEWISH COMMUNAL ASSOCIATION

Ch. Toukatchinsky
Hon. Secretary

„אָרט"
געזעלשאַפט צו פאַרשפרייטן מלאכה
און ערד אַרבעט צווישן ייִדן

געשעצטע פריינט,

Samuel Pianku, Maków-Maz., dla Tow. „ORT"

[Page 202]

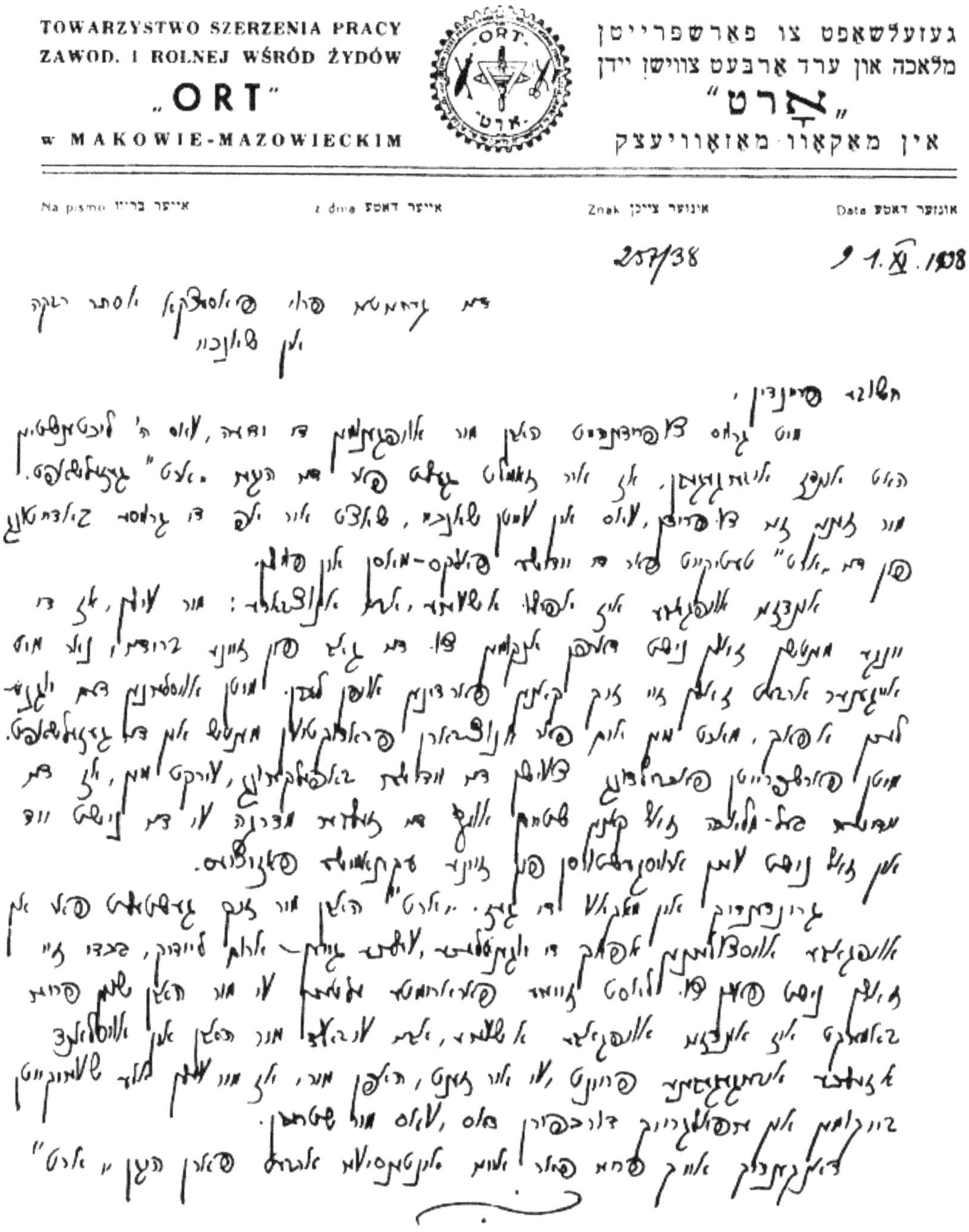

TOWARZYSTWO SZERZENIA PRACY
ZAWOD. I ROLNEJ WŚRÓD ŻYDÓW
„ORT"
w MAKOWIE-MAZOWIECKIM

גezעלשאפט צו פארשפרייטן
מלאכה און ערד ארבעט צווישן יידן
„ארט"
אין מאקאוו מאזאוויעצק

Na pismo אייער בריוו   z dnia אייער דאטע פ   Znak אונזער צייכן   Data אונזער דאטע

257/38   1.X.1938

Activity of Mrs. Piasetzka from Makow in far off Shanghai, for ORT in Makow

[Page 203]

[Page 204] Blank

[Page 205]

Cultural Activities, Schools, Parties

Schools in Makow – Mazowiecki

by Ida Beer – Garfinkel, New York – B'nei – Brak

Translated by Janie Respitz

In memory of my two children, Brokhe and Soreh – Feyge Beer who were exterminated in their blossoming childhood by the Nazi murderers.

Before the First World War when Makow – Mazowiecki was under Russian occupation there were two public schools which taught in the Russian language: one school was for Jewish children and one for Polish.

In the school for Jewish children, the majority of pupils were girls compared to boys who were a small amount. Hasidic parents sent their boys to Cheder (religious school) but the more progressive parents allowed their children to learn in the public school in order to provide them with a bit of secular education, simultaneously with the Cheder.

With the outbreak of the First World War in 1914 the only Jewish secular educational institution was closed. The teacher, who was not from Makow, left the school. The town was left without a public school for a long time, until the German occupation in the second half of 1915.

That same year, Shmuel Pianke who was born in Makow, and his wife Khaye whose maiden name was Nayman, of blessed memory, returned from Vishkov where they were teachers. They reorganized the old public Folk –Shule (public school) in town in the same two rooms at the Rizike's. Shmule Pianke recruited children from all social classes of the Jewish community – from well off and not well off, from religious and "free thinking" homes.

The writer of these lines was one of these pupils. Children of various ages learned at this school, beginning at age 7 and much older, in one class. Pianke was the only teacher and his wife helped him. The work of the teacher was made difficult because the older children, before the war, had attended the Russian school and were able to read and write a bit, but he had to teach the younger ones the alphabet.

[Page 206]

The language of instruction was German and Polish.

With the influx of children, there were also more teachers: Fela Kahana, Geradich, later Feyge Segal and others. Pianke as director of the school now had the opportunity to segregate the children in classes, almost all according to age.

Although the teachers did not graduate from pedagogical institutions, the teaching and education was on a high level. They tried to give the children the maximum.

With the Polish opposition in 1918 the school was broadened even more. More teachers arrived from other towns. The language of instruction was unified. All subjects were taught in Polish. German became a foreign language for students in the higher grades. The public school was called in Polish "Public School Number 2 for Children of the Mosaic Faith". According to the law, Jewish children had the right to attend public schools for Polish children, and Polish children could attend schools for Jewish children.

A class from the public school with teachers Shmule Pianke and Ita Katz, 1928

[Page 207]

A class form the Makow Jewish public school, 1932

Also, Jewish teachers had the right to teach in the school for Polish children but I don't remember one case. If our teachers were permitted to teach at the Polish schools, on the contrary, Polish teachers easily got jobs in the school for children of the "Mosaic Faith".

The differences between Jewish and Polish public schools were the following:

    A.   The day of rest fro Jewish children was Saturday instead of Sunday; "School Number 2" was closed on all Jewish holidays.

    B.   They taught Jewish history twice a week.

In the years 1924–25 a large number of Jewish teachers were allocated to the Makow public school who were locally born graduates of the Makow high school, like: Rayzl Montshkovsky, Dvoyre Blum, Leah Viltchevsky, Avrom Rozental, and a year later, Ida Katz. In the same year, thanks to Pianke's strong relationship with the school inspector, a special teacher was assigned for Jewish religion.

I would like to at this time to remember the teacher Vesolek of blessed memory. As a graduate of Poznansky's seminary in Warsaw, he was a gifted pedagogue. He took his task very seriously. In the 2 hours a week dedicated to teach every class Jewish history, he attempted to give the children the maximum amount of knowledge telling stories from the bible and awakening an interest in the small children. In the older classes he taught the history of the Jews in Poland. He provided the pupils with books in the Polish language.

[Page 208]

As already mentioned, all subjects were taught in Polish. However, the atmosphere in school was Jewish. At recess the children spoke among themselves in Yiddish, the language their parents used at home, although the teachers wanted the children to speak Polish. However they tolerated it. Our children did not lag behind the Polish pupils in any subject.

"School Number 2" had a good reputation in the Makow district. Visitors and inspectors would often use it as an example for other schools, however there was no lack of anti Semitism displayed toward our teachers.

The teaching staff was comprised of mainly local teachers. Shmuel Pianke was the director with a short break when Benyek Ring took his place. After a short time Pianke returned and remained at the helm until 1939.

The local teachers at our disposal at the time made every effort to provide the children with maximum education in order to bring the only Jewish state school to a high level. This was not easy for the teachers because "School number 2" was spread out in various buildings in all corners of the town. The specialist teachers had to get from one building to another in the 10 minute break between classes with no rest between classes.

A class from the Jewish public school, 1930

[Page 209]

An outing of Makow children to Vielitchke after graduating from the public school, 1924

The directors of ORT with students in Makow, 1932

[Page 210]

The classrooms were in old wooden houses, however the teachers and pupils tried to transform these ruins into esthetic classes.

Children from all social classes studied at Public School Number 2. A large amount were from poor workers' and artisans' homes. The school had a so called milk station where all the children, without exception, received a glass of milk and a roll during the long recess. Wealthier children payed for this second breakfast but it was arranged that the poorer children would not feel hurt that they could not pay. Members of the parent's council distributed the milk and roll at the school. They were also involved in other activities.

The relationship between teachers and students was friendly, especially in the higher grades.

The school library was exemplary with a large collection of books appropriate for all ages. Pupils from grades 6 and 7 were responsible for handing out the books under the supervision of our teachers Ida Katz and Kofler.

The drama club ran fine and useful activities and was directed by our teacher Rayzl Rozental – Montshkovsky. She staged actual productions which brought in financial help for the poor students so that they could also participate in and enjoy outings to the sea or the mountains. At the end of every school year, the teachers would organize outings for the two oldest grades either to the Tatra Mountains or the sea at Gdansk – Gdinie.

The public school also had a sports club called "Harcerz". It was organized by the older students and directed by our teachers Avrom Rozental and Ida Katz. Even though it was strictly forbidden, the teachers made the effort to instill in the children the Jewish national spirit.

In the late 1920s the school began to offer evening courses for adults.

[Page 211]

There was a law, that if you could not read or write Polish you could not become a city councillor, and craftsmen could not belong to a guild or craftsmen's union, therefore unable to receive work permits.

This meant, if they took away the work permits of the craftsmen, many Jewish families would be left without bread.

Older craftsmen and their apprentices took these courses. They studied diligently in order to master the Polish language and writing. They did not speak any worse than their Polish neighbours. Shmuel Pianke initiated these courses. The Jewish teachers helped him. They all dedicated their free time, without pay.

The Jewish Public School Number 2 was the only teaching institution in Makow. We did not have a high school for Jewish children.

An outing of a grade 6 class to Danzig and Gdinie in 1930

[Page 212]

Only a small amount of pupils continued their studies, even though there were many gifted children in the school. As already mentioned above, most of the children were recruited from poor homes of craftsmen and workers.

The Jewish High School (Gymnasia)

Before the First World War there was no high school in Makow. A small amount of children from well off homes studied in Pultusk or Warsaw.

Just before the declaration of Poland's independence a Polish high school was founded in Makow called "Komunalne Gimnazjum Powiatu Makowskiego". The school was subsidized by the government for which everyone payed taxes regardless of religion.

Although Jewish merchants payed high taxes, Jewish students did not receive any tuition reductions and were not freed from learning on the Sabbath. For middle class parents who wanted their children to receive higher education, this posed a large financial problem.

In 1918 a teacher named Mrs. Perlman came from Mlave. She had pedagogical experience and was approached to found a Jewish high school in Makow. She called a meeting where parents from all social classes of the Jewish population participated. A parent's committee was formed which helped realize this plan.

With great effort the high school was founded. It was housed in the building belonging to Hillel Shyenberg. The students were recruited from wealthy and middle class homes. The poor could not allow their children to attend as it was too expensive. Not having external material support, only a small amount of poor, but very talented children attend the high school.

Mrs. Perlman was the director of the high school. The classes were filled with students contrary to the third and fourth grades which had a small amount of students. Since the high school did not have many rooms, the development classes were taught in the evenings. Sometimes, the electricity went out and we learned by candlelight.

The director hired the teachers Yuzepovitch and Vegmeyster from Warsaw, as well as her sister and brother for the younger grades, and her nephew, Badilkes as sports instructor.

[Page 213]

Yuzepovitch who was studying medicine at that time was a good pedagogue and did his work with great devotion. He taught two important subjects: Polish language and mathematics.

Later he completed his medical studies and became a well known doctor in Tomaszow – Mazowieck[i].

High School class in Makow, 1918

Although the language of instruction was Polish, Hebrew studies occupied a large part of the program. A lot of attention was payed to this subject. I would like to mention here the Hebrew teacher Vegmeyster. He was not only our teacher and educator, we was also our guide. He was a teacher in God's grace, a great organizer and a community activist. He was one of the most active workers in the "Hashomer Hatzair" in Makow. He spent his spare time spreading the Hebrew language, literature and national awareness among the students. He was the favourite teacher in the high school. After him came the Hebrew language teacher H. Bernholtz.

[Page 214]

The Jewish high school was always in financial need. They did not receive any support from the authorities.

Although Jews comprised the majority in Makow numbering 60 percent of the general population, payed high taxes to the state and the city, no subsidies were given to the Jewish high school.

The situation of the teachers and parents committee was difficult. They were subjected to self help, and not having the proper amount of students, the Jewish high school struggled for its existence and finally had to close.

As previously mentioned, there were two Polish communal high schools in Makow, one for boys and one for girls, under one administration. As citizens with equal rights, Jewish children had the right to attend these schools. However, they were not freed from learning on Saturdays even though, according to the constitution every national minority had the right to observe its religious holidays.

The director Yamrugevitch, a liberal, promised Jewish children would not have to write on the Sabbath. But he did insist they be present in class and listen to the lessons. The teachers however, did not carry out the director's promise.

The parents of the small amount of students who went to high school on the Sabbath were persecuted by religious Jews. A few Ger Hasidim were kicked out of their congregations due to the sins of their children. The Jewish parents intervened to Yamrugevitch asking that Jewish students be totally freed from attending school on the Sabbath. The director finally agreed to their request with the condition Jewish students write exams more often than Polish students. This did not frighten the Jewish students. They were appropriately prepared for high school, especially in the Polish language, and mathematical subjects.

Although we were good students, studied diligently, made every effort to help Polish students, they did not like us. We were harassed at every opportunity by the teachers and students and they always displayed disdain and hatred toward us.

I remember an anti –Semitic stand taken by our Latin teacher.

[Page 215]

This was in 1921 when Professor Albert Einstein was given the Nobel Prize. We, the Jewish students, took great pride in this. The following day we came to class and told the Polish girls about it. When our Latin teacher entered the classroom and heard the noise he asked what was going on. With great joy we told him Einstein had won the Nobel Prize. His reaction was: "What are you so happy about? Everyone know Jews are merchants and know haw to swindle and calculate".

Our professor's answer hurt our national pride. We, the students from the Jewish high school who had been educated by Vegmeyster and the "Hashomer Hatzair" did not keep silent. 5 students: Feyge Borsht, Dvoyre Blum, Rayzl Montshkovsky, Dvoyre Rozental and the writer of these lines went to the director Yamrugevitch. We asked him to give us a certificate saying we were students in the 4th year of high school and we no longer want to learn there. The director asked us in astonishment: "What drove you to this decision?" We told him about the incident with our teacher.

The director calmed us down, asked us to return to class and promised to investigate. A few days later he removed that teacher from all classes where there were Jewish students. With this handling of the situation our Jewish national honour was restored. We were extremely satisfied.

The first class of the Jewish High School in Makow, 1920

[Page 216]

It appears, the director understood that our taking a stand would have influenced more Jewish students who all payed a high tuition. Not one Jewish student, not even the best, received a stipend. On the contrary, Polish weaker students payed less tuition when their parents were not wealthy enough.

The Grzanka forest in Makow

Many of the graduates of the Communal High School in Makow became teachers and received jobs at Public School Number 2. They were the first young local forces in the school and the Cheder "Yesodei Hatorah" ("Foundations of the Torah"). With great devotion to their work they raised the teaching to a high level.

[Page 217]

"The Bund" in Makow

by Leybl Gogol

Translated by Janie Respitz

The "Bund" had existed in Makow from Czarist times. However, then it was a secret party. All meetings took place in the well known Makow forest. We suffered greatly from the Cossacks who persecuted us. This was up until the Germans arrived in Makow, a year after the outbreak of the First World War. This is when all political parties came alive including the Bundist movement.

At that time the "Bund" was the largest movement in Makow. The fact is, from 11 Jewish councilmen the "Bund" had 7 representatives. When the "Bund" stood for election the first time the movement carried out 5 mandates. A strong storm emerged on the part of the other parties: What's going on? The "Bund" received so many mandates? This is not good. We must do something about it. It came to pass that they declared the election invalid.

The bus station in the marketplace

[Page 218]

The first Sabbath after the elections the rabbi, Rabbi Yisroel Nisn Kupershtokh wanted to give a sermon in the old House of Study in order to place a ban on the "Bund" organization. As members of the "Bund" we reacted and told the rabbi if he defames or offends the "Bund" we will disrupt his speech. The next day, Sunday, the elections were scheduled to take place for the second time, in an attempt to reduce the amount of Bundist councilmen. However, the results were even more surprising: instead of 5 councilmen the "Bund" received 7 mandates. We had great satisfaction seeing how almost all craftsmen, small shopkeepers and merchants agitated, to get people to vote for the "Bund" because the "Bund" had higher intentions and were accepted at city hall and the Jewish community.

The 7 city councillors were:

1. Dovid Mnogo who was called "Dovid Torah", his activity he was extremely partial. He was a wheelwright by profession. He always found time for communal work.
2. Avreyml Malakh, the best tailor in the entire region. He was always ready to do someone a favour and was devoted the community at large.
3. Yisroel Shikora, the son of a saddle maker, an honest devoted man, active in the "Bund" movement.
4. Yones Nayman, the son of religious judge, a very active member, a cultured person, loved in all circles.
5. Yankl Shlomovitch, a hat maker by profession, always helping the weak and the downtrodden.
6. Aharon – Yekhiel Aharonovitch, a shoemaker, a worker. His nickname was "Kurtzikof".
7. The writer of these lines had the privilege and honour to serve as a councilman on the Makow city council.

Before the Bolshevik invasion the Polish government arrested all the Bundist councilmen. We sat in the famous Pultusk jail. When the Bolsheviks approached Warsaw all those in jail were evacuated to Lovitch[Lowicz]. We sat there for a few months. When the Bolsheviks retreated, we were freed. We returned to Makow. The work of the "Bund" in town was renewed.

[Page 219]

The "Bund" was situated at the home of Judge Nayman. There was also a cooperative whose job was to support the poor working population of Makow. The cooperative distributed produce, clothing and other helpful items to the needy.

The leaders of the "Bund" Movement in 1929

The "Bund" in Makow also ran a dramatic section. I had the honour of being the director. From all the plays we performed I especially remember "Motke the Thief" by Sholem Asch which I directed and played the role of Motke. We performed this play in Makow and throughout the region: Prazasnysz, Ruzhan[Rozan], Krasnosielc and other towns.

In order to perform "Motke the Thief" we needed permission from the Polish authorities. We could not receive this permit in Makow. We learned this from a member of the "Bund" in Prazasnysz whose name was Nosn Olshever. He said his sister Fania Olshever and her friend Bronia Gzhib could manage to get us a permit from the Starosta (village elder) in Prazasnysz. We actually received it in Prazasnysz and performed "Motke the Thief" two or three times with great success. After the tour they organized a banquet for the amateur actors from Makow. At the banquet I had the pleasure to get to know Bronka Gzhib who later became my wife and gave birth to my beloved son Shmuel Gogol. Unfortunately he died prematurely of heart disease.

[Page 220]

The "Bund" had an evening school where they taught writing, reading, mathematics, history and more. The teachers were: Hershl Zudkevitch, Sender Burshteyn and others.

There was also a large library named for Y.L Peretz with hundreds of books. It was open to everyone.

In general the majority of the Christian residents in Makow were not anti Semitic. The P.P.S party worked with the "Bund". We always found a common language with them.

In 1927 I left Makow. However I remained in close contact with the local "Bund" organization which existed until the Second World War.

Comment: Leybl Gogol of blessed memory, unfortunately did not live to read his story in this Makow book. He passed away on June 18th 1967. May his memory serve as a blessing.

The editors

[Page 221]

With the Current

by Ita Pashut (Rushinyak), Haifa

Translated by Janie Respitz

In memory of my family which was tragically murdered

Who does not remember Makow in the 20s of this century? From one side the thousand year long standing traditions – with Hasidic Rebbes. All sorts of Jewish religious functionaries and all types of Hasidic and Orthodox houses of worship. A tradition with all the beauty of past Jewish life. On the other side- the rise of the youth, ruled by new progressive winds which blew into our town with great force.

The youth organization "Hashomer Hatzair" for the most part recruited school children from well off and respected Hasidic families.

On the other side was the Poalei Zion (Labour Zionist) party. Children from Yeshivas and Cheders (religious schools) joined. They were from lesser well off families. They had already learned a trade (the majority cutters of shoe leather), in order to earn enough to support themselves.

And finally the "Bund". They attracted young labourers: shoemakers, tailors, house painters and similar trades; the children from families of the lowest strata of society. A youth that did not go to school and by twelve years of age already had to go to work in a workshop to earn a piece of bread; a youth which had no prospects for the future, no spiritual baggage. These were the ones that joined Bundist circles thirstily drinking up every new word. This is where they found themselves, became worthy and where their lives once again had value.

I came to the "Bund" thanks to my cousins, the daughters of my uncle Moishe, Lize and Fayle Blum. My uncle Moishe Blum, the son of Reb Dovidl Sofer of blessed memory, was know in town as "Moishe Bubeles". He was popular thanks to his four sons who distinguished themselves with their sharp intelligence and exceptional talents. His daughters did not lag far behind. My uncle lived in an inherited small house not far from the synagogue across from the old House of Study. The house had two rooms and a dark alcove with two entrances. Down the length of the room and alcove stood a large baking oven with a plank bed above. Every Friday afternoon the Makow housewives would come here to bake their Challahs and leave their cholents (Sabbath stews). This was the only source of income for my uncle. In the attic above in the small house lived "Ozer the pauper" (according to what my cousins said). He frightened us children.

[Page 222]

As extremely poor children, all four sons were quickly carried away by the revolutionary current. They all threw away their long black caftans, cut their side curls and became active in the existing parties in town. All of them had to run away from Poland in 1921 together with the retreating Bolshevik army.

Feyvl lived for a while illegally in Vilna and wrote articles in the local daily "The Vilna Day" under the pseudonym "Feyvele". Later, together with his wife, a doctor from Vilna, he moved to Moscow. There he studied journalism and eastern languages. He died of tuberculosis in the late 1920s in a sanatorium in Crimea, a result of years of hunger. His son Oktiaver, lives in Moscow and practices medicine.

The older son, Khaim, left for Oygustov[Augustow?] near Vilna during the Bolshevik invasion and worked as a party functionary of the "Bund". Travelling through Russia and the Far East, he arrived in America without any money.

Velvl, the youngest, was a leader in the Poalei Zion movement. For a long time he worked as editor of the Kharkov "Shtern" newspaper which his party published. Later, when the newspaper was shut down, he was sent to a labour camp for 10 years. He was freed and lives in Kharkov.

And finally, the eldest Rafael Hirsh. He arrived with his whole family in Kovno, (Kaunas) Lithuania. They lived there until the 1940s. Hitler's hordes murdered them all. Among them was my uncle's youngest daughter Fayle, her husband and child.

Feyvl Blum wrote a book called "Samum", stories about the lives of the plantation workers in Sumara, published by "Shul un Bukh", Moscow, 1928. The book and its author are mentioned in Zalmen Reyzen's "Lexicon of Yiddish Writers" without any biographical dates.

[Page 223]

Lize Blum was an amateur actress in the drama club of the "Bund" in Makow. The director was the Bundist Leybl Gogol. With great charm she played the roles of Beylke in "Two Hundred Thousand" and Leah in "Tevye the Dairyman" and other plays. All these performances were great successes in town.

Liza was killed in Bendin [Bedzin] where she lived with her husband and two children.

*

Faye was the youngest in the house. She was born in 1912. She was just a small child when her mother died. Faye was a smart and talented child. She studied in the Polish public school and graduated with distinction. The older sisters were active in the "Bund". Faye joined the "Bund" youth group "Tzukunft" ("Future"). This is where she taught Yiddish and Yiddish literature. She dreamt about studying at the Jewish teacher's seminary. Moishe Blum, whom they called Moishe Bubeles was a good father, not fanatically religious and would have gladly allowed his children to study but he was too poor to send them away to study. The Bundist organization in town took interest in this girl and decided to send her to study at their expense. In 1929 Faye arrived in Vilna at the seminary, joined "Tsukunft" and became a leader in "Skif". She was popular and loved by all. In 1931, when the seminary was closed, Faye returned to Makow. She was active in the "Bund". Not having given up her dream to study, she went to Warsaw, got a job in the administrative office of the Medem Sanatorium and at the same time studied at seminary named for Fagen Luria for a year and later worked as a kindergarten teacher. When Warsaw was captured by the Germans in 1939, she escaped to Bialystok, from Bialystok to Krinki, the birthplace of her husband Rozenblum. She was killed there along with all the other Jews in that town.

From the "Remembering Teachers Book", New York, 1952-1954.

A spring day. The sun shone bright. Everything around smells of grass and flowers coming to life. The nature filled us with joy. We are young and happy. We are preparing for May Day festivities. At this time there was a joint meeting of the "Bund" and the P.P.S., the Polish Socialist Party. The slogan was "Freedom" and "Equality" which stirred up youthful fantasies. "The happy tomorrow" imagined in the fantasy of a young girl whose present did not appear to be so cheerful. She was called to fight.

[Page 224]

This took place the first of May 1928.

We were preparing for the joint meeting with the P.P.S. Our locale (if I remember correctly) was on Prashnitzer Street, in the house of the Makow saddle maker. Hundreds of people, dressed in their holiday best fill the streets in front of the locale. I was standing at the entrance. Suddenly, Khaim Borukh Segal, the son of Yakov – Meir Segal (then a member of the organization) passes me a note: I must welcome the P.P.S in the name of the "Bund". I did not think for long, climbed up on a chair, and when they finished playing the "International", I briefly welcomed everyone.

My father also was preparing to give a sermon that day in the House of Study. My father, Reb Yakov Meir Rushinyak of blessed memory, had been an emissary for a few years, collecting money for the Lublin Yeshiva. He did not have any luck in business. He had been a student at a Yeshiva. When he was 17 he married the daughter of Reb Dovidl Sofer. They had eight children. Together with the parents there were ten mouths waiting for a piece of bread. He was a good preacher. He possessed an innate sense of humour, despite his difficult life. His sermons were rich in content and he always weaved in jokes and parables from the bible. His audience retold his stories with envy. My grandfather was also visiting us. He came from Ostrow–Mazowiecka..

Good friends do not sleep. In no time my father heard the news that his daughter spoke at the meeting.

My father became agitated: such a thing brought about shame. They could kick him off the podium and not allow him to preach because of the sins of his daughter. Luckily, this did not happen. He delivered his sermon with great success.

I returned home around ten o'clock that night. I waited all day at my friend's house, Esther Mikovska, the daughter of the teacher Nekhemieh of blessed memory. When I got home I found my father in bed with a cigar in his mouth. He called me over and asked me to sit down beside him. I was very scared. My father asked me: "Where did you find so much courage to speak in front of such a large crowd?" and then I saw a broad smile, mixed with pride cover his clever face.

[Page 225]

Memories

by Ester Chasad–Elion (Dumbak), Bnai Brak

Translated by Naomi Gal

It is not easy to remember in detail memories from home and from Maków, where I was born, where I grew–up and were I was educated. Many years passed, a period of time that was filled with stress, sorrow, suffering and anxiety. Meanwhile, the greatest tragedy happened to all the citizens of Maków, my family members included, they were martyrs who perished and were exterminated by the Nazi Beast, and my heart is broken and will never be repaired.

Sometimes I see images in my mind as if it happened yesterday. My father, may his memory be blessed, who belonged to a distinguished Hassidic family, was a Torah scholar and we, the daughters of the house, learned from him good manners and morals; he *carved* into us the basics of Judaism and love for its people.

My house was outside the city, among *Goyim* [Gentiles] where the environment was hostile. More than once I came back home bitterly crying, having been beaten and threatened by the *Goyim's* [Gentiles'] children. The daily slogan was: "Dirty Jew, go to Palestine!"

"Havazelet" group before the member Mirel Kirshenbaum travelled to the US in 1927

[Page 226]

I remember school. At first, I studied at the primary school "Yehuda" but for lack of classrooms I was transferred to a mixed school with *Goyim*, although we Jews were a minority there – we always managed to overcome and we excelled in our studies as well as in the confrontations we had every now and then.

The teacher Yenta Schneiderman, may her memory be blessed, who was admired by the children; she organized performances for us and I remember especially one at Hannukah, when the children, with great enthusiasm, performed and expressed their deep love of Judaism and Zion.

Maków youth was very special – warm–hearted, cultured and loyal to the Zionist movement. While still in school I was part of "Hashomer Hatzair" and "Havazelet". My parents were not happy about my being in "Hashomer Hatzair", since back then religious people saw this movement as deviating from the accepted norms [Hasidim were opposed to the State of Israel=Zionism].

In our movement's branch a large number of cultural activities took place. There was a library and I loved reading the Jewish literature classics: Shalom Aleichem, Mendele, etc.

In one of the performances by the JNF, which took place in Lutnia Hall, my sister Tama, may her memory be blessed, read "I Have a Garden" by Bialik. One of the distinguished proprietors in town, the late Pinkas Lipsitz, told my father about the reading and my sister's presentation. Although my father was an Orthodox Jew and adhered the Mitzvot, he accepted my sister's acting as something understandable and in his heart of hearts was very proud of his daughter's talent.

The passage from a religious society to a progressive one was difficult, but still I respected my parents, who inspired me for the rest of my life. I will never forget my father's house – the house that no longer exists: gone are my parents and three sisters – Tama, Dora, and Faige, may their souls be bundled in the bundle of life.

[Page 227]

Death and Heroism

[Page 228] Blank

[Page 229]

The World's Conscience Was Not Awakened

by Yekhezkl Itzcovitch / Tel Aviv

Translated by Janie Respitz

In memory of my dear parents Yitzkhak and Soreh Leah Itzcovitch, my sisters Hene, Fraydl, Perl, Rokhl, Yente and the family.

The destruction of European Jewry began in 1933, when Hitler took over power in Germany. This is when the actions of spreading and deepening hatred against Jews began. The sad and famous Nurenberg laws were enforced which lowered the Jews in Germany to the level of slaves and recklessness. All their possessions were confiscated and in many cities and towns murderers attacked Jewish homes, initiating pogroms, stole their last possessions, beat and chased the Jews from the cities. The same fate was faced by the Jews of Austria, after Hitler, may his name be blocked out, occupied that country in 1938.

Practically all over Eastern Europe terror by the fascist hooligans was strengthening against the Jews. Anti Jewish excesses were renewed in Poland as well. Already in 1936, there was a pogrom in Przytyk, then later in Brisk and other towns. The fascist fire soon swept through all the cities and worsened from day to day. The Polish government followed Hitler's regime with its actions and issuing of edicts. "Ghetto" benches were forced upon Jewish students as well as "Numerous Clauses" concerning Jews and the forbidding of ritual slaughter. Propaganda materials were wide spread against Jewish merchants. Polish signs were hung on Jewish businesses with the following slogans:

"Don't buy from the Jew – he is our enemy". On the roads to the fairs, in the nearby towns, Jewish businessmen and merchants were attacked, robbed and beaten up. Free movement in the evenings was very dangerous for Jews. Here and there fights broke out between Jews and Poles, and in the end, the Jew who defended himself, was punished for "hooliganism" and sent to jail.

[Page 230]

The Jews of Eastern Europe found themselves in a catastrophic situation. The skies above were covered with black clouds. However, nobody foresaw the horrible destruction where one third of our people would be killed.

Spread throughout all European countries, the Jews for generations weaved their lives in the spirit of Jewish and national belief, displaying a rare life force and talent in the fields of economy, science, politics and arts contributing an honourable amount to the countries they lived in. Hitler's soldiers trampled the national borders. The Jews were removed from under various coats of arms and placed under the swastika, and all the differences between religious and secular Jews or rich and poor was wiped out. The murderer's hand united all in poverty, hunger and epidemics until violent death.

All were mixed into one mass, trampled on and killed by the same extermination machine. Of all the Jews of Europe, the Jews of Poland suffered the most, the healthiest core, the greatest national awareness, politically, the most militant, and culturally the most creative. The Jewish community of Poland with its spiritual worth spanned over the borders of Poland and illuminated Jewish life in almost all corners of the world.

Already in September 1939 the Jews of Poland payed a blood tax. Even before a foot of a German soldier stepped on Polish soil, the "Messerschmitt" hailed bullets and bombs threatening death and destruction in the Jewish quarters of towns and cities. This was only the beginning. The great destruction started the moment the German army conquered Poland. Cities and towns were immediately robbed and decimated.

The Germans soon passed a law proclaiming the Jew is debauched. His honour, possessions, blood and life are worthless. Already by December, a few months after they captured Poland, the Germans gave an order saying that all Jews between the ages of 14 and 60 were obliged to do forced labour. They transformed the Jews into work slaves. They captured Jews on the street, dragged them from their homes and sent them to pave highways, chop stones, dry out swamps, cut and load peat and other types of hard labour. In some towns they created workshops where Jewish craftsmen were forced to work late into the night for the German army or German companies. After the western and northern portions of Poland were taken into the "Reich" as a German province, a wave of expulsions of Jews from these regions began. Thousands of families were torn away from their long established homes, loaded into wagons and taken to other cities and towns. There was a flood of edicts thrown at the Jews. The right of movement was taken away as well as the right to use any form of communication. "You are forbidden to possess this, you cannot work in your profession, you cannot read newspapers, you cannot listen to radio etc..."Jews were completely isolated from the rest of the world. But this was just the beginning. The order came to wear the yellow patch with the word "Jude" written on it and after that, this order: Ghetto. The Jewish population was confined to crowded, filthy streets, with walls cutting them off from the surrounding world. The goal was to suffocate the Jews in crowdedness, to let them die of hunger, die from epidemics, exterminate a people through a systematic, slow death.

[Page 231]

To a large extent this was effective. The difficult conditions, moral and spiritual dejection, over crowdedness, hunger, hard forced labour, the lack of medical aid, all of this led to horrible results: mortality for tens of thousands of souls. Despite all of this, Jews did not lose confidence. Religious Jews looked for salvation and hope in the Creator of the Universe. Secular Jews, to the contrary, strongly believed in humanitarian movements and their leaders around the world. "There are powerful socialist and worker's movements, liberals, democrats, humanists, will they allow the extermination of a people?"

Jews patiently suffered, generating a bit of hope to survive this fearful time, and maintain their spirit. One more week, another day, even one more hour "Perhaps God will pity his children and we will live to see redemption".

This is how Jews cradled an illusion. They did not want to admit that the ghetto was in fact nothing more than a death chamber where they kept the condemned before their execution.

[Page 232]

After Hitler's assault on Soviet Russia, millions more fell into Hitler's captivity, from the regions of Vilna, Volhynia and Eastern Galicia, which previously belonged to Poland. The Nazi executioners switched to mass slaughter: killing entire cities and towns, young and old, men, women and children. Hundreds of Jewish communities in Poland were erased off the face of the earth. Hundreds of thousands of souls were shot and burned or buried alive.

An uncontrollable extermination flooded the Jewish ghettos and raged with rising strength. One destruction was worse than the next. The ghettos were surrounded by soldiers. Trucks drove through the ghettos with armed S.S. men, shooting and ordering people to stand at the gathering place. This acts were called "Deportations". They divided people into "productive" and "non–productive". The "productive" were sent to so called labour camps, but in fact the deportation was only a deception so the victims would not know they were going to be killed and to prevent resistance. In fact, the deportations were the final road to death.

They convinced the victims that in the camps they will enjoy better living conditions and they will work in factories and workshops. Once again they vacillated between hope and fear. Perhaps after all...they would survive this destruction...they wanted to live to seek revenge on the murderers.

The victims were brought to the so called labour camp, taken to bathe for "hygienic reasons", handed towels and soap; they were ordered to place their clothes in order and write their names on their bundles so, God forbid, they wouldn't get mixed up with someone else's...could have the Jews even thought that this was a tragic deception?

Could these victims begin to believe that this was their final journey?

Only later, when they were in the corridor which led to the "shower room" did they feel their great catastrophe...

This is where the most horrifying scenes of terror and suffering played out. There is nothing to compare this to in human history.

This is how millions of our mothers, fathers, sisters and brothers were killed together with their last hopes...

[Page 233]

This is how hundreds of thousands of Jewish children, delicate babies, who had not idea what was wanted of them or why this was all happening, died.

Day and night, over a few years, human transports were taken to these death camps: Treblinka, Auschwitz, Majdanek, Dachau and others.

All of this took place right in front of the eyes of the entire world. This all took place in honourable Europe which prided itself on cultural achievements, and great developments in scholarship compared to the rest of the world.

This did not all happen in prehistoric times, but precisely at a time of the distribution of Nobel prizes for peace activists and peace martyrs. Yes, at the same time a murderous nation did everything in order to exterminate an entire nation for one "fault": They were Jews. This murderous work was not done in secret. Out in the open! And the world? Who reacted to this? From near and far, from left to right they watched this coldblooded slaughter and remained silent! They did not disturb the murderers in their dark, murderous work, they did not try to stop the German brutality with warnings and sanctions. They were silent, the nations, even when the heart wrenching cries of tortured Jews reached them. Hundreds of thousands and perhaps millions of Jewish lives could have been saved if the world have reacted appropriately. However, the world's conscience was not awakened, it did not even shudder. Here and there various state institutions honour the tortured Jews with a minute of silence. Here and there, for the sake of appearances, memorial evenings are organized, dedicated to the Jews killed in the camps. But besides this – nothing!

Yes, the German people brutally murdered and the free world remained brutally silent. They were silent and they silenced the Jewish tragedy.

This is the truth and it will remain forever a historic fact.

How many Jews were buried alive after they were forced to dig their own graves? How much pain and suffering did the victims endure during medical experiments? Beatings with iron and rubber sticks on sensitive parts of their bodies; stabbing with long, thin lances in their ears, noses and lips to prove how long a person can stand so much pain...

How many Jews went mad when being taken to the gas chambers; How many mothers poisoned their children with their own hands before poisoning themselves; who is capable of describing these horrific tragedies of the millions killed?

[Page 234]

It must be noted, that despite this nightmare they found themselves in, Jews still had spiritual strength which led them to revolts and uprisings. The heroic battles and uprisings in various ghettos have illuminated their heroism and broke through the dark wall of Jewish hopelessness and brought honour to the Jewish people all over the world. The heroic uprising in the Warsaw ghetto was not the only one.

Jews revolted in Bialystok, Tchenstokhov[Czestochowa], Baranovitch as well as other towns and cities. They fought and distinguished themselves with heroism and honour. Heroism was also displayed in resistances in Auschwitz, Treblinka, Chelmno and others. The following sons and daughters from Maków belong to this heroic group: Tuvyia Segal, Yosef Ludvinovitch, Yehuda – Leyb and Ezriel Glogover, Leybl Katz, Kurnik, Yakov Skurnik and others.

While we are doing a summary of this great destruction, we see how sad our balance is compared to other nations.

It's true, other nations suffered terribly during the war: Russia, Poland, Yugoslavia and others. However, 80% of their victims were soldiers who fought on various battle fields. Contrary to the civilian population, although they experienced difficult times, their family structure was not ruined. The threads of their families were not torn apart. We on the contrary, not mentioning professional losses in comparison to other nations, all our families were exterminated. After the war, there were no Jewish children in Europe under the age of ten. This means the eradication of generations.

Although twenty years have gone by since the great destruction (the Holocaust), you are, without interruption, connected, welded to your old home, attached with thoughts, heart and soul. Your thoughts, memories, longing and grief, all together drill in your mind and do not allow you to rest. People from Maków are always on your mind.

I always see all the fathers in their long black coats and silk hats. The gentle dear mothers in silk dresses, bejeweled and wearing Turkish black shawls on Saturdays and holidays, when the air was filled with holiness, hiding the grey days of the week behind light and joy.

[Page 235]

I see all my friends who were active in communal life. The youth of Maków with their dreams, ideals and revolutionary spirit. The Hasidim, scholars, psalm reciters, the simple people full of love for their people and language. I see this all in a dream, but in reality, it no longer exists. Maków today, like hundreds of other Jewish communities in Europe, in reality, no longer exists. Today it has become the city of the dead. A big cemetery for Jews with no trace of the rich past. With the total expulsion to the crematoria of Auschwitz, Treblinka, Majdanek and others, generations of the well established Maków Jewish community were eradicated.

Farewell party for the Itzcovitch family (at the home of Mr. Avrom Garfinkel)
as they left Germany for Israel in 1949

The burden lies upon us, orphans of Maków, to remember our dear ones with feelings of pain and sorrow. We must honourably remember the pure Maków martyrs, our murdered mothers, fathers, sisters, brothers, sons and daughters, who were barbarically tortured by the German murderers and collaborators and whose ashes are spread over all of Europe.

We have the sanctified obligation to remember our great tragedy. What we earned and what has remained. Remember the date, the 3rd of Tevet, and on that day light a memorial candle for those lives which were exterminated. May the memorial candles tell our children and children's children about the huge tragedy that befell our people. May this memorial book serve as an eternal monument for our Maków Jewish community, which was exterminated in the worst destruction in our history.

[Page 236]

May their memory serve as a blessing!

A memorial to the Maków martyrs. Germany, 1947.

[Page 237]

Beatings, Torture, and Death

by Meir-Hirsch Ciechanower, Tel-Aviv

Translated by Dr. Joseph Schuldenrein

I was born in 1897 in the town of Ciechanow, about 30 kilometers from Maków (60 km from the eastern Prussian border), and 100 km from Warsaw. I ran a seltzer factory that provided a comfortable living for my family, a wife and three children- two daughters and a son.

At the time of the German occupation I was living at #4 Zhiloni Square.

Early winter, January, 1940. It was around midnight, and there was a loud banging on the door. When I opened up I stared at an armed German soldier who ordered me to follow him to the Beis-Midrash, around 50 meters from my house. I had no choice but to follow him. I was accompanied part-way by some of my family who feared I was being led to be executed.

Upon arriving at the Beis-Midrash I saw 20 horses, two or three of which were freed up from their reins, effectively loose. I noticed that the windows of the Beis-Midrash were littered with fragments of Torah parchment. The German ordered me to bind the horses together. Despite the fact that the horses were agitated and rocking wildly on their hind legs, I succeeded in binding them and fastening the reins to wall supports. The German seemed somewhat stunned by my boldness, and said "Hey Jew, go get a lamp because it's really dark in here." I went back to my house to get several lanterns. When my family saw me return they were overjoyed. I grabbed the lanterns, turned right around to the Beis-Midrash and lit them. I noticed that the

German was drunk and wobbly on his feet. Next, he ordered: "Grab the phone and dial up the Commandant." I got to the phone and rang the number. "Who are you? A Jew?"—I heard a stern voice on the other end of the line. "Stay right there. We are coming directly."

[Page 238]

I had managed to tell the Commandant that since he was drunk his counterpart had asked me to place the call and that someone should come and get the horses.

Five minutes later several German soldiers showed up on horseback. They cast a glance at their drunken comrade, lying face down on the ground. They broke out in laughter. Next, they looked at me somewhat approvingly, gave me a slap on the back and told me to go home. I thanked God that the only retribution I got was several slaps.

Rounded up for Hard Labor

In the winter of 1940 the Judenrat (Jewish Community Council) posted a list demanding the conscription of young Jewish men for hard labor. Fortunately, my name did not appear on the list. The next day following the dispatch of the first group of men to work details, I was nabbed on the street. I requested that the German official allow me to go home to pack my clothes and get some food. He went back with me. I grabbed a coat, some clean clothes, and some snacks and returned with him, near the Poviatov House (a landmark circular building), where a group of vehicles were loading up workers, men only. They were poised to leave for the work site. I asked the Jewish police official, Fishel Boorshtayn, if I might obtain a release. His response was "My job is to make sure that you stay by the vehicle".

Maków er Jews digging trenches, 1939

[Page 239]

I removed my jacket and laid it on the seat of the vehicle together with my sack of clothes. I also gave my pass to the same Jewish policeman and went directly to the German on the other side who had not seen that I had stripped down and laid my belongings on the other end. "Excuse me", I said, " I have no clothes, it's cold, might I run back home to get appropriate clothes, some gloves?É.my hands are freezing. I have already left my pass with that Jewish policeman on the other side of the vehicle." I pointed to him. "Please, just let me go, I promise I won't run away and will return promptly."

"Run fast" he yelled after me, "but come right back, as the truck is just about to leave and you will have no way to get out to the site."

I eased up my pace in the distance and stayed home. I saw how they packed in the Jews, bloodied, exhausted, half-naked, clothes in tatters. And I thought to myself: there is no way I am going back.

Once home I found a hiding spot. My wife went over to Avraham Garfinkel the (Jewish) community chairman and chief. She explained to him what I had experienced. "That was the right thing to do. I only wish that the others had done the same." Garfinkel also made sure that I was issued another pass. Shortly thereafter he hand-delivered the pass to my house.

A Head Whipping

Although the Ghetto had not yet been established, the Germans had already begun the process of concentrating the Jews in a formal quarter. On one occasion an official approached and ordered me to leave my home. I ran off to the house across the way and hid myself in the attic. I stayed there together with a fellow named Mendel Kleiner. A German noticed me and there, at the foot of the stairs, and commended "Get down" and I stood in front of him.

"Why did you run away?" he yelled, then beat me across the head with a whip. I felt the blood gushing down my nose. I realized that my nose had split open. More Germans showed up and the beatings continued. They paid a visit to my house and found a variety of luxury items and wares with my name and that of my son on them. They then took me down to the magistrate's office to determine if the suspected items were legitimately mine. A Folks-Deutsch (Ethnic-German) woman responded, "This fellow is a known smuggler". I was led up to the second floor. The inspector examined the items and concluded that they were, in fact, legitimately mine. He bandaged me up and said directly "Since you are already here, please get into the truck which is transporting several Jews to work in the town of Tchervonka[maybe Czerwin].

[Page 240]

```
[Joint 135]                                        2.

Absender A.Garfinkiel              Postkarte
Makow  Südostprussen
Praschnitzer Str.            An Joint Distribution Comitee
Judengemeinde                     Warschau

                                  Jasna 11/5
Otrzymano 1.IV.1940
Nr  101

                        Makow, den 22.3. 1940 J.

        An Joint Distribution Comitee
0/123/40                  Warschau
3/4 podp.

        Wir wenden sich zu Euch schon zum dritten Mal - sendet uns sofort

Hilfe in Form von Geld und Kleider.

        Da leben Juden aus Różan, Krasnosielsk, Prasznitz, Wyszków, Chorzele

Rypin, Pułtusk, Mława, Dobrzyn und Nasielsk in Zahl über 2000 Männer,

Frauen und Kinder.

        Wir können nach Warschau  nicht kommen, denn wir haben kein Passir-

schein. Vielleicht ist möglich, dass Euer Vorsteher uns besuche, und ertei-

le Hilfe aufn Platz.

        Geldsendugen bitte senden auf folgenden Adress: Hilfskomitat für

arme Jüden bei der Judengemeinde in Makow" - Abram Garfinkiel Makow

Praschnitzer Str.

                        Mit Achtung
                        Die Jüdische Gemeinde
                        in Makow.
```

Maków 22.3.1940 document

[Page 241]

They loaded in the sick, women, and children with their bags and linens and drove us to the firehouse. The windows were broken and the cold was bone-chilling.

There were few hundred of us. Several died within days. Those who remained healthy were summoned to dig privies outside. There were no tools or shovels and we had to excavate the dirt with our hands and fingers. I was already ill and had decided to muster my remaining strength to run away. The rest of the group begged and pleaded for me to stay, fearing that they would be killed in retaliation. The fear was such that even those who were able bodied and stood a chance of escaping were afraid to take the risk. Nevertheless, some did take the chance and ran off. They informed my wife of my situation. The next day my wife showed up with a soldier named Brodovski who took it upon himself to get me out. And that's how I got back home.

Several locals from home were with me in Tchervonka[maybe Czerwin} including Moishe Bordovitch with his wife and children and the butcher Yisroel-Meier Petsinash with his wife and children. Some of the locals escaped and were hidden by Poles. Subsequently, when the ghetto was established they moved back.

Twenty Body Blows

We went to work every day. I never avoided the detail because one could count on having something to eat.

One day I returned to the ghetto from work, tired and with my shovel slung over my shoulder. Dressed in work clothes and with my work equipment, I was pretty certain that no one would bother me on my return. I was basically care-free. And then I saw a (Jewish) police official running towards me, closely followed by Steinmetz, the Ghetto Commissar. The German pointed towards me and ordered the policeman, Pavel Rosenberg, to stop me and escort me directly to the Judenrat. I went with him. On the way the German blurted out "You disgust me, you will be cut off". When I arrived at the Judenrat building I was told to stay there and wait until they came back. Steinmetz and the policeman went out and only returned after they had rounded up another 10 people including several women. Ten minutes later Steinmetz and the policeman entered and barked: "You will each receive 10 lashes. Who wants to go first?"

[Page 242]

To which I responded, "I'll be the first"!

Steinmetz ordered me to lay face down and remove my pants. When I stripped down to my underwear and positioned myself I received a stiff blow to the head with a police baton. He then nodded to Rosenberg to begin the round of 10 lashes. The beatings were firm but by the fourth Steinmetz drew his personal rod and whacked the policeman over the head yelling, "You see? This is how you beat him!". Rosenberg collapsed on the floor, and Steinmetz meted out the remaining lashes to me himself. By the time he dispatched the last one I was numb. I had lost consciousness. They dragged me home somehow. Once home, the family started wailing, believing that Steinmetz had killed me. Neighbors began pouring into the house, eventually consoling me: "Don't worry. You'll be OK. This is war."

Amongst the visitors I recall two, Shimshon Blum and Mattes Gutleizer (both murdered subsequently). Mattes told me: "We will all be killed, and I guarantee that only you will survive to bear witness to what will have happened. Don't worry, you will make it through."

Over the course of several days I nursed my wounds and eventually returned to work.

Best Not to Sit Down

Every Thursday men between the ages of 17 and 65 were required to register at the Magistrate's office (this was prior to the Ghetto). Typically, the registration lines were long, as was the wait to process the paperwork. There was a Volks-Deutsch ("Ethnic German") who looked at every ID card and stamped it. If someone had omitted a piece of documentation he would get a beating. Often such violations would result in a person's being led to a separate room to submit to 20 lashes across his bare skin.

I recall one particular instance:

I was summoned to the Magistrate in order to provide an assessment of the value of my house. The clerk, who was responsible for recording the details of the appraisal, asked me to take a seat. I was hesitant to do as she said because it was explicitly forbidden for Jews to walk on the sidewalk and to sit down in the presence of a German. When the clerk insisted that I take a seat I explained the reason for my refusal.

[Page 243]

She then yelled out "I am ordering you to sit down." And I immediately sat down. Then suddenly I felt someone yank away the stool on which I sat. Before I knew it, I was face down on the ground. And then I realized that it was the guard who had pulled the seat out from under me. He screamed out "Jew, don't you know that you are prohibited from sitting?" Suddenly, there was a tussle between the clerk and the guard. She ended up recording the details while I stood and then I hustled out of the office as quickly as I could.

Another time my daughter Rivkah was walking past the town jail. She recognized one of her friends (who worked in the local pharmacy) sitting in a cell. She approached her friend and asked what had happened. A local Pole, who noticed Rivkah approaching the cell, immediately summoned the policeman in charge. He grabbed my daughter and gave her 20 body lashes. And then he ordered her to say "Thank you". My daughter refused to comply. "Go ahead and whip me again but I will never say thank you for that, never."

"Go and bring me 20 (German) marks", he ordered. Bloodied and drained, she summoned every last bit of energy and ran out and brought the 20 marks. They let her alone after that.

The Payback

Once the ghetto was established, I lived together with my family and in the same place as Reuven-Yosef Zafian, (his wife) Freida and their daughter Giteleh and son Hershel. They were model children. Giteleh had an official position in the Judenrat. I was like a father to those kids, and I helped them out in any way I could.

The women in the ghetto were especially burdened and harried. And Giteleh was no exception. This was especially true (in her case) because she had a full-time job. There was an incident when Steinmetz entered the Judenrat and approached her, grabbed her by the hair and saw that the hair was a bit longer than the officially permissible length. He then ordered her to come towards him. Steinmetz led her outside the ghetto walls, sat her down on a bench and struck her ten times with his truncheon.

Giteleh was an only daughter and her brother, an only son. The entire family was eventually dispatched to Auschwitz where they met their fate.

[Page 244]

A high-ranking Gestapo officer took me and my brother-in-law, Leibel Freeman along with another Jew to a farm work-detail. He drove but we walked the entire way. The place was about 1.5 kilometers outside of town. As we approached the farm, he yelled out, "Look here, you filthy Jews, this is where you'll work". He pointed out a group of white-feathered hens and said, "There are exactly fifty hens here, and they better all be here when I return. I also know the exact number of pigs and calves in this farm. If any one of these farm animals goes missing I will shoot you right here."

We worked there for about 5 or 6 days. We cleaned out the manure and did all sorts of menial tasks. And afterwards we were sent back to the ghetto.

German Murderers

The Maków Ghetto was liquidated on November 18, 1942. I bore testament to the ruthless beatings of the Jewish population, the elderly, and women and children as they were all hunted down and concentrated in the central square of the Ghetto sector. Each and every house was searched, and emptied, the sick huddling on benches in the square. I noticed a swollen and visibly beaten fellow stooped on a nearby bench, Moishe-Dovid Fuchs; this was Fayvel Hendler's grandson, a proud fellow. The Nazis beat him ferociously and then shot him dead on the spot. Everyone witnessed the murder.

The bones of 21 souls hanged in the Makówer Ghetto in 1942-brought to burial in Maków

[Page 245]

Nearby we saw Rafael-Hirsch Azrilevitch. As he gazed upon the unfolding scene, the man went seemingly berserk. He stepped out of the line and broke out in a frenzied dance, singing and clapping: "let's all be cheerful, lively and joyful" and he sang "It's wonderful to be a Jew, to be a Jew is greatÉ. I thank God that he made me a Jew"Éand on and on. His prattling continued for a while and then he moved back in the line. We all thought that they would shoot him directly for leaving his place and I kept prodding and pushing him back yelling "Rafael-Hirsch, what are you doing? Have you gone crazy?"

He responded "I am doing this with a clear head, knowingly, and I want them to shoot me; why torture myself to witness this horror!?"

They marched us out towards (the nearby town of) Mlawa; it was quite the scene. They beat us mercilessly, forcing us to run all the while. We didn't even know where or how to proceed; beatings and battering everywhere no matter what we did.

We finally arrived in Mlawa. Families were dispersed and separated, as the march disintegrated into chaos. But the following morning families managed to reunite somehow. The crowds were eventually directed to train cars headed for Auschwitz and among them was Abba Berenbaum. Unfortunately, he was completely exhausted, sapped of strength, incapable of moving further. Avrom Garfinkel ran to attend to him, and lead him onto the train car. Abba Berenbaum responded "Go, in health, dear children, I can't go on anymore." And that was that.

Buna Concentration Camp

On the way to Auschwitz, a group of the Makówer Jews were let out at the Buna camp (adjacent to Auschwitz, part of the complex). My son Mohtel and I were among them. We spent two weeks in quarantine. My fingers were frostbitten and I was hospitalized. From that point on I did not see my son for over a year. I had no idea of his whereabouts, nor what had happened to him. The foreman of my work detail was a fellow named Frantz. He wore special pointy, steel toed boots. He had a habit of kicking everyone across exposed and bare skin to goad them to move faster.

[Page 246]

The man yelled out "faster", "move out". Almost everyone bore wounds and lesions to the point where they could not sit down. Prisoners prayed to God that their wounds would heal quickly, if only that they could tolerate a new round of kicks.

I was transferred from Buna to Auschwitz. We were loaded onto a freight-hauler, the dead together with the living. The dead were laid out on the floor and we had to rest our legs on the corpses as we rode. It was a brutal winter (I believe it was March, 1943). We wore short pants and were generally barefoot. When we finally arrived they ordered us to remove the corpses first. Other prisoners came to take away the dead, while we went directly to the camp barracks. Of all the prisoners in my transport I was the only survivor.

Once at the barracks we were ordered to lay down in the bunks. I shared my narrow "bunk" with another prisoner. There was a single thin cover-sheet for the two of us. The windows were open with the wind blowing through. We lay there until dawn. It was impossible to talk at night because of the bone chilling cold and my fingers fell numb in both hands. In the morning I was taken away from the barracks, and sprayed with cold water, and then my bandages and rags were removed and my fingers were bound together. I was sent back to the hospital and shared a single bed with two other patients. The one's name was Viatrak from Maków, I believe his first name was Simcha, Avrom Viatrak's son. He was a good looking fellow, just 18, and he was suffering from frost-bite on his right toe. The second man was a Mr. Geldi, a Dutch Jew from Rotterdam or Amsterdam, and he told me that he owned a perfume factory. He made a point of asking me that if I survived could I contact his wife and tell her that he died in Auschwitz? On the third day, a car with SS men drove up and took both of my bedmates from the hospital and their fate was clear. They were bound for the gas chambers and the crematoria.

Daily Selections

I was laid up in the hospital for six weeks. During that time there were daily selections as prisoners were taken away to end up in the ovens, the crematoria that took in thousands of Jewish victims daily. I received neither food nor drink during my first three days in the hospital. The explanation was that my papers had not yet been received.

[Page 247]

On the fourth day I finally got my ration: a liter of soup and a piece of bread. Upon release from the hospital I was dispatched to a new block populated with inmates who were either sick or invalids. Both of my hands remained bandaged and the wounds would not heal. The head doctor prescribed a sauerkraut-based remedy to accelerate my recovery. But I only received it once.

In the hospital I was laid up near a Czech Jew by the name of Weiss. He worked at the D.A.V. (German Mechanical Works) as a carpentry foreman. He told me that if I could manage to get assigned to the D.A.V. I'd be able to avoid the gas-chamber. When I left the hospital, I headed out to the central work plaza along with the thousands gathered there. A large number headed off to the carpentry workshops. I stayed back, as I had no idea where to go. I ended up in what appeared to be a light-duty workshop, knowing full-well that I was incapable of performing any hard tasks since my hands were inflamed. It was clear, however, that this particular workshop was heated so that my disabled hands might warm up. I entered the carpentry section. I came up against a Kapo, a Polish Jew from France. He approached me and asked "What are you doing here?"

"I came here because I heard that there is a need for workers", I answered. The Kapo responded to me with a slap across the face. I then collapsed in front of him. The incident was observed by the Uber-Kapo, also a Jew. He turned directly to the Kapo who had beaten me and asked "Why did you hit him? Don't you see that he has bandaged hands and that he is an older fellow?"

He drove me about a kilometer beyond, to yet another municipal square. Next, he summoned a second Kapo to assign me a work detail and keep an eye out for me.

Matter of Life and Death....and a Sewing Needle

When I was in the hospital, I had a tight, ragged jacket that was missing several buttons. Because of my frost-bitten hands and the lesions I was not able to fasten the flaps to keep out the cold winds that blew through the block. But there was a fellow six beds down from me who had a needle and thread. I approached the man and asked him if I could borrow the needle and some thread to fasten the buttons. He gave them to me. Next, I approached another prisoner and asked him if he could sew on several buttons for me since I was incapacitated. When I returned to give back the needle the fellow who gave it to me claimed that the point of the needle was broken. He made a stink about it: "You scoundrel, it's clear that you destroyed my needle, do you have any idea what you have done? Do you think that I can get another needle in this place?"

[Page 248]

A Polish kapo, a doctor in the hospital, overheard the quarrel and approached me. He gave me such a fierce blow to the chest that I collapsed on the floor. I began yelling and writhing in pain on the ground. I thought that it would all end, right then and there. I lay there all night and, first thing in the morning, I awoke and opened my eyes and saw the inmates swarming around me stunned. "Look at him, he's still alive." It turned out that the fellow who lent me the needle got beaten similarly by the same Kapo.

The Death March

On the 18th of January, 1945 we were led out of Auschwitz on foot directly to Gliwice. On the way the prisoners began dropping like flies. Those who could barely move were shot on the spot. Those who collapsed from exhaustion passed out and met their fates.

The Germans destroyed everything in their wake, leaving nothing intact. I marched out together with a fellow from Katzeht. Over the first two days we got no food or drink. The privations caused me to lose my sight. My partner guided me along since I could not see where I was going. I recall that his name was Avrom Mahndershtayn and he was from Mlawa. He did not let me out of his sight for a moment because he knew that this meant certain death for me. Two days after liberation Mahndershtayn himself fell sick with dysentery and died.

Once in Gliwice we were herded into a firefighter-station. We thought that for sure we would be dispatched to be gassed. I remember that Henech Lassek, Avrohom Lassek's son from Maków, stuffed a piece of bread in my mouth because he saw that I was already half-dead. The bread fell to the ground. Thereupon Lassek ran towards a stationery railroad car, on the tracks, and filled a can of water for me to drink. As soon as I guzzled down the water my vision began to return. "Can I get a piece of bread?" I asked him. He stuffed another piece of bread in my mouth and I was able to swallow and digest it. That was the cure that saved me.

In Gliwice we sat outside in a series of open benches. A storm came in and snow started accumulating and covering us. We bunched up together for warmth, drifting off, and imagining that this was finally it, the end: we'd freeze to death.

[Page 249]

But it was probably the snow that insulated and warmed us on the way to the concentration camp at Gross-Rozen, a hell-hole that was even worse than Auschwitz. That's where I saw people wandering around like zombies, almost stick figures. Dead folks walking, that's about it.

The Camp Commandant at Gross-Rozen told us as follows: "You should know that Auschwitz is a vacation spa compared to Gross-Rozen". He led us to a huge auditorium. There were about 2000 people in the place. It seemed overflowing, we were laid out, one on top of the next. We literally had no room to move and anyone who tried to get out never came back in. You also had to take care of your bodily needs in place. We were there for 2 or 3 days. We got nothing to eat. When one wanted to get food in the camp kitchen one returned with nothing, since the kitchen was set on a steep hill and the camp quarters were in the valley. Aside from the fact that one did not have the energy to climb the steep slope leading to the camp kitchen, if one managed to get some food or soup in a container the slopes were so slippery that one collapsed, together with contents of the container that spilled out and disappeared down slope. There were those that tried to slurp the soupy earth directly.

The Trip to Dachau

We got word that another transport was imminent, but we had no idea as to where. We just ran to the assembly site. At this point we felt that we had nothing to lose.

Once we got to the site, there were a couple of thousand people waiting. Everyone got a ration of bread together with a piece of raw, red meat. We were marched to the train station and stuffed into freight cars. When the cars were packed to overflowing an SS officer came by. When he peeked inside he said "There is room here for a few more". They packed in a few more. The train started to move out and we figured again that this was it, the final journey. We traveled for three days in these locked and sealed box cars. The human crush and the noxious air resulted in many deaths. When it seemed that we were finally doomed our luck took a turn for the better. The train cars braked to a halt. Standing in front of us were two women sporting white caps with red crosses on their arms.

[Page 250]

They doled out (paper) cups of soup to each and every one of us. The cups emptied even before we finished swallowing. And we remained hungry.

The train moved on. Within several days we reached Dachau. We disembarked from the freight cars. Once out, we observed vehicles loaded with corpses driving past. The bodies had been dropped off the train and then gathered up on the way in. Those of us that survived the trip followed the corpse-laden vehicles on foot. We were herded into the camp and assigned beds and bunks. We slept three to a bed, two on the ends and one in the middle, feet facing the opposite direction. We stayed there for two weeks in quarantine and were then moved to a camp in the woods near Muhldorf (in the vicinity of Munich). I remained there until April 1, 1945. Subsequently, I was taken to Muhldorf together with another 200 people. Once there, we survived on rations of potatoes. We worked there digging holes and building makeshift shelters. They also made us clean out the remains from the bombed-out train station. I stayed there until approximately April 25, 1945. They put us back on a train, to where, again.....I have no idea. The train took off and moved in circuitous routes since the rail lines were variously bombed out and blockaded. I was liberated at that same train station on May 1, 1945.

"You are free to go"

On the eve of liberation, April 30, 1945, members of the SS entered the train cars and announced "Germany has surrendered, you are free to go." We raced out of the cars and ran several hundred meters before hearing a cry "Not so fast, get back into the cars!" They chased us back, beating us on the way in. Some died on the spot. I made it back to the car, then spread out on the floor and slept through the night. The next morning someone yelled out "The Americans are here". I paused for a while and then slid down from the car that was stationed in the middle of the field. The Americans had already settled in there and brought us boxes of food. We stayed there for two days. Subsequently they came to get us and set us up in a school. Eventually they took us to get bathed and washed, distributed pajamas, socks and shoes. Germans were mobilized to attend to our needs. For the first time in three and a half years I was able to sleep in a normal bed.

[Page 251]

I was able to drink a cup of coffee and eat a sandwich. We stayed in the Feldafing D.P. camp for two years and three months. On May 17, 1947 I arrived in Israel in one of the waves of illegal immigration.

Yosl Makóẇer (in the first row, first on the right) and Meir-Hersh Ciechanower (second row, first
on the right) together with a group of Halutzim for Hacshara, Maków, 1932

[Page 252]

Amongst Human Animals

by Meir Rubin, Herzliyah

Translated by Dr. Joseph Schuldenrein

Friday, September 1, 1939. In Makow Friday was the traditional market–day. At 9 AM, the radio announced that war had broken out–Germany had invaded Poland and bloody battles had begun. I ran out into the street and met up with my friends, Moishe Villenburg and Shloime–Yidel Lichtenshtayn. Moishe Villenburg had just gotten married, about three weeks prior to the invasion. He told me that he had to take off immediately to Yablona–Leghionova, near Warsaw, because his wife was staying there with her family. I used to get together with Villenburg frequently to figure out what we would do if and when war broke out. At around lunch time the peasants scattered from the market–place, planes were flying overhead and the air was heavy with worry and, indeed, panic. That said, some of the local Jews congregated in synagogues, while others huddled in their homes depressed, wondering what tomorrow might bring.

As it got darker, the curtains were drawn, the Shabbos candles flickered out and the houses fell dark.

At the time I was working as a truck–driver for a vehicle owned by Shimon–Meier Rosen. It was part of a trucking and delivery business owned by two partners: Yoel Grossman and Dovid Kasten. There were two freight haulers, I was one of the drivers and the other was a Pole. On the night the war broke out (late Thursday into Friday morning) I pulled into town from Warsaw with a full load of merchandise. The workmen unloaded the wares in the yard. That Friday evening the Polish police approached me with an order to leave immediately to take their families to Warsaw. I tried to explain to them that it was the Sabbath, and that besides I was sick and exhausted and that I did not want to abandon my family at this time. But they responded "Hey, this is war we are ordering you to go, so go!"

That same Friday night Polish policemen and their families began pouring into Makow–Mazowiecki from (the nearby town of) Pruzhnitz. I bade farewell to my mother with a heavy heart and took off with the Polish policemen. We loaded up the officers, their families, wives and children, and their baggage. People sat on top of their bags and belongings and we took off for Warsaw.

[Page 253]

The trip to Warsaw

I finally began to sort out my thoughts about this bizarre trip. While the stress of violating the Sabbath was disturbing that was hardly the worst of it. The police chief from Pruzhnitz, who sat beside me during the trip cradled his revolver and warned me "Look what I have in my hand. If anything goes awry on this trip you'll take a bullet in your head."

It was dark, but I did not dare turn on the headlights as I drove under cover of night back from Warsaw, a distance of about 86 kilometers. Along the way we passed numerous Polish soldiers and military personnel along with crowds of refugees pouring out of Warsaw.

Yet all of us arrived in Warsaw without a hitch. We dropped off the passengers and their baggage at the designated addresses. I was thinking of leaving back to Makow immediately after I let them all off. Just as I was about to depart a Polish policeman approached and said "I am commandeering you and your vehicle. Let's drive and I will tell you where to go." We drove to the Police Station on Tziapla Street, but immediately after the policeman got out, I started the engine and took off. I drove all the way to the house of Israel and Nathan Montcheckovsky (currently in Israel, adopted name of Shachar); they owned an auto–parts store behind an iron gate. I bought a car battery from them and then on to get petrol at Franzischkahner street so that I might make it home.

The Montcheckovskys asked me to get word to their brother–in–law Ezra that he should send his family food to Warsaw. As I was about to leave, there was a searing sound from German airplanes overhead. And then a horrific explosion. When the air fell silent I began the drive home and by 9 AM on the Sabbath I dropped off the vehicle at the garage in Makow.

I did not head home directly for fear that I would get mobilized for yet another trip out. Instead I went to my uncle Yosef Hendel's house to sleep. I dispatched my cousin Shmulik to my mother's house to let her know that I had arrived home safely, and that should anyone inquire as to my whereabouts she should tell them she had no idea where I was.

[Page 254]

Bombs Raining Down

As soon as the police learned that I had driven off, they arrived at my house to look for me. When the search came up empty they summoned another driver, Srulik Skuza, and commandeered him along with my vehicle to drive–it was not clear where. At some point Skuza made his way back to Makow without the vehicle. He told us that during the bombardment the car caught fire near the Romanian border.

That Sunday morning an order was issued from the Magistrate that all young men were to leave town immediately and show up in Pultusk for military service. I left for Pultusk along with my three brothers and several friends. And so we were enlisted. However, there was nothing they could do with us as there were no available arms or weapons. They told us simply that our mission was to defend Warsaw.

Along with my three brothers, my sister Michaeleh and cousin Shmulik Hendel and Moishe Bachrach we packed up our bags and loaded them onto a wagon and headed to 41–43 Chlodna Street in Warsaw, the address of my sister's brother–in–law. There was an empty room on the sixth floor. We were to stay there temporarily. Ultimately we were there for 4 weeks during the German bombardment. Each evening we lined up at the bakery for bread rations. One night as we were waiting in an alley way for our bread the Germans began blasting the neighborhood with artillery fire. I told my brothers that we had best get out of there immediately because from the direction of the firing, it was pretty clear that we were the targets of the assault. As soon as we left we saw a shell fall at the precise spot where we had been standing immediately before we ran off. Those who remained there were killed on the spot and many others were wounded.

There was an incident when I was with my brother Pinyeh and his brother–in–law Fishel Lichtenshtayn on Smotcheh Street. Bomb blasts ensued. We began running past the gate at Leshna–Passage and I noticed someone racing past on a bicycle and pointing hurriedly. I understood that he was signaling us that the Germans were right there. We ran frantically through the gate and the shell exploded directly behind us.

Two or three weeks thereafter we were visited by one of our hometown friends, Tuvia Sehgal. He told us that while retreating from the front he threw away his rucksack and all of his belongings (except his rifle).

[Page 255]

On the way back he found a pair of Tefillin, put them on and began to pray. He claimed that this act helped him to avoid the bullets. He told us of the horrific battles at the front and reported that the Germans had broken through every line of defense.

On Rosh Hashanah and Yom Kippur our delegate, Councilman and Jewish Community leader Meyer Ostroff, organized a Minyan at Chlodna Street at the home of our relative Mr. Tannenbaum. During the day, when the Germans were around, the streets were deserted. It was a scene of consummate devastation. Broken streetlights and dead horses, interspersed with human corpses, littered the streets. We stood by the city gates and watched as the Germans arrested Polish officers. They ripped off their badges and medals and began beating them mercilessly. Several days later bread trucks came in with deliveries. The Germans yelled out "Jews Away". I hid my hat, so as not to be recognized as a Jew, then stole a piece of bread and took off running. Shortly thereafter the Poles began informing on the Jews. The Germans began shooting. I barely made it out alive.

Return to Makow

The Germans put up notices on the streets declaring that all refugees were now permitted to return to their homes. My brother Yerachmiel, Shmuel Hendel, Moishe Bachrach and myself got together, along with several other friends from home– Shmuel Dzhenkevitch, Moishe–Yehuda Freschberg, and others–and made the trip back to Makow. We left Warsaw around 5 PM. We got to Yablona–Legionowo. That's where I ran into my friend Moishe Villenburg. I was so happy to meet him. He offered me a piece bread. He gave the same to the rest of the group and told us that his motorcycle lay hidden away. He suggested that we both ride back home to Makow together. I responded "No, it's probably best to go on foot. Come along with us."

We set off on the way together. When we got to the train station the Germans stopped us and put us in jail. We came across many others in the same situation. The Germans held us in detention several days. During the day they put us to work polishing machinery, cleaning the rooms, and shining soldiers' boots. We also "organized" bread loaves and packs of cigarettes. One time they had us dance around the machines and told us to sing Jewish songs. Moishe–Yehuda Freschbergen performed a "Pshepooska" (dance) for 10 of the older Germans. The next morning we headed off in the direction of Makow.

[Page 256]

When we got to the River Narov we saw that the wooden bridge was destroyed. We got as far as a pontoon bridge that the Germans had put up. However, the German patrol refused to let us across and we turned back to Nowy Dwor by way of Nashelsk, where we came up on another bridge about 20 km from Nashelsk. The Germans refused to let us make that crossing as well. However, Moishe Freshberg reached out to the German commandant who let us go and we finally reached Nashelsk.

Nashelsk was the home of my grandfather and he lived there with my grandmother Esther–Itta. They owned a bakery there together with my uncle Yechiel. When we got to their house my grandfather was standing in front of the oven baking fresh loaves. When he saw us coming he burst out in tears and began doling out warm bread "fresh out of the oven." We ate it heartily. Grandfather invited us to spend the Sabbath at his place.

That Sunday afternoon, around 5 PM we left for Makow. We got to within 5 km of town and ran into some peasants who asked us (in Polish) "Jews, where are you going? There isn't a single Jew left in Makow!" We decided nevertheless to continue heading into town. We came across my mother and her cousin Golda Hendel. I asked them "Mamehleh, where are you going?" And she replied "A certain family just got in from Warsaw. I wanted to go past your place to pick up a grinder (for food preparation)". I told her what the peasants had just relayed to us and she retorted "That's a bold lie. Everyone is here and everything is just fine."

We went over to the Hendel's place. The Bachrachs were also there. Everyone, the Bachrachs included, visited together at the apartment on Grobarskah Street.

Getting a Job

My older brother Yerachmiel was terrified of the Germans. He did everything he could to avoid going out in the street. I was a lot more open, however, and knew how to interact with the locals. That said, my mother would often lock us in the house (she shut the lock from the outside). That was because the Germans would dash around town like forsaken mice and round up people for work details. I took on a job as an electrician.

[Page 257]

```
AMERICAN JOINT DISTRIBUTION COMMITEE, WARSAW


                              Warschau, den 2.Mai 1940

No.O/419/40

An die
Jüdische Gemeinde
z Hd.des Herrn A.Rozental
M a k ó w
Rynek 31


     In Beantwortung Ihres Briefes vom 22.v.Mts. teilen wir mit, dass

Ihnen in den nächsten Tagen die bewilligte Subvention überwiesen werden

wird.

     Wir würden Sie bitten, nachstehende Personen in die Verteilungkom=

mission einzuberufen, und zwar:

     Herren:  Chilinowicz Szymon Chaim
              Berenbaum Abe
              Garfinkiel Abram
              Monkacz Piszel

     Ferner bitten wir, uns einen Bericht über die Tätigkeit des Hilfs=

komitees zugehen zu lassen.


                    Hochachtungsvoll

                American Joint Distribution Commitee


JS/ak
```

American Joint Distribution Committee letter,
sent through the Jewish Institute of Warsaw to Israel

[Page 258]

When the ghetto was set up I had the opportunity to get out and, more importantly, to get back in. That allowed me to bring in food from the outside for my family.

On Yom Kippur 1940 the German issued an order to create a ghetto for Jews within the town limits. Subsequently a harsh wave of hunger broke out. Typhus ran rampant. I was to remain on the job per the instructions of a German officer named Schuman, recently arrived from Germany. He was dressed in civilian clothes and became the overseer in charge of the electrical facilities in town. He also took over a stately house ("Potshekalnia"), formerly the home of Yakov–Moishe Skurnik, who had already left town before the war broke out. The building now housed an electrical supply store as well as Schuman's office.

One day I was asked to take in an assistant, Fayvel Skaleh. I took him in gladly. It turned out, however, that he engaged in an escapade of intrigue against me with Schuman, and in the end I was deposed from my job along with my brother, and Skaleh took my place. After removal from my position I was demoted to forced labor details. Next, I was dispatched with a group of 40 other Jews to small towns across the countryside about 15 km from town. We were tasked with the removal of huge boulders from the surrounding sandy landscape. This is where we ended up sleeping and the only daily meal we had was a couple of potatoes with watered down kasha.

When the Germans came into Makow, they began to ransack the biggest and oldest synagogue in town. They ripped out the Ark, the beams, the wooden flooring and benches and they replaced it all with a school. Eventually, as the Germans began building houses for themselves they tore down the school and dismantled the entire building. It was transformed into an empty lot. The German ghetto commissar eventually turned the lot into a "playground" for his sadistic pursuits. In the evenings he used to round up young men and women and meted out whippings and beatings. Among his victims were Abraham Blum (of blessed memory), Tovtsheh Rosenburg and her sister Chantsheh (of blessed memory), a girl from Dshinkevitsch, and many others. The severity of these beatings was such that the victims were temporarily paralyzed. They had to be treated with cold compresses for hours at a time.

An Edict to Shave Beards

The ghetto Commandant also issue an edict that all Jewish men shave their beards and that the women shave the hair off their heads.

[Page 259]

The first woman who cut off her hair was Avraham Garfinkel's wife. Garfinkel was the Chairman of the Judenrat and therefore called on his wife to serve as an example for the women.

I shuddered and was overcome when I saw how frightening the women looked with their shaved heads. Tears streamed down my face to my neck. I thought I took leave of my senses, as I was ashamed to look the women in the eyes. To fulfill the German orders the men went ahead and shaved off their beards. Even the older men complied. There was only a single Jew, one of the most prominent men in town, Yaakov–Dovid Hendel, a Torah scholar and brilliant leader, who steadfastly refused to shave it off. "I refuse to give them the pleasure" said he. Day and night he slept down in his basement, not daring to stick his head out into the street. He ignored the gossip as well. "Look here, in the darkness of the grave, I will get myself up and out and not a single hair from my beard will be removed". So he claimed.

I have no idea whether or not he had the opportunity to fulfill his wish. I never saw him again, because he was led off to Chiechanow, to a concentration camp, and I don't know what happened to him. As for the rest of the God–fearing Jews, they were forced to respond to the edict and were left to shave their beards. This was done by the Chasidim from the Alexanderer Shtibel (small and intimate synagogue), the Gerer, and the Amshinover shtibels as well.

Makow 1945, a look at the murder site

[Page 260]

"We are putting our trust in the Almighty. We trust he will take heed over our wrath and frustration."

I recall an incident one Friday evening when the Germans rounded up some Jews and placed them under arrest. The German police officer in charge of guarding the prisoners entered the detention center in the middle of the night and beat the Jewish prisoners. Later, a second police officer came in to take his shift and relieve the first. He found the guard ostensibly asleep, face down on the table. He approached the unresponsive officer and nudged him with his hand. Before the second officer uttered a word, the first fell over and collapsed on the floor, like a corpse. He was dead.

The Jews were up against another threat, namely that they would be accused of killing the German officer. Instead a miracle happened. The doctors who conducted the post–mortem on the dead policeman declared unequivocally that he died of a heart–attack. The Jews saw the hand of God in all of this. Specifically that he, the policeman, met his fate because he falsely laid the blame on the innocent Jews and therefore paid the price.

The Dead Hero

Three young guys from Pultusk happened to be in the ghetto. One time they ventured out in search of food in the town of Shelkoveh[?], about 9 km outside of Makow. I remember one of the guys, his name was Yosef Rubin, also known as "Scap". The police caught them in Shelkoveh and planned to shoot them square between the eyes, in the street, and in front of the crowd. The three begged the police for mercy and not to shoot them publicly but to take them into the woods and to execute them there. Once they reached the forest, "Skap" and his two friends assaulted the policemen, disarmed them, beat them up and ran off. All three made it back to the ghetto, although "Skap" had suffered a severe head wound. A Jewish doctor from Berlin, who had been dispatched to Makow to attend to the sick, ended up tending to Rubin's injury.

Three days after the incident Steinmetz, the German Commissar for Makow, made it his mission to find "the wounded Jew". He called out the doctor and asked him if he had attended to the injured Jew. The doctor responded that no, a Jew fitting that description had not turned to him for medical help. Shortly thereafter Steinmetz went to Yosef Rubin's home and confronted the bandaged Rubin.

[Page 261]

Steinmetz ordered him to get out of bed and come with him. "Skap" was then tortured in a most sadistic manner. When he could take it no longer, Rubin sent word to Avraham Garfinkel asking him to intervene with the Germans to have him shot and thus put an end to it. But the torture continued for several days until the Germans drove him out of town. When "Skap" sensed that he was sufficiently distant from Makow, he mustered whatever energy he still had, tore out of the grasp of the three police who had held him down, and bolted out of the back of the vehicle. The Germans opened fire on him and he fell dead.

But that was not the end of it. Ghetto Commissar Steinmetz was out for revenge. His rage and anger remained unabated. Back in the ghetto he found 20 Jews and sentenced them to a public hanging, all as payback for Yosef Rubin's ("Skap's") brazen act of defiance. In addition, he sentenced the Jewish doctor to hang. In all 21 Jews paid with their lives for this defiant act against the German police.

In Chiechanow

I headed off to work in the town of Chiechanow along with 300 other Jews. We had a number of jobs working for various German firms. They divided the group into three barracks. Each morning they did a roll call and broke us up by group and by firm. Each group was headed up by a representative whose assignment was to greet the Germans. One time I was selected as the head of my group. On our way to work we passed a field, where we were tasked with digging holes in the peat deposits. The area was patrolled and overseen by a division of the Hitler–youth. These hooligans split up amongst us and brutally beat each and everyone. We brought this to the attention of the (German) camp chief and he personally escorted us away from them to avoid further violence.

The Gestapo headquarters were in Chiechanow. The place was effectively a slaughter–house. Whoever had the misfortune to end up in that building did not make it out alive. Whenever you passed by the house you were required to remove your hat and keep it off 10 meters before and 10 meters after passing the building. If the German guards noticed that for whatever reason someone did not comply with this order, that individual was taken into headquarters, never to be seen alive again.

[Page 262]

There was an incident in Chiechanow wherein the Germans came across a prayer Minyan. They led these Jews, wearing their prayer shawls, into Gestapo headquarters. It was mid–day on Shabbos. They ordered the Jews to bring their Teffilin and to pray in front of them. After this spectacle they beat the Jews while driving them out into the street.

I remember another occasion in Chiechanow when they hanged a group of Jews in the municipal sports stadium. The Germans issued a public invitation for an event that would be taking place in the stadium. The admission fee for this event was one German mark. The German public grew very agitated; why should they pay an entry fee for a spectacle which should have been free of charge?

"No Work for Me Today"

There was the case of an 18 year old fellow by the name of Kviteyko who claimed to be sick and refused to report for work. "I have had it with the Germans", he claimed, "and I refuse to do anything for them. They will ultimately murder us anyway, so why should I let them exploit me?"

The camp commander assembled a number of us (Jewish prisoners) and warned the young man that if he continued to defy the work order he would be shot directly. The Germans urged Avraham Garfinkel (of the Judenrat) as well as the young man's parents to persuade the young man to report for his work detail. None of those interventions proved productive. Despite all pleas to exempt the young fellow nothing worked. And up until the evacuation of the camp he never worked again. After a while and once he had settled in, he decided that he really did want to work but this time his entreaties fell upon deaf ears. The camp commandant unequivocally refused to sign him to any detail. Around September of 1942, on an afternoon, the first evacuees of the camps in Chiechanow and Mlawa began to trickle in. The commandant informed us that the entire Jewish community of Chiechanow would be arriving in our camp. He gave a speech ordering us not to mix and mingle with the new arrivals. We were not to conduct any business with them, nor undertake any dealings involving money, gold, silver and other valuables. He warned that anyone participating in such activities would be immediately shot.

All of Chiechanow's Jewish residents were subsequently brought to the camp. The next morning, at the break of day, we were driven to Mlawa. They transported us by car. Earlier on they transported the Chiechanow Jews and then us, the last lot to evacuate the camp. Over the course of unloading the transport several Jews were shot to death.

[Page 263]

The Jewish Police Chief's Wife is Shot

The Jews from Chiechanow were taken to the Mill while we, the workers who had just returned from the work camp, were marched away to a barn. There was a selection. The Chiechanow Jews in the Mill included men, women and small children. Anyone who straggled was shot on the spot. The work detail group in the barn were dealt with after everyone else. In the evening I managed to sneak out of the barn in search of a place to sleep. I had a friend from Mlawa who was a policeman in the Jewish force. His name was Alter (I don't remember his family name). Later that evening he brought me to the police station. While I was there the Jewish police chief and his wife came by to see the place. A pair of German policemen showed up immediately thereafter. They exchanged some words with the Jewish police. The Jewish police chief's wife called out to her husband "I am heading home." Her husband remained at the station headquarters. Not two minutes later we heard two shots ring out from the outside. One of the Jewish police ran out immediately to see what had happened. The officer returned, his head lowered, to report to the Jewish police chief the horrific news, that the two German police who had just visited the station shot the chief's wife.

I asked my friend, the Jewish policeman, to please take me back to the barn. I couldn't sleep at all that night. I couldn't help but think and shudder at what happened only hours earlier.

The next morning I witnessed yet another murder. Several German policemen headed up by the Chiechanow police chief marched into the barn. They took out the Kvietko kid (the one who refused to report to work for the Germans) and shot him. The German police came all the way from Chiechanow exclusively to fulfill that mission.

The Transports From Mlawa

Shortly after Kviteyko's murder, rumors began to circulate that a transport from Mlawa was imminent (the entire Jewish population of Makow remained unaffected at the time). In fact, one transport from Mlawa had already departed.

[Page 264]

We were in the second transport. We appealed to the Judenrat of Mlawa that since transport from Makow would eventually be scheduled, we had hoped to stay behind and unite with our families before departing. But our appeals fell on deaf ears. Their response was "You must leave with the next transport taking off tomorrow morning." I really wanted to stay back and wait for my mother, brother and the rest of the family–in–laws, aunts and uncles. But they herded us down to the train station together with the Chiechanower and Mlawa groups and loaded us into the cars. They chased us down and beat us brutally. Anyone who resisted or hesitated was shot on the spot. The desperate screams and beatings reverberated to the skies, it seemed. I was the only one of my family who survived the ordeal– solitary, broken and helpless. I never saw any of them again.

We traveled past Radom, Czestochow, and Czestochowa, and saw the horrific destruction; broken doors and windows, mattresses, pieces of furniture, shattered kitchen wares, linens, scattered and strewn everywhere. This was utter destruction as one would expect in a battle. At that moment we began to realize the extent and magnitude of our fate and misfortune.

That night we arrived at Birkenau, exhausted, beaten up, delirious from lack of food and drink, physically and spiritually decimated. Over the course of this trip we had absolutely nothing to eat and drink. The children succumbed to hunger and thirst.

In Birkenau we stared at the illuminated barbed wire that lit up the area like daylight. We knew what awaited us, although we still hoped against hope that we were being taken to a labor camp.

The SS thugs were lined up at the train car. They pulled on the levers of the train doors and yelled "Everyone move out of the train cars". One of the SS men issued orders "Right, left....". We were then mobilized in lines and led to the camp. Men were grouped separately, and then children, women and the elderly separately. During the selections children were torn away from their mothers, wives from husbands, and the elderly from children as well. The yells and shrieks were other worldly. I was among a select few that were marched directly to a camp. However, we were not led to a barracks. Instead we spent the entire day and night outside. This was in October, 1942. It was a very severe cold autumn, as I remember. It rained non–stop. We stood under a steady stream of water as in an endless downpour where the cold water kept on pounding, completely soaking one's clothes and penetrating the flesh. I was shivering from the cold and my teeth did not stop chattering.

[Page 265]

That evening they led us to the bath house and ordered us to strip down. When we bent down to take some water to quench our thirst, they clubbed us and warned that whoever dared to drink would be shot then and there. The water that came down from the shower was cold as ice and then one by one we exited and went to a nearby station where we were given "striped robes", the prisoner's uniform. And from there we went to our blocks.

My Name, My Number: 75267

We were tattooed on our arms as soon as we were assigned to our blocks. My number was 75267. And that became my name and identity. Whenever that number was called out I had to present myself. Immediately after being tattooed they doled out our food rations: a portion of soup with unpeeled potatoes. Even though I was absolutely ravenous, I simply could not bring myself to put that food in my mouth and I gave it away. Next they chased us out to our "bunk–beds". They were stacked vertically on four levels, one on top of another. I ended up on the fourth level, together with four other inmates (five of us to a bunk–bed). The bunks were made of circular pieces of stock wood layered with straw. We were laid out like sardines in a flat–can. When any one individual turned on his side, the other four had to turn over in unison. Each group of five was given two covers; they were called "Canadian cots".

Those who slept on the lowermost level could barely breathe, because the air was so vile from the crowded and sweaty bodies; the windows could not be opened and the stale air created a most awful stench that permeated the entire barracks. Some of the inmates simply did not get up the next morning; they died overnight.

Human Animals

Overnight men turned into animals. They scrambled and scuffled to claim a place to sleep, a piece of bread, a cup of soup. In the wee hours, at around 2 or 3 AM (of course no one had a watch!), they parceled out bread (a part of a loaf, divided into strips). They also issued a stick of margarine with a spoon of jam.

[Page 266]

In the morning they counted and lined up the prisoners for the work detail. If this were a work camp the operation would be led by a Kapo and Assistant Kapo. If we were outside the camp we would be led by SS men. For every 50 inmates there were at least 4 SS men; with companies in excess of 50, more SS men.

As I was heading out to work that first day, I notice a dense and heavy odor. At first, I had no idea where it came from. But then when I returned to the barracks and met up with the other inmates and inquired about the unusual, pervasive smell I was informed that there were deep and extensive pits in front of the camp where people had been incinerated. They were set on a wooden platform, the pits were dug and trucks came by and dumped off live bodies. Germans armed with machine guns were at the ready on both sides of the truck and shot into the pits and then the bodies were incinerated. So now I finally understood where the overwhelming stench originated and what was really going on in the camp.

Upon my return from work to the camp barracks I witnessed countless inmate corpses sprawled out. Bodies were steadily dragged from the work detail, many of them already dead, some dying. No one made any attempt to save or attend to them, they were just dragged across the leafy way right in front of us.

When I headed off to work on the second day, I saw two Polish foremen assault one of the Jewish inmates. They beat him fiercely with wooden clubs as long as it took for him to expire. And we just stood there and stared at the bloody spectacle. And not a one of us said a word.

And on the third day–the same thing, different group. This time two Poles grabbed one of us and beat him over the head. When he finally fell over one of them set the club across the victim's neck and stomped on both sides of it, choking him to death. This was all done simply to terrorize us.

Arrival at Auschwitz

That was the situation over the course of my two weeks in Birkenau; I was assigned a variety of jobs. Soon after, my number was called out for transport with another 300 inmates (I was 27 years old at the time). They marched us out on foot directly to Auschwitz. I found out that I was brought there to work on electrical operations (when I was tattooed I was asked if I had any specialized training and I told them that I was an electrician).

[Page 267]

Upon arrival at Auschwitz I went through the shaving and body hair removal process again. Not a hair was left on my skin. They made us smear our bodies with a gel like substance. Then they issued us new "clothes" (the "striped" inmate wear) and assigned us to blocks. The next morning they dispatched us to our work assignment: demolition of old structures. Next they sent me to a detail that dealt with water and plumbing operations. We dug out drainage basins in open fields and laid down pumps and pipes, etc. The routine in Auschwitz was much the same as in Birkenau: torture, death, and beatings. It seemed a bit more straightforward here, more surgical, if you will. Previously, we slept two in a cot (a mat underlain by wood). Subsequently, it was a one person set–up. On that first night we ate and were ordered to go directly to our bunks. Barely a half hour later a yell rang out "Everyone up immediately and strip down". The commands came directly from the "house orderlies". We roused ourselves up and were chased and herded outside butt naked and ordered to run to the shower dorm to wash ourselves without washcloths, towels or soap. We took an ice–cold shower and were herded right back to the cold barracks. That routine was repeated five days in succession. Get naked, run to the shower, and run right back outside in the cold and snow to the barracks. This "stroll routine" was too much for many and some gave up; eventually more and more ended up as corpses laid out along the way. I got paired up with a partner, Yitschak Yonastovitch from Makow, and we were dispatched to dig pits. As we were working, the Uber–Kapo passed by (a husky German) and yelled at us to pick up the pace, and to emphasize the point he threw a rock at us. The rock hit me hard and dented my head. The blood poured out over my face but the frost caused it to freeze in place. The Unter–Kapo (a Czech) inspected the wound and said "there is nothing you can do." That evening I felt the pain worsen, and went down to the barracks floor, found a heated spot, and warmed up. A Polish fellow helped me cleanse the wound so that it would not become infected.

Shot…Shot

Some of the Jewish inmates tried to escape. They were caught and summarily shot dead. The next morning, as we were marched out to our work detail, we saw that their bodies were laid out at the camp gates and covered with scraps of paper and shredded book fragments to emphasize that they were shot and discarded. After that incident the Germans added a triangle beneath the tattooed numbers to isolate the "Jew". They also issued an order that we were not allowed to wear any cap or hat during cold and rainy weather (they took them away from us) and we were exposed to the elements hours at a time, bareheaded. It was especially trying during the freezing weather. Over time, inmates periodically tried to escape and the routine was to line up all camp inmates near the kitchen area where the captured escapees were rounded up; a public hanging followed. We watched the entire procedure. It was a public warning that whoever tried to escape would meet their fate either by a bullet or a public hanging.

[Page 268]

After a month or two in Auschwitz, I learned that the Makower Jews were routinely taken to Birkenau. I started to ask around if anyone had heard word of my older brother Yerachmiel.

While looking for him I ran into Yitzchak Philut. He was in very bad shape, barely breathing. I said to him "Yitzchak, hold on as long as you can, don't give in, maybe we will make it out of here." I managed to get him some bread and left him, knowing full well that a similar fate awaited me.

Subsequently I found out that Zaks, a 15 year old kid, was working in a masonry "school" (training shop). A few days later word got out that he was shot and killed. The reason: they found a cup of butter in his work bag.

I also came across Yakkov Shteinberg and Avraham Garfinkel. As I walked through the camp one evening, I saw that Garfinkel put out a call to assemble a Minyan for the Mincha–Mayriv daily prayer.

There were days when orders were issued prohibiting movement out of the camp. I used this opportunity to move around the compound in search of relatives and friends (from home). I got friendly with a fellow from Pruzhnitz. It turned out that he was well acquainted with my parents and worked in an SS facility sorting out their uniforms and outfits. When I told him who I was, we got closer and one day he invited me over to his area and gave me a quarter of a loaf of bread!

The Krupp Factory

I was assigned to do interior wiring and electrical work in the Krupp Factory. One day I got injured on the job and could not return to the job sites immediately. I took advantage of the lay–off to ask my cousin Moishe Bachrach, then at Birkenau camp, to come see me at my barracks if an opportunity arose.

[Page 269]

Several days later he came over to our kitchen to get food and supplies for a German officer stationed at Auschwitz. He brought me a pull–over and then told me that (cousin) Yossef Hendel and his family of 7 managed to jump off the train to Auschwitz and escaped to the town of Bendin[Bedzin]. They stayed there until Bendeen was evacuated and were then taken to Auschwitz.

My cousin told me that many of the Makower Jews ended up working in the ovens and crematortia complex. They told him that they collected the ashes and filled up urns, pots, and cups laying them out in pits beyond the perimeters of the crematoria.

For the longest time I heard nothing about my older brother Yerachmiel. Subsequently I learned that he was dispatched to the coal–fire furnaces at Buna where he was murdered. I also found out that all five of the Lichtenstein brothers were murdered in Birkenau.

On the Eve of Rebellion

As soon as my wounds healed I went back to my job at Krupp. There was clandestine talk about preparations for revolts at both Birkenau and Auschwitz. The timings and logistics were unclear. What was clear was that when the word came down we should be at the ready.

I had a friend from Lodz whose name was Mietek Halberstam. He called me over one day and said that since I was an electrician my job would be to get ahold of pliers and wire cutters, as necessary, to facilitate the operation. One morning shortly thereafter we heard powerful explosions in Birkenau. We did not know exactly what was going on and where the explosions were taking place. But something was happening. Suddenly, a wave of SS men broke into the plant. It seemed like there was one SS man for every inmate. They surrounded the factory (the factory had about 1400 workers). The SS ordered us to stay quiet and not to speak amongst themselves. I was outside at the time along with my German supervisor. Most did know the details of these explosions. Then Camp Commander Kaduk entered the factory and threatened that if we did not disclose the names of those who headed up the explosives operations in Birkenau, all 1400 workers would be dispatched to the ovens and crematoria. Naturally, we stayed silent.

[Page 270]

And even if we had known who the leaders and explosive suppliers were we would never have given them up (the SS remained convinced that the explosives were issued and delivered directly from the Krupp factory).

4 Young Women are Hanged

In our factory there was a Jewish Kapo by the name of Schultz who worked with us on the night shift. He gave up the names of the 4 young women who supplied the explosives. It turned out that each evening when the women left work for Birkenau barracks they got ahold of explosives material and brought them back to work they following morning. They supplied the explosives to the inmate leaders and revolt planners. The aforementioned 4 women were taken by the SS and hanged in front of everyone. We subsequently found out that the "brigade" (revolt leaders), consisted of crews working in the crematoria, and they had planned the entire operation. If memory serves me, this all happened in 1944. We eventually learned that the revolt was structured as follows: When the German Uber–Commander came to the Sonder–Commando and announced that there was an imminent transport (code for execution) they grabbed the Nazi murderer (the first one who got his hands on the German was Yaakov Skurnik) and they threw him in the oven directly, grabbing his revolver. They powered up the coal furnace and seized other weapons from the SS men. Absolute panic ensued. The other SS men in the area began to run away, not knowing where the billowing fire came from. Prison inmates had grabbed SS weapons and opened fire. Some of the Sonder–commando managed to escape. Eventually, however, all of the revolt participants were caught and shot to death.

The Red Army Closes In

It was in January, 1945 as the Red Army approached Auschwitz, that the evacuations began. The Germans moved us out towards the train station. They loaded us onto freight cars and we headed toward Mauthausen, Austria. I was among the last inmates in Auschwitz. We began to remove tripods and equipment from the plant but the Germans could not get mobilized and organized. They ended up leaving equipment, machinery and everything. As we abandoned the camp we heard the artillery barrages from the Soviet advance. It took us the entire night to walk the distance to the train station. Countless inmates collapsed and died on the way out; they were simply too depleted to drag their feet any further. Those who fell were shot in place by the SS men while those who could move on were loaded onto (the train) platforms. And that's how we made it to Mauthausen.

[Page 271]

We stayed there several days, crowded one atop the other in the camp barracks. We were naked, barefoot, and starving. We lay in the barracks for two days. Next, they dispatched us to Ebensee (Austria). They put us to work in a factory on a mountain–top but the echoes of the bombing were in earshot there as well. A few days later they transported us again, this time to the Gusen camp (Austria). They put me to work on an electrical detail at a Messerschmidt factory. An order was issued one evening that instructed us to appear at a location marked "Entry for all Jews". We immediately assumed that this was a liquidation order. Each of us grabbed a piece of bread on the way in, thinking "let us at least not perish because of starvation". The German "house–orderlies" then came in muttering "if only we were Jews".… Word got out that we were being turned over to the Red Cross. Each one of us was issued a ration of bread and a packet of butter and we marched on. We ended up back in Mauthausen, which had by then been occupied by Gypsy inmates. Once there we saw corpses littering the camp–grounds all the way to the base of the mountains. They led us to a barracks for the overnight. Once there we met up with newly arrived Jews from Hungary. They had just come in with a new transport and were still in possession of their belongings and food supplies that they had prepared for the trip in. I remember one inmate who approached an unsuspecting new arrival and robbed him of all his food. He pointed in the direction of Mietek Halberstam, my friend from Lodz. At that moment Camp Commandant Kudek entered the facility, took out his revolver and shot him on the spot. The incident occurred three weeks before the liberation.

We were next taken from Mauthausen and ended up in the camp at Gunskirchen (Austria). As we proceeded to march in the pouring rain we took notice of the approaching vehicle of the Red Cross. The team in the vehicle began to observe us carefully. However, they took off in the opposite direction just as quickly and we were left and taken to the barracks in Gunskirchen, where we remained until liberation.

Several days later I was in the barracks and suddenly I received a package with food and supplies. It was to be rationed 1 packet for every 20 people. That rationing was clearly insufficient for a camp population that was slowly dying of starvation, which we were. And yet we began to feel that somehow, in this final hour, someone would come for us and our fortunes might turn. It was certainly high time for that.

The SS Runs Off–Liberation!

On a bright Shabbos day we were issued rations. All the while there was heavy fire in the background. We received word that we were free. There were no Germans around anywhere. The SS took off like mice. Even the sadistic murderer Kaduk was nowhere to be seen.

[Page 272]

But we were so beaten down, decimated, and downtrodden that our responses to the wonderful news of our liberation were muted. No strength to move or act. Our memories of a warm home, a clean bed, a tasty meal, and even civil human interactions….these were long gone. We just wanted to hang on to life a bit longer and to take revenge on our oppressors. I, along with Hersh Leib Kurnik from Makow and Fishel Yatzentovski from Pultusk, decided to go to the SS barracks and to spend the night there. Once there we slipped into the clean sheets and warm covers and slept like babies. The next morning I turned to them and said "light up the fire, I'm off to get water, sugar, and we'll make a nice hot glass of tea." On my way back with the water I ran into an American soldier. He turned to me in Yiddish and asked "Who are you?" I told him who I was and where I was from and it turned out that he was a cousin of Dr. Soloveichik from Warsaw. He took out a bag of biscuits, sugar, and sweets and gave it to me. I became ecstatic in the barracks, after all the dark years of suffering this was the first time I could freely enjoy a hot glass of tea and biscuits….Later we received rations of canned meats. I warned my buddies that we needed to be careful and not eat the meats since our stomachs had adapted to such extreme hunger over the years. My words were not taken seriously, however, and we cooked up a mid–day meal. Before long the three of us got sick. The two responded very badly and my reaction was somewhat less severe. I took them to the hospital. After that I never saw them again. I was informed that both of them had passed. Along with other camp inmates we were moved to Linz, Austria. I spent two weeks in the hospital there. After recovering somewhat I made my way to Bindermichl D.P. camp and I stayed there until 1947. And then during the "Brichah" [illegal immigration of Holocaust survivors to Palestine] I got on the ship "Hatikvah" to Genoa. However, the British captured the ship and diverted it to Cyprus. I found myself in yet another camp where I remained until 1949, and that same year I finally arrived in Israel. I was married in 1950 in Ramat–Gan. I currently have a wife and two children and am settled in Herzliyah.

I remain the sole survivor of my entire extended family.

[Page 273]

From Death and Destruction

by Moshe Aba Kamen, New York

Translated by Naomi Gal

On Friday night the Polish radio announced that the war had begun. Since this news, we Maków citizens, were frighten and terrorized. And then airplanes showed up and passed over our heads, we were scared that in a moment bombs would be dropped on us. The alarm sounded every fifteen minutes – and so it went on all day long. The streets emptied; everybody searched for a hiding place close by as soon as the alarm was heard. Then the radio announced the bombing of Częstochowa, Lodz, Warsaw. But the speaker soon assuaged the listeners saying that the cities were not ruined and that Polish airplanes chased the enemy away. And so, he went on relating the Germans' advances and then broadcasting news about successful counter-attacks. Among other information he said that thousands of Polish, British and French airplanes raided Berlin and almost destroyed her. And although they declared loudly on the radio that justice will eventually win, the doubts filled the heart and instilled fear that the Germans might win…

* * *

After Kabbalat Shabbat came the rumor that the community of Przasnysz headed by their rabbi were approaching Maków – fleeing the enemy that was getting closer to their city. In the morning the town was filled with refugees, men, women and children, some naked and barefoot. They ran away from Mlawa, Chorzele, Przasnysz, Mishnitz and Krasnosielc. They all passed through Maków, wanting to continue to Warsaw. People sitting on top of cars, willing to desecrate the Shabbat in order to survive – but staying in Maków with no other choice. Each one eyeing with envy a friend who managed to escape. The buses were close to toppling with so many passengers, but whoever managed to squeeze in was considered lucky.

When evening came, villagers arrived. They too were escaping barefoot, their clothes torn and in tatters, amid them old people and babies, all crying bitterly. One came riding a horse, another one driving a cow and a third one dragging a reluctant pig.

* * *

On Saturday evening Przasnysz was engulfed in flames. Maków's police and the municipality personnel left the city. Great panic reigned and no one knew what to do. When darkness descended, thousands of people began to flee the city. I thought that there was no need to leave the city yet. But when morning came a regiment of the Polish cavalry arrived and they told us that the enemy was approaching. The officers issued an order that every man between the age of 18 to sixty who knew how to hold a gun needed to leave the city and get to Pultusk. We left together, my father and I, uncles and cousins trying not to separate from each other. The only people remaining in the city were elderly, women and children. "What would become of them when the Germans enter the city?" we all asked ourselves. "Would they spare them? Would they stand any chance of not being killed, burned?" These thoughts tortured us to death.

[Page 274]

When we arrived at Pultusk on Sunday at one o'clock in the afternoon, we went to the offices of PKW - the enlisting offices - to enlist to the army. But they responded that one cannot fight with sticks and we had no guns. "Go back to where you came from," they said.

In Pultusk they took all the men to dig fortifications. They declared that this is going to be the battlefield. From there the Poles will push the enemy away.

At the house of our relatives in Pultusk everything was packed, ready to leave. While we were talking the enemy airplanes begun turning up in the sky above the village and when night came, full blackout was imposed. The day after, we began our escape from Pultusk. My father and I tried in vain to get a carriage so that we could go back to Maków. The road leading there was declared an "army only" road. We were looking for vehicle to get to Warsaw, in vain. We had no choice but to walk…

* * *

We were getting close to Serock. A few kilometers before the town I decided that it was not worth continuing to Warsaw, which would be probably bombed more than any other place and we would not be able to find food there. I convinced my father. We left the road to Warsaw, heading in the direction to Wyszków. We had to cross a bridge on the Bug River, we hardly had time to cross it when airplanes arrived and blew it up.

We spent the night at a Polish farmer's hut in one of the villages and in the early morning we continued on our way to Wyszków. Near the town we were again surprised by German airplanes. They passed right over our heads. The bombs were dropped so frequently that the earth under our feet trembled. We hid under the trees until the bombing stopped. We then met people who were running away from Wyszków. They told us that there were many dead in the city as a result of the bombing.

We entered Wyszków. The streets were empty. Broken electricity and telephone poles filled the streets that were sown with broken glass from shattered windows and everywhere – dead bodies in pools of blood.

"Get into the houses" – a stranger was pulling my sleeve. "They are coming back. Can't you hear the airplanes? Get in quickly."
We entered a Jewish home. I stood and prayed. But the airplanes interrupted my prayer. Shots were heard and bombs were falling. We decided to run away from the city.

[Page 275]

When we left Wyszków and arrived at the edge of the bridge the sky darkened, all of a sudden, filled with airplanes. We prayed that we would be able to safely cross the bridge. And indeed, as soon as we crossed it, we heard terrible explosions in the city, that was now covered in dense smoke. Dozens and hundreds of airplanes were now circling above the smoke and our heads.

Tik-Tik-Tik – all of a sudden machine guns begun firing from the airplanes aiming at multitudes of people – thousands and tens of thousands – the citizens of the many villages who were escaping their homes. Men, women and children fell dead and wounded in front of our eyes, and there was no one to dress their wounds, to give them some water. Screams were heard from all sides: "hide in the forest".

We entered the forest. But the destroyers found us there too and started to sow death among us. They dropped bombs. They set the forest on fire with firebombs. Where could we escape? We fell flat on the side of the road, on the other side of the forest, under the trees and we prayed for our lives. And all around us blood and fury.

Suddenly a falling bomb was heard. Earth was thrown on my face. The bomb did not detonate. We were saved by a miracle.

* * *

We encountered this kind of danger time and again on our way. We often saw death up close. When the airplanes left, we found a wagon. As soon as we climbed on top of the wagon the death angels were again above our heads dropping bombs and showering machinegun fire. We descended quickly from the wagon and found shelter, as much as we could.

When dark came, we continued on a road filled with fleeing people. We were afraid to open our mouths. We looked with terror at the stars shining in the sky. Finally, we arrived in good time - after midnight – to Węgrów.

The village people welcomed us graciously. They fed us and gave us water, but they were worried: who knows what tomorrow will bring. Day after day the airplanes arrived, dropped a few bombs, in Węgrów too, people were killed. Yet it did not suffer like other villages where the death angels poured all their wrath.

In the week before Rosh Hashana, on a Monday, at nine o'clock in the morning, Węgrów fell into the German's hands. A woman and a girl who took a peek through the cracks of the door paid for their curiosity with their lives.

After spending the days of Rosh Hashana in Wegrow we took the risk and went back home by foot and we arrived safely at our destination.

* * *

The fate of the villages in our district was bitter: Wyszków was completely burned. Not one house remained standing, the same was in Różan. All Jews were evicted from Pultusk. They were ordered to leave the village in ten minutes. Immediately afterwards the German begun showering fire into the windows and in the streets. Hundreds of people perished that day. Those who were able to reach the bridge were thrown into the river. The shooting went on and on. The villagers were ordered not to give the Jews shelter nor food – to let them die of hunger and cold. Five hundred Jews who were expelled from Pultusk were murdered cruelly, probably in Ostrów-Mazowiecka. Before the Germans moved on to an area ruled by the Russians, they [the Germans] put the Jews alive into the graves that they had dug for themselves and they [the Germans] shot them.

[Page 276]

In Goworowo they pushed all the Jews into the synagogue and set it on fire. They also burned all the houses in the city and shot the citizens who were expelled from their houses. Many fell [dead] on their doorsteps.

Some who were locked in the synagogue were lucky: a German general was passing through the city and when he heard their cries, he felt pity and ordered the synagogue be opened and released those who were locked inside. "Do not burn so many people at once and in one place" he said. But their fate after their release was bitter as well. They were expelled from the city naked and barefoot. For three days and nights they wandered the fields eating only uncooked turnips.

In Przasnysz they put the Jews on buses and made them cross the River Narew, which is in Różan. They let them out in the fields across the river. When they crossed Maków on their way, the men, women and children on the buses were begging for a piece of bread…

Murders and sufferings were the fate of Jews in many other places.

* * *

The rabbi of Goworowo, who is now in Vilna, describes the slaughter in his city. In a letter to a relative in Tel Aviv he writes:

"…the Germans slaughtered 72 people in front of me, the most prominent of my landlords. Like sheep to slaughter. Women and children were burned alive. The rest of the village Jews, about two thousand people, were pushed into the synagogue which they burned. Everybody would have burned but for a miracle. A German officer passed by and when he heard the screaming coming from the synagogue, he ordered to release the people from the burning house. The survivors crossed the river to the fields where they remained without food for three days. I was hiding at the cemetery but the Germans found me and begun to torture me, I was able to escape and go to Russia…"

hat was the beginning of the destruction of Am Israel in Poland by the Germans, may their names be forever erased.

[Page 277 - Yiddish] [Page 305 - Hebrew]

Red Flowers

by Yehezkiel Itskowicz

Translated by Anita Frishman Gabbay

Red flowers…when I see you, I break out into a sweat remembering those horrible days.

Red flowers…I don't want to see you again, but you follow me step by step with your red, bleeding appearance. I can't turn my gaze away from you, the bloody sword still hovers over you, that killed the blameless child, in one blow. Young, pure blood poured into you…and your whiteness was transformed into a purple– red dye. Who can reveal so much, like you, red flowers…

This happened in the autumn of 1939, when the murderous Gestapo men took control of the towns and villages of Poland. At the time, I, together with hundreds of Jews from Maków, left my home in the direction of the Russian border– to save our lives. The highways and roads, that led us "*to the other side*" were flooded with Jews–refugees: with wagons and packs, or by foot without baggage, young and older mothers holding frightened children at their bosoms; everyone's eyes emitting fear and confusion. Everyone escaping from the murderous sword.

The sky began to fill with dark clouds. A hailstorm was brewing.

[Page 278]

First events. How they encircled us and when the shooting stopped, wild, bewildered faces laughed:

— Raus"[out] to the road

— "Raus"[out] you accursed Jews!

We went out to the highway, and assembled in rows.

A small group of us remained. Hundreds of people disappeared.

A larger part–shot. And the remainder–ran away into the forest.

The murderers patrolled us from all sides. Some of them went into the forest and resumed the shooting: they returned and then led us further.

Depressed from this great misfortune, we dragged our feet with our last strength. A woman next to me had a child in her arms. She whispered quietly: Dovid, where is my Dovid?…

After a march, which lasted at least an hour, they led us into a fenced yard, in which they were several large beautiful houses. The area along the way was covered with green grass and white flowers.

As I later discovered, this area, in peace–time, was a sanatorium, near the town of Ostrolenka.

The Murderers are Coming

Several S.S. officers appeared and with loud voices called out, everyone needs to give up their gold, dollars and other valuables which we are confiscating. Whoever hides it and he who is later found with these valuables, he, together with nine other men, will be shot–as punishment. If we freely give up our valuables, they will bring us to the Russian border.

Everyone of us gave up their life's savings in order to buy their freedom: watches, rings, earrings, golden coins, dollars :we were stripped of our material goods, except for our spiritual being.

After they accumulated their spoils of war, they brought us to a wet cellar, which smelled of rotten potatoes and we were locked in for the night.

In the cellar the whining and silent crying resumed.

One person asks: "where is my father?": where did my sick mother die?"

[Page 279]

Names of men, children and wives were called out who got lost in the forest. An older Jew with a black– grey beard shook himself like it was "Yom Kippur at the synagogue" and cried laments to the Almighty: "*God–enu*, why did you rain upon us your anger?" the wife, next to me, still held onto her child in her arms. The small girl was still sucking on her mother's breast, holding the mothers dress with her small hands. No fear, so her Mommy should not lose her. She fell asleep from tiredness. Her cheeks were red. The mother deliberates with heartache her unfortunate child, hot tears falling from her eyes.

We spent the entire night in the cellar. Between *fear and hope*, between *wake and dream*, in the early morning a soldier opened the door and ordered us to go out into the yard and to sit in rows, to remain silent and await new orders.

"Where is My Dear Father? [My Daddy]"

Feebleness and fatigue cloaked our entire body. The daughter sat next to her mother and trembled from the cold. Fear and loss mirrored in her cherry–like eyes–she remained silent and threw glances at the strangers and couldn't understand what was happening here…she quietly asked her mother" "where is daddy?"…when is he coming?…"and when her mother, quietly, answered her, "tomorrow" and asked her to remain silent as Germans are coming, she could unfortunately understand this, she understood and promised herself with all her strength not to cry. She trembled like a small fish…

Soon the murderers showed up again and reported to us, they were leading us to a place, nearby, where there were potatoes. There we needed to gather and place them in sacks and bring them to the cellar, where we spent the night. The quicker we carry out this work, the quicker we will be set free.

Finding ourselves in the open, we considered our work a miracle. We worked with all our strength, to end our work as soon as possible and leave this bloody hell. Together with us, the small girl was also busy at work: for one she held the sack and for another–helped gather the potatoes, until her mother asked her to finish and sit to rest. She listened, sat down, watched how the birds were chasing one another. Her lips opened in a child–like manner as the birds were fluttering over her head with their spread–out wings, swishing and sitting on a branch covered in white flowers, and cheerfully rocking herself. Seeing the beautiful flowers with the green leaves, the little girl sprang up smiling like a reborn child. She caressed and smothered the little flowers and pressed her nose against them, smelling them, her eyes lit up.

[Page 280]

A Shot from the Window

Suddenly there was a pop from a window opposite us. Everyone's eyes flushed with a shiver and we saw how the child fell among the flowers. We ran towards her, but several shots flew through the air. We were warned not to approach the child. We looked from a distance, how the little girl convulsed, curled up in anguish. At the same time, she was clinging to the branch, as if seeking salvation. Among the white flowers we noticed red spots…

The birds returned and began again to fly over the child, this time not in a friendly manner. Suddenly they flew away into the sky. Perhaps they sent a message to the Almighty as a protest against these murderers on behalf of a blameless child.

The unfortunate mother fainted. We tried to revive her, poured water on her, but couldn't revive her. She stared at us with glazed eyes. We thought: she is dead.

"Work and stay quiet!"–an other order came. With frail emotions we completed our work.

It was now night. The gloomy sky fore warned, it is going to be dark. The murderers tell us again to line up in rows. Another person and I were given the task to remove the dead child and clean the spots off the white flowers…

We go to retrieve the body and a horrible picture unfolds, which I will never in my life forget: immersed in the bloody flowers lay the child with a worried face, her teeth fractured, with half open eyes, from which emanated abyssal shock.

[Page 281]

Taking the Victim

We gathered the child, together with the flower she held in her closed hand, wrapped her in a coat and returned to our row. The mother was still unconscious. We held her under her arms, muttering and spraying her with water.

"Forward!" – an order was issued.

We went forward with the little strength left in our bodies. The dead body we carried in our hands. We were wet from our own sweat. It seemed to us as we are going to our own funeral.

–stay still–we are commanded. We are told to continue with the same road without anything? F Another few hundred meters, we soon enter a town. The murderers remained behind us with their guns aiming to fire, warning us. They waited several minutes and then disappeared.

The last of the hundred people passed this moment literally with their last breath. The accumulated pain was like lava erupted and pored over us.

With heartache we came across the first Jew who we met in this town, as if we arrived to our *savior*. We told him, in short, about the events that we survived. He immediately took us into his home and gave us tea and bread. The unknown Jew with his family showed us deep compassion, in particular to the young, dear *sacrifice*. They prepared our sleeping arrangements, and their two young daughters took care of the unfortunate mother.

A conference of the remnants of the Maków survivors in Germany, 1946

[Page 282]

Tired and broken–hearted, we dropped down on our bedding and fell asleep.

Early the next morning, when we entered the room, where the unlucky mother slept, we saw a doctor sitting next to her, helping her with various injections. He forbade us to enter the room and let her rest.

Coming to the Burial of the Small Flower…

At the Jewish cemetery of Ostrolenka, we dug a small pit and buried the small child– the small flower in her hand that she held so tightly, she didn't want to part with it, even after death. We buried both our little flowers….

The elderly Jew with the black–grey beard said the Kaddish [prayer for the dead]. We all cried.

When we returned from the burial, we didn't find the mother. In the meanwhile, she was sent to the hospital, where she hovered between life and death.

The doctors and nurses did their best to save her, unfortunately–without avail.

Flowers…red flowers…she clung to until the last moment. And with these words on her lips she quietly passed away.

[Page 283]

A Bundle of Sad Memories

Told by Shmuel Taub (Haifa): Written by Itche Shlomovitch

Translated by Janie Respitz

A few days after the war began the Germans marched into Maków. Immediately after they began to persecute the Jews, robbing Jewish businesses, grabbing people for various types of work as well as cutting off beards. All Jewish businesses were robbed and then finally closed. There were line ups for bread but Jews were thrown out of line. Already in these early days of German rule Jews suffered from lack of bread. A few Maków Jews managed to escape to regions captured by Russia. These were rarely entire families. They were mostly men whose wives and children remained in Maków. A large portion of these men returned when they fell into the hands of the Germans when they captured parts of Russia.

The persecutions in Maków increased and the situation worsened. One of the first mass murders the Germans carried out in our city was of cripples, crazy people and others they captured. They took these people somewhere and killed them. Until today, we do not know where.

In those days, the Germans would grab men and women and send them to work, mostly to the surrounding villages. This work was never payed. This continued until January 1940. After that Jews had to wear yellow patches. This way the Germans and their Polish collaborators could easily identify them. I would like to state that the majority of the Polish population gladly helped the Germans carry out the persecutions against the Jewish population.

In those days, Jews who lived in the gentile quarter where moved to Jewish living quarters. A crowded Jewish neighbourhood was created. At the same time they worked to enclose the ghetto. All the fences that were within the Jewish area were taken and used to enclose the ghetto. All the windows and doors that looked out of the ghetto were boarded up.

[Page 284]

It was strictly guarded and no cracks remained through which one could look out. The streets were enclosed. The ghetto was connected to the outside world with three gates: one gate was near Piasetsky the blacksmith led to the cemetery. The second gate led to the Ozhitz River.

Certificate given by the U.S military to former inmates at Dachau

There were three wells in the ghetto and a great shortage of water. Once a day, for one hour, the gate which led to the river was opened in order to get water. This one hour was strictly observed resulting in long lines and unjustified suffering. The third gate was at the exit of the marketplace between Payshe Lipovitch and Shmuel Yosef Ezrilbitz. This was the main gate which was guarded by the Jewish police. Life in the ghetto was run from this gate. Twice a week on market days (Tuesdays and Fridays) the people were permitted to go to the market for one hour. However this was extremely dangerous because the Gestapo and their Polish collaborators would beat up Jews. However, hunger forced Jews to risk their lives in order to buy or trade for food.

[Page 285]

The Germans forced the Jews to do hard labour which included: highways, cutting stones, digging peat among other things. There was no salary. Very often people would return from work dejected and bloodied. There were some stores in the ghetto that only Jews were permitted to buy from. At first there was one bakery (Lumanietz). The bread baked in that bakery was by far not enough for the population. So they opened a second bakery in the new House of Study at the spot where the Holy Ark once stood with a fenced in oven. When the Germans entered Maków they ripped up the floors of the synagogue and turned it into a riding school. On the spot where the holy words were inscribed: "this is the gate to God, all the righteous will arrive through it", they hung a large sign, in red, with a Swastika and the following inscription: "Everything for Germany". The Maków painter "Leybl Kider" was forced to paint that sign. By the end of 1940 the synagogue was torn down and the stones taken away. The lecterns, benches and everything else were stolen by the Poles for heating. The place where the magnificent Maków synagogue once stood remained empty, levelled, vacant.

The living conditions in the ghetto were very difficult. People lived in horrible crowdedness. The situation worsened day by day. The Germans continued to bring more Jews from the region into the Maków ghetto. People were placed in warehouses, stalls and attics. There was nothing to heat with. People suffered from the cold. Garbage was not removed from the ghetto but thrown into dug out pits. The bad living conditions, cold, hunger, terrible sanitary conditions led to epidemics, first and foremost, typhus. Practically no one was spared. Tens of people died. They created a hospital, but due to lack of space a patient could only remain 2–3 days.

At that time there was no doctor in Maków. The only medical help was provided by the medic Brodavsky. There was also a huge shortage of medication. With the permission from the Germans, a doctor was brought from Warsaw. He was a religious Jew and a devoted person.

[Page 286]

<u>Bescheinigung.</u>

Es wird hiermit bescheinigt, dass in der Stadt M a k o w eine jüdi-

sche Bevölkerung von zur Zeit 3527 Köpfen wohnhaft ist und dass sich

unter diesen 517 Flüchtlinge befinden. Die Anzahl der als hilfsbedürf-

tig anzusprechenden Juden beträgt 1950.

Makow, den 22. April 1940.

Der Bürgemeister.

/podpis nieczyt./

Okrągła pieczątka
ze znakiem hitlerowskim

w obwodzie: Der Bürgemeister der Stadt

Makow /Südostpr./.

[Page 287]

He worked day and night to ease the lives of the population.

The ghetto commissar ordered an empty lot in the ghetto to be plowed. This sowing of the area helped ease the lives of the Jews in the ghetto since it provided a bit of green space. I was chosen as the ghetto gardener. I had to wear a white band with the words: "Ghetto Gardener". This provided me the opportunity to move freely, often outside the ghetto when I was sent to work in the gardens of the Gestapo. This also gave me the privilege not to be sent to do other forms of forced labour. On the lot where the synagogue once stood I was ordered to plant tobacco. I would like to mention that all the commands from the Germans and the Judenrat were brought to the people by a drummer. The ghetto drummer was Rafael Rozenberg, the writer's son.

I remember one day, very early, the ghetto drummer came to me with an order to remove the tobacco from the synagogue lot because they were going erect gallows for 20 Jews. I immediately carried out the command. They actually built the gallows on that spot and hanged Jews. This act was carried out by the ghetto commissar Shteinmetz.

After the Germans murdered the only Jewish doctor in the ghetto they brought an older doctor from Germany. However, on the day we learned the Germans were going to liquidate the ghetto, the doctor and his wife committed suicide.

In November, they gathered all the Jews working in the region and brought them to the ghetto. The ghetto, which until then was guarded by Jewish police, was now surrounded by S.S. men. Leaving the ghetto was now impossible. In the middle of November the assistant rabbi (Langfus) gave a speech through the window of the rabbi's former house, and shared with the population the news that the ghetto was to be liquidated and we will be sent to work. We were advised that we had to gather very early at the gate which leads to the cemetery. Each person can take one bundle, their house must be swept, the beds made and the doors were to be left unlocked.

Tens of horses and wagons awaited the people. S.S. men stood on the outside of the ghetto gate beating and hastening the Jews.

[Page 288]

People began to run. Families got lost because everyone, wanting to avoid beatings, ran quickly to the wagons.

We rode all day and at night we arrived at Mlave. Maków was now cleansed of Jews. A Jewish community which had existed for hundreds of years was eradicated.

In Mlave we found a few hundred more Jews. Most of the houses were empty and they placed us there.

A few days later they gathered all the women who had lost their husbands in previous operations and took them away with their children. Not one person from that transport survived.

On the 6th of December, half of the Jews were transported to Auschwitz and the following day, the second half. The departure looked like this: from Mlave to the train, a distance of 2 kilometres, we were led by foot. From there, threatened by frightening beatings we were packed into cattle cars. It was so crowded, people were lying on top of one another. There was no air to breathe. When we arrived at Auschwitz on the 10th of December, many in the train cars were dead.

We arrived at Auschwitz at night. They lined us up and took us for selection. From the thousands in this transport, 525 men were sent to Birkenau, accompanied by S.S men who beat up the unfortunate. The rest of the Jews who arrived in that same transport were immediately burned in the "ovens", there were as yet, no crematoria. Not one Jewish woman from Maków who was brought in the above mentioned transports survived. The two Maków women that did survive Auschwitz arrived there from Warsaw and Lodz, not Maków.

When we arrived in Birkenau we were stripped naked and everything was taken from us. Then they shaved our heads, sent us to bathe, tattooed numbers on our arms and gave us camp clothes. Many Jews from Maków fell victim that same day. Dead bodies lay on the roads. At that time, we were, from both transports, more than 1000 men, the strongest, including 70 from Maków, were chosen by the Germans for the "Sonderkomando", work units. Many of us were sent to Buna, a camp 7 kilometres from Birkenau. We were there for two weeks. Due to epidemics almost all of us were sent back to Birkenau.

[Page 289]

The amount of people from Maków was decreasing. There were new victims falling every day. Some committed suicide by jumping on the electrical wires (including my brother Yekhiel). Many were killed by gunshots and beatings. Some froze to death and others died of hunger. In the two winter months, December 1942 and January 1943 90% of the Jews from Maków died. I was sent with a group of others from Maków to Auschwitz to the so called "Bricklayer's School". Four months later I was sent back to Birkenau where only a few Maków Jews remained. Some Maków Jews were still in the "Sonderkomando". We were forbidden to go near them but they bribed the KAPO and thanks to that, from time to time we were able to go them. They helped us with food and to get better work assignments. And more: during a selection we would hide among them. I remember the Maków Jews who were in the "Sonderkomando": the assistant rabbi Langfus, Berko and Yidl Tofer, Meir Piekartchik, and Vevl Fuks.

On a summer day I received the news that 4 Jews tried to escape Birkenau and were caught. Among these four were Henekh and Shloime Gromb. From this experience I learned this was punishable with immediate death. At the investigation Henekh Gromb took the full blame upon himself. The others were sent to the S.K punishment commando. A few days later he was hanged. He gave his life to save the lives of the three others. I know that two of them are alive (Shloime Gromb in Australia).

At that time my job was to clean the sewers. This allowed me to go to all the places like: the crematoria and the women's camp. I saw with my own eyes the devilish murder of Jews and other nationalities as well. I saw gas chambers with the opening for gas, the iron wagons they used to bring the people to the ovens as well as the iron sieves to sift the bones. One day I came to the gate of the "Sonderkomando" with my sewer cleaning wagon. Langfus, the assistant rabbi from Maków came running toward me and shouted: "Litman's son, God sent you". Then he continued: "You cannot enter the area of the crematoria, we're blowing it up".

[Page 290]

He continued: "We received news that some of us have to be killed. We decided this time to resist the German murderers and blow up the crematoria. We really have nothing to lose".

He also told me he wrote down all the transports, where they came from, how many people were in them and buried these lists in tin boxes. Until today I don't know if these lists were ever found.

I said goodbye to the assistant rabbi. On my way back to the camp from the crematoria I heard an explosion followed by shooting. People started to run (in the camp there were four crematoria, one was blown up). Dozens of S.S. men surrounded us and pushed us into the camp. All those that were found in the crematorium were shot. As far as I know, the heroes who destroyed the crematorium succeeded before the explosion to throw the German KAPO, alive, into the oven.

The resisters eased up life in the camp with their heroic act. The selections were stopped. They stopped sending the new arrivals straight to be burned. You could now see middle aged people in the camp. Children's blocks were created (before this there were no children in the camp as they were taken straight from the transport to their death).

I remained in Birkenau until January 18th 1945. I saw how the Germans wanted to wipe away all vestiges of their murders by destroying the crematoria. We were then sent by the Germans on a march to Glayvitz. I was liberated by the Americans in May 1945 in Dachau.

[Page 291]

The Makówer Youth in Auschwitz

by Ida Kac-Beer-Garfinkle, Bnei-Brak-New York

Translated by Anita Frishman Gabbay

1944. The war in Poland is still raging. The cruel beasts, the Germans, their name should be erased forever, were mobilized on all fronts-in the east and in the west. The Russians are at the gates of Warsaw. This we learn from our secret sources who enter the ghetto and by various other means.

I was still in the Lodz Ghetto-Litzmannstadt- as the German occupiers called it.

Suddenly rumors spread that the Lodz Ghetto is going to be liquidated-we will be evacuated to work camps. From these rumors, reality soon set in. All the workshops were closed, machinery, working tools, tables, benches were taken away. These were prepared for transport, where to, no one knew. This was to masquerade their true intentions. There was great confusion in the ghetto.

The leader of the Lodz Ghetto at that time, (Hans) Biebow, his name should be blotted out forever, arranged mass rallies in several sections of the Jewish neighbourhood to appease the population, saying-we are being transported to other work camps and nothing bad will happen to us. Actually, he is doing us a *favor*. The murderer emphasises: "the Russians are nearby and are attacking Warsaw. In a short while they will advance to Lodz. They will murder you all-the entire Jewish population. You obviously had good jobs here and were productive for the German Army [war effort]."

With this speech he motivated the evacuees to depart quietly, to go like sheep, wherever they lead us.

Without sarcasm about our fate: first, we were the "dirty, lice-infested Jews, swine, dogs". Now these people spoke to us politely, as if we are *normal* people. At the last minute the murderers didn't want to arouse a panic, fearing the population would seek reprisal.

Nevertheless, people sensed something was wrong. If one could, they hid themselves, not going of their own free will.

I, together with my husband, Yechiel Beer, of blessed memory, hid. We couldn't hide for a long time because our food supply was limited, barely for a few days- barely enough to sustain the soul.

[Page 292]

In Closed Horse-Wagons

One time, at night (we were afraid to go out in the daytime), in complete deprivation, we left our hiding place to find something to eat nearby, in the already abandoned Jewish houses. We were successful in hiding for some time, but in the end the Germans found us and dragged us out of our hideouts. They transported us to the train station "Morishin" where we met thousands of Jews. They shoved us into closed horse-wagons, about 120 Jews to a wagon, without windows. There was no air to breathe. All our bodily functions had to be relieved in the wagon. The stench was unbearable. This is how we rode for 2 days. We went frontwards and backwards, and when the train stopped, we had several dead among us in the wagon.

My husband, Yechiel managed to peek through a crack and recognized the area we were passing through, Upper Silesia, the region of Katowice.

Hearing this, I remembered the postcard I saved in the Lodz ghetto, [received from my never forgotten parents, Rochel and Pinchas Kac, of blessed memory], was still with me. It was a farewell letter written in Mlawa, dated November 1942.

In this postcard, my mother wrote "thank God, we are able to work, even the children (their grandchildren) and now the Germans are sending us to a work camp in Upper Silesia". I held the card tightly, like a Holy souvenir from my parents. At this moment, I couldn't imagine the cruel acts the Germans, the Nazi murderers, carried out against my parents and children in those horrific gas-chambers (crematoriums).

After a 2 day journey from hell, the train stopped at a station, this was Birkenau-Auschwitz, in Upper Silesia.

In Birkenau-Auschwitz

With great feelings of despair the doors were finally opened. The S.S. men were screaming with angry voices: "Fast, *heraus, get out you swine-animals, leave everything behind*".

Trembling with fear we jumped from the wagon, leaving everything behind, even our last piece of bread.

[Page 293]

The selection started on the platform. Young inmates dressed in striped clothing, like prisoners, their faces and their eyes were filled with both compassion and fear. I recognized them as being Jews. I remember the postcard from my parents of 1942. Of the first inmate in front of me, a young fellow, I asked him about the fate of the Jews of Maków Mazowiecki, my parents and my family- I say, "they must be here".

He turns his head away, not looking at me, as not to draw the attention of the S.S. men (he wasn't allowed to speak to the newly arrived prisoners), and asks me who I was?

Simultaneously, he asks me: "do I have bread?". I answer "no". He enters a wagon, brings 2 pieces of bread for my husband and myself, and says to us: "eat this bread before you reach the place where the Germans are standing, pinch your cheeks, bite your lips so they appear red and when then ask your age, say in your 20s". It is redundant to mention those people who were brought from the Lodz Ghetto looked like skeletons. The fellow [the one I questioned] was one of "ours" from Maków, who had been in Auschwitz-Birkenau since 1942.

His name was Leibel Fuks, son of Velvel (the butcher). His mother's name I can't remember. Leibel looked after my husband and I, until we arrived at the selection where the S.S. men sent us to the "Right". "Left" meant straight to the crematoria. When we went to the right, we were sent for "delousing", then to the "bathhouse", where the women were separated from the men.

There, in the bathhouse, we were told to undress (totally naked) in front of strange men. They didn't spare us any humiliation, they studied our bodies looking for lice, shaved our heads, took away our clothes (undergarments, clothes and shoes)-those things which were among our last possessions.

One Dress-No Wardrobe

After bathing, they threw one dress at us, which was to serve as undergarment and overgarment-and a pair of "Holland clogs" (wooden shoes).

After this, they placed us in rows of 5 and led us to the *lager* [camp], this was the famous "*Lager C*" in Birkenau-Auschwitz.

[Page 294]

Here we met thousands of women who had arrived on earlier transports from all over Europe. At this camp no one was sent to work, also no one was tattooed. Our camp had to present itself several times a day (roll call) for selections. This was directed by Dr. Mengele, his name shall be erased forever, with his helpers. This camp was overflowing, so each day a selection took place with new victims, in order to make room for future transports. Part of us were sent to the various camps, the others, the largest part, were sent to the gas chambers.

They sectioned us into blocks. I had the good fortune to be placed in a block which had 2-story wooden bunks. On each one, 8 women slept, 4 at the head, 4 at the foot. In other blocks, there were no bunks and the women slept on the lime floor.

As we realized later on, Leibel Fuks, when he came back from his work told-on the same evening-the young people from Maków (who were also in this camp) that I, Ida Kac-Beer, from Maków, had just arrived in a transport from Lodz to Birkenau and I am now in "Lager C".

The word spread among the Makówers. Each and every one of them looked in on me. They all knew when the children from the Maków transports arrived and were sent straight to the gas-chambers. They took it upon themselves- the task to save the Makówer women who arrived from other ghettos. This was their main objective, to help. It wasn't an easy thing to do.

Actually, the next morning after my arrival at Birkenau, in Lager "C", the first one to look for me was Yitzhak Granievitch, the son of Shlomo and Etel, may their memory be blessed. He was able to come into the Womens' Camp because he worked as an electrician. We didn't recognize one another. He, my former student, dressed in grey-blue overalls, like a prisoner, I, skin and bones like a skeleton with a shaved head. I was embarrassed to leave my barrack, because my dress, which was also my night-clothing, tore while I was lying on the hard bed.

The Makówers are Coming to Look for Me

Holding my torn dress at the back, in order not to expose my naked body, I left my bed. First I asked about my family.

[Page 295]

But again no answer. He begged me, with tears in his eyes, however difficult the road ahead will be, to keep myself strong-physically and mentally. I had already prepared myself for the worst, I was now indifferent to all things to come-my husband, my children, my family were gone. He himself, the Maków er, will do everything in his power to help me stay alive.

Most important, he spoke to the block leader (I noticed he gave her something) to pay extra attention to me, to let me disappear during a selection and give me more to "eat". The whole daily meal consisted of: the morning meal -some black water they called "Kave", for lunch-soup with some pieces of potatoes swimming in the so-called soup, sometimes some cabbage or beets and when we received a bread-soup, it was a "celebration", at night, a portion of bread, hard like clay.

After Yitzhak Granievitch found me, other young folk from Maków came to me with help and to give me courage.

The second one was Mordechai Ciecanower, the son of Meir-Hirsh and Rochel.

Seeing my torn dress, my shaven head, he brought me a new dress, I don't know from where, a kerchief to cover my head and especially- a bowl of food-sweet noodles. Such a "luxury" I had not seen or eaten in quite some time [it seemed a lifetime].

Several days later Josef Ludvinovitch, the son of Mates and Perel, of the Pianke family, entered the Womens' Lager "C" to see me. He didn't hesitate to seek me out, even if the punishment was severe. He worked in the "Gendarmerie" (police). He didn't have permission to enter our lager, this could even be punishable by death.

When I met them both I began to cry. We reminisced about our days as neighbours, our families were very close. I asked again: Josef, where are my parents, my sisters, my brother-in-law and my children? He answered: "Now we must keep you alive". From this answer I understood that my nearest and dearest, my 2 children (I also understood) Bracha and Sara-Feige all met the same fate. The Nazi-murderers tore them away from me during the deportation of the Pabianicer Jews in 1942.

[Page 296]

The young people of Maków in Auschwitz took upon themselves with great devotion the responsibility to look after the welfare of their fellow Jews (landsleit), especially those women who were still alive.

Tuvia Segal, the son of Fishel and Liba, provided me with warm clothing, an overcoat and a new pair of mens' shoes. Very much in demand. This protected me from the cold while standing for long hours during the "Apel" [roll call] in rain and snow.

Procuring this clothing wasn't easy. Words cannot express my gratitude for all these kind deeds.

Yehuda-Leib Glanover, the son of Chaim-Yitzhak and Raske, almost every day after his work, [who pushed a cart of bread (provisions) for the S.S. men], passed by the lager where I lived. Whenever he passed by he threw a bread through the barbed wire, there were times he wasn't able to do it because those cruel S.S. men followed him around; to throw a piece of bread meant endangering himself. When Glanover wasn't able to provide me with the bread, news spread in the block among the Maków ers, and early the next morning, leaving for work under S.S. guard, one of them managed to throw over a package of cigarettes (which could be traded for bread). I became very familiar with their schedule when they left for work, and I returned to stand by the barbed wire fence. This is how the young Maków ers learned what to do.

Throw a Purse Over the Fence

I remember one time, Israel Zion, the son of Nahum and Rochel, threw a paper purse with a few carrots and cucumbers to me. Because he had to throw it up high to be able to pass through the wires, the paper purse tore and the "precious treasure" of carrots and cucumbers scattered far from me. The inmates, like wild animals threw themselves upon the scattered treasure, one on top of the other- I couldn't move from my spot, I cried. This picture awakened in me feelings of despair because I lost such a precious cargo. I didn't ask them to return it. One of them brought me several pieces of carrots and cucumbers. I saw her destitution in her empty eyes, so I shared the small portion with her, this coveted food. I was one of them, the hungry ones. Thanks to the dedicated souls of my Maków er friends, my situation was slightly better than the others.

I remind myself: once a Ciechanower friend, Noah Zabludovitch, looked for me in my *lager* and gave me a package of food, courtesy of the Makóẇer friends, which consisted of cigarettes, margarine, marmalade and a piece of salami. The margarine, marmalade and salami I ate, but the cigarettes I hid like a precious cargo. Later, during my *March*, they were my salvation.

[Page 297]

Thanks also to my Makóẇer friends who worked in "Kanada" [a warehouse for goods confiscated from the inmates of Auschwitz], where Zundel Beer, the nephew of Yechiel my husband, worked. He was informed of my whereabouts in Lager "C". He was assigned to work in this warehouse and managed to smuggle food and clothing from the newly arrived transports. In 1944, transports were still arriving from Holland, some of the last to arrive. They brought with them many containers of canned goods, which they had to leave behind in the wagons, just like on the earlier transports. Zundel volunteered to "steal" these containers, which he shared with me and others from Pabianice.

His sisters' friend, I often shared soup with her.

Now I have to mention another friend from Maków called Riback, it is a great honor to write about him, he symbolizes brotherhood, the task of performing Holy deeds (mitzvot) that all the youth of Maków performed in the death-camp of Auschwitz, to keep alive each and every one of us with whatever means available to him, hoping that perhaps one of us will remain alive.

He explained to me, he was a simple young man, he comes from a poor family called "*yokpers*" [orphans], an apostate family who lived behind the town. He brought me a bowl of soup and told me to eat it right away, which I did. Hunger always tormented me. Then he brought me another bowl, advising me to hide it for later. At the same time he told me he didn't have any bread.

After liberation, when I was reunited with the Maków survivors from the concentration camp of Auschwitz-Birkenau and told them the story about Riback's help, they wouldn't believe it. How was it possible, he didn't have enough food for himself, he went hungry very often.

The Big Help

And here I have to mention another source of help which I received from the Makóẇer youth in Auschwitz. Thanks to this help for me and the other Makóẇer women we were able to survive.

[Page 298]

The warm clothes and especially the heavy-soled boots, which I received from Tuvia Segal, protected me in those terrible winters of 1944/5 with their deep frost and snowstorms.

The warm clothing protected me from getting sick. And the thick boots from slipping, which happened very often going on the *March*. Whoever broke a foot or incurred another setback couldn't continue on the *March*, so he got shot along the way and we had to bury the body in the snow.

Again I remind myself: a few days later, after my arrival in Auschwitz-Birkenau, my cousin Roize Shremer, on a transport from the Lodz ghetto, arrived here. She was the daughter of Yeshaya Dovid and Itke, my father's sister. I told Yitzhak Granievitch about her. He immediately took interest in her and introduced her to the block elder, a Czech girl. She helped her as well not to go hungry. I have to mention, although she was born in Maków, the Makóẇer youth didn't know her because she left the city at a young age. But they helped her anyways. Now Roize-Shoshana Goldberg lives in Ber-Sheva. She arrived in the Land in 1948, got married and has 2 talented children.

Our Makówers Were One of a Kind, Honor Their Memory

In October 1944, after the uprising and the attempt to destroy the gas-chambers, in which many Makówers participated, I didn't hear from them very often. The Russians were approaching Silesia. The German murderers started to evacuate Auschwitz-Birkenau and various other concentration camps, and drove us deeper into Germany. At this time together with 3000 women, the last of Lager "C", we were transported and divided into 3 groups. My group consisted of 1000 women. We arrived at a camp, on an area of felled forest and erected buildings of boards which became overcrowded. At night, when it snowed, we were covered in snow as we slept. The forest belonged to the village *Birnbaumel*, near Trachenberg, not far from Breslau. We belonged to the horrible concentration camp Gross-Rosen. Every day, in our wrapped *schmates* (rags), they took us to work about 4 kilometers away, in open fields, covered in snow. We had to dig ditches in the frozen ground, even in snowstorms.

[Page 299]

When the snowstorms were impossible, even when the S.S. and other guards could no longer endure the cold, even with their warm clothing-long, leather coats and high boots-they sent us back to the camp. This was the greatest pleasure for us. Nevertheless, in these buildings we were somewhat protected from the snowstorm, even under a roof of branches. Not once did the winds blow away the roof, and we remained under the open sky.

The March

After 3 months in this "Gan-Eden", our camp was again evacuated. Of the 1000 women, only about 900 left. They others died from hunger and cold.

We marched for 13 days, surrounded by heavily guarded S.S. men with their strong reflectors. However, at night, they drove us into horse-stalls, or pig stalls, fearing that we would escape into the nearby forests. The murderers didn't tolerate any panic, they did everything orderly and quietly *with silk gloves*, not to arouse suspicion from the wider population.

At night, on the 14th day of the March, we arrived at Gross-Rosen. Here, we all thought, we will meet our end. Dragged, with frozen hands and feet, after the long March in deep snow, no one had any hope to remain alive. The Germans actually believed we would die. But to our good fortune, the Russians were already waiting at the gates of Breslau, and time didn't allow the murderers to carry out their final plan: to continue the March. This time we resisted, praying: shoot us here on the spot, we can't go any further. The Obersturmfurher of Gross-Rosen showed "pity on us" (the bullets were more dear to him) and he told us, a group of about 3000 women, to continue on a train. He actually kept his word. He didn't want a standoff, it was already January 1945. The Nazi-murderers already saw, they lost the war on all fronts, though they didn't give up on their devilish plans, to annihilate us, us Jews. They didn't leave us alone until the very last minute.

[Page 300]

On the Road Again

They again loaded us into horse wagons, this time open ones. At the train station, they gave us half a kilo of bread, some margarine and 100 grams of salami. These were our "provisions" for 4 days.

Along with our train, another train carrying male-victims, drove us deeper into Germany, in the region between Hanover and Celle, we were bombarded by American airplanes. From above they didn't see that these trains were carrying *extinguished* prisoners. The bombs didn't fall far from our wagon, falling closer to the train with the men. Many of the prisoners were hit by shrapnel.

After driving around for 4 days, we finally arrived at Bergen-Belsen. There were many dead in the wagons from the bombings along the road, many frozen and suffocated from the lack of space and air. Some were taking their last breaths. All of them were left at the train station, and the living were marched into a death camp (almost 4 kilometers away)- Bergen-Belsen.

Bergen-Belsen-the death camp, full of typhus and diphtheria, piles of dead, scattered bodies without burial. A shiver runs through my body, when I remind myself about this, my nerves are weakened, not knowing if I'm able to survive this. I had to focus on two things: access a water-pump and find bread.

The Plan to Survive

10 days before liberation, the devils already saw the forthcoming defeat. They didn't reveal their plan for freedom "one minute before 12" (like they said) they still wanted to kill the few remaining Jews. Finally they closed the water pumps in the camp, (only one pump worked for the entire camp when tens of thousands of people were). The needy portion of bread was stopped. The only food was watery soup, with some hard pieces of potatoes swimming around. With this we had to maintain our *soul*.

The administration of the camp was handed over to Hungarian hooligan soldiers who beat us at every opportunity. The Germans went into hiding, knowing their end was close.

[Page 301]

The American and British Airforce bombed the region day and night. For us this was the most beautiful "concert" of our lives.

Not far from the Bergen-Belsen camp, there was a camp for political prisoners. One of them, a German doctor, revealed their secret; he was also in Bergen-Belsen (besides Jews, there were prisoners of different nationalities). They prepared poisoned bread, at the last minute, to be distributed to the "half-humans". The German murderers didn't manage to carry out their plan.

After our liberation, the leftover bread was given to the dogs, and it was seen, that the bread was mixed with poison.

End of March. Shorty after liberation, I became sick with tuberculosis. I didn't receive any medicinal help. Somewhere I managed to find a piece of sugar among my things, which I had exchanged for a cigarette. The cigarette I had received from the Makówers, who threw it over the barbed wire with "luck". I only licked this small piece of sugar from time to time. This was the recipe for my survival. I couldn't swallow the turnip soup. With warm water I, moistened my burning lips. My dream then was-to receive a glass of tea with a piece of bread.

A memorial service for the martyrs of Maków, Germany, 1945

[Page 302]

The Liberators Are Coming

April 15, 1945, we were liberated by the English and Canadian Army, but I couldn't greet the liberators. My feet were swollen and my body was exhausted. I was 28 kilos. Several days later in the camp, some S.S. men were discovered in a hideout, many of them had come from Auschwitz. With Dr. Klein and Irma Grese, "the blonde beast", [also "the beautiful beast", the Hyena of Auschwitz], this is how we called her in Birkenau. She was the overseer of "C". The English brought them in a army truck to work nearby the block where I was. Everyone went out "to look them in the face", these murderers. I also wanted to see them, to throw a filthy rag at their tyrannical faces, but I didn't. My feet couldn't move. A Russian girl, Maria, helped get up. She helped me see the former proud assassins- and now-the downtrodden and harassed, like previously we were their helpless victims. I now watched the former S.S. men gathering the dead bodies, the victims of their shameful atrocities. Thousands of dead bodies littered the *lager*. Later a group of 18 S.S. men appeared before a court in Lubeck. They received an honest deserving verdict: death by hanging.

It took a long time before I became "*human*" again. I was physically and mentally broken. A little time later, when I felt somewhat stronger, I began to look for my family. I thought: Maybe someone is still alive. We were 5 sisters. All with families. Only one, Miriam, remained alive, thanks to her emigration in 1935 to Eretz-Israel.

End of 1946, I left Bergen-Belsen and went to Firstenfeldbruck, near Munich, where some Maków survivors were located. We lived like one family. Actually here we organized the first memorial for the Maków victims.

I wed for the second time, Avraham Garfinkel, the son of R'Moshe Yosef and Mirl. End of 1949 we left the soaked German land for America, where my husband had a brother, Israel-Yitzhak. Arriving in Brooklyn, we received a very warm welcome from the first Maków *landsleit*, especially I want to remember one family-my mothers' cousins, Batia, from the house of Frankel, and her husband Meir Ostri, of blessed memory, and also their children, They welcomed us like parents receiving their own children, and their daughters and son-in-laws, like sisters and brothers. They integrated us into their family, provided us with courage to carry on a normal life and to rebuild our home. At that time this was the greatest moral help.

[Page 303]

Achtung!

Makower Jden in Umgegent:
Pultusk, Przasnysz, Rozan, Chorzel

Dermit machen mir bekant, dos

Monteg 15. XII. 47 J. 6 a Zajger N. M.
in Sztod Fürstenfeldbruck bei München

Kumt For A

TROJER AKADEMJE

Gewidmet Di 5 Jorzajt
Fun Di Tragisz Umgekumene Makower Kdojszim
in Umgegent.

Es is A Flycht Fun Jeden Farinteresirten Antajl cu nemen.

Mit Achtung

Makower Komitet.

The last memorial assembly in Germany...In 1947

[Page 304]

May these few lines serve as a memorial for the perished friends of the Makówer youth, who died at the hands of the Nazi murderers in Auschwitz.

Honor Their Memory!

[Page 309]

Along Blood-Drenched Roads

by Mordechai Ciechanower, Ramat-Gan

Translated by Dr. Joseph Schuldenrein

The day the war broke out–September 1, 1939–intense anticipation spread across the local population, as our town was at the German-Polish border. That same day we took off from our homes, places we had lived in for years, abandoning familiar surroundings and fleeing to safety in unfamiliar towns and villages; as far away from the burning wreckage as possible. But it was near impossible to escape from the stealthy German enemy–the planes–which began bombarding the area from the outset of the invasion. They targeted towns as well as defenseless fleeing citizens; there were corpses strewn in fields and everywhere.

Beginning on Day 1 escapees and refugees streamed out of their homes from all over, Pruzhnitz and the surrounding villages, and not just Jews. A number of folks remained in Makow, while some kept moving further east and south. That said, many of the local Makower Jews remained in town. Those who stayed took in the refugees willingly and provided them with lodging in their homes. Based on experiences during the First World War, the Makower Jews believed that their town would be safer than others. That is what they felt initially, lacking any notion on what the next day might bring. No one had any idea of the speed of the German onslaught, the suddenness of it all. Schools shut down immediately, people were out of work, folks wandered the streets as in a daze, transfixed to the German news updates blaring across the radio waves. No one could imagine that the Germans would murder defenseless and unarmed citizens in plain sight. Then there were those who felt that the Polish army would turn back the assault. Beginning on Day 1 stores were closed up and the loss of food supplies and inventory was felt directly. Merchants began hiding their products for fear of break-ins and looting. The Makower Rebbe, Rabbi Eidelberg, left town that Friday for Warsaw. The roads both in and out of Makow were sealed off immediately. A general sense of panic overwhelmed the populace. And it wasn't only the Jews who stole away from town, but also Christians who loaded up their meager belongings on wagons, and in some cases packed in their animals as well.

[Page 310]

But most of the refugees poured out on foot. Small contingents also departed by buses, making their way through the clogged crowds; everyone doing whatever they could, to distance themselves from the front. Those running away included rich and poor, healthy and infirm, young and old, families as well as individuals. Nevertheless a large group--perhaps the majority–remained in Makow. The rich and the middle class appeared to rely on their capital as well as faith and God. And the poor felt "What can they possibly take from me? Surely they will supply us with food, at least." The fear, however, was pervasive. By nightfall no one had the courage to venture out in the street. That first Friday night and Shabbos there were only isolated minyans in the synagogues. Subsequently, minyans were held solely in private homes.

The Polish Army in Retreat

The radio broadcasts formally announced the German bombardments across Poland. Warsaw was hit as well. The news from the front was equally dire. By Monday, the fourth day of the invasion, we knew that the Polish military was already in retreat. On Tuesday morning there was a deafening explosion. We assumed that Makow was in the throes of the bombing offensive. As we were running away we knew what was going on; that the Poles blew up the bridge over the River Oziscz. In addition to the military, the Town Council elders, the mayor, and various police divisions took flight as well. The town fell into complete chaos. The sounds and screams of panic were everywhere. And the Germans kept streaming in. Most locals took to locking themselves into their homes; no one dared as much as to poke his nose out the door. At most we peered through open windows to get an idea of what was about to unfold. It was Tuesday, September 5, between 11 am and noon, that the initial vanguard of the German army formally entered Makow. They drove in on motorcycles and armed vehicles mounted with machine guns; the soldiers were heavily equipped with hand grenades. They yelled out "Have no fear, nothing will happen. There is nothing to worry about". The onlooking residents along Pruzhnitz Street bore witness to the scene, as they peered through the cracks and shattered window glass facing the boulevard.

That same evening, September 5, a German car drove down the street and proclaimed through a loudspeaker, in Polish and in German, that "the German army has occupied Makow and will continue to advance". And further, they continued, under penalty of death, the residents were ordered to surrender their guns and small arms by 6 pm that same day. They were put under a strict curfew at that hour as well.

[Page 311]

All the while the drone of motorcycles echoed through the streets of town uninterrupted. No one slept that night and well into the next morning. By sunrise those walking outside were confronted with signs bearing the Nazi swastika on both sides of the street. They contained instructions on how residents were to behave going forward (surrendering arms, etc.). That same day Jews entered town from Krasnosheltz and surrounding villages, reporting on horrific acts of violence perpetrated by the Germans upon local Jews as they began round-ups for work details. They caught me and 10 of my friends the next day and drove us to Ruzhan, 20 km from Makow. When we got there, we were instructed to unload blocks of coal from a set of small wagons and to load them up onto other vehicles. No one at home had any idea as to what happened to me. We were forced to work until midnight and were then driven back to Makow.

On September 7 the placards on the streets announced that the Jews no longer had any rights, they were forbidden to walk on the sidewalks, just on the streets, and not in groups, only separately. We were to take off our hats when encountering German soldiers, etc. It became clear that here and there Jews would be randomly seized and beaten for no reason, if only because they were walking in the streets. That said, in the beginning there were no horrific or mass acts of violence. It got to the point where merchants and store owners gradually began to re-open their stores and shops.

Several days later vehicles passed through the main streets announcing via loudspeakers that all Jews between the ages of 14 and 65 were to gather in the market square. Once they assembled, the new German mayor made the following announcement: "You no longer have any rights. From this day on you are subject to German authorities. You have an opportunity to depart now to the Russian zone and you can make arrangement to leave in that direction. The border is open and the Russians will take care of you." Immediately thereafter several groups of Jews were given limited supplies and crossed the street. Those who opted out began walking in the direction of the Soviet border. There were those who made it there safely. Others encountered bands of thugs and were robbed but they pushed forward. The first stop along the way was the town of Lomzhe.

Those Jews who remained in Makow and had been taken in by Gentile families were ordered to abandon their houses, businesses and workshops and were displaced to the Jewish section.

[Page 312]

The Germans Begin Their Dirty Work

The Germans established an Agency for Jewish Affairs (precursor to the "Judenrat") that was under Jewish management. Management was responsible for attending to displaced Jews and reported directly to the German authorities. There was a steady flow of Jews returning to Makow from the Russian front. There were also refugees who poured in from surrounding towns and villages. There were those who returned to quarters now occupied by the Germans and they had to be resettled. No one knew the revamped layout, which areas were "good", which were "bad", nor could former residents navigate for appropriate places to stay. Many wandered aimlessly through the streets, assuming they would eventually find some kind of shelter. But the Germans overran most of the city and the ominous sight of soldiers in every corner of the city made the situation worse.

In the meantime, the border between Russia and occupied Poland was hermetically sealed. The contact between those on the Russian side and the sectors under German control was completely broken off. The Jews felt surrounded by dangerous enemies on all sides without the possibility of moving safely in any direction. And then the Germans exposed their true character: kidnapping citizens for work details, beating, and muggings the local Jews, forcing them into near bondage at the Walter Kaiser company that built concrete pavements and roads. Former merchants, intellectuals, grandfathers, and children were forced into the lowliest and dirtiest forms of labor. After work they were subject to merciless beatings. That was the grim state of Jewish life in town.

In time the situation deteriorated from bad to worse. The Germans took to enforcing more sadistic and humiliating tasks. On Yom Kippur 1939, the German gendarmes removed Torah scrolls from synagogues, tore them to pieces, spread them out in the street, stomped on them, and continued to rip them to shreds. It's impossible to describe the pain and humiliation that the Jews felt watching this violation of holy objects as these events transpired. The new Beis-Midrash was completely destroyed.

The Germans transformed the place to a stall for horses. At the same time the old Beis-Midrash was turned into a shelter for homeless refugees.

In November, 1939 a band of German soldiers captured a young Jewish girl and violated her. She was subsequently found collapsed and unconscious. The local Jewish pharmacist, well-known in town, recounted that he went to attend to her and gave her a prescription. The young lady took the medicine but later died. The Germans found out about the incident.

[Page 313]

They went to the pharmacist's house, seized him and his wife and tried them (in a makeshift court). They were later released thanks to the intervention of the head Polish pharmacist, Mr. Pizarski.

Fayvel Koval

There was a fellow named Fayvel Koval who lived in the village of Chociwel with his wife and two daughters. He had a Christian partner with whom he jointly owned a mill in the village of Dobzhankov. On 21 October he drove towards the Russian border and attempted to cross it. However, the German forces stopped him and ordered him to turn back.

In February 1940 the German gendarmes suddenly surrounded our house and inquired as to the whereabouts of Fayvel Koval and his wife from Chociwel.

Initially the Germans approached the Jewish Agency Command (Judenrat) in order to get the address of Fayvel Koval. At the time a senior head of the Jewish Agency Command was one Avraham-Michoel Adler also from Chociwel. He was also a refugee. As soon as the inquiry was made, Adler dispatched a messenger to our place to warn the Kovals that they were being pursued and that they should take off immediately. They did that. Shortly thereafter the Gendarmes burst into our house and started beating us mercilessly pressing us to divulge the Kovals' hide out. We didn't give it up. The Germans then took away the two Koval daughters, aged 18 and 20. Additionally, the Germans demanded a sizeable "contribution" from the Jewish Command. They warned that for each day that the Kovals failed to appear in front of the German authorities the Jewish Agency would be compelled to provide an increasingly higher "contribution". The two daughters were in lock-up for two weeks. They were eventually released but were subject to constant surveillance. A month later the Germans threatened to hold the leaders of the Jewish Agency (Judenrat) hostage. But shortly thereafter the Germans located Koval and his wife in Chiechanow and placed them under arrest in the town of Wlozelavek. The daughters had an opportunity to glimpse at their parents through cracks in crates that impeded direct observation. The senior Kovals eventually disappeared. Apparently they had been murdered by the Germans. No one had any idea why the Kovals were so ardently pursued by the German authorities. However, it was known that Mr. Koval was well-connected in East Prussia. It was assumed that he was targeted by the Germans because of his valuable holdings in that area.

[Page 314]

The First Labor Camp

It was late 1940, or perhaps early in 1941 when the Germans began to dispatch young men to the first labor camp in the town of Gansevoh. Around 300 of us were loaded onto vehicles for the initial transport. As I said, this was the very first group of young men that was designated for displacement from Makow. They set us up in an abandoned schoolhouse and, consistent with Nazi protocols, they stuffed us in there well beyond the capacity of the building. The routine was stressful; up before dawn, roll-call, and off to work detail. The work itself involved digging up stones in the fields, and breaking them up for pavements and pathways. It was grueling labor. With minimal rations, the Polish guards pushed us mercilessly, prodding and beating us with wooden clubs, slugging us at will, and pushing us to the limit of endurance. We grew increasingly desperate. Most felt that this is where and how we would meet our end. Men would collapse and faint on the spot. This scenario played out for six months, until June, 1941.

One of the earliest victims in Makow was a Jew from Pultusk by the name of Velvel Skurka. He was sent to the work camp at Nova Wiej along with another group of prisoners. One of the camp guards, a "Volks-Deutsch" (Ethnic German), beat him so mercilessly that he was completely spent. The poor fellow screamed and pleaded "I beg you, please spare me, I'm a father of three young children", but the brute beat him to death.

There was a Jew from Warsaw in the camp, his name was Mayorek I believe, who composed a song dedicated to the memory of Velvel Skurka. While I don't remember all the words to the song, two stanzas remain fixed in my memory:

> In Nova Wiej, Nova Wiej,
> That horrific camp,
> A voice still echoes
> From the deepest bowels.
> It weeps, it shrieks,
> Grief blows in the wind,
> Velvel Skurka is beaten again,
> The clock strikes 3, three more blows,
> Velvel Skurka is the guard's victim yet again,
> And he begs and pleads,
> "Spare me, my life,
> I have three little kids
> And they need to be fed"

[Page 315]

Over time the local Jews were dispatched to labor camps in neighboring villages and towns occupied by the Germans. I was able to maintain contact with Makow. When one of our people fell sick we found ways to send him back to Makow for treatments.

However, as the occupation endured, conditions in Makow grew increasingly more difficult and dire. The local bath-house was turned into a jail, and many of the locals (Jews) were locked up and beaten randomly.

By June, 1941 entire families had vacated Makow, dispatched to work details in the town of Tchervonka. The young Poles were transferred to work assignments in Germany.

Wanted: Farm workers for Germany

One day while on a break from stone-splitting, the gendarmes encircled us and and gave the prisoners the once over, eye-balling each and every one of us. No one had any idea of what precipitated this sudden inspection. But everyone was scared: how was this inspection going to end? We all wondered.

The gendarmes finally selected two of us: Henech Lassek and me. They ordered us to leave the group and follow them directly. They led us to the command-center where we encountered several dozen horse-drawn wagons. The wagons were filled with groups of Poles (Gentiles) with their belongings; they were to be dispatched as farm workers to Germany. It turned out that two wealthy Poles had succeeded in buying their way out of this assignment and appropriate substitutes were needed directly. Apparently both Lassek and me conformed most closely to a "Gentile profile" so we were selected. When the wagons arrived in Makow, we were immediately recognized by several (Jewish) passersby. Not knowing what was going on, they immediately ran to Jewish Council headquarters (Judenrat) as well as to our homes to inform the locals that we were sighted in town.

The gendarmes took us to a makeshift hut which they had converted to a temporary jail. We stayed there for two days. The Council had us released and we were subsequently sent to Biedzitzeh, which turned out to be the harshest and most dangerous labor camp in the area.

[Page 316]

The Ghetto is Built

By Yom Kippur day, September, 1941, the Makow Ghetto was completed (the Judenraat had already been established by July, 1941). The Germans had already rounded up the Jews, settled them within the Ghetto confines, and had issued the yellow Star of David ID patch. The ghetto perimeters had been cordoned off: the southern border was the market; on the east, Grabova street; the northern edge was the Old Cemetery; and on the west Pruzhnetz Street. They packed in 2-3 families per room, which is to say that the entire Jewish population of 5000 was crammed into a space that amounted to no more than 20% of the area of Makow proper.

They clustered all the Jews in the ghetto, local residents and refugees, as well as stragglers who made their way to town from elsewhere. The ghetto was demarcated by barbed wire. Broken windows and boarded up openings over long stretches also marked the ghetto boundaries. The enclosed area was further offset by high walls ringed with barbed wire. The Germans issued a proclamation that any Jew found without the Yellow Patch (which had to be fastened and displayed on the front and shoulders of each Jew's garment) was to be shot. The economic situation in the Ghetto was dire. Bread rations were meager. We were able to make some adjustments, figuring out ways to smuggle in Kosher meat. However, the filth and sanitary conditions were deplorable to the point that there were frequent epidemics. By March of 1942 a severe epidemic of stomach-typhus broke out. Dozens of people died, a situation exacerbated by severe shortages of medicine and the absence of medical care. Once the epidemic became uncontrollable the Germans began to fear that the maladies would expand beyond the Ghetto walls. At one point they brought in a Jewish doctor from Warsaw along with his wife and child. The Germans issued an order that all men and women shave their heads. At the same time food was in short supply. People stood in lines for endless hours–officially from 3 pm to 8 am–with cups and containers to obtain their meager rations. It was not uncommon for people to wait in line overnight only to find that the rations had run out and that there was nothing left. The gates of the city were at southern margin of the ghetto, offset by the market on Rivneh Street. The gates were routinely patrolled and guarded by two Jewish policemen, but the German Commandant of Makow, Steinmetz, came by for spot inspections. He would appear without warning, escorted by two German gendarmes and the Jewish police. Often he would randomly stop Jews and beat them, eliciting perpetual fear and terror whenever he showed up.

[Page 317]

Jüdische Gemeinde
  in Makow   p. Melman
dn. 19. XII.1940
L.dz. 49/40   Do
               "Joint Distribution Committee
                       Warsau
                     Jasna 11

Z wielkim zadowoleniem potwierdzamy niniejszym odbiór Waszego pisma

z dnia 10.XII.1940 r. N.O/1459/40 w sprawie szczegółowego sprawozdania

z działalności naszej na polu opieki społecznej.

Wysłaliśmy do W.P.P. list dn.14 b.m., w którym wskazaliśmy na koniecz=

ność niezwłocznego przyjścia nam z pomocą materialną.

Pisma W.P.P. nadeszło - wobec tego - na czas.

Pozwolimy sobie przede wszyszkim kolejno odpowiedzieć na poruszoną

w piśmie sprawę:

1. Liczba Żydów w Makowie wynosi 3800.-

2.   "   " uchodźców około   2000.-

3.   "   " pozostających pod
           naszą opieką   1235.-

4.   "   Rückwanderer/?/

5-7. Żadnej kuchni ludowej nie posiadamy, a to z braku funduszy.
Natomiast zorganizowaliśmy u miejscowych rodzin wydawanie obiadów biednym
i uchodźcom w liczbie 100 dziennie. Jestto jednak kropla w morzu nędzy,
gdyż faktyczne zapotrzebowanie wynosi 800 obiadów dziennie.

8. Opieka nad dzieckiem nie istnieje u nas. a to również ze względu
na brak możliwości finansowych.

9. Nie ma żydowskiego ambulatorium, szpitala, schroniska. Udzielamy
jednak pomocy lekarskiej bez wydawania lekarstw, do czego oczywiście moż=
liwości nie ma.

10. Budżet miesięczny Opieki Społecznej przedstawia się następująco:

a/ wydaje się 3000 kg chleba,

b/ "   " na pomoc lekarską - 200.- RM oraz

c/ "   " 200 śniadań dla dzieci, składające się z bułki i mleka.

Przeprowadziliśmy akcję pomocy zimowej zbiórką odzieży, bielizny, pościeli

Polish document: Jewish community of Makow (19.12.1940) to the Joint Distribution Committee,
Warsaw 1940

[Page 318]

2.

itp. gdyż brak ten dotkliwie daje się we znaki uchodźcom pozostającym tu. Wasza pomoc w tym kierunku jest nieodzowna.

Reasumując powyższe uprzejmie prosimy - ze względu na okropną nędzę panującą tu wśród wielkich rzesz uchodźców i biednych - przeznaczyć dla nas:

/pieczęć:
Otrzymano 2?.XII.1940
      Nr 2479/

a/ jednorazową subwencję na zakup opału na wysokość kilku
       tysięcy RM.

b/ większą subwencję miesięczną dla:

1/ uruchomienia kuchni ludowej względnie zakupu dla ludności
produktów żywnościowych;

2/ Zorganizowania należytej opieki nad dzieckiem.

3/   "   schroniska.

c/ przesłanie nam jaknajrychlej paczek odzieżowych, bielizny
itp. koniecznych dla prawie nagich uchodźców.

d/ przesłanie większej ilości medykamentów.

W oczekiwaniu pozytywnego załatwienia naszych życzeń kreślimy

Z poważaniem

B. Ryzyka
A. Adler
Berenbaum
A. Faskowicz

pieczęć:
Jüdische Gemeinde
in Maków

Sekratär

/podpis nieczyt./

Polish document (second page) signed by B. Ryzyka, A. Adler, Berenbaum, A. Faskowicz

[Page 319]

Sadistic Entertainment

In May of 1942 100 young men were transported out of the Ghetto and taken to Ruzhan, about 20 kilometers away. About the same number were sent off to Karnievoh. The work camps there were among the cruelest and most debilitating. In Ruzhan the laborers were housed in what is best described as a fortress; they slaved away from dusk to dusk, and their labors were rewarded with beatings by wooden clubs and whips. The Germans did everything in their power to break the Jews' spirits, and to humiliate them to a state of despair. On Sundays the Commandant from Ruzhan camp would invite "guests" to celebrate these acts of hooliganism. They orchestrated "shows" for the honored "guests". The camp Commandant would chase us down, and beat us as we ran while the guests clearly took pleasure in witnessing these spectacles. Every Sunday they selected 5 inmates from the worker details and they meted out 30 lashes on their bare bodies. The victims shrieked and screamed in pain as the Germans were overcome with perverse glee. We longed to get back to the Makow Ghetto, even though we knew that the epidemics were spreading and people were dropping dead from hunger there.

In Karnievoh, a village 8 kilometers from Makow, 30 young men were working in a field under the supervision of a German Commandant. Early one morning the Commandant suddenly appeared on horseback, stiff whip in hand, and began mercilessly flogging random laborers as he rode. And as this was going on the laborers continued to work.

Back in Makow social and community life had effectively ceased. An atmosphere of helplessness pervaded the town. No one thought about the Torah or anything when there was no flour, people were starving, running around in fear, and the spectre of imminent demise was persistent. Nevertheless, a group of 20 young and pious young men found shelter in an attic and managed to go on with Torah study.

The First Uprising

The following incident occurred in June, 1942:

There were three Jews from Pultusk, the first was named Skop, the second Rubin (I don't remember the third's name). They made it out of the Ghetto and wandered about the poor neighboring towns to procure food. Along the way they encountered a German officer approaching them on horseback. They immediately sensed an imminent confrontation with a probable negative outcome. They realized that it was useless to take off and instead chose to stop short ahead of the officer. Aware of both the futility of the situation as well as the immediate vulnerability of the soldier, they felt they had the upper hand and decided to take him on. They diverted the soldier and his horse to a side alley and threw him off his mount in front of the horse. He ended up lifeless, on the roadway.

[Page 320]

Just as the three felt that they were free and sufficiently removed from the scene of the incident, two soldiers mounted on horseback pulled up. The three Jews, sensing calamity, took off on foot as fast as they could. The soldiers drew their revolvers and began shooting in the direction of the escapees. Two of the guys fell dead immediately, but the third–Skop– survived but took a bullet in the neck. With his remaining strength he turned back and disappeared into the Makow Ghetto. Somehow he managed to find the local doctor who helped nurse him back to health.

The two gendarmes who had shot the two escapees dead hastened to report the incident to the Ghetto commissar. The commissar took off to the doctor's house to inquire whether he had just treated someone who had been recently wounded by gunfire. The doctor realized that he could not sidestep the incident. He confirmed that he had, indeed, attended to the wounds of a Ghetto resident and that his duty as a doctor mandated that he provide medical assistance.

Once the Germans extracted additional details on the incident they surrounded Skop's house and forced him out. Skop made an attempt to burst through the cordoned off area. His attempt was unsuccessful. The Germans seized him and drove him to a Christian cemetery in the nearby town of Shelkoveh where they shot him dead.

After Skop's death the Makower Jewish population assumed that the case was closed and resolved. As it turned out, the blood-thirsty German thugs continued in pursuit of additional victims. Several days later the Ghetto Commisar, accompanied by an SS detail, moved into the Makow Ghetto again. He brought with him a list of old, weak, and disabled Jews who had been excused from work details for health reasons. According to "orders" all names on the list were scheduled to appear. Once the first 20 names were announced the Commissar stated that no more individuals were needed. Subsequently the Commissar noted that those 20 were to be hanged in punishment for the gendarme that died in the ambush outside the Ghetto walls.

The 20 were locked in a cell at the Jewish Council headquarters. They remained under 24-hour watch by the Jewish police.

[Page 321]

In the meantime a stage was being outfitted, across from the Jewish Council building, as a gallows for the 20 selected Jews. They had a clear view of the construction activity from their holding cell, fully aware of the fate awaiting them outside. They were in a holding pattern for four months as the gallows were being built. On a bright September day, a large vehicle with a mounted loudspeaker drove through the ghetto announcing that all Ghetto residents–men, women, and children–were to appear at the plaza near the synagogue to witness the public hanging of the 20 Jews. The announcement specified that no children were to be left behind in their homes. Anyone who did not appear in the "Execution Plaza" would be shot on sight.

The Public Execution of the 20

The entire Ghetto was surrounded by German soldiers and gendarmes armed with automatic weapons. When the "Execution Plaza" had filled up with spectators a second announcement warned that no one was to speak and that any signs of disturbance would be met by a mass shooting. That morning the Jewish police were instructed on the procedures for making and fastening the nooses around the victims' necks and how to kick out the stools from under the victims' feet. Amongst the 20 sentenced for hanging were the two sons of Moishe Gogol, the brother of one of the Jewish policemen. The depressed and defeated crowd gazed at the scene, fighting back tears–in silence. The condemned 20, hands bound, were marched to the gallows.

Corpses of the 21 murdered

This tragic event broke the spirit of townsfolk.

[Page 322]
It was September, 1942.

In early October 1942 the German police arrested the Jewish doctor (who had assisted Skop) and marched him directly to the gallows at "Execution Plaza", where the original hangings had taken place. The Germans issued the following accusation: "When Skop came to you to attend to his wounds, you did not inform the authorities, and on that basis you are sentenced to hang."

On the day the hanging occurred, the doctor's wife went berserk. Subsequently she met her end in Auschwitz together with many more Makower Jews.

Later in October word got out that there would be an imminent evacuation. People would be moved out en masse but no one knew where or when. Folks wandered the Ghetto streets aimlessly, like the living dead, not knowing what was about to happen. The Judenrat itself had the feel of helplessness and despair, a holdover from the public execution of the 20 that only grew deeper as the days passed.

On November 1 the tragic news broke that the Makow Ghetto would be liquidated. Rumors began floating, about places like Auschwitz and Treblinka but no one really knew what any of that meant. Two days later it came out that older folks would be executed and that the younger people would be dispatched to work camps in Germany. But the details were not known at the time. Just rumors.

"Black Sabbath"

On November 5, an edict came down that the Jews from the surrounding towns like Ruzhan, Karnievoh, Nove Wiecz, Thchervanka, Bieddzhitza, and others would evacuate the labor-camps and return to the Ghetto. They came back that same day. On the one hand the news was joyous since families would be reunited and there would be no more indentured servitude in the labor camps. On the other hand there was a suspicion, bordering on fear, that the Jewish population would be re-interred in the Ghetto. Before evacuating the Germans allowed us to take not only the daily rations but also any bread that we may have otherwise stored. This gesture was also a source of suspicion.

We were escorted and marched back to the Ghetto by the German Commandant along with Polish guards. As we approached the Ghetto check-point we noticed that the entire place was surrounded by the German gendarmes.

[Page 323]

When we mentioned this to the locals they didn't believe us, since the gendarmes were apparently stationed exclusively outside the Ghetto walls; ironically we were the ones who brought the sad news for the residents on the inside.

When we got in we were met by sobbing relatives who told us that they (the Germans) were making preparations to take us to an unknown location.

I recall that it was a brisk fall day, a heavy rain came down, and the sky was overcast; the dreary weather was a reflection of our situation. Young people gathered in groups to discuss coping strategies and even potential escape plans. We were clearly locked into a dreadful and hostile situation. We found out that the local Poles, in the cities and towns, were warned by the German authorities that, going forward, if they were to hide or shelter Jews they would be hanged.

The day became known as "the Black Sabbath", November 14, 1942.

That same day there was a selection. The Chief Ghetto Commandant, Steinmetz, along with several SS men, were stationed opposite the "Judenrat" building on the corner of the "Zhiloni Rinek", the Market Square. Steinmetz ordered the Jews to appear directly in front of him. The Germans had prepared and handed him two separate lists. No one had any clue as to what these lists meant. The only thing we knew is that we needed to appear young and healthy. Those 16 years old and beyond were registered per family names. Those under 16 went with their parents. There were those who grouped themselves together on the spot "as families" in order to look young, fit, and presentable. The feeling was that these groups would be selected for the "young and fit list", assuming the lists segregated the living from the dead. The registration/selection procedure took place all of Saturday and well into the night. When the process ended we all returned to our homes, not knowing what fate awaited us. People consoled themselves by saying "I'm pretty sure I looked healthy enough to be among the living...as for the others, heaven only knows!"

The next morning the official order came down to prepare for the evacuation. All money, gold items, and valuables were to be surrendered to the authorities. Most other items could accompany the individuals to the destination. The situation was such that folks hid, tore up, and even buried their cash and personal valuables. It was a scene that approximated absolute chaos.

[Page 324]

The Evacuation

The official edict came out on Monday morning, November 16, 1942. It stated that on Wednesday, November 18, at 6 AM the gate at the Pruzhnitz Road would be opened. Wagons would be there ready to transport the Jews to the town of Mlawa. Practically no one slept over the course of the next two nights, except for some individuals who managed to sneak out of the Ghetto.

Late Tuesday night, November 17, and into the next morning folks were busy packing their belongings. No one really knew what to take, some buried their valuables, others destroyed them completely.

By 5 AM residents had already abandoning their homes and began marching toward the gate at the Pruzhnitz road, which had basically been forced open by the Germans. We were informed that if anyone remained in a dwelling after 6 am they would be shot directly. Obviously, there were those too sick and disabled to leave; they stayed back, as there would be no one left to care for them. Rumors circulated that they were eventually killed off.

At the Pruzhnitz Road gate, the German gendarmes announced again that all cash, gold, and valuables were to be surrendered. On-site counters were set up for that purpose. The wagons were loaded up, two families to each horse-drawn wagon. The wagons themselves had been mobilized from Makow and the surrounding region. In all there were 5,150 people that made the trip including Makowers and Jews from the countryside and villages. The Germans packed the folks onto the wagons as quickly as possible, armed with clubs and prods. The wagons took off as soon as they were full. The people were so despondent and forlorn that there was not even a hint of resistance. Anywhere. Up until the last wagon took off isolated individuals, especially those who could not walk, were dragged out of their homes. That task was undertaken by the Jewish Police. And so the town of Makow became "Judenrein", (Free of Jews). The entire Jewish population of the Ghetto, in excess of 5000 souls, was led out on their final journey.

The trip lasted the entire day and well into the night. It was around 7-8 PM, when the Ghetto evacuees arrived in Mlawa (about 50 km from Makow). The Mlawa Ghetto was empty, as the evacuation of that town had occurred several days earlier. The only Jews in Mlawa were holdovers from the Judenraat, the Jewish police, and their families. They served as the intake officials and designated temporary residence, one family per room, within the former Ghetto area.

[Page 325]

When we arrived we saw that the last (Jewish) residents had hurriedly abandoned their homes; we saw that household items remained in place, as they were left. There was uneaten foot on the tables, unmade beds and the like. When asked what happened to the Mlawa Jews, the Judenrat and police responded that they had no idea. One fellow retorted simply "Nothing good, that's for certain."

We stayed in Mlawa several days. At night we would occasionally hear painful screams. We looked out the windows to see where they noise was coming from, as no one dared to venture outside. We witnessed the German gendarmes and the Jewish Police dragging individuals out of their homes. By morning the majority of the older remaining residents had been removed. From my quarters, I peered into an adjacent house and saw a couple bidding their last goodbyes to their three children, not knowing where they were going to end up. They put on their coats, held back tears, and then went off. The children effectively became orphans then and there. By the morning after, the Mlawa Ghetto was deserted. Word was that thousands had been transported to Treblinka.

Folks were led out and marched away as if to a funeral service. By then it was obvious that the Jews were heading towards their final resting places.

The Road to the Extermination Camp

This was the situation that the Makower Jews found themselves in. We remained in the Mlawa Ghetto for the next few days, until December 8, when the order was issued that the remaining residents, numbering around 4000, were to show up at the local mill site. The first transport included 1000 people. The second transport was scheduled to be dispatched on December,

10, this time numbering 2300. The third and final transport contained the last 700 individuals. The second transport also took in the Judenraat members and the Mlawa Jewish police. Once we saw that the officials were being transported it became clear that the entire town would be evacuated. The third transport of 700 included workers and skilled professionals that served the Germans in maintenance and technical capacities; they were moved out at the very last minute. The transports were organized by family, with each unit taking its possessions to the central dispatch quarters at the mill. People waited there through the night until 5 AM when the German gendarmes arrived and ordered that everyone assemble at the Central Ghetto Plaza to be dispatched to their destinations. At the Plaza we were instructed to break out in rows, 5 persons per row. Then it was announced that we were to march to the railway station from where we would be transported by train to specific labor camps.

[Page 326]

The Germans again ordered that we empty out our money, gold and valuables immediately. They laid out deposit boxes for these items. They followed up by saying "Where you are going there will be no need for any of these items." I noticed that very few individuals offered up these items this time around. Next we were chained together, 5 people per row, and forced to run at a steady pace the entire 1.5 km distance to the train station. I supported my mother on one side, my father on the other, and my two sisters were alongside them as we made our way. We got to the ramp where there were "passenger" and freight cars. We were stuffed into these cars, prodded along by Germans with clubs who liberally beat us and ordered us to speed up the pace. People hustled to position themselves into the "passenger" cars since these had benches and space to breathe. In contrast, the freight cars were simply stuffed with as many people as possible and there was no room to move. Folks were simply piled one atop or adjacent to another like piles of firewood.

Those poor souls who did not have the strength to walk were simply dragged and pushed into the cars. When they were packed to bursting the Germans locked and sealed the doors from the outside. The cars began to move. At that point people started to wail and scream in desperation, cursing, and yelling, and then pushing and shoving and gasping for air. It was nearly impossible to breathe.

This was the situation for about three days. Through the windows we could see that we were passing through Warsaw. We stopped in Czestochowa for about a half hour. A Jewish workman, with a Magen Dovid (Star of David) around his wrist managed to bring us a cask of water. The train went past the city of Radom and approached Bieletz. It was around 6 PM on December 12 when we arrived in Birkenau. It was there that the German gendarmes transferred us directly to the SS authorities. They swung open the doors of the cars. They moved us out quickly, clubbing us indiscriminately, accompanied by dogs. These murderers yelled at us and beat us down to move quickly and evacuate the cars. As I descended from the "passenger cars" which I (fortunately) occupied with my family I saw how they beat those who vacated the freight cars. As the train doors flew open the scene was like a boiling pot with vapors and smoke streaming out. People were freed up after having been crushed and cramped from three days. It was like a block that decompressed and separated out; and then there were those who were dead and fainted lying still and trampled in the rush…. Despite that the SS men went about their business clubbing people and beating them as they made their way out, apparently relishing the scene that unfolded in front of them.

[Page 327]

The Selections

The dead, frail, and sick were grouped together, loaded onto freight trucks and driven away. The living remained on the ramps and platforms, beaten, screaming, and subject to selections. An SS officer stood by and pointed with his finger, to the right or to the left, determining who was to live and who was to die. Fathers were torn away from their children, wives from husbands, as separations were the objective. The same fate awaited my family. My father and I went off to one side, and my mother and her two sisters to the other. I saw them drag the women away. I cast a glance towards my mother and offered her a piece of bread. I told her, "We are men, after all, we will figure out a way to get by. But what about you?" An SS man beat me across the hand with a club, knocking the piece of bread to the ground. I retreated. Later my mother picked up the bread and ran towards me and my father, saying, "It's clear to us where we will wind up. Please take the bread. We won't need it anymore." And those were the last words I heard my mother utter. I stared as her image faded farther and farther into the distance. I stood there frozen and holding back tears and emotions, as if my heart was being ripped out from my insides, disappearing, forever gone.

Out of the 2300 Jews from the second transport, the largest of the three, 524 men were removed. The rest–dead, sick, frail, wounded, as well as women and children and the old–they were directed to the other side by the SS officer on site. We saw the freight trucks heading towards us with steps leading up to the hold. They told the men to climb on. We saw the trucks driving up, one after the other. The men who could not make it on to the trucks were shot on the spot, their bodies loaded on to the trucks with the women and children. They told my group of five to climb into a truck. And the SS men drove us directly to the camp. And in the distance we saw the electrified barbed wire strung between the posts bordering the camp. It was still, quiet, like a cemetery. The hairs on my head stood up from fear. They drove us straight into the camp (it was 1 km distant from the train station). They jammed all 524 of us into a single barracks. They brought in a load of striped clothes. A manager along with an SS man greeted us with the following words: "You are now in the death camp known as Birkenau. You will work very long hours and have little to eat. And you will behave yourselves. You will be here three or four months, and if you can't hold up you will die.

[Page 328]

Should you have any money, gold, dollars, and any other valuables you shall surrender them directly. And now I should inform you not to inquire about your families because you will never see them again."

Later that day the assistant to the manager gave out the assignments for the camp and work details. He said:

"No one can leave the barracks. That is where you sleep. Anyone who has to "attend to his (personal) needs" will go to one of two places in the barracks and will not come in contact with anyone else in the barracks or the second camp until the next morning."

Those terrifying words, spoken in such basic and simple terms, allowed us to recognize exactly where we were and what to expect from this horrific place. We also learned precisely what fate awaited our families. We felt that sooner or later the same end game was in the cards for us.

Working in the Shadow of the Crematoria

The next morning we were assigned to another barracks. We were escorted by two block-captains and an SS man. They told us to strip down naked and leave everything in place. They shaved us clean of all head and body hair. Then they instructed us to rub some sort of fluid across our bodies that burned our flesh like fire. Next we took cold showers. Then they issued us the striped clothing–outerwear, long johns, and the striped pants, a jacket, a skull-cap of sorts, a pair of socks and wooden shoes. We were not permitted to measure the clothes for size, just to take whatever was issued. Eventually it got confusing as to who owned what. As for our previous belongings, we had no idea what happened to them. They remained where we left them.

The 524 members of our transport were then sub-divided into groups. One group was transferred to Buna and the A.G. Farben factory. The second, directly to Auschwitz. The third group was further sub-divided into two. One segment stayed in Birkenau and the second was led away by the "Sonderkommando".

The camp was hemmed in by electrified barbed wire. There were guard posts every 10 meters. Alongside the barbed wire there were wide channels infilled with water, on the inside, where there was yet another barbed-wire barrier. The SS guards had a barracks at the camp gates and entryway.

[Page 329]

Birkenau occupied a setting that was underlain by a dense, clay-rich soil. Whoever stood on the surface after a strong rain felt as if he was sinking in mud. When you tried to extract your foot from the mud, the second foot got stuck behind you. Our food rations were as follows: bitter coffee in the morning, a liter of soup by mid-day, an occasional piece of meat, and for dinner a 250-gram ration of bread with a few grams of margarine.

Inmates awoke at 5 AM since roll-call was at 5:30 and the protocol lasted for an hour. During the count we stood out front for the duration in the cold and rain. Next the block commander along with SS men undertook yet another count-off. Once the counts were completed they divided us into work details and we headed out of the camp to our work stations. An orchestra was set up at the camp gates and played marching music. As we marched out each kapo reported the number of inmates in his group to the SS officers stationed at the gate. We shared the roadway with the truck transports that streamed in and out of the camp on their way to the crematoria. We were forced to stop in place intermittently to yield to the trucks bearing the bodies for the crematoria. The crematoria were outside the camp gates; it was an empty plaza manned by SS guards who oversaw the traffic and the workings of the operation.

Our work consisted of building barracks, digging holes and drainage basins, dragging stones, and moving heavy boulders from one location to another. The inmates worked in order to clear space for additional barracks to house future inmates or even themselves as the camp expanded. All of this work was under the direct supervision of the SS. The combination of minimal food rations, back-breaking work, and the stifling air replete with the stench of death, made it clear that we were not long for this world. My Makower brethren began to drop like flies–the victims of hunger, cold, and disease. My father and I were dispatched to Buna, a camp 10 km from Birkenau. The work there was even more oppressive. In addition to harder labor and reduced rations, we were mercilessly beaten and abused over the course of the work day. We were out in the cold barefoot and almost naked and my father got frostbite in his fingers and toes. He was taken to the infirmary. After that I turned completely despondent. I grew so weary that I could barely stand up. One day as I was walking towards the infirmary ital I caught a glimpse of my father. I approached him and passed him a piece of bread.

Sometime later there was a selection. I was led off to the crematorium. I was in a group with corpses, cripples, and sick inmates and they stuffed all of us together in vehicles headed to Birkenau.

[Page 330]

When we approached the camp the SS officer told the driver to "bypass the crematorium because a new transport has just arrived. Proceed directly through the camp gates" (this was in April, 1943). So we were back in Birkenau. Those who could walk exited the vehicle. They were told to line up in groups of 5. But I could no longer stand on my feet. By that point I had grown so indifferent and apathetic that I felt I could not get to the crematorium fast enough.

An Encounter with Hometown Friends

As we were lined up together, we noticed the inmates wandering about the work-camp grounds. One fellow approached our group, looked at us intently up and down, and then approached me directly and asked: "You wouldn't by chance go by the name Motl Tchikhanover, would you?" To which I responded in the affirmative. Since I had not seen the fellow in over five months, I did not recognize him. It was Noah Vitzoker. He was holding a tin of soup, and turned to me saying "Motl, I can't eat any more of this, I have dysentery, so please take this soup and finish it. Perhaps this bit of sustenance will save you."

I took the soup from him, finished it, and licked the sides of the tin and felt somewhat revived. I could stand on my own two feet again. Noah Vitzoker stared at me with his sunken eyes and told me that there were still some surviving Makower Jews in the camp. Perhaps I would run into them and he would certainly spread the word that I was alive.

Immediately thereafter another Makower Jew approached me. He was holding almost an entire loaf of bread and said to me: "Here, take a chunk of this bread". It was Dovid Wolfovitch. "Eat", he said. I ate it lustily, tearing up as I consumed it. With each bite, I wept more, but this was the recipe for my body to revive and gain strength. I got the feeling that these two Makower Jews were my guardian angels and that God dispatched them my way to avoid death by starvation.

We stood around the cleared plaza several hours until an SS man ordered us to return to the barracks. And I met yet another Makower there–Hershl Karlinski, who was known as "the butler". He offered up some more food saying

[Page 331]

"Here's hoping that you have the strength to survive because you are young and I will take it upon myself to help you in any way I can". He went on to inform me that my mother's brother (uncle), Itcheh Segal, had been alive and well until a week ago, but then he suddenly passed.

Mass Transports

In April, 1943 mass transports from Greece began arriving. Two rabbis from Salonika were ushered into the camp in one of the groups. While they were deliberately segregated from us we were able to communicate with them through windows in the barracks. They were apparently forced to write back to Greece saying that while they were, in fact, stationed in a work camp, there was no shortage of food and drink and that they were treated quite well. Thanks, in part to these letters, the Greek Jews felt there was no need to oppose or organize against the transports. In reality, the Greek inmates suffered the worst treatments in the camps because the language barrier pre-empted communication with the Germans. They were given orders and specific tasks to fill and they did not know what was being asked of them. The Germans simply thought that the Greeks were resisting and were unusually non-compliant. And for that reason, they were beaten senseless, killed and sent directly to the crematoria.

It was around May of 1943 that transports began to arrive from Warsaw, shortly after the Ghetto uprising there. The recent arrivals mentioned that with their evacuation, Congress-Poland (the provincial population and administrative center) could now be declared "Judenrein" (or free of Jews). They also reported that Warsaw's "Umshlag Plaza"), or central dispatch center, was now the site of dozens of daily transports to Treblinka and Majdanek. During the months of June and July other towns and cities that transitioned to "Judenrein" included Bendin, Sosnowiec, and their surrounding metropolitan areas. The lone surviving ghetto was that of Lodz. All the while transports continued to arrive from places like Belgium, Holland, France, Latvia and Estonia. In general, families were slated for extermination, while the healthy males were selected out and brought into the work camps.

Henech Gromb

There was an incident involving a fellow named Henech Gromb. One clear day he simply disappeared. He succeeded in escaping from the camp along with his brother and three Soviet prisoners. Hundreds of SS men along with dogs and kapos were dispatched to hunt them down. In retribution, the SS forced the camp prisoners to stand in place without a break, while the search was in progress. In two or three days the escapees were caught and we witnessed their entry back to the camp. They barely resembled human beings: beaten to a pulp and bloodied beyond recognition.

[Page 332]

Henech Gromb himself took the blame for his younger brother, anticipating his fate (the brother was only 17 years old). About a week later Henech and the three Russians were brought out in front of all the camp prisoners. The four were led to a public space to be hanged. The younger Gromb remained in a holding cell and while he witnessed the tortuous and humiliating scene, he survived the war (he is currently living in Australia).

In December 1943 a transport from Therezenstadt arrived and the Jewish families were led directly to the camp. An SS man was brought in to serve as the block-officer for the latest arrivals. Amongst the newcomers he recognized a young woman with whom he was friendly during his school-days. One fine day he entered the camp decked out in his finest SS uniform, approached her and they ran off together. The authorities were alerted to the incident and pursued them but the two were never found.

The Endless Flare of the Crematoria

Over the course of a month there was a massive transport from Theresienstadt–men, women, and children. They were all exterminated. The barracks that housed them lay empty.

There was a barracks, near ours in Birkenau, that was populated by Gypsies. It was surrounded by electrified barbed wire. The Gypsy barracks included entire families. They appeared to have better food and were able to purchase foodstuffs somehow. The Gypsies remained in the camp for several months until one night several thousand families were led out of the 30 or so barracks that they had occupied; then they were exterminated. We saw endless clouds of smoke emanating from the four chimneys of the crematoria, that stood a half kilometer from the Birkenau camp. The crematoria ran all night, non-stop.

It was February and March, 1944 when the mass extermination of the Hungarian Jews took place. Transports came in daily and often the victims were marched directly to the gas-chambers. The crematoria ran in waves, but incessantly. The two facilities (gas chambers and crematoria) were adjacent to each other.

A camp known as "T" (letter "Tzaddik" in Yiddish/Hebrew) housed the Hungarian Jewish women and it was close to our camp. Every day when we took off for work we saw the women head out to their assignments as well. They wore pants and since their heads were shaven it was difficult to determine if they were men or women.

Block 7 (known as "the Seventh"), an infirmary, was subject to visits by the SS every second or third day. They would inspect the sick and remove the most dire cases directly to the crematoria.

[Page 333]

I myself suffered a bout of malaria. For three weeks I ran a high fever, afraid that I would be spotted and taken to Block 7, where the inevitable fate would be a trip to the crematorium.

The Lodz (Poland) Ghetto was liquidated in June, 1944. The last transport from that city arrived in our camp immediately thereafter.

The Rebellion

Birkenau had a Sonderkommando unit. The most able bodied, young men from Makow were forced into this unit and their assignment was to perform and maintain the incinerators in the crematoria after corpses were transferred there from the gas-chambers. After a 6 month term these commandos (consisting of 200 individuals per crematorium) were re-assigned to another camp where they were summarily executed to guarantee that there be no living witnesses to the horrific crimes that had been committed.

In July or August of 1944 word got out that the entire Sonderkommando unit was slated to be transferred to another camp (and to be exterminated).

At the same time the Sonderkommando personnel began to plot a rebellion in the death-camp. They decided that in the long run it was better to die with dignity–to quote the Bible "Better that my soul expire along with the Phillistines".

Preparations for the sabotage was hatched secretly over time. It was devised in conjunction with members of the Resistance outside the camp. Co-ordination was implemented through civilians who worked inside the camp but lived on the outside. And they were well paid for their efforts. There was a young woman who was actually caught by the Germans smuggling out gunpowder from the ammunition factory. The powder ended up in our hands and we buried it beneath the block floor, where Tuvia Sehgal worked. Separate groups were able to bring in powder and other materials to build improvised explosive devices. When the time to strike came, each group was notified by a designated group leader. The specific hour for the rebellion was finalized once each group had made its way into the camp. A signal was given to begin the operation. As it turned out when "zero hour" approached the organizers called a last-minute halt to the operation. Tuvia Sehgal and some of the others in the Makower group did not receive the last minute cease and desist warning and they began the operations on their end. A huge explosion went off. One of the crematoria was blown up. Members of the Sonderkommando began to take off in several directions.

[Page 334]

One of the Makower group, Hershel Kurnik, ran right into the arms of an SS officer, grabbed his weapon and began firing randomly as he sprinted out of the camp. Tuvia Sehgal did the same as did Leibel Katz, Vladek Frenkel, Yisroel Lefkovitch, Moishe Fuchs, and other Makowers in the group. They assaulted the SS men directly. Several were killed in place while others were wounded. The uprising was ultimately deemed a failure. Viewed in context however, and given that millions were murdered in the long run, it was the Makower group that initiated one of the more memorable revolts against the German enemy.

The Germans issued an alarm once they realized what had happened. All inmates were instructed to stay in place and not move, under penalty of death. The SS men themselves began to panic and some took flight. For a brief period it seemed that the situation could spiral out of control. But the matters began to stabilize shortly after the initial shock. Within minutes hundreds of heavily armed SS appeared with dogs and surrounded the crematoria complex. All inmates, including the Sonderkommando and others were rounded up and driven. back to the barracks. The SS burst into the crematoria and opened fire on the Sonderkommando. Many were shot dead on the spot and those who had taken off were eventually hunted down and killed. Some escapees who had survived the shootings were brought back to the camp. The German high command issued an order to redistribute the inmates in the barracks, to minimize the possibility of a follow-up rebellion amongst the survivors. Of those who had escaped and re-captured none ultimately survived.

By September, 1944 evacuations of the Auschwitz-Birkeanau complex had begun. Outgoing transports were unscheduled and seemingly unplanned since the Russians had begun to close in. I was on one of the transports together with my compatriots, Shloime Reitchik from Makow and Yakov Frost from Pultusk. We were packed into freight cars, together with 30 or 40 inmates. The SS, armed with machine guns, were stationed in the last car of the train. No one had any idea as to where the train was going. When the train departed, around noon (September, 1944), one of the inmates approached me and said "We should be arriving in Radom, around 8 PM this evening. At that point we will assault the SS escort, grab their weapons and kill them.

[Page 335]

This action will occur simultaneously in each car. At that point we will all disperse and take off to the surrounding woods and countryside."

Word of the planned action was apparently co-ordinated and spread across all the cars in the train. Each and every one of us was understandably apprehensive about the planned action. On the one hand, we considered that here it was, the end of 1944, we had already made it through Birkenau for two years, and just maybe liberation was a possibility. On the other hand we considered that perhaps this action itself was our best chance of actually surviving.

The Women End up in the Crematoria

The arrival time at Radom was overestimated and the train got in at around 7 PM. We had already decided which inmates would attack the SS men. But 30 minutes before "Zero Hour" the same fellow who informed me of the plan told me that the action was scuttled and that everyone should be informed immediately since we had just learned that our final destination had changed to the camp at Stuthoff. We got to Stuthoff (near Danzig) at 3 AM. We were there for about two weeks, during which time a major transport of women arrived. Peering through the barbed wires we saw that these women were marched directly to the extermination complex. It was October 1944. We saw that the doors to the gas-chambers had been locked and apparently the gassing was about to start, when an order was issued to cease the procedure and to march the women back to the camp. The doors to the gas chambers were opened and everyone was let out. At that point the SS men informed us directly that there would be no more executions by gassing. Subsequently, cremation became the disposal method for the dead, the shot, and the expired.

The Russians were closing in quickly and the Germans decided to evacuate Stuthoff as well. I together with my friends, Shloime Reitchik and Yakov Frost, were on a transport to Tubingen, close to the French border. We were taken to an airplane hangar. We joined another 500 or so individuals and were informed that this would be our accommodation while we worked in the new camp. We were led to our work stations by members of the German "Luftwaffe" (Air-force). Our work consisted of digging up huge unexploded bombs (ordnances) of American, British, and Russian origin. We loaded them onto freight trucks and they were driven away. We remained in Tubingen through December, 1944 and were transferred to a camp called Dortmeringen (near Stuttgart, Germany). There we were under Ukrainian supervision. The camp also had a significant contingent of Gypsies.

[Page 336]

While the food rations here were minimal, the work was relatively easy. As February drew to a close we were transferred to Bergen-Belsen. Our shoes had fallen apart by that time and we used rags to cover our feet. They loaded us up on freight cars for the trip. Many inmates simply expired on the trip out (my friends Shloime Reitchik and Yakov Frost stayed behind in Dortmeringen). We were assigned barracks in Bergen-Belsen. We were not assigned work details but there were no food rations either. Many more individuals expired that first night. Those who passed were removed from the barracks the next morning. We packed ourselves tightly in the barracks to keep warm. One night I literally slept on top of one of the prisoners just to keep from freezing. The next morning I realized that he was dead. They led away corpses in a procession of large-wheeled wagons, almost non-stop, directly to the crematoria.

We remained in Bergen-Belsen until April 15, 1945, the day that we were liberated by the British army.

Since my first day in captivity at Birkenau I formed a friendship with a fellow from Novidvor, near Baranovitch. His name was Leibl Chayat and he was 20 years old at the time. In Bergen-Belsen he approached me one day and said "Motl, help me, I have come down with dysentery."

I responded "Look at me. I am practically dead myself. What can I do to help you?"

Leibl responded "There is a Norwegian doctor in this camp. He has a medicine that is effective for treating dysentery but he will only accept gold in payment. Listen to me Motl, we are on the verge of being liberated. Please help me."

Now the camp was littered with corpses, in the back areas, that had not yet been removed or incinerated in the crematoria. I thought to myself: "I can survey the camp, search the corpses and perhaps I can come up with some gold. I could barely work my way through the mass of bodies, but I managed to extract some gold fillings from the teeth of victims. Whatever I got I took with me and ran straightaway to the Norwegian camp doctor. I pleaded with him to have mercy on my friend and to accept the gold that I had recovered. The doctor gave me the medicine. I took it and ran back to Leibl Chayat and gave it to him. He passed the next morning. I was completely shattered. It was a feeling of complete helplessness, followed by apathy and despair.

[Page 337]

I was 21 years old when we were liberated and weighed 30 kilos (66 pounds). I was told by an English doctor that were it not for liberation on that day (April 15, 1945) and had I not been treated immediately, I would have survived another two days at best. On Liberation Day we were completely dazed, forlorn, and hopeless. We could not even process what liberation meant.

On that same day, the SS men ran out of the camp. They passed on "authority" to the inmates.

The Liberation

Inside the camp we had been guarded by Hungarian soldiers, formerly partnered with the Germans. The British took over and kept watch on all four sides. They cut the barbed wire and burst through the camp in tanks. We hadn't eaten a thing in over two days.

The British brought in help and supplies directly. They drove across the camp-grounds in vehicles with loudspeakers announcing in seven languages "The Germans have lost the war. We are liberating you. Going forward you will receive everything you need. Please stay where you are."

And the British kept their word. The next morning hundreds of Red Cross doctors entered the camp. Every survivor underwent an immediate medical examination. I was taken directly to hospital. I was there for 10 days and when I was sufficiently recovered I got up, left the hospital and began my search for family. My feeling was that maybe, just maybe, I might find someone that survived.

The number of dead, immediately after Liberation, was enormous. People even dropped dead during the act of eating. The British used bulldozers to empty the road and pathways of corpses. They attended to the sick who could not move, and fed the survivors as called for by their medical conditions. Life at Bergen-Belsen began to approximate a new "Normal" as a rehabilitation setting.

Over the course of my searches and wandering after leaving the camp I ended up in Munich (Germany). Once there I made inquiries as to where the Jews lived. I was directed to Don-Pedro Square. Once there I found out that many Jews were housed on the second floor of a building there and I encountered a young man from Czestochowa. He delivered the good news that my father was alive and living in Feldafing (DP camp). That next morning at 6 AM I hopped on the first train heading there.

[Page 338]

I was ecstatic that my father had survived and that I was indeed, not the lone survivor in this world and that I was on the verge of reuniting with my father. I was also hopeful that there might be other family members who made it through the war.

In the train car I met yet another Makower, Yitzhak Itzkovitch, and he requested that I allow him to deliver the news that I survived to my father directly and in advance. When we arrived in Feldafing he ran to my father and informed him. Subsequently I got to my father's place and he recognized me immediately. We embraced and wept long and hard. And then I asked him: "What about mother and her sisters?" There was a long, protracted pause. I looked in my father's eyes and saw only tears, endless tears streaming down his face.

Ultimately, I made my way to Israel, under the auspices of the Jewish Brigade. I was active in the War of Independence, fighting for the establishment of our newly declared State.

In the Terrifying Years

by Shloime Raytchik / Natanya

Translated by Janie Respitz

When the war broke out in 1939 we left Makow and wandered until we arrived in Vengrov[Wegrow]. We had just managed to cross the Vishkov Bridge when the Germans began to bomb and destroy.

I escaped with my parents, sister and brother. There were already many refugees in Vengrov. It was difficult to get settled. We remained there until the Germans occupied Poland. Then we returned to Makow where we met the Germans. They had already taken over our house. It was the only house in town connected to the municipal sewer, there was a bathtub and other comforts. Clearly, the Germans took it right away. The house had two floors. They allowed us to live on the second floor. However it did not take long until the Germans removed us from there.

We moved to another apartment and tried to once again earn a living from the leather factory which we ran. Since the Germans had not yet taken it away form us, we removed the leather at night and finished the work at home in an attempt to make a living.

[Page 339]

A Commemorative Gathering for the Martyrs, 1946

After a short time we received a list from city hall and the Gestapo with my father's name on it. My father hid and on that same night escaped to Russia. Other Jews whose names appeared on that list also escaped and they were not caught. One of the municipal employees, a Pole by the name of Piontek had warned us that they were coming for my father and that he should escape quickly.

10 Lashes for Gold and Jewelry

Knowing the Germans would steal everything we decided to hide gold, jewelry and other valuables. We dug a deep hole at night and placed everything there. Our neighbour, a Pole by the name of Pigelsky, who worked in our leather factory, apparently saw us digging at night. In the morning he came to us and demanded half of our possessions. If not, he threatened to inform the Germans. We did not believe that this Pole who had worked for us for years and received an honourable salary, would denounce us to the Gestapo.

[Page 340]

Therefore we did not hand over what he demanded, what we had worked for our whole lives. Pigelsky went to gendarmerie and informed them. A gang of Germans soon came to us and told us to dig up the gold and jewelry and I had to carry the tin box with our treasures to the command centre. When I handed everything over, as a thank you, I received 10 lashes from a braided whip.

Together with my mother, brother and sister, I remained in Makow. Just like all the other Jews they captured me and sent me to work. The work was not far from Makow. I worked there for three weeks and then returned to town.

While still in Makow we received a letter from relatives saying they were going to Trieste and from there to the Land of Israel. They said we should come and take some of their possessions they were leaving behind and perhaps we too will have the opportunity to emigrate.

My parents sent me to our relatives in Warsaw. I crossed the border illegally as a gentile. I arrived in Warsaw however the plan to travel to the Land of Israel came to nought as the road to Trieste was blocked and my relatives remained in Warsaw.

In Warsaw

At the beginning of 1940 there was not yet a ghetto in Warsaw. Since we owned a few buildings, I went to collect rent rom the neighbours. They informed me they were already paying rent to the German trustee.

While in Warsaw I made use of my time and went to a trade school to learn to be an electrician. There were many candidates but I passed the exam and was accepted. At the same time they began to build the walls of the ghetto. My father bribed a Polish guard at the gate and he allowed me to leave the ghetto. I arrived at the Danzig train station, took the train to Ciechanow, and from there travelled by wagon to Makow.

By this time Makow had changed completely. You did not see any Jews on the street. Jews had to walk on the left side of the highway and not on the sidewalks.

[Page 341]

This left a horrible impression on me. I felt dejected.

My uncle Raytchik and his partners Likhtenshteyn and Hertzberg had a mill. One of their employees, a Pole, later became the manager. His brother lived in our house and brought us flour, butter and other products, of course for an obscene amount of money. All the Jews were registered in the work bureau and had to work. My mother arranged for me to work for a German who came from Konigsberg and built a new house in Makow. I worked there installing the electricity. I had permission to come and go but since the house was outside the ghetto I had to stop working there and return to the ghetto.

As I mentioned, I had permission to leave the ghetto. This provided me the opportunity to get some food for me and my family.

I believe in was the eve of Yom Kippur when they locked the ghetto, you could not go in or out. The Germans announced we were to be evacuated. They no longer took anyone to work and the ghetto was hermetically sealed. The exits were guarded by Jewish police and the Germans.

Selection in Birkenau

The wagons arrived in November 1942. The Jews were ordered to climb in. They were pushed with sticks and were beaten mercilessly if they did not climb fast enough. They took us to Mlave where we remained for about three weeks. Then they took us to the train. I climbed aboard with my mother, sister and brother. They chased us into the train cars while beating our heads and faces and shoved us in. One of those helping to shove us into the train cars was the commander of the Jewish police in Mlave. When all the Jews were loaded in, the Germans shoved him in as well. He shouted to them: "You are throwing me in? I helped you with your work. I am the commander of the Jewish police in Mlave. We worked together". They answered him in German: "Dirty Jew, get in there with the rest!"

[Page 342]

The night of December 12th 1942 we arrived at the ramp in Birkenau. The S.S man standing beside us gave an order: "Women and children to one side and all men over the age of 18, to the other side".

Standing there I had the opportunity to speak to a German. He said to me: "you will be going to a work camp. You will be able to see your parents on Saturdays and holidays".

They made us put down our bundles and line up. I saw how the German officer carried out the selection: to the right, the healthy, to the left the old and weak men. They sent me to the left. Since I saw the healthy men on the right, I ran, in the darkness and stood among those on the right. I went to the camp with them. This was the last time I saw my mother, my younger brother and older sister.

Hunger, Torture and Death

They took us to the bath, made us undress, took away our good shoes and clothes and gave us camp clothes: a shirt, a jacket, pants and a camp cap. We saw the Germans looking for good shoes.

Beside the Old House of Study on the road to the cemetery

[Page 343]

In the meantime I tore my bootleg so they would not take my boots away. There were French Jews working in the bath. One of them, Maurice, told me that among us there was someone who did really bad things and had been chief of the Jewish police in Mlave. Maurice beat him and warned him not to behave as he had in Mlave. We entered a half round fenced in barrack, 10 men to a bunk. The block elders were Jews. We were ordered to write letters to our old addresses and say we were healthy, feeling good and working. The police commander came into our Block. He was handed over to the Block leader. He received a beating every day and three days later he was suffocated.

Every morning, when it was still dark they woke us for roll call. We stood from 5 until 7 in the freezing cold and waited to be counted. Then we received some water – breakfast – in deep red bowls. I worked carrying bricks to build a building which turned out to be the crematorium. Anyone who ran away from work was liquidated. From hundreds, only dozens remained. People were broken and none other than the weak held out, in comparison to the heroes who fell like flies.

I decided to continue working as along as I could stand on my feet. I hoped that eventually I would be saved. In the evening after night roll call they distributed food: a quarter of a bread and a bit of soup which you could only receive with a beating so I never took any.

A Freezing Cold Bath, Naked

When I became sick with dysentery and had to use the toilet they did not let me go because anyone who was seen outside was shot. The Block elder said to me: "You are lucky, you are young, and that's why I'm not going to kill you".

For six months I did not change my clothes and did not wash. My skin was covered with wounds. A while later they called all the young men, lined us up in a row for the commandant to do a selection. Together with others I was sent to Auschwitz, to Block 7/A. First I was quarantined, then they took us to the bath.

[Page 344]

We washed and were given striped clothes. It was the first time in 6 months I washed with warm water and changed from dirty to clean clothes. I went to a fenced in school where they taught us to build houses. The Block elder was a German sadist. Every night he would kill a few inmates. He was obsessed with cleanliness and said he would not tolerate anyone being dirty.

They made us wash completely naked, with cold water in frost and snow. He stood on the steps and watched. If one of the inmates did not wash and was not wet, he shot him. He would take men up to the attic, pour cold water on them and kept them there until they froze to death. He enjoyed giving beatings. If you shouted, you received 20 lashes. If you were quiet and withstood the pain you only received three lashes.

I was in Auschwitz for half a year and did not go through a selection. After we completed the building course they took us back to Birkenau, to a new place where they had built the men's camp in Block 21. I was sent to a building crew. I went out to work every day. I was an older inmate, I had many acquaintanceships, even in the "Sonderkommando". (Prisoner work units).

There were many Jews from Makow in the "Sonderkommando". They helped me a lot. We received from them gold teeth and gold dollars which we took with us to work and bought bread, cigarettes and alcohol. There were regular selections. I was lucky and was saved. I worked the entire time. We built a potato market and had friends in the "Canada Crew". Boys from Makow whose work was, commanded by the Germans, to take away people's belongings when they arrived in a transport, brought us clothes, shoes and most important, food. Soon after we arrived we knew that women and children were immediately burned in pits since the crematoria had not yet been built as opposed to the gas chamber which already existed. They gassed the people then burned them in the pits. Often, when walking by we saw how they burned the people. Day and night we saw and smelled the smoke. The whole camp was black from smoke. If someone escaped we would have to stand for twenty four hours outside in the cold, without food or drink.

[Page 345]

When there was fog they would not take us to work out of fear that someone would escape. They guarded us with big wild dogs.

Early in the morning we would leave for work outside the camp, built the potato market and other buildings outside the camp and returned at night.

The Last Selection

The last selection I remember in Birkenau was in January 1944. I remember it as if it just happened. Dr. Mengele ran the selection. He declared me unfit due to a wound on my leg. The same day they transferred me to a block with everyone else who was to be sent to the crematorium. When I arrived at that Block I met someone from Makow, my friend Shloime Glogover who was the "house servant" in the Block. He encouraged me and said he will do everything possible to save me. He told me his uncle and other people from Makow were working in the crematorium and they will try to get me out. Thanks to him I succeed in leaving that Block and connected with acquaintances as my file was sent through head "house writer" in the Block. My number was 81736. I met someone from Makow who was the messenger for the head writer in the camp. He went and asked for me and returned with this response: if I gave him a bottle of alcohol, 20 gold dollars and a few other things he will try to take me off the death list. However on that day no one was permitted to leave the camp, therefore no one could bring me the bottle of alcohol.

I connected with someone else from Makow, Henekh Gromp, who had a good relationship with the Block elder, a German, (also an inmate). Through his connections Gromp brought me a bottle of alcohol. I received the 20 dollars as well and gave it to the messenger. Twelve o'clock that night I received an order to return to the Block where I was before the selection. The writer in my Block met me with the following words: "Dirty Jew, you got lucky".

Later I worked building the Gypsy Camp.

[Page 346]

There it was easier to arrange to get something to eat. My friends in the "Sonderkommando" helped me the entire time.

In 1944 the bombardments began. All night we prayed to God that the Allies would bomb the camp and destroy the gas chambers, crematoria and the Germans, even us, as long as they will put an end to the German's extermination work.

Meanwhile, we were beaten by the Germans and their people every day not knowing how or for whom to watch out for because the beatings came from all sides.

One day, we suddenly heard explosions in the crematorium. We later learned the head KAPO of the "Sonderkammando", a German inmate, sadistically treated the commandos. At a certain moment, they grabbed him and through him alive into the fire. We also received information that other members of the "Sonderkommando" who tried to blow up the crematorium were shot trying to escape.

Transferred to Stuthoff

In September 1944 they began to evacuate Birkenau. They sent me to Stuthoff near Danzig. It was then I learned there was an order to no longer use the gas chambers and crematoria. We worked in the forests. The exterminations were now carried out through beatings. They searched us for gold and diamonds. People were dropping dead.

From there I was transported to Stuttgart. We built underground hangars for airplanes at the Egenfeld Airfield. We lived in a large covered market and worked hard from dark to dark. It was cold and our striped clothes did not keep us warm. We received one bread for twelve people and a bit of water. That was our food. From there they transported us to Dartmeringen. We worked cleaning the stones outside the camp. One night they removed all the Jews from the Block and stripped us naked. Everyone underwent a strict search to make sure he was not hiding gold or diamonds somewhere on his body. The searched in the most intimate body parts. They inspected us all night and only allowed us to put on our striped clothes in the morning. We had to sleep naked not even with something to cover ourselves.

[Page 347]

From there they took me to Halach, near Dachau. There I met a Pole from our town. He helped me with food. He helped others from Makow as well.

From Halach they took us by train to Tyrol. On the train everyone received a parcel from the Red Cross, the first time since we were transported to camps. They took us back and forth on the train and we understood the earth was already burning under the Germans feet and they did not know what to do with us. We noticed the Germans were changing their clothes and running away and we felt liberation was approaching. Those who devoured their food did not live to see liberation.

Salvation is Coming

On April 30th 1944, in Stalag near Shternberg [Sheemberg], we were liberated by the American army. I did not know what to do or how to live. They told us to go, but where? I was completely broken. I walked as if in a daze. I came to a small German village. The Germans were suddenly so kind and sweet. Everyone complained about Hitler saying he brought tragedy to the Germans and all other people. First I lay down on the floor in order to sleep and rest. There were German military camps there. We broke in and took clothing and shoes. We received food from the military kitchen. We were not organized and everyone did everything on his own. After two or three weeks UNRA trucks arrived and brought us to a camp in Feldafing. There the Jews were organized according to their countries of birth. I ended up in a Block with Lithuanian Jews. There I met a fellow townsman Yakov Sheynberg and he began to take care of all of us, like a father. This is where I learnt that so few Jews had survived. Nevertheless I began wandering with the hope that I would find a member of my immediate family or other relatives.

Before I was separated from my mother she told me that if anyone from our family will survive, our meeting point would be in the Land of Israel, at my aunt Zlate Makover in B'nai B'rak. I decided to carry out her will. I immediately sent a letter through the Red Cross to my relatives in B'nai B'rak. I did not have their exact address and I wrote: "B'nai B'rak, Makover, Palestine".

My letter arrived and my cousin, Yehuda Makover, who was in the Jewish Brigade, was given the task to look for me in Feldafing and bring me to the Land of Israel. It did not take long for him to find me. He gave me military clothes and left me with his friend in the brigade. He taught me English and also how to salute as a British soldier. They took me through Paris and Brussels to Antwerp where the base of the brigade was situated. I stayed there for half a year as a "co – soldier" at the expense of the English King. From Antwerp I went to Marseille and from there, with the second Aliyah, to the Land of Israel. My relatives received me warmly. I lived with my aunt in Rehovot, the Avrahami family. I lived there as if with my own parents. For half a year they did not let me work. They wanted me to rest. I found work in the electric company where I still work today. I got married and now have two children who I named after my parents. Let the chain continue.

In March 1948 I volunteered to be mobilized in the Palmach and fought in the War of Independence. I participated in the battle to conquer Beersheba and Eilat and was released after two years with the rank of sergeant major.

[Page 348]

Number 81434

by A. Eisenberg

Translated by Janie Respitz

The number 81434 is burned on his arm.

He was born in Makow. He was a student at the "Yavneh": School. He was called Motele, in Birkenau they took away his name and gave him the number 81434.

In Israel his name was returned to him. He is called Mordkhai Ciekhanower. You can see him every morning coming to work. A tall man with broad shoulders and blond hair, light blue eyes. There is a quiet smile on his face, because he knows that when he arrives at the office he will give work to the unemployed. This was a part of his life, helping those who were suffering.

[Page 349]

When he sees a number on someone's arm he sees before his eyes, Auschwitz – Birkenau.

He was brought to Auschwitz when he was 18 years old. The young Motele, a quiet Jewish young man was carrying a knapsack on his back. Among the things his mother packed for him were his phylacteries and her steaming tears.

When they threw him into the camp at Birkenau he saw these were the last boundaries of life. He arrived there with a lot of Jews but only few remained.

This terrifying scene stands before him: a child's cry mixed with the words: "I want to go to my mother"… A German releases his dog on the child. The dog runs, he is its prey. But the dog stands before the child and looks at him in his eyes. Even the murderers were moved with this scene. Another shout: "Bite"…But the dog does not bite. The German shouts at the dog and the dog looks at his chief and at the child. One shot, another shot. The dog and the child are thrown onto the heap of corpses…

…Motele is in the Block. The Block KAPO says: "This is the death camp Birkenau. People only last three months here. And after? Do you see the chimneys?…"

Time had no meaning. Why wait 3 months? Day, night, there was no difference. You received soup, a piece of bread, roll call, again to the right, to the left. There was more space after every roll call, place for new victims.

Another few months. Motele is already a "Muselman". Wooden rattles, shaved hair, striped clothing. Hard labour. All signs of humanity are gone. He looks like the other "Muselmen" wandering around. Downcast eyes. Open mouths. Lips whisper and quiver. Limp bony hands. When you hear a word spoken it is: "bread, a bit of soup"…

One thought chases the other away. His father is not here, his mother and sister, burned. What is there to live for?

A selection. Dr. Mengele and a couple of other murderers observe Motele. He pretends to limp. Mengele calls out: To the right.

"I'm asking for left" says Motele.

"Dumb kid, your body is clean, you're young, you can still work for the Wehrmacht".

[Page 350]

"I want to go left" cried Motele, "Left".

"Good, go left. That way leads to the crematorium". And suddenly another transport appeared.

"We must kill them first" shouted an S.S. man. "Yours can wait two hours".

Another voice: "whoever feels well should come work with us". Motl turns his face. A group of 30 Jews were standing at a distance. They were wearing clean clothes and looked much better. One fell and couldn't eat his soup. Motl finished it.

Motl is with these 30. They are the roof workers crew. Unknowingly, Motl takes a piece of wood from a broken wagon to repair a roof. He hears a shout from an S.S man: "Sabotage, what is your number? 81434. This means death!"

Mordkhai comes to the Block and takes his mother's pack with his phylacteries and clutches it to his heart. He begs God for a quick death.

They call his name. Everyone looks at him with compassion. They say goodbye with their eyes. Mordkhai is in the punishment house. His hands and feet are tied. Two robust murderers beat him with leather whips braided with lead. "Take down your pants!" But before he can even think: "One, two, three, four, it irritates, it burns. No, he can't count anymore. Suddenly he feels a pain in his back. Darkness before his eyes. He becomes cold and wet. Those beating him poured water on him. The 100 lashes must be recorded with German accuracy.

"Stand up!" the beaters laugh, "you withstood this, you will not burn. Quick, run!"

Until today he does not know where he found the strength to run. God only knows. He lay for three days. After, he worked on the roofs. During the day he inhaled the smoke of thousands of souls.

On hot summer days or calm winter days, when the smoke did not rise to the sky, but fell to the ground, men and women would go out from the camp, stretch out heir arms, absorb the smoke and shout:

"Father, mother, my child, my soul! May your smoke at least rest in us". Bony hands embraced the smoke, hearts breathed deeply.

He remembers a night.

A Jew suddenly cried out: "Jews, why are you sleeping? Come out and bless the new moon. God has given us four moons. Come out, look at them in the sky. Do you see them? I do".

[Page 351]

And he laughs out loud. He shouts: Sholem Aleichem! Greetings". A bullet silenced him forever.

"This I will never forget" said Motl.

The suffering flowed and time stood still. Again day and again night. Again sun and again darkness.

When they ripped his nails off his hands with pliers he remained silent; when as S.S. man threw him off the roof for sheer entertainment, he remained silent; he was even silent when he listened to the laughter and crying of dying Jews. However he stopped being indifferent when he learned an act revenge was being planned.

Spring 1944. He was sitting on the camp roof. It was noon. He knew something was supposed to happen today. Suddenly, a powerful explosion! It was the most beautiful sound he heard in his life. Sirens began to wail. People were running and shooting. Concentration camp inmates were chasing Germans. The Sonderkammando were fighting bravely. A short yet bitter fight. A pure Jewish battle organized only by Jews. KAPOS were running, S.S men were shaking. Jews were shooting.

The flame coming from the crematorium was bright. The smoke was different. Oven number three will no longer burn Jews. Hershl Kurnik from Makow runs by, grabs a machine gun from a German and shoots him on the spot. He runs until he is hit by a bullet. There is Leybl Katz and Tuvia Segal. They are fighting with their fists, knives in their teeth.

That day Mordkahi became a new person. He too was prepared to die in battle.

At they end of 1944 they brought them to Bergen – Belsen. It snowed the entire journey. The roads were covered with dead people. Airplanes were bombing. A thought: which liberation will come first, perhaps by a bomb?

April 1945 – liberation. Motl is 21 years old and weighs 37 kilos. His blond hair is now white and grey. There is a hole in his shoulder. A number on his arm. His heart is empty, life has been extinguished. He is lonely in Munich. What next?

[Page 352]

"Meir Hersh" he heard someone say, "I brought you a visitor" said a city Jew.

"Father, you don't recognize me?"

Two people embraced each other, trembling and crying for along time.

"How did you get of hell?" the father asked his son Motl.

"Noyekh Visoker's soup saved me" said Mordkhai, "and you?"

"Ask God" replied his father.

Sitting, Mordkhai examines the number on his father's arm. He reads it and turns pale. "81433. This is my number father, 81434". Is this a coincidence?"

Today father and son live under the blue skies of Israel. He is free and has a family. However those horrifying experiences in the death camp oppress him. He cannot forget.

This is why he has done everything to ensure that at least a portion of that terror will be recorded in this memorial book for future generations. He witnessed everything that took place in the death camps.

It was as if he returned from the after life.

And he, Mordkhai Ciekhanower, could not be at peace until this book saw the light.

[Page 353]

The Holocaust and its Lesson

by Rafael-Tzvi Baharav, Kiryat Motzkin

Translated by Naomi Gal

To the memory of our city Maków-Mazowiecki Martyrs, May Their Memory be Blessed

Time is pulling us away from those horrible days, from the dreadful days of staggering atrocities and in order to avoid forgetting them we are committed to remember and never forget, so we need to tell ourselves time and again what happened to us back in those ghastly days, so that their memory would stay with us and with all future generations.

For this important goal here are the things to remember:

The grisly massacre that the *defiled German people* performed on us with the assistance of their henchmen and their allies is so sordid it is impossible to measure, the human mind cannot begin to fathom the diabolic horror and cruelty of those events. It is shocking that this massive murder was done in front of the whole world, undisturbed, and even those who were not directly part of the slaughter, were accomplices all the same, since they saw us bleed and *did nothing*. It is a fact that in every country where the German murderer arrived, there were people of these nations who helped the German murderers and assisted them exterminating the Jews. And the slaughter was scientific. Educated people, decorated with academic degrees, planned and executed it; writers, poets, artists, musicians. And the benefit of this murder-factory was two-folded: sadistic satisfaction and huge compensation for these murderers, enriching the vaults of the German treasury and their henchmen's vaults as well.

The long road of suffering that led our sacred victims to their last station of death is soaked with tears and blood.

Locked in ghettos, hard-labor, systematic starvation, torture of body and soul even the devil could not envision - everything was calculated so that the sadistic murderer and his henchmen in the conquered nations would *quench their thirst* by their satisfaction of humiliating men to no end; shattering everything cherished by them, beating and kicking, slaughtering children in front of their fathers and disgracing daughters in front of their mothers, abusing women in front of their husbands and children, and other calamities the human language cannot even speak about.

In extermination camps, where gas chambers were built, millions of martyrs were granted a so called "Humane" death, that *German science* invented for them.

It was not always the same way in some of the Polish towns or other countries conquered by the Germans; there the tortured and starved martyrs were taken outside the town, were forced to dig deep pits and then their clothes were stripped, their hair cut for the mattress industry in Germany, their gold-teeth extracted from their mouths, and soldiers opened fire on them with their guns. The wounded fell into the pits and before they died another group of Jews were brought, shot and fell on top of the first wounded ones. And so, one layer upon another, a third, a fourth, a fifth – one layer on top of another until the long pit was filled and a group of Jewish undertakers was ordered to cover the mass grave with earth to hide the signs of this horrific murder that was executed precisely and quickly.

[Page 354]

A grove named after the Martyrs of the Maków Community in the Martyr Forest in Jerusalem

[Page 355]

Later on, big machines were sent, the mass-graves were opened and the bones were grounded to dust which fertilized Germany's and Ukraine's *earth,* that was *soaked with blood* and from the *marrow* of the victims flesh, they made soap.

"HaTzofe" – March, 1964

The fate of Maków, our city, was the same as for all of Poland's Jewry; a third of the nation drunk the Nazi poison and was sucked into the vortex of the cruel and diabolic sea-of-blood, and our nation was swallowed and disappeared.

For the elevation of the souls of its martyrs and victims I want to mention in order to illuminate their praise and glory, that they were faithful and innocent, believed with all their hearts, they were modest and honest in their ways of life, they kept Mitzvot and paid their dues to God and others[society] equally. And although they were busy with mundane tasks like modest living and striving for their livelihood, they took care of each other, the same way they took care of themselves. Hence, they established charity and assistance institutions and helped every needy and poor soul; services that in those difficult years were far more important and necessary and because of their importance should be mentioned by name. The ones I remember are: "Talmud Torah" for poor children; for free, a hospice for poor and sick people who had incurable diseases (Hakedsh); "Hachnasat Orhim (Welcoming Guests) for poor visitors, "Hachnasat Khala", "Pidyon Shvuym", "A guest for Shabbat", "Giving Anonymously", "Boxes" Charity Galore and to R' "Meir the Miracle Maker" and the "Tzedakah Company" and others; these establishments were maintained by donations and contributions and could only exist due to the generosity and charity of the majority of Maków Jews. Even those who could not afford it, deprived themselves to support these charitable institutions. We should also remember the public activists who worked diligently and persevered with their generosity for no personal rewards.

They lived by the principle of modesty, Maków Jews were satisfied with basic necessities that they earned honestly and justly, they were happy with their destiny and their concerns were their faith, their dreams, their hopes and desires- to see their off-spring blessed and productive, becoming an honest generation to live peacefully and harmoniously- these were their treasures.

Due to its merits and advantages, our city Maków gained a good name and despite being small, it was famous as a place-of-Torah, due to the Yeshiva is sustained and was known as an organized community with charity and assistance organizations, for being quiet, serene, and blessed with fresh air, which was healthy, Maków was dear and beloved by all its citizens.

Hence, the sorrow and pain are great for the loss of this excellent community that was furiously swept away, decimated and gone. How the heart aches and breaks for the fate and the bitter end that came at once upon its sons-citizens, the pure treasured souls, among them my late brother Shraga Faibel, his wife and their household, and all my relatives, who were led like sheep to the slaughter and were slaughtered, murdered, shot, burned, suffocated in gas chambers, exterminated and drowned in the sea of blood of the Nazi inferno and were not even granted a grave, lost forever. With them went the gifts and the talents and their ancestors' legacy, the sacred spiritual skills and valued cultural treasures, assets and labor of many generations – everything annihilated with nothing left, only a deluge of suffering, terrible tragedies and a sea of tears.

[Page 356]

Although we are getting further away in time from those tragic days, days of destruction and horror, which we did not experience since we became a people [creation of the state of Israel] – still the blood of the martyrs' screams, demands vengeance proclaiming their blood that was shed freely like water, proclaiming their tortures, sufferings, insults and shame – this demands justice from the known and the secret murderers who were not yet punished. And as long as the nests of the [home]base blood-thirsty murderers are with us, multiplying and growing, as long as the contaminated and defiled hand of the Nazi monster has not been amputated – the blood of the martyrs will not be quiet and will not know peace.

This horrible shocking tragedy, that has no similar one in the history of the world, nor in the painful history of our people [who knew difficult afflictions, sufferings and experiences] – more than asking for revenge and retribution, it warns and alerts by sharing this bitter lesson about the duty and responsibility we have to safeguard our country, the fortress of our revival, our safe haven; to strengthen and reenforce her, because only in her strength, our exitance, safety and future are guaranteed. And in face of the empowerment of our enemies our duty is even greater to concentrate all our efforts and energies to increase our power and achieve this with all our dedication and as fast as possible, so that all our scheming enemies who want, God Forbid, to destroy us, would be thwarted. We have to be diligent and keep the most treasured asset we have, the essence of our existence, which is our country, our homeland, that will save us from extermination and guaranties our eternity, which our generation was granted, something that generations before us did not have. We should repay her for all the good and blessings she bestows upon us and thus, we will keep the testament of the innocent martyrs, and with their martyred deaths, sanctified heaven and Israel, and with their last "Shema Israel" commended us to cherish life and peace.

May the memory of the martyrs always beat in our hearts and prompt us to good-deeds and blessed activities, and energize us to rally all our forces to the sublime aim and goal of building our nation in our homeland. Thus, we might find consolation to our broken hearts and Israel's Guard will assist us. We will dwell safely in our country, we will extol her, and renew our lives like it was in ancient times, and the name of the sacred martyrs will be memorized and become known and famous. May their lives be bundled in the bundle of eternal life of the nation.

Kiryat Motzkin - 1965

[Page 357]

Makow in Ruins
A Visit to Makow, Right after the Holocaust

by Yehezkiel Itskowicz, Tel–Aviv

Translated by Anita Frishman Gabbay

At the Warsaw bus station there was an never–ending tumult and it was still dark outside. I was overcome by a feverish expectation and a considerable amount of alarm.

I was standing at the bus–stop, on my way to Makow and remained in a corner, so to be less visible and–God forbid–not to be recognized. Just like a criminal, as one who had escaped from jail.

We started moving, [as for my luck], perhaps the bus will not reach its destination. The memory still pains me, how to hide my face, when daylight appears. My neighbour is already asleep, like a dead person, snoring heavily. His head leaning on my shoulder, as if I were his best friend. The rest of the gentiles around me talk among themselves, laughing. One of them recounted joyful anecdotes and every time a spontaneous laughter broke out. I don't have any patience to listen to their conversations. Although I'm curious to know the thoughts of the Makower Gentiles, what they are speaking and joking about in these days [post war].

My thoughts are intertwined with much anxiety. Something is disturbing me, like in a mill [possibly in reference to wheels spinning]. The early morning, grey light, is piercing slowly through the darkness of night and with every minute I notice, daylight is arriving. I pull out a newspaper from my sack and open it. As much as possible, I hold it with my two hands, so that my face is hidden from all sides.

1937, Toz–colony [camp] for children

[Page 358]

In an hour and a quarter I arrive in Makow, my town, which fate forced my expulsion of nearly nine years– torn from my home, father–mother and my nearest ones. During the stormy years I wandered through many lands, through forests and scorched steppes, over oceans and continents: years of longing and drudgery, in poverty and in work–camps. But my home, my town, I never forgot!

I heard and read about the barbarism and murder that descended upon my town, descriptions of survival, about their martyrdom.

My brain couldn't comprehend this. I now arrived in Makow, so that I can see with my own eyes this destruction.

We drove into the town. My blood is pulsating to such a tempo, as one who is condemned to death, when a bullet will hit him at any second.

The bus turned right, then left and stopped. My neighbour in the meantime awakens. He crosses himself, opens his mouth with a wide yawn.

I descended from the bus and stood confused– not knowing what is happening to me. My eyes are confused and I can't orientate myself. Where was I? I continued, not knowing where and for what?

All around me there was an empty void with mounds of rubble. Such a sight of where all the houses of study used to be, the Hasidic Shtiebels, the party–headquarters of all the youth organizations, to which I looked forward to participate [with such enthusiasm], in their various problems and decision–making.

[Page 359]

Orzyc River

Nothing remained! In a dead cemetery, our Jewish Makow lies motionless! Almost our entire market–place is buried in rubble.

[Page 360]

I approach our steps. How sad and bitter–darkness surrounds us! Shall I enter my house? Shall I even encounter anyone?

I knock at the door. A gentile with naked feet and wild hair looks at me with frightening eyes. She doesn't say a word, as if she lost her tongue, she wants to say something, but something is not allowing her. She motions to me with her hand to sit down, and calls her husband (Bundkovski) from the other room. A face appears before me. It becomes clear to me.

He looks me over from head to toe and with intentional flattery invites me "to go to the second room".

— "I remembered you at once"–with a fake smile–"where are you coming from? Mrs. Itzkowicz? We heard rumors that you were burned in Auschwitz"…

I tell him briefly where I came from and want to know the fate of my family?

He pulls his pipe out of his sack, makes himself comfortable and lights his pipe. He says to me:

— "I helped your parents, with whatever means possible. I basically put my life on the line for them…but you know, Mrs. Itzkowicz, what type of hooligans the Germans were… the fate of your parents was the same, as the fate of all the other Jews of Makow "…"yes!"–he continues–"I have something for you."

He gets up and tells me to remain for several minutes. I remain in the room alone. I remember every corner, every piece of furniture, various images spin through my memory. The same tapestries with flowers are on the walls. The same dresser, the table…even the same iron hooks sticking out of the walls, on which our pictures used to hang: here was the picture of my parents, there across, –my sisters. In the corner our old fashioned gramophone was still standing…everything remained in its place. Only the *character* [ambience]of everything died. Like the fate of my family…

Soon the peasant returned carrying something, wrapped in a piece of newspaper.

— "You see"–he says to me–"I hid this for many years, especially for you…take this and remember, who gave this to you."

I thank him and impatiently unfolded the newspaper wrapping: I held before my own eyes my father's Holiday–Prayer Book [Machzor].

[Page 361]

A shiver tore through my bones. Tears formed in my eyes…with nervous gaze and nervous movements I looked at the book, as if I could find their last words among those pages. Perhaps their last wish…I now see ink writings. As a young girl I wrote them.

The pages are yellowed and moist. Who knows? Perhaps from tears…I felt, I can no longer remain in this house. I thanked him and bid them farewell.

With the *machzor* in hand I returned to the bus.

It is still nearly an hour until we depart. I feel completely broken and depressed. I wanted to collapse and break down in tears. But how can I do this in front of the goyim?

My feet dragged me unknowingly. I threw stares in all directions, as if I were inhaling all the sights. My mind wanders over the half–forgotten pictures of my former, dead world. Here I recognize signs of the boulevard, where I used to sit and read. I recognize every corner, every small piece of grass, each concealed lane. Once the blooming acacia trees secretly adorned the benches and, their aromatic smell made us dizzy , aroused tears… from the secrets of so many lovers …these same acacia–trees, once upon a time overheard?…

I approach the known river.

Ozycz, my dear one, my old friend, how well I remember you! Times before, in the summer–days, on your green shores, without worries, without angst, I spent my time wild and free– playing! Reflecting in your blue crystal clear waters. In winter–on your frosty glass body–dancing on the ice with joy. Now nothing remains of my former feelings[life], only memories ..perhaps now you can remind me! Perhaps you can reveal some secret to me. My dear river?

Boringly calm the river Ozycz continues to flow in its direction. The swallows swooping down and kissing you with their tiny beaks– rushing, fluttering, circling over head. They are lazy and agitated now, as if they were screaming[lamenting] the great–cry of woe of the destructon of Makow. But perhaps they say instead, together with me, the "*Yisgadal v'yisgadash, Smei Rabba*"[magnify and sanctify–memorial prayer] for the tragic– murdered Jewish souls, of the Makow community.

May their memory be blessed!

[Page 362]

A Visit to My Town

by Moishe Katz / Tel Aviv – Jaffa

Translated by Janie Respitz

After years of bloody slaughter and suffering
I had the good luck to be in my town
To my town, my Makow I returned
With a quivering heart, and astonishment before my eyes.

The people looked with curiosity at me,
At my soldier's green uniform.
The asked: who is he? From where did he come?
Why is his face so bitterly deformed?
A soldier should be proud, always ready for battle and look,
He walks like a drunk…

The people sense my piercing glance,
Which drills into them with accusation. They pull back.
My heart is aching, my mood is bitter –
Are there really no Jews left here?

I see my home in front of my eyes;
I touch the walls with trembling fingers,
I run up the steps and knock at the door,
A dismal nightmare is chasing me.

A strange woman stands before me
And does not let me into my house.
I hear some laughter from the other room
Which carries me into a dark pit.
Men and women dressed up fine,
Flowers on the table, cakes and wine;
Glasses are lifted for luck and joy,
Their celebration is disturbed by my piercing glance.

[Page 363]

They ask with amazement what I desire,
Perhaps I'd like to drink some wine?
Soldier, please, sit down at our table –
The cake is delicious, sweet and fresh.

I do not respond, my glance is focused
On the wall where my grandfather's picture hung.
And now on that wall
A strange image hangs.

Here is the bed, the mirror the chair.
This is where I felt my mother's affection.

And there in the corner the clock still stands
And calmly tick tocks the time.

A woman is laughing heartily at my side,
As they are accustomed to fine manners.
And here stands a soldier, impudent and wild,
And looks at the wall, as if crazy and dazed.

Why has he come here? One asks very boldly,
He's walking on our carpets in dusty boots.
A woman laughs heartily by my side,
And the clock over there continues to beat out the time,
The time that beats me with suffering and shame
And I clench my fists of my hardened hands.

Why does she laugh so poisonously, why stab with your
glance?
This is my home, my room and my joy;
This is where my yesterday blossomed and bloomed –
Why do you your eyes stare at me so?
The bed and the mirror did not cost you a thing,
This was my for–father's labour with blood and sweat,
This is where my mother and father stayed,
Oh God, who chased them from here?

[Page 364]

I gave you freedom, after all, by means of battle
So you can live here sweetly with a comfortable life.

The men and women draw back
My heart is bitter, my glance now dark.
A force is pulling me toward the door
The dismal nightmare continues in me.

I run from my house in sadness
This ends my visit, my joy.

[Page 365]

A Matzevah
[Headstone]

by Tsirl Bejlem (Aczech)

Translated by Anita Frishman Gabbay

If a Jew survived the Hitler–Years, together with his parents–it was a rarity. Not many Makower families were saved. During the war, when we met a Makover or heard about one, we became overjoyed. Such a small thing: A Makower! The "*rich*" one who possessed a piece of bread, divided it with his *landsman*[those coming from the same town].

Many from Makow escaped to Slonim (White Russia). We couldn't get any lodging there. I went to Slonim several times and each time I spent the night at Mordechai Blum's. Everyone offered to help, but it didn't happen and I endured many heartaches that we couldn't be together with the Makowers.

The end was, very few managed to survived in Slonim and Michashevitch, where we lived. I remember, going to Tashkent in 1941, on the sixth vaksel?, I met Yolke Grozman. What joy: A Makover! I was the "rich" one then. I gave him a kilo bread and he continued on his journey.

When my father discovered that a Makover was here in Arkhangelsk [Russia], the family of Alter Burstein, and Avrahmel Kviteika, he immediately sent them a parcel of food.

After the war, my husband and my daughter, then only 1 year old, left for Sweden. Being there we searched for Makovers. Through Yankel Segal, in Germany, we discovered that Rochel Blum was in Sweden. I immediately wrote to her and she invited us to visit, but it was impossible to go because we lived far away from her. There were approximately 200 refugees in Sweden, I was the only one that didn't need to be an "orphan" because my family survived.

My luck didn't last long, 3 months after arriving in America, beginning 1954, my dear father died. I was very depressed and thought, "I will not survive this". I survived and became stronger. Four years later, I lost my beloved mother. In those days my younger sister, Tema, became sick. One year after my mother's death, my brother Avigdor in Australia died. And 3 years earlier, after 6 difficult years, my sister Tema died prematurely– all the survivors o the Holocaust.

[Page 366]

Several years ago we began to speak with our *landsmen* about a Yiskor Book. At a memorial service for Makow in New–York, Rabbi Shmuel Hilert and Yacov–Chaim Sobel, spoke and praised the worth of such a book, a memorial for the martyred souls and remarked, that no money in the world could suffice [the sacrifice] and there will never be a more meaningful memorial–as there are no graves to visit. The only way is to memorialize their names is in the Makow Yizkor–Book, all the souls from our destroyed community.

[Page 367]

At the Day of Mourning

by Rafael-Tzvi Baharav, Haifa

Translated by Naomi Gal

At the day of mourning, suffering and terror, to the prophet- listen.
Do not strain your voice with crying and spare your tears,
Stop being melancholy and lamenting;
Your pain will not pass, your sorrow and suffering will stay intact;
Tears are precious, but they cannot extinguish the fire, the flames.
Look, your tears are falling on an arid rock,
They will not soften a hard heart-of-stone.
Stop crying, no one hears you cry, nor sees your brokeness;
Wipe your tears so that Amalek, the enemy,
Would not amuse himself with them, would not rejoice and gloat,
Would not see them as weakness, lack of strength,
Look, here is the hater, the corrupting devil, sharpening his weapons,
Sharpening his sword to devour you,
And he is so close, relentlessly threatening and horrifying.
Hence, be awake and agile, to beat him, to quickly win,
Disperse his soldiers, amputate his serpents' heads, behead them,
And if you are just a few, no matter, you had already proven,
And more than once, that not quantity but quality counts, that is decisive!
And you have the advantage of knowledge and talent, and thus, victory is yours.
To be safe come together, unite, be all as one, no one should be amiss.
Do not ask, nor demand honesty and justice from evil villains,

Whose eyes are for greed only, their hands to steal and robe, their mouths
lie, and their tongue is poisonous;
And not from the wayward, scheming and harboring intrigues,
Who turn justice into injustice, law into lawlessness, and jury into injury.
You will forget the help of others,
they have no interest, no need of you,
we recognized them in the horror days when your blood was shed like
water,
when you were tortured, murdered and burned
and they watched indifferently, idly.

[Page 368]

 They did not nod their heads, did not look, did not open their mouths
telling the murderer: Stop,
Since they had no profit nor use – why should they care about rivers of
blood, the love of the sword?!
Yes, without a shred of conscience, feeling and responsibility,
They proved the lie, the hypocrisy,
And to increase suffering and sorrow, they now add insult to injury,
They distance themselves from us, they are evasive, they approach our
enemies,
They turn their backs on us, deprive us from help,
And our haters-enemies they enrich by billions,
Purifying the vile.
If any help, only from loyal, devoted and sincere friends, and if non are to
be found, be ready on your own,
With all your strength, might and courage,
With all your experience, knowledge, the fruits of your brain,
Like a hero gather your power, and with your strong arm teach Amalek
your enemy his lesson,
So that he will know your force and recognize that you can defeat him,
disperse and expel him.
Trust your power and your just fight,
Be sure of your victory,
And with the help of the God of Israel you will succeed,
Achieve the aspired and desired goal,
In your homeland, complete rest, peaceful life, and true security.

Kiryat Motzkin, April 28, 1963
Yom HaZikaron

[Page 369]

The Road of Agony
From Poland, Russia – Until Israel

by Ruchl Pomeranec, Haifa

Translated by Anita Frishman Gabbay

September 1, 1939, Friday morning, I suddenly heard yelling and screaming coming from people in the streets. I left my house, and one of the first I met was a Christian, Sobieski, who told me the horrible news while was crossing herself and with a crying voice said: "God, we are doomed. The Germans invaded us, the war has begun!"

There was a panic in town, some people ran to Warsaw. They immediately mobilized the young men. Among them was my brother, may he rest in peace. The next morning, we heard planes overhead and all the men still remaining in Makow were ordered to leave the city– to go to Pultusk, to enlist in the military. My husband Chaim, together with his brother Yacov, and with many other men, departed for Pultusk. But they were not taken into the military due their age. So they continued to Wishkov and then further to Wengrow. When the Germans approached this area, they ran away to Ostrowa. The Germans caught them and put them in prison for several days and later freed them. They made their way back to Makow, by foot. The Germans by that time invaded all of Poland. The mood in the city was very strained. With fright and worry we awaited the following day.

Lawlessness in All Areas

Several days later the Germans declared, all the Jews must present themselves, 8 o'clock in the morning, in the market– place with their belongings, only what one person can carry. I locked the house, gave the key to a neighbour, a Christian, and left with my husband and children to the marketplace. Here I met all the Jews of Makow. A German officer gave us a speech– from this day on, all the Jews are surrounded. Only those that want to leave for the Russian border–they can be given permission. In the marketplace, wagons[trucks] were ready to drive the Jews to the border, only a small number went with them. Most held back, as no one believed, that such a disaster will descend upon us. Some men, as some said, left, and left "temporarily" their wives and children at home. This is what happened to me. My husband gave the key of the bakery to the magistrate. And afterwards, they didn't even want to take him back as a worker in the bakery, he then decided to depart for the Russian side, to see what opportunities awaits, and later bring over his family. With heartache and pain I departed from my husband and remained behind with my children.

[Page 370]

In the meantime life in Makow became more difficult and dangerous. Every day brought new troubles and new decrees. Also the border–crossing to Russia was closed. By some miracle I managed to break through and together with my children we arrived in Lomza where my husband was. Later we went to Bialystok, life there, like for all the refugees, was very difficult. We were, nevertheless, comforted by being together, and eventually, in peace–time, we will return to Makow and meet again our dear Jewish and Christian friends of Makow .

Command to Seize Soviet Territory

At a given time in Bialystok, it was proclaimed– all "refugees" must register and report if they want to become Russian citizens and receive Russian passports. Or, if they want to return home, to the Germans. Most of the Makowers in Bialystok wrote they wanted to return home, despite, knowing what awaits them back home. We didn't want to receive passports out of fear, because this meant, they will never allow us to return home. On the contrary, the Makowers, who lived in Lomza, most of them took Russian passports and they were resettled in Slonim. Among them was my brother–in–law Yacov Pomerantz with his brother and family.

Those, that reported to return, included my family. At night they took us from our home, loaded us with our meagre belongings onto electric–wagons, and took us in an unknown direction. We rode for days and nights until we arrived in *Kotlum* [maybe Kolyma]. There they deposited us onto barges and distributed us in different regions. For weeks we *swam* and then *rode* endlessly. Contact with my family in Lomza was cut. We encountered many problems, especially loneliness and pain along the way.

[Page 371]

Our place, where they dropped us off, in Severnaya, in the U.S.S.R. by the White Sea, is where we were forced to start a new life, in the cold of 60 degrees Celsius. Winter was 8 months, and the short summer we were covered in mosquitoes, which simply tore pieces [of skin] from the camp–workers. Many workers froze as they worked in forestry, at cutting trees. This was actually the only work there, under inhumane conditions. We ate *kasha* [porridge] and fish soup. Also for this humble substance we had to pay by working the usual labour in the forests.

Fortunately, my husband was able to secure work in the bakery and thanks to this our life became somewhat easier. We had a piece of bread and some flour at home. I supplemented as well, by helping many people with flour and bread. And we almost got arrested because of this. Half a year we lived in this Siberian "*Gan–Eden*" [Paradise], isolated from the world. Not knowing anything about the war. We lived with the security that perhaps God himself will have pity on us and bring us a miracle and deliver us from this hell. We didn't know at this moment what was happening to the Jews of Poland and Makow.

We Are Released From the Work Camp

One day we received an order to be released on the orders of the regime, which General [Wladzyslaw] Sikorski and the Russians agreed to. They provided wagons and allowed each one of us to go wherever we wanted. All the Jewish–refugees decided to go to warm places, to central–Asia. On the way my children became sick and without medicine, we had to stop in Kyrgyzstan. Many people got sick on the way, many died along the way. We arrived in a kohlkoz [*collective farm*] with our children and some others. We arrived at a clay hut. My husband broke down and immediately became sick. I had to attend to a sick husband and children. We didn't have any means. Each time we had to sell another piece of clothing to meet the basic necessities of life. We fed ourselves with grass and soon remembered the "*good times*" of Siberia.

Later, when my husband and children recuperated, we started working in the kohlkoz, but we couldn't manage to make ends meet from this work. There was not "*enough to live and too much to die*".

[Page 372]

Then my husband was mobilized into the Soviet Army. I was left alone with my 5 children. My life was a chain of torment and hardship. I didn't know what to do. But God gave me the strength and I survived until the end of the war. In 1946 my husband returned from the army and thus enabled us to go to Poland for repatriation. Immediately after crossing the Polish border we received a "*reception*" from the Poles. They threw stones at us, into our wagons, where we were sitting. Seeing the reception of the Poles, we immediately began rethinking of leaving this land, the sooner the better, which abundantly produced the crematoriums and gas–chambers in which Jews were murdered. We temporarily settled in Szczecin and enrolled the children in "Gordonia". The Polish regime at the time still tolerated these Zionist organizations. After some time we managed to cross over to live in Germany, where the *road* was easier to reach Israel. We settled in Ulm and the children left to learn a trade and study Hebrew.

We Are Leaving For Israel

In 1948, when the state of Israel was created and the war with the Arabs began, my eldest son volunteered to enlist and was immediately sent, through various routes, to Israel. Arriving in the Land he was mobilized and fought for Jerusalem. I went to the agency in Germany and asked them to allow our family to join my son in Israel. Here they told me that my youngest son will go first, then the remaining family will join them [both sons] later.

The second son made Aliyah and they sent him to kibbutz Ein Harod, shortly after we also arrived in the Land. At the same time my eldest son was free from army duty, my youngest came home often from the kibbutz and slowly life became more normal. We settled in Haifa, our youngest son joined the military where he excelled. He also played the accordion in the air–force orchestra. We were very proud of him. But this luck didn't last too long –

[Page 373]

August 24, driving from home to the base in a military vehicle, a severe automobile accident occurred where my son and other soldiers were killed. This misfortune broke us completely. Even today we can't fathom the loss–we looked after him in all the difficult years of wandering, from Siberia to central–Asia and when fortune came, and we arrived in the Jewish homeland to begin a new, dignified life, this tragedy suddenly befell us. My only comfort, though, that makes the heartache somewhat easier, that my son died in the Jewish homeland and is buried in this holy land.

אימפאזאנטע הזכרה נאך די קדושים אין מאקאוו און אומגעגנט

מאנטיק דעם 15־טן דעצעמבער 1947
(אור ליום ג בטבת תש"ח) זיינען זיך
אין פירסטענפעלדברוק ביי מינכען צו־
זאמענגעקומען די "אודים מוצלים מאש"
— דאס על פי נס ניצול געווארענע
רעשטל פון דער אלטער, מיוחסדיקער
פוילישער קהלה ואם בישראל מאקאוו
און איר אומגעגנט וואס איז היינט צו
טאג צעשפרייט צווישן די שא"הפ אין
גלות גרמניה. כדי אין א נאענטער
סביבה באערן דעם הייליקן אנדענק
פון די טויזנטער מארטירעריש אומגע־
קומענע בני־עיר.

נאך מעריב און יאר־צייט קדיש
וואס ווערט דורכן גאנצן עולם געזאגט
בציבור, ווערט דער אפיציעלער טייל
געעפנט דורכן אנגעזעענעם לאנגיערי־
קן מאקאווער גבאי, טויער (היינט פרעז.
פון מאקאווער לאנדסלייט אין דייטש־
לאנד) ה' אברהם גארפינקעל וועלכער
לאדט איין אין פרעזידיום די ה"ה:
פרעז. סימאן צוקערמאן און ראזענ־
בערג (פאריס. פונעם ארטיקן יידיש;
קאמיטעט). די לאנדסלייט: י. מ. דא־
ביעט י. סעגאל. ש. שילדערניין (מא־
קאוו). גויהא (רוזשאן). הענדעל (פול־
טוסק) אריאס (פראשניק) און גלי־
קאווסקי (ראזשל). ביי א שטילקייט
וואס ווערט אפט איבערגעבראכן דורך
ספאנטאנישע געוויינען. ביי דער טונ־
קעלער שיין פון די "יזכור"־ליכט הערט
דער שטייענדיקער עולם אויס דעם
"אל מלא".

ה' שמחה שולדענריין זאגט: אין אט
די פאר אונדז הייליקע הזכרה־מינוט,
באהערשט אונדז אלע דא. די פארבלי־
בענע. איינזאמע זאנגען פון נאכן בלוי־
טיקן שנים. דער איין און איינציקער
אימהדיקער געדאנק. אז נישא שוין
אויף אייביק אונדזער היימישע משפ־
חהדיקע ערה. אפגעמעקט און מינדעסטן
שפור אונדזער יידיש שטעטל. חרוב
געווארען מאקאוו. חרוב געווארן א
מאמע־שטאט פונעם פאלק ישראל ביי־
זאמען מיט אירע פילצאליקע שוועסטער
קהילות פון מזרח און מיטל אייראפע.
נאבן אלגעמיינעם איבערבליק איבער
מאקאווער אלטערטימלעכער קהילה
אירע מערקווירדיקייטן. רבנישע גדולים
און פערזענלעכקייטן פון וועלט רום
ווי ר' נחום סאקאלאוו. ד"ר יעקב אראנ־
סאן, רעד. בן־ציון בילינאוויטש א. א.
דערמאנט דער רעדנער דעם לעצטן דור
מאקאווער בעלי־בתים חסידים. בעלי־
מלאכות און אינטעליגענטן. וועלכע
האבן באשיינט דעם נאבעלן נאמען
פונעם מאקאווער ייד בכל תפוצות הגולה
באזונדערס אין א"י. נים דערלעבט
האבן אונדזערע בני־עיר. די אויסגע־
טרוימטע נחמת ציון! דעריבער וועט
דער אויפריכטיקסטער תקון פאר זייער
הייליקן געדעכעניש זיין — מיטבאטיי־
ליקן זיי אינעם אויפבוי פון ציון. נאכן
אויסטערים פון די לעבנגעבליבענע מא־
קאווער יונגט־אקטיוויסטן פלאטוי און
ווישניא. ווערט באערט דער אנדענק
פון די בני־עיר. אומגעבראכטע נאך
אין נעטא אויף דער מאסן־תליה אין די
טרעמבלינקער און אשוויענטשימער גאז־
קאמערן. מיט באזונדערן יראת הכבוד
ווערט דערמאנט דער געוואגטער אויפ־
שטענדלערישער פריוו. פון די העלדן
מל"צ הרב לאנגפוס טוביה סעגאל.
באשע פלאטקא תי"ד א. א.. וועלכע
זיינען אבזרייתדיק אומגעבראכט געווא־
רן, גרויס אנזען האט ארויסגערופן דער
בריוו פון דעם בן־עיר ד"ר קאציאק.

דער פארשטייער פונעם ארטיקן קאמי־
טעט ה' צוקערמאן דריקט אויס זיין
מיטמיטגעפיל.

די טרויער־אקאדעמיע ווערט געשלא־
סן מיט התקוה.

יש. בן חיה.

Recognition of the martyrs of Makow and surroundings
Jewish newspaper, 1947

[Page 374]

I See You, Mother

by Yehezkiel Itskowicz

Translated by Anita Frishman Gabbay

In memory of my bereaved mother, Sora Leia, of blessed memory

I see you, mother, your small eyes, with unknown glare,
When you embraced me while sucking at your breast,
You covered my heart with a red ribbon.
Stroked my head and caressed my skin.

I see you, mother, at the side of my cradle
When you sang a song to suppress my crying,
With practical symbols for my confort, goats and sheep.
Until I became tired, and plunged me into slumber.

I see you, mother, in your present condition,
How you treat me, your only son, taking my hand to Cheder,

Your face shining with joy and hope,
Seeing this great pleasure, which you had lived to see…

I see you dressed and decorated for the holidays,
Your face shining with pleasure, with joy without end,
On the day of my Bar–Mitzvah, you blessed me and cried
With tears of pride, the whole world is yours…

I see you, mother, in the days of my youthfulness,
When throughout my destiny, you worry and ponder
For my tomorrows, various plans are weighed
And in the middle of the web–our dream is shattered…

I see you, mother, in the days of the horrible days of thunder,
When you blessed me to continue on my road,

[Page 375]

Hearts were torn, between hope and longing…
The last hot kiss that separated us both.

I see you, mother, from a faraway place
Where murderers killed you with rifles and swords,
Your eyes diminished with pain and sorrow,
Your face is tarnished like the color of lead…

I see you, mother, when you grind your teeth,
From your daily struggle and constant pain…
Your lips murmur: woe is me
Forget not, my kaddish[heir], take revenge, my child.

I see you, mother, so clear…so good.
Among the clouds in heaven, you float in blood.
In storms I hear your laments, your weeping…
In fire, I see you how your soul continues…

[Page 376]

A Tombstone for my Town

by Moishe Katz / Givat Aliya, Jaffa

Translated by Janie Respitz

Makow, my small Jewish town,
Where I spent my youth;
The place where my dearest were murdered
And the children were slaughtered in front of their eyes.

I will plant a tree in your memory,
A tombstone for your communal grave,
Arched by the blue sky by day
And with the starry eyes of children at night.
I hear the voices of my beloved as the wind blows,

Their secret conversations through the rustle of the leaves
And in the sad song of the bird among the tombstone leaves
We hear the cries of suckling children.

In the early morning with the sun rays on the dew of
surrounding fields
The brightness of the children's eyes, the stars, disappear.
With them – the drops of dew on the trees – their tears.

[Page 377]

Who Has Not Swallowed Tears

Translated by Janie Respitz

Who has not swallowed tears instead of bread,
Who has not wrestled every moment with death,
Who has wavered every day from hunger and cold,
The you who does not know – oh, cruel world!

Who has not crawled on all four over the wet ground,
Who has not had his life cut to pieces with a sword,
Who has not thirstily given up his last aspirations,
The you who does not know – Oh, a weary cursed life!

Who has not dreamed about a longer darker night;
Who has not cursed God, His world with all its splendor,
Who has not blasphemed His Torah and His commandments,
The you who does not know – Oh, almighty God!

Who has not spent months and years on life's deepest decks
Rolling to the end of the abyss, without a shore
And did not lose the last – the only shadow,
The you who does not know – Oh, world, oh life, oh Satan!

[Page 378]

At Dawn

In memory of my parents and dear brothers

Translated by Janie Respitz

At dawn spitting flames
A black rooster crows.
Jews, young and old together,
Prepared to die!
A lovely morning arrives
With bloody steps,

A thorn bush burns in the desert.
God is hiding…
On the roads lie slaughtered sunny demands…
There was life but it is now broken –
Is anyone sorry?
Heavily weighed down and without strength
We plod along the road.
The murderer lies in wait,
Sharpening his axes.
The first springtime swallows circle –
Behind barbed wire.
Corpses lie in the houses
God is hiding…
Springtime laughs
In a flower – hat…
Corpses lie in the streets,
Jewish blood is flowing.
Spring was accompanied by hot fever…
We know where we are going –
Crematoria. Mass graves.
Thirst and hunger death…
A cricket sings on the road

[Page 379]

The song of a dead miner.
He recites the blessing for the dead
The Jews dies.
He lays a sunbeam on the road
Stretched out like a worm…
The spring spreads out webs
On the fresh graves.

[Page 380]

Only your gaze remains

Shmuel Burstein / Netanya

Translated by Mira Eckhaus

Dedicated to the memory of my teacher and friend
the late Reb Avraham Yitzchak Zilberberg one of Makow's hollies.

I will still remember you
in the land of Jordan and Mount Hermon,
you and your gaze
on that last Yom Kippur,
before your extinction, you and your people.

* * *

In those days, when you returned from Ger,
wrapped in silence and loneliness,
I felt unconsciously
in the Holy Spirit that dissipate from you,
in the stream of longings that flowed from your heart.

* * *

I saw you then wrapped in tallit,
praying ... and I opened my eyes,
and I saw your inner world, the holy world.
Your gaze has penetrated me, and your world wrapped me
and since then I have no rest.

* * *

Look, rivers of trouble that flooded me
did not wash away your gaze!
The flame of anguish of life did not burn it!
With renewed force
it dominates me.

* * *

Tonight I saw you in my dream,
standing by the Orzysz River,
and your penetrating gaze passed through me
even more forcefully.

* * *

I will still remember you
in the land of Jordan and Mount Hermon.

Netanya, 26 Elul, 5722

[Page 381]

[Page 382] Blank

PERSONALITIES AND IMAGES

[Page 383]

The Memorial Prayer Kaddish for my Friends

Your tragedy is as large as the sea, who will heal you. Lamentations 2:13

by Yakov Khaim Sobol / New York

Translated by Janie Respitz

It is simply impossible to comprehend that the majority of my friends are gone. It is hard to make peace with this fate, that they are no longer among the living, although I think about them at every opportunity. They appear before me and I see them and talk to them. However the bitter truth is that they were brutally murdered. All that remains are the memoires of the past…

Who can one forget? Can one just wipe away almost 30 years of life? The longing tugs and my heart aches.

We were raised from childhood together, lived together from our days in Heder, later to other schools and then communal organizational life, always together like brothers and sisters, like the children of the same parents in our town, where we lived, celebrated and dreamed of a better tomorrow. Now they are gone.

The great destruction (Holocaust) arrived. The Nazi murderers, without any pity or human feeling killed them, burned and gassed.

I do not know if the traditional Kaddish, mourner's prayer, is appropriate for so many pure, holy martyrs…

They did not die a natural death. They do not have tombstones. Only their ashes soar through the air demanding salvation of the soul and demanding that we never forget.

In all the Holocaust literature we have not yet seen the modern Jeremiah, the appropriate mourner who will cry for all the martyrs, the annihilated children, the future and hope of our people.

[Page 384]

I am doubtful if I will be in a position to list all of them, but I will try to remember at least a few:

Who can forget!

Yakov Khaim Goldshteyn, the dark haired charming young man, an intellectual, a magnificent speaker, who for years held a respectful place in the leadership of "Hechalutz", "Hechaluts Hatziar" and other cultural organizations.

Meir Fishl Likhtenshteyn, the successful businessman who ran his father's business and was always ready to help others. He was the permanent treasurer of "Hechalutz". No trace of his family has remained.

In a postcard written at the time he cursed the day he was born. This shows how terrifying his troubles were.

Itche Segal, the simple Itche, who could not speak loudly, was a regular active member on the committee of "Hechalutz".

The committee of "Hecahlutz Hatzair", Makow, 1928

[Page 385]

Hershl Vaysberg, the talented artist, who enriched and brightened all Zionist events.

Sender Hertzberg, my Heder friend, an active worker in YIVO and the Folk University. He was immersed in Yiddish literature. His entire family was killed.

Khaim Leyzer Freshberg, a son of sickly parents, an active member in "Hechalutz", and one of the founders of "Hechalutz Hatzair".

Yosef Krukever, filled with wisdom, had great organizational talents, the permanent treasurer of "Hashomer Hatzair", honest, precise, and worked closely with Berke Hendel of blessed memory.

Khaim Borukh Segal, had a great sense of humour, always prepared with a joke; always made everyone happy and entertained us all.

Henekh Blum, my school friend, a great and serious student. He left to study in Belgium and was killed there.

Moishe Rozenberg, (Shmuel the writer's son) my Heder friend. A quiet boy fluent in many languages. He ran his father's office (writing requests).

Yosef Shamovitch, the talented Yosl, with a great sense of humour. He was an employee at city hall. Not a trace remained of him or his family.

Moishe Yehuda Preshberg, the simple, sincere, gentle Moishe Yehuda, a devoted Zionist. It was never too difficult for him to fulfill a Zionist mission or work toward the Zionist goal.

Yakov Yedvabnik, the devoted worker in the Sholem Aleichem Library and an active member on the committee of the Jewish National Fund.

Yakov Likhtenshteyn, an intelligent quiet student. He was one of the first students to receive a diploma. Later he became a teacher in the state public school.

Leyzer – Khaykl Preshberg, the simple Khyakl, a devoted member of "Hechalutz", never refused to participate in a flower day fund raiser for the Jewish National Fund. He regularly attended all meeting of "Hechalutz".

Frida Vengerko, aware and well read, she secretly attended meetings "Hechalutz" against the will of her orthodox father. She was a member of the committee and led a group of young girls.

Alteh Hendel. (Berke's sister), modest, gentle intelligent Alteh, who led a group in "Hashomer Hatziar". She was also a member of the committee of the Jewish National Fund.

[Page 386]

Esther Piekartchik, beautiful, smart Esther, wise and intelligent. She was a regular member in "Hashomer Hatzair" and sat on the committee of The Jewish National Fund.

Yente Shnayderman had a beautiful voice. She enriched all Zionist programs with her singing; she was a devoted teacher and educator in the public school.

Kaytche Vilenberg (Vaysberg), beautiful Khaytche with her sweet smile. She always worked for the bazars for the Jewish National Fund.

A group of members of the "Yugnt" ("Youth") movement in Makow in 1924

Feyge Rivka Raytchik (Garfinkl), the beautiful blond woman who always helped out at the Jewish National Fund bazars.

Gitl Ostri, the intelligent quiet Gitl. She later worked as a cashier at the Jewish Cooperative Bank.

Feyge Soreh Glogover (Kurkover), the charming Feyge Soreh led a group at "Hashomer "Hatzair". She never refused to participate in a flower day for the Jewish National Fund.

Basheh Platko, an intelligent student, a great martyr who took revenge on a Nazi murderer. Her name will be eternalized among the heroes.

[Page 387]

Who can forget the beautiful youth of Makow? Although most of them did not have higher education, they had inborn intelligence and were autodidacts. They were talented and active in all areas and played an outstanding role in cultural and communal life in our town.

Who knows what personalities they would have become; who knows how large their contributions would have been to Jewish cultural life.

The loss is immense. We will never forget them!

Magnified and sanctified be God's great name…(First line of the mourner's prayer).

[Page 388]

Makow in Heaven…

by Rabbi Ben – Zion Rozental / Chicago

Translated by Janie Respitz

During the great destruction (the Holocaust), pious, spiritual Makow was tragically annihilated by the German murderers together with all the pure Jewish souls from our town. I have taken upon myself the task to write about the great personalities who influenced and led our Jewish community, those who contributed to the spiritual, religious physiognomy and shape of Makow and to where Makow stood among the other Jewish communities of pre–war Poland.

When I received a request from Mr. Yakov Sobol, general secretary of the Makow Association in New York, asking me to participate in the memorial book which people from Makow in America and Israel were preparing for publication, I thought it would be a very difficult task. He asked me especially to dedicate my article to the dear holy souls of the orthodox portion of our town who were so closely connected to me in the religious life of our town. This was a difficult duty for me as I had to bring back to life, in my memory, all my former good friends with whom I prayed, belonged to the same organizations and worked together for Torah and Judaism: in "Agudas Yisroel" in the Heder "Foundations of the Torah" and in "Beys Yakov". We studied Talmud together at the Ger little prayer house every Thursday night. Oh, how hard it is for me to describe such dear, holy Jews, our devoted friends. We were so completely devoted to God's word and educating the new Jewish generations to continue on the same path as our ancestors. When I remind myself that they suffered such tragic deaths at the hands of wild murderers, may their names be blotted out, some at the sacrificial alter in Treblinka and Majdanek, how could one not break down, how can one stop from wailing? Oy vey, what has become of such pure souls!

Not even a single bone has remained from them, their ashes have spread over seven seas. Perhaps, I thought, it would be better for me not to write about them so that during my thought process I won't, God forbid, have any doubts about my faith and the creator of all worlds. But I thought it over and I remembered the commentary about Isaiah the Prophet and Hezekiah, saying we should not ask questions. Therefore it is my obligation, if there is no one else, to give a review about these beautiful Jews, the "face" of our town which they represented.

[Page 389]

The "Beys Yakov" School and the girls from Agudas Yisroel in Makow

And perhaps, I thought some more, this is part of my goal in life, which God willed, that I will be the only one that can share this with future generations. To tell them who these Jews were and what they accomplished. If not now, when? And if I don't write now, when will I have the opportunity to leave some memories about these holy men from our town. Let these lines which I will dedicate to all those who I remember serve as a memorial for these holy souls eternally. Let this be recorded for future generations of Makow Jews everywhere, wherever they live. Let this be passed down to our children and children's children.

[Page 390]

Let them learn how the elite of Makow lived and how they tragically died.

Rabbi Yitzkhak – Zvi Adelberg of blessed memory

It is worthy and proper that I first write about the spiritual personality of our last rabbi of blessed memory, Rabbi Yitzkhak Zvi Adelberg, may God Avenge his death, who was a close friend of mine. We studied together in the first years after my wedding when I still lived with my father in law Motl Yismakh of blessed memory. He arrived in town to be our rabbi the week of my wedding in 1933. He came from among respectable rabbis in Poland: he was a scholar and knew the language of the land – he spoke a beautiful Polish. I remember when he gave a speech in the middle of the marketplace from the balcony of Meir Ostre's house in Polish, the gentile neighbours were amazed. Also, when the cardinal from Plotzk came to Makow, he went with the delegation, led by the head of the Jewish community Mendl Klyen and welcomed him with bread and salt and made a blessing in Polish before entering the town. His sermons, which from time to time he would deliver in the large House of Study made a great impression.

He was a great community worker in town, both in religious and social spheres, helping people in need. He was a student of the great rabbi Rabbi Tuvye Gutentag (Tovyami) of blessed memory, from Sochotchin[Sochaczew], who was a Talmudic genius and was known throughout the world by the title of his book "Tel Yisroel". The Makow rabbi was the son–in–law the Yablon rabbi of blessed memory. We left town together on a Sunday, the first night of Slikhes (prayers of repentance) in 1939 after the Nazis arrived. I never saw him again.

Unfortunately it is not known where he and his dear family, his wife and seven children, were killed. May his soul be bound among the living. May God Avenge his death.

Reb Yisroel Segal of blessed memory

Reb Yisroel Segal was the most respected Jew and Hasid in the Ger Hasidic prayer house. He was the president of "Agudas Yisroel" in Makow. He was also a member of the executive of "Agudah" in Poland. He was a student of "Avnei Nezer", Reb Areymele Sokhochover[Sochaczewer] of blessed memory. He did a lot of work for the Heder "Yesoday Hatorah" ("Foundations of the Torah"), and everyone came to him for his opinion on Jewish matters. What can I say about Reb Yisroel Segal? He was a clever man and you could consult with him on all matters, both spiritual and secular. He was a successful leather merchant working all week in Warsaw and returning home only fro the Sabbath. Nevertheless, he never let a page of gemora or the writings of Maimonides out of his hands. You could discuss the most complicated passages with him. He would sit at many arbitrations, with many rabbis, and interpret difficult rabbinic lawsuits. He was a regular at the table of the Ger Rebbe of blessed memory, which was considered a great privilege not many obtained. He came from Mlave. His father was Khaim Shmaya, the esteemed teacher, of blessed memory. He married the daughter of Reb Zalmen Urlik (Zalmen the tanner). At the start of the war we met almost daily in Bialystok and spent a lot of time together, telling each other our problems, how we escaped from the Nazis to this part of Poland which was captured by the Soviets. He was alone then, without his family. Later, when they sent us from Bialystok to Siberia in 1941, I never heard from him again. Right after the war I met his son Shmuel Dovid and one of his grandchildren from his eldest son Reb Leybl who got married in Ostrove. They now live in America, in New York. They are carrying on the traditions, thank God, of their father and grandfather.

[Page 391]

Reb Shimon – Khaim Khilinovitch of blessed memory

Reb Shimom Khilinovitch[1] and his wife Bas –Sheva of blessed memory were people who did not live at all for themselves, but for others. They earned a respectable living from their poor store. If anyone needed help they neglected their business and busied themselves with helping that person. They both had dear, good souls. He had an important father, Reb Notele of blessed memory the head of the Makow Yeshiva.

[Page 392]

After his father of blessed memory died, Reb Shimon Khaim ran the Yeshiva. He was a student of the Kovner Rebbe and studied with Reb Yitzkhak – Elkhanan of blessed memory, but he was a Ger Hasid. We were very close friends despite a big age difference. He was charismatic. Our friendship did not take age into account. May their souls be bound among the living.

Reb Aron Bulman of blessed memory

Reb Aron Bulman was dear Jew and a respected Hasid, and guarded every word he said; he taught the daily page to everyone, read from the Torah in the small Hasidic prayer house, had a difficult life in the years before the war, but this man accepted everything with love, was always happy and lived with great faith in God. He had no demands from the Creator. May God avenge his death.

Reb Pintche Toyman of blessed memory

He was a nice young man of illustrious descent, the grandson of the Nowy Dwor Rebbe of blessed memory, and related to the Ger court. He was one of the guards of the Ger prayer house. "Language of Truth" by the old Ger Rebbe of blessed memory, was his main source. A word from the last Ger Rebbe or a letter received by the Hasidim was a holy treasure for him. He would walk into a fire for a word from the Rebbe. He was the director of "Beys Yakov" and spent a lot of time travelling to Ger, to the Rebbe of blessed memory. May God avenge his death.

[Page 393]

Reb Eliezer Likhtig of blessed memory

Reb Eliezer Manker was the father–in–law of Reb Pintche Toyman. He was a member of a prestigious family, the Sherentzker Rebbe's son, a passionate Jew. He would give away his last groshn to perform a good deed. On the eve of Sukkot he would buy his own Etrog and Lulav even though he should not have spent the money on this good deed as he would not have enough money left to celebrate the holiday with his family. He was a great Talmudic scholar and was able to study day and night. He was always preoccupied with Torah. His children had good reputations in town and in Poland.

May his soul be bound among the living. May God avenge his death.

Reb Yerukham – Fishl Munkarsh of blessed memory

Reb Yerukham Munkarsh, my uncle, Reb Bezalel Vilenberg's son in law, was a man with a large Jewish heart. There was never a time when someone asked him for a favour and he refused. Not willing to help someone was not part of his nature. He was a dear soul of good character, gave charity with an open hand, above his means. He came from the finest family in Nashelsk. The Pultusker Rabbi of blessed memory, Reb Meshulem Koyfman, the well–known genius of the previous generation, was his in–law. His sister was the rabbi's daughter– in–law. The Zamosc rabbi, Rabbi Blum, was related to them. Reb Yekhiel – Fishl died with his entire family among all the martyrs of Makow.

May his soul be bound among the living. May God avenge his death.

Besides all these nice Jews from the Ger prayer house, Hasidim, community workers, and Torah scholars who stand before my eyes is Reb Avrom Yitzkhak, my teacher from Heder. He was a young man, a righteous man. He sat every Friday night in the prayer house until midnight and studied with my uncle Dovid Zomerfeld, Bezalel Vilenberg's son in law, may their memories be blessed. The rabbi and genius, the righteous Reb Dovid Hendel of blessed memory was also a teacher in Heder and was the son in law of the righteous Hasid Reb Moishe –Yosef Garfinkel of blessed memory. He became the rabbi in Volyie, near Warsaw after the death of his great father the Rabbi and genius Reb Avrom – Aron Hendel of blessed memory. His father also came from Makow. He was my brother in law's uncle, Reb Elazar Hendel of blessed memory, who is also no longer here with his family. May God avenge his death.

My uncles, Moishe Vilneberg and Yisroelche Vilenberg of blessed memory, were very charitable people and supported Torah study with an open hand and guided their children down the straight path.

[Page 394]

The Mizrachi Jews from the Amshinover Prayer House

Rabbi Velvl Feyntzeyg from the Heder "Foundation of Torah" was a learned Jew and a Hasid who came from Ostrove, where the Feyntzyeygs were one of the most respected families in town. In 1934, after the death of the rabbinical judge Reb Shmuel Yosef Rozental, he was a candidate for the position of rabbinical judge in town. He was the candidate from the Hasidic side but he lost to the other side whose candidate was Reb Shmuel Yosef's son in law, Rabbi Langfus of blessed memory, who was married to the daughter of the judge. He remained the judge in town until it was destroyed. Reb Khaim Dovidl Melamed was a righteous Hasid and modest although he was extremely knowledgeable in Torah and was very devout. He always had a smile and a kind word for everyone. May God avenge his death.

Reb Kalmen the ritual scribe[2] was a Jew who understood the world and was known in many towns for his accuracy and protection of his holy task of writing Torah scrolls. He was very learned and devout.

Reb Yakov Leyb Ablodziner of blessed memory was one of the most respected Jews in the Hasidic prayer house. Even though he was a merchant and a busy man he studied a page of Talmud every day.

And Reb Meir of blessed memory and more. May got avenge their deaths. May their memories serve as a blessing.

The Polite Jews from the Alexander Hasidic Prayer House

My father in law, Reb Motl Yismakh of blessed memory was a successful merchant whose word was always trusted. He was not capable of telling a lie, fooling someone or swindle. He was loved by everyone and as was very charitable. Who ever would come as an emissary for the Rebbe of Alexander, or for the Yeshiva, they always stayed with my in laws of blessed memory. My father in law was a man of virtue and had devoted children. May their souls be bound among the living.

Reb Sender Beker of blessed memory was a great Talmudic scholar, always studying Torah. He was highly respected for his knowledge and devotion. My uncle Reb Yosef Vilenberg who died a few years before the was, among the most important men in the Hasidic prayer house. He gave a lot of charity for holy causes in town and all around.

[Page 395]

Reb Manes Ingberman, the town beadle also prayed at the Alexander Hasidic prayer house. He was a dear Jew whose children were geniuses. His son, who was a rabbi in America was killed in the catastrophe when an airplane flying to Israel over communist Bulgaria and was shot down. He was a young man. They spoke about his ingenuity in all the Yeshivas in America and his great scholarship. There were more noble Jews from the prayer house. May God avenge their deaths.

The Jews of the Mishnah Society

I would like to mention the extraordinary good Jews from the "Mishnah Society" with whom I studied Talmud for years, every day upstairs in the large House of Study.

Eliyahu Dovid Rishelevsky was a man of virtue. He brought the following with him from Lithuania: Reb Shmuel Rozenberg (Shmuel the candle lighter), a dear Jew; the Freshbergs, Sender, Gedalyie and Moishe and his father. Hardworking Jews. All week they travelled to the villages to do business, but they never missed a Saturday or Sunday to come learn and listen to Mishnah or bible. Of all the other Jews from the House of Study who are racing through my mind, the dear Hillel Shaynberg of blessed memory, a great scholar. He would tell me that even though he was a "Mizrachi" he still studied a page every day from the "Agudah". He was a Lithuanian Jew who followed the Shulchan Aruch (Code of Jewish Law). He was the brother in law of the great Zionist leader Nokhem Sokolov of blessed memory. They were both sons in law of Mrs. Dobeh Segal, who if I'm not mistaken had her estate in the village Podesh near Krasnosheltz where Nochem Sokolov lived with them after his marriage in Makow. At the same time he founded a bank, but due to financial reasons had to liquidate. Then he left for Warsaw and founded "Hatzfira". His biography is known to all.

It is worthwhile mentioning a very important Jew, an Amshinov Hasid, Reb Yakov Dovid Hendel of blessed memory. He was a great scholar and spent a lot time learning in his older years. He had good children who held respectable positions in town.

May God avenge his death.

[Page 396]

I hope I will be forgiven by the families of the martyrs, who were among the religious and pious, but I have forgotten to mention here. Everyone should understand that after so many years, and experiencing so many troubles and suffering of my own, it is impossible that the angel of forgetfulness would not control my memory. As much as my memory serves me I accepted this holy obligation to remember these holy souls and I beg forgiveness from all the others and God forbid, they don't think badly of me, or that it was, God forbid, intentional not to mention them. It was only because I do not remember and I ask forgiveness.

It would not be a complete or correct picture of religious life in Makow if I would not show appreciation of these two men: one was a Hasid who was not only well known in Makow, but in the entire region, and perhaps throughout all of Poland for his religiosity, devoutness and good heart. And the second, the wealthiest man in town, who was known for his philanthropy which he displayed his entire life.

Although they left this world before the war broke out, I would like to say words about them from the prophet Isaiah chapter 57: The righteous perish and no one takes it to heart". Both of these righteous men died before evil befell upon us.

The first was Moishe Yosef Garfinkel of blessed memory, or as we called him in town "Moishe Yosef the baker". When I came to Makow Reb Moishe Yosef was no longer among the living. But when I was a young student at the Yeshiva in Warsaw, on the eve of Rosh Hashanah I wanted to travel to Amshinov. I simply did not know which train to take. A man with a gentle appearance came to me and said: "come with me little boy".

Boarding the train I noticed he felt he was already at the Rebbe's. He took off his overcoat and under he was already wearing his Sabbath sleeping jacket. He took out a bit of schnapps and some food. I was also in a different mood swept into another world. When we were in Amshinov I found out who this man was: he sits in Amshinov for weeks and does not leave until the Rebbe calls on him and then tells him to go home.

[Page 397]

He comes to the Rebbe just before Rosh Hashanah and stays until the interim days of Sukkot.

Once, his wife came and went to the Rebbe shouting and asking why her husband was sitting there: "the work in the bakery cannot continue and it is too difficult for me to run the business by myself". It was also like this in their home. He would pray all night, sometimes until midnight, and when he had time to leave the bakery he would bring poor widows, the sick, weak poor people who did not have anything to eat, baskets of his baked goods and distributed them to the needy, saving many from hunger and destitution.

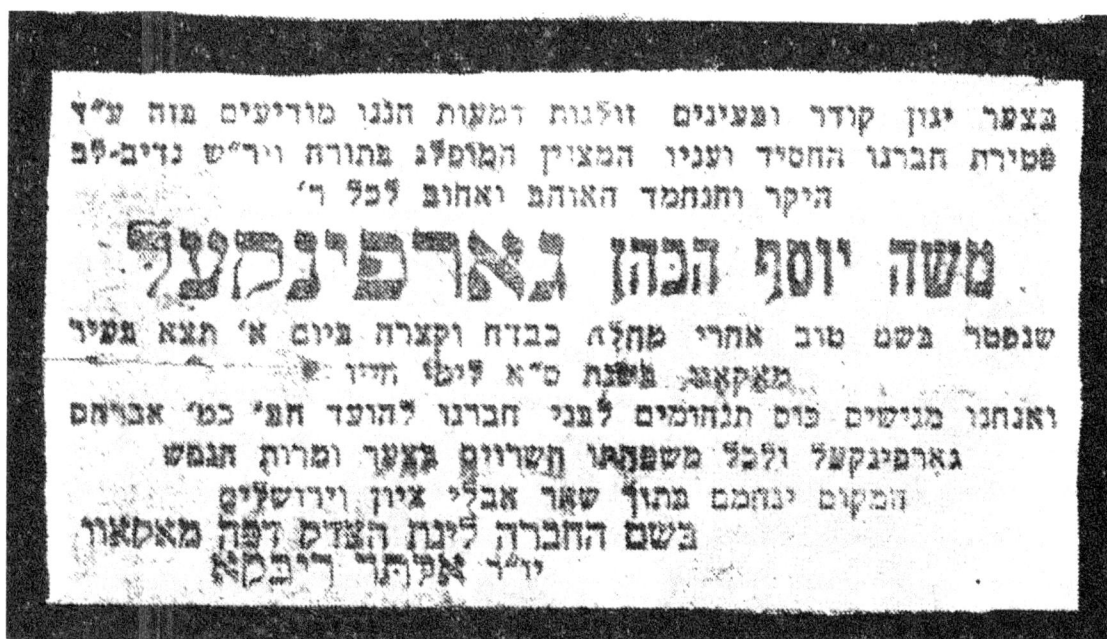

The obituary of the deceased Reb Moishe Yosef Garfinkel of blessed memory

[Page 398]

Avryml Malakh the tailor, who was a passionate "Bundist" once told me the only religious Jew he respected was Reb Moishe Yosef the baker. He said that when he learned of his passing he felt they snuck someone out of his household.

This was the type of man Reb Moishe Yosef of blessed memory was. May his soul be bound among the living. May he be an intercessor on behalf of his children. They should be proud to have had such a father.

Reb Bezalel Vilenberg of blessed memory

He was a rare man. I don't know if you would find another like him among one thousand men. He was the wealthiest man in town. More charity left his home than the rest of the town combined. Every Wednesday and Thursday, the poor people in town would receive a few kilos of flour from him for the Sabbath. This went on for years. All the profits he earned from Passover flour he donated to the "Beys Yakov" School. The smallest Jewish sigh moved him. He would always help someone get back on their feet.

I am a witness as I was present when one day when the Broker Rebbe's grandson, Reb Eliezer Broker of blessed memory came to town to collect money. When the old man Reb Bezalel saw on Friday, the eve of the Sabbath he was wearing a torn coat he went to his closet and took out his new silk coat and gave it to him as a gift. He wore his old one.

Every important guest that arrived in town was the guest of Reb Bezalel Vilneberg, room and board. Every week he would send flour to the Radziminer Rebbe of blessed memory in Warsaw to feed the children in his Yeshiva. He was the most trustworthy person in town. He was entrusted with all the dowries, even without writing them down. When the Makow Society in America would send aid, especially on the eve of Passover to distribute among the poor for Passover Matzahs the money was sent only to Reb Bezalel Vilenberg. He was not only the Jews who trusted him but gentiles as well.

When the farmers would com to town on market days to sell their grain, they would not do business with anyone until "the grandfather" came out to the marketplace and offered a price, because they were sure the "grandfather" would not try to cheat them even out of one groshn. Before he arrived at the marketplace he would call Warsaw and find out the price. Then he would calculate how much to pay for the wheat.

[Page 399]

The Talmud Torah Heder in Makow, 1924

[Page 400]

It is worthwhile mentioning that the day he died in the summer of 1937 there was a fair in town and the Christians asked if the funeral could be postponed until the evening so the fair would be disrupted since so many famers would leave to go to the funeral. And that is what actually happened. Hundreds of Christians came to his funeral walking with bowed heads until the cemetery. Among them were many noblemen with whom Reb Bezalel did business. Even the local judge Olshevsky took part. He was a good friend and did many favours for the Jews thanks to Reb Bezalel. Some of us remember the story about Shimon Meir Rozen of blessed memory. He was sent to jail and Reb Bezalel bailed him out.

On the day of his passing he was fully conscious. He called all his children to his bedside and asked them to pardon all debts owed to him. This is what his children did. There were hundreds of Jews at his house when he passed away including the rabbis from Plotzk, Sokhatchin[Sochaczew] and the rabbi from our town. They delivered eulogies in the synagogue. The rabbi from Plotzk eulogized him at the cemetery. For many years Reb Bezalel was the manager of the Burial Society. I remember when the women from The Society to Spend the Night with the Sick wrote a Torah scroll. They brought the Amshinover Rebbe for the conclusion ceremony. Simultaneously he had to collect money in Makow. Reb Bezalel of blessed memory and other respected men went to greet him. He arrived from Ostrove where he had spent the Sabbath. We travelled to Ruzhan and had a celebratory meal at the home of an Ashminov Hasid. I believe it was Yisroeltche Zilberberg of blessed memory. Reb Bezalel had been to the Rebbe a few times. Later, when I went to the Rebbe in Ahminov he told me that when he returned home, he called his family together and said, that he saw a Jew in Makow that put his respected Hasidim to shame. They could all learn lessons in morality from him.

[Page 401]

Their factories in Lodz operated on the Sabbath on credit and this Jew, Reb Bezalel won't accept this rabbinic authorization. This is how he was his entire life, when he was rich and even before he was successful. He was always a devout Jew and loved scholars and learned men who upheld the Torah. He built the Heder "Foundations of the Torah" from his own money and later signed it over to the central "Agudah", in the name of Reb Shayke Roznboym who was the president. He paid the rent for "Beys Yakov" school every year of its existence. This man set an example for the town with his great virtues and noble work, for God and for people. May he never be forgotten by us and by anyone from Makow, and by us, his grandchildren who had the privilege of having such a dear Jew as our guide. May his memory serve as a blessing.

One of the most beautiful Jewish communities in Poland was wiped off the map by the despicable, evil hands of the Germans, may their names be obliterated. Along with hundreds of Jewish communities, large and small that were so tragically annihilated. But our community, our town will always be remembered in the books which were created by the important people who lived and held important positions in our town. Like the Rabbi of Makow from more than 150 years ago, the great genius Reb Leybish Kharif who later became rabbi in Plotzk. During his lifetime he wrote 24 books about the Torah. Another great rabbi in Makow was Reb Eliezer Pultusker of blessed memory who was known throughout the world for his brilliance and devotion. Another rabbi in Makow was the genius and righteous Reb Feyvele Gritzer of blessed memory, the first Rebbe of the Alexander dynasty, the father of Yekhiel from Alexander, and he is actually buried in the Makow cemetery. He was a student and follower of the first Vorker Rebbe, Reb Yitzkhak of blessed memory. Makow is also written about in history because of a dispute which took place more than 150 years ago with the preacher Reb Dovid Yerzolimsky. He wrote against the great leaders of Hasidism of the day, against the Koszheniter preacher of blessed memory, against the "Visionary of Lublin" and Rebbe Elimeylekh of Lizensk of blessed memory and other Hasidic leaders. He wrote various pamphlets. Reb Yisroel Segal of blessed memory showed me one of these pamphlets. I don't want to judge the preacher here for his opposition to Hasidism because this is not the place and as we know he was misguided together with all the others who opposed Hasidism. Let us not assume the preacher was an ignorant non believer. I heard a story that once, on the morning before Passover, when it was the last chance to sell your goods that were not kosher for Passover, as the law prescribes, he called for the owner of the brewery to come and sell all his liquor. That guy ignored him and did not come. After a short while he sent another beadle to get him, but he did not answer. The preacher said: "the law says all non– kosher for Passover food must be burned". Moments later there was a fire and everything he had went up in smoke.

[Page 402]

The first Yeshiva in Makow was founded in 1897 by the genius and righteous Rebbe of Rabbi Hertzog of blessed memory, Reb Nosn Noteh of blessed memory. My father of blessed memory was one of the first students in this Yeshiva. My uncles, my father's brothers studied at this Yeshiva. This has all remained in the history of our town. Also, such a giant like Nokhem Sokolov, whom I mentioned earlier, grew up in our town of Makow as well as other writers and scholars. And so, our dear Jewish town will remain spiritually and will exist eternally, although physically, the town no longer exists.

All of its holy souls will remain with us forever, for generations, and this must be our oath to these pious souls: we will never forget you and will never forgive the murderers who spilled your innocent blood.

The land will not be covered in blood!

Original footnotes:

1. Shimon Khaim was the brother of Ben –Zion Khilinovitch, a contributor to the Warsaw newspaper "Der Moment".
2. Reb Kalmen the ritual scribe was the brother of the well known writer and poet Yisroel Shtern.

[Page 403]

My Makover Grandfathers

by Yehuda Rosenthal, Ciecanow

Translated by Anita Frishman Gabbay

With my modest contribution, I want to rescue from the abyss, two Makower families, from which I find myself descended; one its grandchildren.

My grandfather, on my mother's side, was the grain-broker Gedaliah Fridman, (with a characteristic Makow nick-name: Gedaliah Gorgel"). He was an Amshinover Hasid. I remember him as in a fog. We left Makow for Mlawa when I was only a small child. I remember only, that he was very tall and thin. He died several years later, after we arrived in Mlawa. My father said Kaddish [memorial prayer for the dead] for him in the Gerer shtibel. My grandmother Pesia, the widow, survived my grandfather until the end of the First World War.

Several weeks after the outbreak of the war, when the Germans began their offensive against the Russians, we, together with my three sisters, ran from Mlawa back to Makow, where we spent the High Holidays and Succoth at our grandmother's. When the Russians began their counter-attack we returned to Mlawa. I didn't return to Makow anymore, which I regret until today.

Already in America (in 1939) I received news from my brother Baruch Itzel (Bernard) that our grandfather Gedaliah, already in his 80s and had come to America, spent 5 years, peddled, saved some money and returned to Makow. Grandmother, Pesia, had many children. They didn't all survive, they died young. Only my mother survived, Feiga-Rivke. My grandfather returned from America with money for a dowry for their only daughter.

He wanted to buy a "pedigree"; his daughter should find a suitable match, a smart student and that was my father, the son-in-law, Meir-Shloime Rosenthal![1]

In those 5 years, in America, he didn't eat meat. Our mother never told us children, about his life in America, it was so wasteful, those years, in her eyes. She was ashamed of this, although she often told us, that half of Makow fled to America.

[Page 404]

But that was the "fate of our people". She also told an anecdote, how a Jew goes out, that is, in the evening, to close the shutters and takes with him in secret his Talis and Tefilin, knocks on the shutters and yells out: Soreh, goodbye (stay healthy), you should know that I am going to America....

I have no doubt, that the impression that the 80 year-old grandfather Gedaliah returning from America made on my mother. When my brother Baruch-Itzel in his early twenties, wanted to take us all to the United States, she categorically refused. She didn't want to go to the "*treifen* [non-kosher] land".

Grandmother Pesia, whose maiden name was Blum, had two brothers who ran away from Makow because of conscription. One of them, Yitzhak, changed his name from Blum to Apelboim. He went to Germany where he married and his children served in the German Army, during the First World War; and then they became wealthy merchants. Yitzhak Apelboim remained very religious. He then went to live in Basel and immersed himself in an Orthodox life. His youngest daughter, (Charlotte), studied in Italy. There she met Dr. Yacov Blobstein (Sale), the brother of the Hebrew poet Rochel Blobstein. She married him, Dr Yacov Blobstein and moved to Eretz-Israel, where he immersed himsef in a cultural-social life, founded the "Beit-Hem" in Tel-Aviv. He knew Latin and Italian. He translated Shlomo Ibn Gvirol's philosophical work " Source of Life" from Latin into Hebrew. He translated pedagogical works from Italian to Hebrew. Dr Sale died in 1906. Yitzhak's daughter, the widow, lives today in Holon.[2]

A second brother of my grandmother Pesia settled in Bordeaux, France. I don't know anything about him, only, that after World War 1, two of his unmarried daughters lived in Bordeaux with the family name Blum.

My grandfather from my father's side, was called Berel-Itche (Yitzhak) Rosenthal. When my father was born, about 1870, my grandfather was over 50 years old. From this I can see, that he was probably born at the beginning of the 19th century, that is 1820. The family's leanings' were those of the Mignagdim- [the opposition of Orthodoxy]; this was the family of Reb Dovid of Makow, a Jew, a scholar, a great "Believer".

[Page 405]

In his elder years, he became a widower and wed a second time, the widow, Dina Malka from Proshnitz [Przasnysz]. And here he died. My father was the "youngest-son" of my grandmother Dina-Malka and grandfather Baruch-Itzel, both had children from previous marriages. As my mother used to tell me, my grandmother Malka was already close to fifty when my father was born. This was considered a "blessing" received from the Ciecanover Tzadik, R'Avraham Landau. The only book I inherited from my father's great library and brought over to America was, "Pamphlet to Fulfill the Shortcomings of the Shas".[3] Such a book could only be found in the home of a wise-scholar. On the front page of the book is written: " Belongs to the "Sage", Rabbi, who is an expert on Torah, the genius Rabbi Baruch Itzhak Rosenthal, [May his light shine on], a gift to Meir Shlomo Rosenthal". In his old age, when he lived in Proshnitz, the Proshnitzers gave him the nick-name "*Gotie*" for the sake of his "*fear of heaven*".

About R'Dovid ben Benzion Yeheskel of Makow, the grandfather of my grandfather Baruch -Itzel, much is written about him as it relates to the history of Hasidim; those that are interested [study] in the "struggle" of the Misnagdim against the Orthodox community.

After he "converted" to Hasidism he became one of the fanatic defendants of Hasidim. Reb Dovid of Makow was first and foremost a follower of Reb Menachem Mendel of Vitbesk, a student of Rabbi Reb Ber from Mezrich. Then he changed course and became a fanatic campaigner for Hasidim and joined the circle of the Vilner Goan's students and played a central role in its struggle, he was a great Talmud-*chacham* (scholar). [This was also added by his opponents]. He left behind 23 books, of which the largest part were lost. The remaining writings are now being prepared [from the latter period] for print by the known professor Mordechai Vilenski of Boston.

The Magid [preacher] R' Dovid from Makow came from Roznoi[4]. He got married in 1759, in Makow, where he was judge and Magid [preacher]. He lived from 1772 until his death [in Makow] in 1815. He had 3 sons: R'Yeheskel, who was rabbi in Radzimin. After the death of R'Dovid, he [R'Yeheskel] was the rabbi in Makow for several months and died in the same year, 1815. R'Aron Rafael and Yitzhak lived in Makow, he also had a daughter Rochel, who was engaged to be married to the Magid and Talmud-scholar, Reb Yehushe Rosenthal. Nahum Sokolow, who was a Makower son, writes about Reb Yehushe Rosenthal, the father of grandfather Baruch-Itzel, "the great rabbi, the late Rav Yehushe, was a merchant and also a great scholar in Torah, there was never a rabbi who served in Makow who was so sharp and proficient"[5].

[Page 406]

A brother of my grandfather was R'Avraham-Yosel (Yosef) Rosenthal, a scholar with a penchant for secular education. He was a friend of Nahum Sokolow. When Abraham-Yosel died, Sokolow dedicated to him a heartwarming eulogy in the "Hatzfira".[6] Our grandfather Baruch-Itzel had a son called Aba Rosenthal with his first wife, who was a Jew, a "Ben-Torah" and patience with children. However, he didn't have any luck in business. He wandered around America in the beginning of the century. After he brought over his family, he was a prayer-leader In the Ciecanower Beit Midrash in New York. He knew all the *davening [prayers]* by heart. Even the prayers for Yom Kippur. All his children became Americanized and became absorbed in the larger American world.

Our grandfather also had two important sons-in-law, one was Sholom Solarz from Ciechanow, a sugar manufacturer and a *parnass*. He also became a widower in his elder years. His children, several daughters and a son (Baruch-Itzel-Bernard) emigrated to America. All the children remained pious. Several grandchildren became active in the conservative movement. One son- in-law of Sholom Solarz, Max (Menachem-Mendel) Terkeltaub was privileged to lead a long life. He over a hundred (to a hundred and twenty), is derived from Radziner Hasidim. He still remembers his youth, as a young Cheder boy, going by foot to the funeral of R'Dovid Kotzker (a son of Reb Mendele). Max Terkeltaub was once a respectable landlord (*a husband to his people*) and very active in the Orthodox life in New York. Sholom Solarz's children in New York became very successful and integrated. They mostly disappeared [assimilated] into the great American melting-pot and the grand-grand children began to mix with non-Jews.

The second son-in-law of grandfather Baruch-Itzel was the Magid Afroim Perelmuter of Makow. He lived for a long time and died in Mlawa at the old age of 93. Part of Afroim Perelmuter's family saved themselves by leaving for Eretz Israel. Zionism and education were deeply instilled in the homes of his children, in Warsaw, Mlawa, and Makow. One grandson, Baruch-Itzel Perelmuter left for Israel for several years before World War 1, then left for America where he became actively involved in the *Farband*, [Labour Zionist Association] In New-York. A second grandson, Berish Perelmuter, was the *spirit of life* of the Zionist organization in Mlawa. Chaim Eliahu Perla, a son-in-law of Afroim Perelmuter and a son of the known Talmud genius R'Yeruchim-Fishel Perla, was the "Rosh Hahaim" of the "Mezrichisher" movement in Mlawa.

[Page 407]

Berish Perelmuter and Chaim Eliahu Perla enriched and developed modern Jewish education methods in Mlawa, between the two world wars. Afroim Perelmuter"s grandsons were very dedicated to the "Hashomer Hatzair" movement in Mlawa. We can now find all over Israel grandchildren and great grandchildren of Afroim Perelmuter, in kibbutzim, Hashomer HaEmek (Guard of the Valley, Kfar Menachem and others), in Ranaana, Holon, Haifa, Tel-Aviv, Jerusalem and others.

Some great grandchildren of Afroim Perelmuter, children who had worked their way up in the Land, now can be found in America.

Some great-great grandchildren of Afroim Perelmuter, those who worked way up in the Land, are now showing up in America.

Several grandchildren of Berish Perelmuter, the pioneer of Aliyah to Eretz Israel, who before World War 1 sent his children to agricultural schools to prepare for Eretz Israel and who was one of the first to leave "exile-Poland" with his entire family to settle in the Holy Land, eventually found their way to the Golden Land of America.

Great grandchildren of my grandfather Baruch-Itzel today live in America (also from my fathers' side). These are the children and grandchildren of my brother Baruch-Itzel (Bernard) of blessed memory. A daughter with her family lives in Mexico and a daughter and 2 sons live in New York and Los Angeles.

And also the writer of these lines, the last grandchild from the 2 Makover grandfathers.

Two Makover Rabbis from the 18th Century

The names of these 2 Rabbis are well known, who gave *agreements* for their books. One was called Moshe Ben-Gershon. His *agreement* for "Eliahu's Letters", a commentary on the patriarchs (Pirkei Avot) of Eliahu, son of Rabbi Aryeh of Kobrin, printed in Hamburg, in 1715. The book was written in Tishrei 18 [1713].

The second was called Avraham Baruch son of R'Chaim [?]. He gave an *agreement* for the book "Aven-Shoham", a commentary by Rabbi Moshe Bar Yehuda Mameschlev, printed in London, 1772. The agreement was written in 1767.

See *Index approbationum,* Index of agreements, *number 34, 2548.* Leopold Lowenstein (Berlin, 1923)

Footnotes:

1. I wrote about my father in the book of Mlawa (1950)
2. See Dr. Yacov Blobstein (Sala), David Tidbar, Encyclopedia Pioneers and builders of the settlement, A. 260
3. Polemic of Rabbi David of Makow against Hasidim, Proceedings of the American Academy for Jewish Research, vol. 2591956), 137-156
4. And not from Rovno, according to a private communication of Professor Vilenski
5. Hatzfira 1888, #181 last side
6. Hatzfira, THERE

[Page 408]

The Jews of Makow

by Yakov Khaim Sobol / New York

Translated by Janie Respitz

The shame is great and the pain is great, which is greater? Tell me, human being! (From "The City of Slaughter" by Chaim Nachman Bialik). In memory of my father and teacher Yeshayahu, son of Avrom Sobol. Dedicated to the memory of those from whom not a trace remains.

The Jews of Makow, the victims of the great destruction, were respectable, simple, kind hearted Jews; poor, middle class and rich; businessmen, workers and craftsmen. Each one live according to his own standard, some better, some worse. They are no longer with us, together with one third of our people.

The great responsibility to eternalize their holy memories lies upon us, the survivors.

Let us remember barely a small amount of individuals from among the murdered. The truth is, that each one had a unique personality, each one possessed goodness and good virtues, the Hasid, the Zionist, the Bundist, the folksy types, and the simple ordinary Jews. All of them together were our unforgettable Makow Jews.

We Will Remember:

Yekhiel Meir Plato, with his majestic appearance, an honest businessman, the permanent chairman of the Zionist Organization, the councilman whose word was respected. Even the gentiles treated him with great respect. His beautiful home was always a meeting place for meetings of a communal nature.

Shmuel Pianko (Shmulke Pianko) the director of the State School for Jewish Children, the quiet intellectual, director of the Jewish Bank, councilman and devoted community worker, always ready to help another.

[Page 409]

Moishe Rozenberg (Rivka Menashe's son–in–law), the secretary of the Zionist Organization, leader of the yearly campaign for the Jewish Agency, city councilman and active participant in all Zionist activities.

Meir Ostri, the devoted member of "Mizrachi", cashier at the Jewish Bank, energetic volunteer and warm man.

Khaim Mantlok, the successful businessman, a good Zionist, regular contributor the Zionist funds.

Yosef Hendel (Yosl Hendel), the small carefree Yosl, who together with his wife Leah had the best restaurant in town. His inn or candy store was the gathering place for everyone. This is where the Jews discussed politics. This is where they took care of the Jewish situation and town problems.

Yitzkhak Vesolek, the non–partisan modest intellectual, teacher the General Jewish Government Schools, represented Jewish interests in various municipal institutions. He was in general a nice person, friendly to all.

Yosef Rekhtman, Yosl, a good devoted Zionist, participated in all fund raising campaigns for the Jewish National Fund and the Jewish Agency.

The board of directors of "TOZ", Makow, 1937

[Page 410]

Ezra Rozhanek, the grain merchant, owner of the mill in Smorotzk, devoted Zionist, member of city council, a generous Jew with a warm heart.

Mordkhai Blum (Reb Feyvl's son), a respectable Jew, a smart successful businessman, always ready to lend money to the Interest Free Loan Society, one of the biggest contributors to the Zionist funds, a great philanthropist.

Yitzkhak Dobres, a respected businessman, an active Zionist and was active in t he Merchant's Union.

Avrom Rozental (son of the rabbinic judge Reb Shmuel Yosl of blessed memory) an intelligent young man, a teacher in the General Government Schools.

Dovid Minoga, a leader in the "Bund", city councillor, a kind hearted fellow, a wheelwright by profession. He was always ready to leave his workshop to do a favour for someone. He was an active member of "TOZ".

Avrom Malakh, everyone's good friend, the best tailor for men in town, a fanatic Bundist and a happy person.

Henekh Vaysman, a leader in the "Bund", city councillor, member of the executive of the Jewish Bank, represented the interests of poor craftsmen.

Yehuda Meir Raytchik, one of the younger leaders of the "Bund", a shoemaker by trade; his parents were poor and sick; a warm, kind person.

Matisyahu Ludvinovitch, his brothers in law were Yitzkhak and Arke Pianko. This was an original family. They were horse dealers. Good hearted proud Jews. They knew all the high officials in the surrounding villages, always ready to represent Jewish honour and defend the Jews.

Let us remember Hershl Khunovitz, Dovid – Berl Kurnik, Sholem Yoine Yonasovitch, Motl Krukover. The last, a pure, tidy, smiling Jew with his Sabbath boots; Notke Kashtan with his round lovely beard, always with his hand in his pocket ready to give charity, always quoting biblical and psalm passages.

Naftali Shuster with a red beard, a decent man with many children, on the Sabbath and holidays he would dress up with a watch and chain. On the Sabbath before evening prayers he would recite psalms at the podium of the old House of Study.

Shmuel Vayntroyb (Shmule the cantor's), a small man with a beautiful handwriting, wrote requests for the Jews to various municipal and government offices.

[Page 411]

Matisyahu Lasko, a carpenter by trade, also dealt in animal skins. He was not simply a carpenter, he was an artist: his hands made what his eyes saw.

Velvl Volfovitch, (lame Velvl), a tailor by trade, a tall man, very poor. During the week he prayed at the podium of the old House of Study.

Avrom Skala, Tuviye Skala, two brothers, honest decent people, good mechanics, talented craftsmen, big jokers, great senses of humour. Avrom Skala was the only Jew who worked as a mechanic in the village Shtshik.

Hillel Hendel (Hiltche), a smart man, a man who required little and was happy with what he had. Active in the Mizrachi Movement, educated his children in the spirit of Jewish nationalism.

Pinkhas Katz, a businessman, always neatly dressed. He was always ready to do someone a favour.

Asher Yosef Grinberg, prayed with all his heart at the podium in the tailor's prayer house and the old House of Study.

Hershl Lasher, Yitzkhak Gogol (the lame Yitzkhak) Shmayee Piekarchik, Avrom Rozonek, Rafael Hirsh Azrielevitch, Hersh – Yitzkhak Getzelovitch, Yankl Dovid Shelsky, Meylekh Vaysgarber were craftsmen, simple, kind– hearted folks.

Eliezer Likhtenshteyn (Lozer) was a businessman, travelled to fairs, did good deeds, never refused a request for charity.

Itche – Meir Likhtenshteyn, always smiling, he was active in the Society to Spend the Night with the Sick. He was the only Jew in town to represent the state lottery, he was in good standing with the gentile officials and use these contacts to obtain favours for Jews.

Yitzkhak Itzkovitch, a small man, a smart businessman, also travelled to fairs. You could always get a loan from him.

Moishe Kleynhoyz, (he was called Moishele the screamer). In fact he was not a screamer, he couldn't even speak loudly. An observant Jew who knew how to study. When the craftsmen were packing up their goods at dawn to go to the fair, you could see him and Reb Yankl Dovid Hendel going to study in the Alexander Hasidic prayer house.

Friday afternoon, long before candle lighting, he began to push his customers out of his manufacturing business in order not to desecrate the Sabbath.

[Page 412]

Mendl Kleyner, a smart educated man, a member of the Jewish town council, an active community worker.

Dovid Goldvaser, a tall handsome Jew, a businessman, active in the Interest Free Loan Society, always ready to help those in need.

Shloime Henekh Albek, a Talmudic scholar. He was a Ger Hasid but also a folksy guy. He was friends with everyone. Anytime there was an arbitration in town he was the arbitrator due to his wisdom and logic.

Mendl Student, a smart Jew, an outstanding businessman, a member of city council, was known in town for his anonymous donations.

Shmulke Yerozlimsky, a handsome Jew a businessman and an active member in the Society to Visit the Sick and the Society to Spend the Night with the Sick.

Moishe Nisn Rubin, a good hearted person, he had a sweet voice, prayed at the podium on the High Holidays in the Alexander house of prayer. People came from other prayer houses to listen to him.

Hershl Orlovsky, a member of Mizrachi, councillor on city council, owner of a saw mill. He was the first to hire Jewish workers in this field. It is important to mention that the first training camp for young Zionist pioneers was at his mill. He donated regularly the Jewish Agency.

Yosef and Yisroel Vilenberg, (sons of Reb Bezalel) were businessmen with good hearts and an open hand to help others.

Shloime Modrikamien with his sons and Zalmen Fogelman, the town Klezmer Band that played at all Jewish weddings.

Zalmen Fogel, a small Jew with a black and white beard, a little deaf, added a lot of charm to the band. They provided great joy at celebrations.

Let us remember the active kind hearted women who donated so much of their time to the Zionist movement in town like: bazars, the Jewish National Fund, fund raising flower days and worthwhile causes. Zvia Fliato, Shayndl Rekant, Khaye Shuldenreyn, Raysl Mantlok, Feygl Dobres, Khave Ribak, Khaye Pianko, Sotche Blum, Rivka Rekhtman, Golde Vilenberg, Mrs. Rozhanek, Yakhet Sheynberg, Gitl Vilenberg, Frimet Azrielevitch, Rivka Blum, Perl Skurnik (we called her Perl the righteous) who were dedicated to visiting the sick, poor women, bringing a Challah to a poor family for the Sabbath and making a sick person feel better with a bit of homemade jam.

[Page 413]

Let us remember the Sabbath in Makow. Jews would return from prayers from the synagogue, the old House of Study, the new House of Study, and small Hasidic prayer houses, all dressed in their best. Faces shone. Throwing aside their financial worries, carefree Jews with pure souls, as if the Divine Presence was resting upon them. The Hasidim in their silk long coats, the craftsmen wearing polished boots, the Yosls, Dovids, Yishayahus, Moishes, Avroms, Mendls, Shmuels, Meirs, Hershls, Khaims etc.

These are the Jews of Makow, these were the community activists, the businessmen, the craftsmen, these were our fathers, mothers, grandfathers and grandmothers.

The oak trees fell, but their roots have remained. Their spirit is our inheritance. We will never forget the genealogy of our fathers. The will remain forever in our memory, and engraved in our hearts.

May God avenge their deaths.

Eulogy for the late R' Avraham Yosef Rosenthal

From an article published in "Ha-Tsfira" no. 181
On August 22, 1888, by Nahum Sokolow
Printed by M. Zinovitz

Translated by Naomi Gal

The city Maków (located in Mazovia Province in Poland) lost its treasure, the great Rabbi of Torah and wisdom, an exemplary man of merits and gifts, the remains of a noble family of *Israel*. Our great Rabbi Avraham Yosef Rosenthal left his heartbroken congregation, his family, his friends and those who knew him near and far. This noble man was for me like grapes in the desert, a great and excellent man in every respect, who was in the city in which I lived for several years.

[Page 414]

My soul was connected to his with deep love, so much that parting with him was painful when I left this city, especially this last parting…

With an aching heart and shaking hands I am writing these few notes to commemorate this Jew, so that I, and maybe some others could appreciate his worth.

The readers are not used to read bitter eulogies for the death of people they did not know in their lifetime and they have not heard their names, but the wise ones recognize that sometimes these people "who are hidden and unknown" are better than many famous people, and one of those special personalities was the late R' Avraham Yosef! He combined all the merits and gifts that the old generation possessed, and he was a brilliant genius for all who knew him.

His grandfather was the sacred and admired genius who was named by his contemporaries R' David "The Maggid from Maków" a scholar of the late Vilna Gaon known for his devotion and abstinence and his strong objection to hypocrites. His father, the great Rabbi R' Yahushua, was an important merchant and at the same time a great scholar of the Torah, to the point that not one of Maków's Rabbis could argue with his brilliancy and knowledge.

The late Rabbi Avraham Rosenthal was a faithful descendant of these two *greats*. He did not have an air of importance, did not feel superior to the *Landlord's Party*, but was by far more exceptional, due to his spiritual merits.

He was busy with Torah and commerce, wisdom and work all his life and his heart was open to every resource. His wisdom was pure and honest, the kind you cannot find among thousands of men. His judgment was brave and outstanding. His views about the world and in people's eyes were those of a great man's views and it was amazing to hear this man, who spent his life in a small town, talk with sharp logic and words that resonated with wisdom and *leaned* on experiences[life's lessons]for his teaching, so that he was considered by the masses a wizard of advice, and his rhetoric were like words of an enlightened.

R' Avraham Rosenthal, the late righteous, was the epitome of pure glory, an enlightened orthodox Jew, educated and devoted to God, who combined deep faith and love for people with all the might of love for his people and the country where he was born, a loyal citizen and many of his own people craved his friendship and were attracted to his light.

R' Avraham Yosef was a modest man, who deeply resented laziness, pride, luxuries. He had the Stoics'[characterized by tranquility of mind and certainty of moral worth] merits and their spiritually.

He was seventy-seven when he died and until the day he fell ill, he was healthy body and soul, his eyes sharp and his manner young. At nine o'clock, the second day of Elul he was led to his resting place accompanied by all the city's people, they all wept and the Grand Rabbi of Maków eulogized him.

[Page 415]

Let us hope that his spirit, the spirit of faith, wisdom, education, peace and patience still lingers in the mourning city. There is no telling how great was the loss of the late R' Avraham Yosef Rosenthal.

The activities of the Zionists
in the city in the years 1917-1918

From the news in "Ha-Tsfira" weekly
Copied and edited by Moshe Zinovitz

Translated by Naomi Gal

"Ha-Tsfira" April 19, 1917

On March 25 the "Zionist Lodge" was opened in Maków in its special abode. That same evening the establishing meeting took place under the presidency of Mr. M. Bejozo, this, was too the general meeting of the previous Zionists Youth. According to the report given by the chairman it was clear that the Zionist endeavor in the city progressed excellently, materialistically and spiritually. The number of members increased to eighty, and participants to 104. Throughout the year the association organized seventeen important lectures about Zionist and Hebrew subjects, which helped propagate the Zionist idea among the youngsters, seven balls were held to celebrate different occasions, and one Flower Day in the last Lag B'omer.

Mr. Isenberg, the representative of Zionist Youth in Warsaw, on his visit to Maków in 1917

[Page 416]

The association's income for the year was 1512 Mark for Zionists goals like planting trees in Herzl's Forest, helping the Hebrew workers and for the benefit of those hurt by the war in the Land-of-Israel, 641 Mark for a local charity and the rest to assist different public establishments like Beth-Yaakov, evening Hebrew classes, Bit-Haam etc.

After the meeting a farewell ball was held in the honor of Mr. Bejozo who was leaving the city. The best of the Zionists participated in the ball and while toasting and praising his devoted work for Zionism, which he headed for seven years with unparalleled courage devoted to its success with his youthful energy. All the assembled decided to establish a Hebrew Library bearing his name and many of them contributed large sums.

A second useful establishment was opened in the city lately, it is the soup kitchen that distributes around tree hundred meals a day for free. The young Zionists are doing most of the work in this kitchen and they deserve deep gratitude.

*

"Ha-Tsfira", May 31, 1917
Maków

On the last Lag B'omer the committee held in our city a special Flower Day, raising money for the National JNF, where they sold JNF's tags with blue and white flowers.

The revenue was 237 Marks and half was allocated to a local charity.

That same day the "Zionist Lodge" organized a great event and a day trip to the forest in which the three Hebrew Schools participated and there were three hundred students, all the students, girls and boys, of the Hebrew evening classes, the members of the Zionist Lodge and the members of the Hebrew Book Club, around five hundred people.

On Saturday of Lag-B'omer Mr. Kirshenbaum visited our city, invited from Warsaw by the local Zionist Lodge.

At noon on Saturday Mr. Kirshenbaum spoke in Hebrew to a small group of young men and women about "The role of the Hebrew Woman in general and the Hebrew Daughter in particular".

On Saturday evening there was a big public meeting in Beit Haam, the hall was full to capacity and more than 200 people attended. Mr. Kirshenbaum gave a meaningful speech about "The situation of the Zionist Movement nowadays". His words, delivered in popular and coherent way with lots of enthusiasm, made a huge impression and were loudly applauded by all attendees.

Afterwards Mr. Bejozo read the two famous resolutions about demanding equality in Poland and guarantees to free Jewish colonization in the Land-of-Israel, which were unanimously accepted.

The meeting ended in high spirits and with the singing of "Hatikvah".

A few weeks ago, the election for the municipal consultants were certified and from all three districts nine Jews were elected, among them three Zionists, Mr. Meir Austri, Shlomo Gernevitz and Aba Birnbaum, the three consultants are members of the Zionist Lodge and among the rest of the elected there are three permanent members.

[Page 417]

The Jews, whose number mounts to seventy-five percent of the city's citizens, bargained with the Poles before the elections and were willing to give up three or four mandates, but the Poles declared in no uncertain terms that if they will not get a leading majority in the city's council, they will not participate in the election. And indeed, they did not and hence only Jewish consultants were elected in our city.

Still, the Jewish consultants opted to elect four members to the magistrate: two Poles and two Jews (one of then a Zionist).

In the last meeting of the city's council, while they were approving the city's Polish and Jewish school's budgets the consultant Meir Austri raised the question: what is the difference between the Polish and the Jewish schools "since there are no special Hebrew studies in the Jewish schools" and demanded to implement such Hebrew studies. The Pole Stach Artifikwitcyh supported this suggestion, but the "Orthodox" consultants were against the proposal claiming that although Hebrew studies have their place in the Cheder, not so in schools where girls study as well. Yet, the majority decided that the Jewish teachers who until then taught general studies, will in the future teach the Jewish language and would make an effort to include for the next scholar year a special Hebrew teacher for Hebrew studies.

*

"Ha-Tsfira"' July 5th, 1917
Maków

By the initiation of the local Zionist Lodge two weeks ago a Hebrew "Kindergarten" was opened, headed by the expert teacher Mrs. Oshorovsky from Warsaw.

Last Saturday a general meeting was held with all the children's parents under the management of Mr. Bejuzo. After an update and in light of the educational and social value of the kindergarten a PTA was elected including Mr. Y. M. Pliatoi, I. Recanat, S. Gerenevitz, I. Muskin, Y.M. Vilenberg and Mrs. P. Birnbaum and L. Vilenberg.

By initiating this Kindergarten, where around thirty children are now studying, once again a step forward was taken in the normal development of the Hebrew language in our city. Let's hope it would grow and improve with time and will reach the level it deserves.

This past week a new department of beginners was opened in the evening's classes.

"Ha-Tsfira" October 25, 1917
Maków

On the second day of Passover a general assembly was held in Beit-Haam's hall by the association of the local "Tzeri Zion". From the report given by the chairman one can see that the Zionist work is growing In our city in an excellent way materialistically and spiritually. The number of members is already hundred and the number of interested is close to one-hundred and seventy.

[Page 418]

During the summer the association organized thirteen public lectures that helped to spread the Zionist idea among the youngsters. Five balls were held to celebrate two holidays and two Flower Days; on Lag B'Omer and on the Fifteen of the month Av last year.

The association's income in the last six months was 1202,76 Mark out of which 615,25 Mark were allocated to JNF and war refugees in the Land-of-Israel and the rest to establishing a Zionist Lodge and supporting Hebrew evening classes and Beit-Akad.

In the meeting were discussed as well the program for the future Jewish Confederation and the outline for the Zionist work in our city. A few important decisions were accepted among them: 1) to assist in establishing a Mizrahi Association in our city. 2) to open in the beginning of the winter a shelter for the tree-hundred destitute children who became beggars. 3) To establish a "Zion Flowers" Association for young members, boys and girls, from the age of thirteen to eighteen. Lately a Zionist Council was elected whose members are: Zevi Orlowski, Gittel Vilenberg, Favel Bloom, I. M. Skornik, Nathan Muntchkovsky, Haim

Montliak and Shimon Rosenthal. The council elected six committees: for income, JNF, Hebrew Language, publicity, charity and supervision.

Bazar for JNF in Maków, 1934

[Page 419]

To the Zionist Convention that will take place in Warsaw on October 28 were elected two members who will represent the Zionist Lodge of our city: Aba Birnbaum and Moshe Bejozo.

*

"Ha-Tsfira" June 6, 1918
Maków

Beit-Haam in our city became during the last days part of the Zionist Council together with its library that contains around thousand books. This increased the value of "Tzeri Zion" Association and the number of members is already higher than one hundred and fifty. Different lectures are given every now and then at "Beit Haam" about national issues. Lately the lecturers were: Mr. Lipman and Dr. Miralas from Poltusk, Mr. Israel Stern from Ostroleka and the local members: Mr. Moshe Bejozo, Teacher Kochiak, Favel Bloom, Israel Munshkovsky and others. The committee of the National Pound works diligently, they committed to raise this year two thousand marks and they already collected half, while till now they collected for JNF around three, four hundred Marks per year. The "Zion Flowers", whose members are teenagers thirteen to eighteen years old, is also thriving and the number of members exceeds eighty. In the evening classes that were opened there are eighty-four students, young men and women, who study Hebrew with two teachers. The association has its own lodging and a library for the youngsters. Heading the association is a council with several committees.

The Zionist Union of Poland organized in the summer of 1917 a petition collecting signatures for a declaration that The Land of Israel is for the People of Israel.

Each one who signed committed to contribute for the war refugees in the Land-of-Israel. In our city 1034 signatures were collected and the sum of three-hundred and ninety Marks.

The History of the Rabbinate in Maków until 1881

Copied and edited by Moshe Zinovitz

Translated by Naomi Gal

This article was published by R' Moshe Naaman from Maków in "Ha-Tsfira" in 1990 issue no. 281. These were his words.

Our city is famous for generations due to her Rabbis, geniuses, and brilliant personalities whose *light* was followed by many and whose *water* we drink until today. Among them are: the genius M. Avraham Avish, who, according to lore, was the brother of the genius Zevi-Hirsh Ginzburg, the presiding judge in Miedzyrzec, the father of the great Torah scholar M. Avraham Avish[1] [Abusch], the presiding judge (in Frankfurt on the Main) died in 1753.

In his days the Gaon M. Moshe Hacohen was the Maggid in our city. (From Kohelet Moshe).

[Page 420]

In the following years the Gaon R' David was Maggid in our city. He died in the year 1815. A bitter eulogy was held for his memory by Moshe Ze'ev of Bialystok and it was printed in his book "The Ezov Association" (Bialystok 1924 in "Alon Bechot").

The famous Gaon R' Aryeh Lieb Zuenz who wrote the books: "Ya'alat Chen", "Get Mekushshar'" "Penay Aryeh" and others. In his book "Penay Aryeh" he writes: "We were debating this question in our holy community in Maków in 1827... he died in Warsaw on September 25, 1833". Thousands of Jews accompanied him on his last way. In the book "Even Habohan" by the speaker R' Nathan Haim from Ural. These are his words eulogizing the late righteous Gaon R' Lieb Zuenz.

The holy Rabbi, R' Nathen' the son-in-law of the holy Rabbi R' Haim Haykel from Amador, a disciple of the holy Rabbi from Lublin ("The Prophet from Lublin") had many students (in the forward of his book "Life and Grace" and "In Name of the Greatest").

The holy Rabbi R' Avraham Avli Rosen, the author of the book "Avraham's Blessing" about the Kabbalah was the student of the Holy Rabbi from Amador, the Gaon Mr. Favel Danziger, the disciple of the holy Rabbis of Simcha Bonham from Przysucha and Rabbi Yehuda Ben Bezalel from Warka (mentioned in the book "Hemdat Shlomo" Shulhan Arouch Even Haezer, page 8) and he is the father of the late righteous Rabbi R' Yehiel from Alexander.

At the end of the forward in the book "Avraham's Blessing" by Rabbi Avraham Avli it says: "And this composition is completed, on a Tuesday, when it was said it is twice as good, on February 22, 1820 in Maków close to Warsaw."

The Gaon R' Moshe Zevi Zinger was the author of the book "The novelties of R' Meir of Rothenberg". In the second part, on page 28 he writes: "Most of these I preached in Maków when I was accepted there as a Rabbi. This was a community used to greats of *Israel* and hence I had to prove my worth." In the forward to a book written by his son he writes: "Many were drawn to his pleasant ways, stemming from his pure heart in three courts: in Maków, later in Sokolow, and then in Siedlce."

The Gaon Mr. Eliezer Hacohen who wrote the book "Fathers of Rabbis Elazar" was at the end of his life the head of the court in Sochaczew.

The Gaon Efraim Fishel Solomon, a greatgrandchild and grandchild to the luminaries Meir of Rothenberg and Solomon Luria, served here from 1856 until his soul ascended to heaven on January 20, 1881. He was not just a genius in Torah and famous all over the world, he was generous as well, and was always the first to help with each charity in his city and was the initiator in every establishment and charity endeavor.

Footnote:

1. Aryeh Leib ben Moses Zuenz(1768-1833), author of Ya'alat Chen, Get Mekushshar, Magen ha-Elef (Shem Chadash), She'elot u Teshubot Gur Aryeh Yehudah, Birkat ha-Shir, Melo ha'Omer, Tib Chalitzah, Tib Kiddushin and others.

[Page 421]

Kahan (Yechiel) Michaeli[a]

Y.M.S.

Translated by Anita Frishman Gabbay

Edited by Janie Respitz

He was born in Makow in 1867. His father Avraham Yitzhak Michah's was a simple Jew, his trade was a carpenter, a passionate Misnagid [opponent of Hasidism], which was seen in our city. For many years he was the member of the community council playing the role of purveyor of government highways. In addition, he was a wood–merchant. He received a strict Jewish upbringing, studied in the Cheder from the age of 3 and Gemara with Melamdim. At 12 years old–with the Rabbi in Goverove (Ostralenker municipality)– he excelled in his studies due to his intellect, persistence and piety. Although he persevered to carry the heavy burden of the Cheder, at 13 years old he ran away from home to Vilna. He studied at R' Melech's Kloiz [small prayer hall], in R' Shmuel Peskind's class, and he spent his poverty–years. He endured many hardships in the Yeshiva due to his Polish accent, even though he studied with great diligence. As he was preparing to travel to Volozhin, he reached the age for military service and left for America. He arrived in Boston and peddled, removed snow from the streets. Then he became a tailor, in the meantime studying English, then he left Boston, gave lectures and then enrolled at the Latin University. At the time (1886) he made his debut in the "New Yorker Yiddish–Folk Newspaper", published by M. Mintz and Dr. Broslovski, about the impressions of the trial of the Chicago anarchists, November 1887, (which made a commotion in the land) thus strengthening his involvement with the anarchists. He began to speak and agitate, since the inauguration of the newspaper "F.A.S[Frayer Arbiter Shtime–Free Workers' Voice]", June 1890, where he became an active member and at the same time, became a student in the medical faculty of the New York University and left for Baltimore, where he studied medicine, while leading intense agitations on behalf of the Anarchists. He was jailed twice, where he wrote his impressions and other accounts in several articles for "Friends of the Workers". He became involved with the Orthodox weekly "The Israelite", which Alexander Harkavy then published in Baltimore. But, because of his collaboration, the printer Zilberman stopped the newspaper, in order not to antagonize the Orthodox, who were bitter towards Kahan and his wife, whom they boycotted. Then he participated in Harkavy's radical magazine "The Jewish Progress", and became the leader of the struggle against the Jewish Orthodox in Baltimore, and for a fiery speech got arrested. Not caring about the consequences or his welfare, he, thanks to his wife, who worked as a seamstress, ended his studies and about 1893, relocated to Brownsville, New York, then several years later to Brooklyn, where he practiced as one of the first Jewish immigrant doctors. He went to Europe several times, studied in Berlin, worked in the Charite and other hospitals. His last trip, 1923, as a correspondent of the important English newspaper "The New–York Evening Mail", he wrote a series of articles describing the "Frayer Arbeiter Shtime", the exhibition in Paris of 1900, and participated as a delegate for the Anarchist Congress.

[Page 422]

He wrote countless articles in the "F.AS", (in which he was one of the first members of the Anarchists of America, a member for 27 years of its existence), journalistic, political–economical, sociological, cultural–history, a series of articles "What do the Anarchists Want", 1921, which tackles the theory and the history of how Anarchism evolved, its various tendencies and representatives of this movement. He also translated [Edward] Bellamy's "Looking Backward" (in the London "Friends of the Worker", Pytor [Peter] Kropotkin's "Memoirs of a Revolutionist" (in F.A.S.) and a larger collection of songs of I. Bowshover. Also he wrote a book "Religion and Science" and a book "The Measures to the Purpose and What is its Purpose".

Visit of Ben–Zion Chilinovitch, with associates of "The Moment" , Makow, 1919

Original footnote:

    a.   a. From Zalman Reisen's "Lexicon of Yiddish Literature", vol. 3

[Page 423]

Ben–Zion Chilinovitch,
May God Avenge his Death

Y.M.S.

Translated by Anita Frishman Gabbay

Edited by Janie Respitz

He was born in Lomza in 1889. His father, Reb Notele, a Jew and Torah authority, founded the illustrious Yeshiva of Makow. He was the head of the Yeshiva and director for a long time, where he made Makow his home with his family. Ben–Zion received, like all the youth in that time, a traditional, religious upbringing. He studied in the Cheder, then in his father's Yeshiva and then in the Yeshiva of Ger and Sochachew, preparing for the Rabbinate. Under the influence of the Revolution, in 1905, he stopped his studies in the Yeshivas and began with secular studies. For this he had to depart from his religious home and went to Bialystok. There he learned to become an agitator. In 1912, he became a contributor for the daily newspaper "The Moment" in Warsaw, publishing journalistic articles, daily–pictures, references and others.

After Poland's Independence in 1918, was the Sejm–correspondent for " The Moment", "Vilner Times, Lemberger Daily News" and other newspapers.

He published under the pseudonym Ben–Adam, Ben–Zion, Ben–Zamach, willow names.

During the Nazi occupation he was in the Warsaw Ghetto, was the leader of the so–called Workshop Commission. Together with Kipnis, who led the press apparatus of the "Joint". In the beginning of 1942 he receives a pass from the regime to publish an evening newspaper in Yiddish, where despite reports, there was also news and information, which lifted the spirits of the Jews of the ghetto. At the Aktion of the summer of 1942, together with a group of Jewish writers who lived in the same house with their families, were sent to Treblinka and there they were murdered.

(Lexicon of the New Yiddish literature, 3rd volume)

*

Ben–Zion Chilinovitch came for Passover and Succoth, often in the hot summer months he would come home to Makow. For the Zionist organization meetings he delivered speeches and lectures on various themes, literary and political. Being very friendly with the great humorist Yosef Tunkel ("the dark one"), editor of the humorous section of "The Moment", and having as well his own sense of humor and instinct for pranks, Ben–Zion was invited to gatherings and banquets, with his monologues and parodies from Tunkel's rich repertoire. He also taught us to sing Hasidic and satirical songs.

[Page 424]

His older brothers R' Shmuel–Chaim Chilinovitch, May God avenge his death, followed in his father's, R'Notele's footsteps. He inherited the management of the Yeshiva until it was liquidated in 1914, at the outbreak of the war.

Their two sisters Feigel and Leitche were both active in the community. Leitche for many years was involved with Zionist causes. She was involved in "Keren Kayemet" and on the culture committee. In their home, many Saturday gatherings of young people took place, in order to learn Jewish history and literature.

Leitche and her family saved themselves from the work camp and settled in America.

A Road full of obstacles and hardship

by Y.M.S.

Translated by Naomi Gal

From the book "Tenuvat Zsiyon" by Rabbi Ben–Zion Rosenthal, May his Light Shine, the Rabbi of "Sharai Torah Anshe Ma'arav" Chicago 1961

…It so happened that I married my first wife, the late Mrs. Chaya, may she rest in peace, the daughter of the famous late Hassidic Rabbi Mordechai Shmuel Ismach, God avenge his blood, from Maków.

After the wedding I accepted my father–in–law's invitation and stayed at his house for about five years while dedicating myself to Torah and work.

For several years I was a pro–bono teacher in the city, since my generous father–in–law and Rabbi Bezalel Vilnberg provided for my needs abundantly.

"If it were not for your Torah as my livelihood [game], I would have been lost to poverty" this saying by King David may he rest in peace, comes to mind when I am writing my painful memories.

When the horrible Second World War broke, we ran away, myself, my wife and our household members, escaping the Nazis, may their name be obliterated. After many wanderings and hardships, we arrived in the Siberian forests of Russia and there we were prisoners for a year and a half. We left by a miraculous intervention and went to Uzbekistan. For more than two months we moved from one place to another on a bumpy road sowed with adversities. On this torturous road my two darling daughters died, suffering from thirst and hunger. After a year of mourning, sadness and pain, my wife, too, passed away, may her soul rest in heaven, and I was left all alone as a stone in a life filled with sorrow and a tortured soul. I again began to study with great devotion so that I would not submit, God Forbid, to depression…teaching Torah to some youngsters.

When I lived in Asia, in the city Raterji near Samarkand, I made many changes for the Sephardic Jewish community who were living there. Since they were Orthodox, they had no one to guide them in Torah's ways... and they trespassed unwillingly[unknowingly] the holy Torah's instructions...now all the improvements and the teachings of the Torah in Communist Russia were dangerous for me and those who followed me.

[Page 425]

When I returned to Poland I was accepted as the head of "Netzach Israel" Yeshiva for the remnants[survivors] of Jews in Lodz and later in Katowice(Poland) until I traveled to France and from there to the USA. In 1948 I was accepted as a Rabbi in the community "B'nai Avraham, Warsaw Jews" in Chicago.

After two years I was nominated as a Rabbi in the community "Sharai Torah Anshe Ma'arav" which sustained me with honor and also helped me come to the USA.

And I remember and lament my daughters who died in the days of the terrible fury, who died in poverty, suffering and hunger in Asia.

My daughter Frida who was 5 years old, went to heaven on October 24, 1941. My daughter Faige, may she rest in peace, was 7 years old and her soul ascended to heaven on October 22, 1942. May their souls be bound together in the book of life.

I want to memorialize the name of their mother as well, my first wife, the modest and righteous Mrs. Chaya, may her soul rest in peace, the daughter of the late Hassidic Rabbi Mordechai Shmuel. She died on January 14, 1943. May all their souls rest in peace.

Memorial to the Saints

I wish my head would turn to water and my eyes become a source of tears so that I could cry day and night lamenting the destruction of the people of Israel that were destroyed in Europe– six million saints and the purest of our Jewish brothers and sisters, one million children, the purest of souls, who were burned by the accursed German murderers, may their name be forever erased. They were led to crematoriums, among them the holy community of Maków (Poland); our people were defiled and taken to their slaughter to Majdanek and Treblinka. It used to be a Jewish city; famous Rabbis sat on its throne; the Gaon R' Laibitch Harif, may his soul rest in peace, from Plock, R' Elazar Poltusker, may his soul rest in peace, R' Favael Grizer, may his soul rest in peace, and the late R' Nathan Netta Hilinovitch, the Gaon and the righteous from Lomza, may his soul rest in peace.

I will mention in memoriam the names of my friends: The late Rabbi Gaon R' Ishak Zevi Edelberg, may his soul rest in peace, the last Rabbi of Maków. The late brilliant Gaon, a remarkable Hassid, R' Israel Segal, may his soul rest in peace, and the Gaon Rabbi Ze'ev Finzeg who was the head of the Cheder "Yesodai Ha'Torah" and especially the souls of my family members: R' Yeruham Monkrash and his family, R' Zevi Orlovsky and his wife, R' Mendel Student, the last manager and the Hassidic Rabbi R' Aaron Bolman, R' Yaakov David Hendel, the knowledgeable Hassid R' Shimon Haim, the son of the late Gaon R' Netta Hilinovitch and his late wife Bat–Sheva, may she rest in peace, the head of "Linat Tzedek" and other *landlords* [elders or prominent community leaders] and yeshiva students– all God fearing, Hassidic and practical men. May God remember them with the rest of the saints and the righteous of the world.

Do not forget their blood and their cries until God will avenge their deaths and lead us redemption. Amen.

Copied from the book with some minor changes by Y.M.S.

[Page 426]

Words of Mourning and Condolences for the Passing of Rabbi R' Mordechai Finkel Of Blessed Memory

Y.M.S.

Translated by Naomi Gal

(Ha–Zfira, July 24, 1903)

We heard the sad news that Rabbi Mordechai Finkel died after a long illness in his city Ostrava next to Lomza district.

Rabbi Mordechai Finkel was a survivor of the Cossack Riots, he was the brilliant son of the late Rabbi Fishly who was the Chief Judge in Maków and spent most of his life in Brisk Litovsk, he was a merchant and a Torah student, and also read secular books, a real Talmudic man, spirited and wise, a son to a distinguished family and for most of his life Rabbi Mordechai Finkel was a prominent and generous *landlord*.

At the end of his life he moved back to Maków and made her his home again after his father died and he was the first for every public endeavour, combining Torah and work. He was highly regarded by all the city's citizens.

In his late years he became weak and an illness bent his strong spine and although he was not yet very old, only seventy years old – his illness progressed and his life changed, he lived in his brother–in–law's house in Ostrava and there his illness became grave until he surrendered.

He left his saddened son, our distinguished writer Mr. Elazar Dovid Finkel, his sons' descendants, the family of his late wife, may God console them and may his soul be bound in the book of life forever and ever.

From the activities of "Keren Hayesod" in the City A letter published in "HaYom" newspaper in September 1925

Translated by Naomi Gal

They are writing to us from Maków:

On Thursday, August 20th, we were visited by Rabbi Itzhak Burg and Dr. Yosef Shulman who came to fundraise for "Keren Hayesod".

The economic crisis and the uncomfortable local conditions could not create a welcoming atmosphere for this important work and the local board even demanded from the Central Bureau to postpone the fundraising. However, the delegation ignored the decision of the local board and came to Maków and we were delighted to find out how baseless our previous desperation were, since despite the dire straits, people remained loyal to the idea of the Land–of–Israel and it became crystal clear[our moral duty] during Keren Hayesod Week that took place in our city.

[Page 427]

The distinguished guests successfully held three large assemblies and awakened the hearts to the Land–of–Israel idea. The real results of their work exceeded everything we achieved and the number of contributors was 50% percent higher than the previous year.

We find it important to mention the dedicated work of Mr. M. Austri, A. Barenboim, Y.M. Lowe, Sher, and Recanat who assisted the delegation and worked all throughout the fundraising with high energy and great success. The practical work was also assisted by the members: Y. M. Skornik, M. Rosenberg and the members of "HaShomer Hazair".

The elected members of the new committee were: S. Recanat – chairman, A. Barenboim – vice chairman, M. Austri – treasurer. Y. M. Skornik – secretary, Y.M. Lowe, S. Pianko and M. Rosenberg.

Maków Jews will remember for a long time the impact of such a successful fundraising event for the building of the Land–of–Israel.

A Makovian writes

All the participants in this fundraising for "Keren HaYesod" mentioned in my letter, except me, the one writing these notes – are all respectful, educated Jews, who worked for the public with faith and diligence, they all perished during the Holocaust. May their memory stay forever.

Y.M.S.

[Page 428]

The Writer Elazar [Leyzer]
– Dovid Finkel of blessed memory

by Yacov M. Skornik

Translated by Naomi Gal

His father, Rabbi Mordechai David Finkel, the son of the famous late Rabbi Efraim Fishel was, according to his friend Nahum Sokolow "A wise Torah scholar who read as well secular books, a man of integrity, a real Talmudic man, spiritual and with profound opinions". During the eighties of last century, the letters of Rabbi Mordechai Finkel were published in Ha–Zfira", he writes about the city's happenings in good taste and clear language, which testify that he not only was a wise scholar but was as well immersed in languages' intricacies. His son Elezar[Leyzer]– Dovid was born in Maków in 1862, studied in Brisk Litovsk, the city to which his parents moved, he studied Torah and Talmud and was famous as a brilliant student. He followed his father's footsteps, and he too, dedicated himself to research and science. He mastered languages easily and knew well the classics and the spoken languages, including Arabic and Japanese. He translated world's literature into Hebrew. After his grandfather, the late Rabbi Efraim Fishel died, his parents went back to live in Maków.

In "Ha–Zfira" of June 12, 1881, during the riots of Jews in South–Russia, a letter by Leyzer– Dovid was published and these were his words:

Maków.

Distinguished publisher,

Please accept the sum of nine Rubal (silver Rubal) for our robbed brothers in the wilderness' cities, collected by the following people: (here came a list of contributors among them his father, Rabbi Mordechai Finkel, 3 Rubal and from the writer himself 2 Rubal) and he ends the letter with these words: "I hope that by the time this is published my friend Nathan Avigdor will hurry and send the remainder of the funds raised, about 20 Rubel".

Elazar [Leyzer]– Dovid (the son of Rabbi Mordechai, may he rest in peace) Finkel

That same year he married the daughter of the distinguished Nahum Halberstat from Warsaw who was a devoted and Hassidic Jew and he chose Elazar[Leyzer]– Dovid as a Torah son and a scholar to marry his daughter so that he could fend for him while he studied the Torah, as was the custom among Polish Jews. But his son–in–law, instead of studying the Talmud, read secular books and learned foreign languages. This caused disputes between him and his Hassidic father–in–law until they separated from him, and he went on with his studies.

He begun translating scientific writings from other languages into Hebrew and published them in "Ha–Zfira" and the "Melitz". He also participated in the translation of[Gustav] Karpeles's big book "The History of Jewish Literature"[Toldot hasfirut haivrit] and many other books into Hebrew, until he became one of the main contributors of "Ha–Tzfira", where he worked about twenty years. Later he worked for the Yiddish newspaper "Haynt" in Warsaw. At the same time, he published articles in "Ha–Tzfira" weekly. A collection of his original articles and translations were assembled in his book "Chapters of Leyzer's Ways" (Warsaw 1904–1905). He studied the Torah all his life besides working and acquired deep wisdom and knowledge, as his father before him. He was liked and admired by his friends and acquaintances since he was modest and innocent in all his ways. He exceled with an encyclopedic knowledge and frequently turned his attention to philological research.

During World War I, when the German governed Poland, he fell ill with typhoid and died young on June 9, 1918.

There is an Aramaic saying: "It is sad to lose an unreplaceable person".

Sources:

G. Karsel: Lexicon of the Hebrew Literature in the last generations, second volume.
"Ha–Tzfira": July 24, 1903
"Ha–Zefira": Weekly April 25th, 1918

[Page 429]

The Late Rabbi Efraim Fishel Nyman
– The rabbi of Maków People in New York

Translated by Naomi Gal

He was born in our city in 1882 to his father R' Mordechai Nyman (the late R' Fishel's grandson) he was a teacher and Chief Justice for many years. (Died in 1914). Efraim Fishel studied in Maków Yeshiva under the direction of R' Nettale and later with his father and with R' Haim Hertz Halperin, the Chief Justice in Bialystok where he learned the state language and the laws concerning the Rabbi and his flock. He studied in Vilna, too, with the Gaon's Beit–Midrash and in Moscow. After receiving his rabbinic certification in 1920, the rabbi, Batya, his distinguished wife and their two gentle daughters Golda–Raisel and Matil arrived in the US and he was nominated as a rabbi at the Maków People Synagogue in New York.

Rabbi Efraim Fishel Nyman may he rest in peace, the author of "Beit Efraim", the
grandson of the righteous Gaon R' Motelle from Maków

[Page 430]

He served as a rabbi for close to thirty years and was loved and respected by his congregation, always busy with public needs and active in the Rabbis Association in New York as a management member, talented as a writer, he published articles about religion, Judaism and the history of Jews in periodicals that appeared in the USA and Poland in Hebrew and in Yiddish. He also authored books, among them the book "Ways of Life" about the non–Jews' laws, their ways and manners (New York, 1948). In the pamphlet "Beit Efraim" (New York 1922) Rabbi Efraim Fishel writes: "I am sending a greeting and blessing to my native Maków residents who now live in the USA, the distinguished and dear, who excel in the love of Torah and deep faith, who love me and take good care of all my needs". And the Rabbi concludes: "And I pray for them so that God will repay them as they deserve and bless them with success and grant them all their wishes and fill their hearts with goodness."

The grave of the righteous Gaon Rabbi Mottele May he Rest in Peace with other righteous in Maków

[Page 431]

Khil [Chil] Aronson,
of Blessed Memory

Melekh Ravitch

Translated by Anita Frishman Gabbay

Edited by Janie Respitz

He was born in Makow, Poland in 1900. He left for Paris in his 20s. There he passed all the trials and tribulations of the war years. He died in November 1966.

Perhaps the greatest amongst the connoisseurs in the plastics[1] arts– great art among the Jews was unbelievable on one hand, but real and reachable on the other. His extraordinary group admired him throughout his life. His family name was simple and plain: Aronson. But Aronson simply put it: Khil (probably for Yechiel). In French they called him: Shil–Shil Aronson. He didn't care for these trivialities. He was immersed in the arts in general with a focus on Jewish art. He served as an art critic..and this I don't know very well.

I didn't know him very well. He never approached an acquaintance. He always waited like a shadow until he was approached. It seemed he always had plenty of time. All his problems were art related problems. He didn't take seriously his food, dress, or place of residence–they were only an infection for him–something only foolish folks worry about. Also he–Yechiel Aronson–so be it. And–what is most important–without life one cannot admire the art of Jews and non–Jews.

[Page 432]

How did he–Khil Aronson–appear, do you want to know? Thin like a starving artist, should he open his mouth–it should be only to eat. In order to describe a brief encounter, or to describe part of his art world, while working as a secretary for the society of Jewish journalists and writers in Warsaw– I sat at one occasion immersed in my thoughts–I didn't notice, someone entered behind me and stood there not saying anything: I apologized, but this didn't seem to affect him–Aronson. He had only one problem: he wanted to go to Paris because this was the center of art for the entire world.

He left the office–and left me with this problem…despite all, it was a miracle to receive a visa or pass in those years in Poland–especially for a Jew–one who had to deal with it really knew.

Several weeks later Aronson was in Paris and began his struggle–Jewish art in the art metropolis of art. His dream was–to release a representative album featuring reproductions of many Jewish artists concentrated in the mecca of the art world–in Paris between the two World Wars–he introduced their color, line and dynamics, displaying their God blessed talents, while at the time, others had a bit of reservation for this grandiose plan–Aronson didn't seem to care. He assembled several hundred portraits and profiles of Parisian Jewish artists. He gave each one of them the means to partake in this collaboration, each contributing a minimum of 3 paintings, in total seven hundred oversized pages, a glorious panorama of bohemian Paris unfolds here–its cafes and characters, literary banquets, gallerists, painters, and models. There is something quite Proustian about Aronson's elegiac and detail–laden re–creation of a vanished world. His voice is by turns gossipy and analytical–he had both the curiosity of a tabloid journalist and the mind of a scholar. But above all, this is a portrait of Montparnasse as a Jewish cultural space, Aronson's Yiddish lens brings into sharp focus the common bonds of language and identity that linked in other, overlapping circles–French, Russian, or Polish. Arranged large portfolios with a minimum of three pictures. The profiles are short, clear and especially– are written with great enthusiasm. The books are read and the pictures are admired–because Aronson understands art, especially Jewish art. Among the great artists of the world–that the plan will be realized–was Marc Chagall. A book–no, a fundamental book about and from the most famous Jewish artists in Paris. A book–no, a great work and precisely in Yiddish in print. Just as the commentaries and essays, through this book, became a reality. And so these hundreds of reproductions later were reproduced in black except two. But this should not diminish the value of the book, that only Khil Aronson could bring to fruition. How? You may ask yourself? Quite simply, it's a miracle for the Jewish Montparnasse in between the two wars.

This was a monumental work, let's look at it from the physical side: the book weighs 12 pounds…printed on the most durable paper. The colored reproductions were only for two pictures. One from Chaim Soutine and the other of Marc Chagall.

Still like a shadow he arrived from a Polish town to Warsaw–still like a shadow he left for Paris in 1926– and there, still like a shadow he slaved over his life–work–pictures and exhibitions from Montparnasse.

Earlier on Khil Aronson continued his life's work according to his vision– a vision that encompassed his entire life. I corresponded with him for a short period. My letters to him were full of praise of his life's work. But his letters to me–full of bitterness. First–about his work–about his life's dream. Was this a struggle to achieve his goal?

Forty years he wandered in the desert of disbelieving the achievements of the work of Jewish artists, in life of the entire human race–but he had achieved his dream. Through him Jewish artists achieved greatness and world fame.

One of the most renowned Jewish art books and surely the most detailed book of Jewish artists in the plastics period, and even written in Yiddish.

- Khil Aronson, wrote extensively on modern art in Yiddish, Polish, and French. He was a Polish art critic who offered a unique perspective on the Ecole de Paris–the extraordinary constellation of Jewish artists who flocked to Paris in the early decades of the twentieth century. He was an established art critic for the Polish Yiddish press by the time he moved to Paris. He was captivated by the émigré art scene in Montparnasse, he became its devoted chronicler. A gregarious and popular figure, he visited painters in their studios and homes, gossiped with them in cafes, and reviewed their exhibitions.
- Excerpt from the Yiddish Book Center."The Big Green Book"

Translator's footnote:

1. Plastic arts are art forms, such as sculpture and ceramics. It is also a term used broadly for all the visual arts (painting, sculpture, film, photography) as opposed to literature and music.

[Page 433]

The Kotzker Rabbi Asks a Klezmer from Makow to Play at Jewish Weddings

Dr Yehuda Rosenthal

Translated by Anita Frishman Gabbay

Edited by Janie Respitz

From "The Daily Morning Journal" February 4, 1968, the Kotzker writer Menashe Unger writes a story about our town. Printed in the book "Amud Haemet", page 127

The father of the Hasid R' Yehoshua Yacov of Makow, was a deaf Jew. His livelihood came from playing at weddings. In the regulations of the Makow community it was written that no one can play at weddings, except for this one Klezmer, who relied on this for his livelihood.

When this Klezmer died, the notables of the city wanted to make his son, R' Yehushe–Yekel the Klezmer, to play at weddings. However, he wasn't able to convince himself to play where women were dancing. So R' Yehoshua–Yekel decided to go to the Kotzker Rabbi for advice. The Kotzker rabbi said: "…there is more written concerning this, that one should enjoy being in good health, than from piety… but it should be only for the well– being, and the brain should be concerned with spirituality." So R' Yehoshua–Yekel resigned himself to play at weddings, but he played facing the wall in order not to gaze upon the women dancing. And when the Kotzker rabbi married his second wife, he played at the Rabbi's wedding.

[Page 434]

Dr. Yehuda Rosenthal

I. M. Skornik

Translated by Anita Frishman Gabbay

Edited by Janie Respitz

The author of "My grandfathers in Makow", son of Meir-Shloime Rosenthal, scholar and Ger Hasid, was born in 1904 in Makow. While still a child, his father with his family relocated to Mlawa. Yehuda Rosenthal received a traditional Yiddish upbringing, studied in Warsaw, later in the universities of Berlin and Leipzig and in the College of Judaism in Berlin. In 1939, he arrived in the United States, studied medicine and there received his doctorate. From 1942, professor in the College of Jewish Scholarship in Chicago. In his field, Dr. Rosenthal published research papers in scientific journals in Hebrew, Yiddish, English and German.

C. Kressel: Lexicon of Hebrew Literature
Recent generations, pg. 842

His great work of 700 pages in 2 volumes "Research and Sources", published by the Midrasha of Judaic Studies in Chicago in collaboration with Reuven Mess Publishing, Jerusalem. This work received great reviews from genuine critics of the Hebrew press in Israel as well as in other cities. The renowned Hebrew researcher and scientist Ephraim Shmueli offered a great critical dissertation on the book in the "New York Post", under the title: The research results of a Hebrew historian". At the end the interesting and scholarly words of Ephraim Shmueli: "Dr. Rosenthal's book is a treasure trove of innovations and summaries of Jewish Wisdom. Dr. Yehuda Rosenthal is one of the luminary students of the High Beit Midrash in Berlin (to which he consecrated an informative and important article in the second volume of the book). After feasting on Mishna and Talmud he learned science and combined Torah, wisdom and good manners". The author of this article adds: "he is one of the only researchers in this country who writes in Hebrew. And who knows, he might be one of the only ones in the last generation of the wise Jews in the USA who writes mainly in Hebrew".

[Page 435]

In the Pinchas of Mlawa one finds a resume of his father Shlomo Rosenthal, which is of interest for all of us from our city. It is told, after the death of the "Magid" the children and grandchildren had to endure burning troubles from the Hasidim. Several times the Makover Hassidim burned the Ohel of the tomb of the Magid. The Magid's daughter, who called the Hassidim, played a prank[1] on them, on the eve of Pesach [they] smeared the entrance of her house with resin and she smeared her holiday clothes with resin".

Dr Yehuda Rosenthal,
Pinchas Mlawa, New York 1950

Translator's footnote:

1.   Could not verify

[Page 436]

Berko
(Dov Hendel of Blessed Memory)

Dr Menachem Gur–Kotziak, Haifa

Translated by Anita Frishman Gabbay

Dov Hendel z"l
(Berko Hendel z"l)

He stands before my eyes as if he were still alive, my pal and young friend Dov Hendel, who we in our town, called: Berko.

He came from a well–to–do family, the son of R'Hillel–Hiltche Hendel. He studied in the Cheder, in Perelman's gymnasia [high school], and then he began his revolt against the concepts [what was expected of us] of our small shtetl–he went to learn a profession.

There were few professions in Makow: shoemaker, chimney sweep and tailor. And this is how Berko came to tailoring in a workshop of the best–known tailor in our town, Avraham Melach.

But this was only a small part of his work. The main goal of his life was dedicated to his immigration to Eretz Yisroel; and Zionism, which he expressed through his activities in the youth movement "HaShomer HaTzair".

The "HaShomer HaTzair" was founded in 1918 in Makow by Meir Kanarek, who then lived in Plotzk and later he became known as the social activist[representative] in Mlawa.

Berko joined "Ha'Shomer Ha'Tzair" in 1918 together with Avraham Rosenthal, Yankel Sheinberg, Alter Kotziak, Vove Reitchik, and other brothers and sisters from the shtetl. At the head of the "HaShomer HaTzair" was Shmuel–Zelig Hendel and Yacov–Moishe Skornik.

Suddenly Berko *stands out* from the others and becomes one of the leading colleagues in the district membership of Mlawa.

[Page 437]

Later he made Aliyah to Eretz Yisroel, arrived at the Ein Shemer Kibbutz of "HaShomer–Ha Tzair" and here he died from an Arab bullet, in 1938.

He had the features of a talented leader, the soul of an artist with a great love for humanity and nature.

If it were normal conditions, he might have achieved great goals and important deeds. Berko was tormented to lead another life which he did not find in the poor, wooden houses of Makow; he used to wander through fields and forests where he basked in the glory of nature.

If the Heavenly–One had endowed the Kingdom of Poland with lovely landscapes and monuments, a large part of Makow was endowed with this beauty.

This shtetl was in the heart of Mazovia, the sandy, poorer part of Poland, but outside the city beautiful pine forests grew, fields stretching along the banks of the Orzyc river, which snaked and cut through the shtetl itself.

Saturday, early morning, everyone is sleeping, only the young girls and boys of "HaShomer–HaTzair", under the leadership of Berko, leave the shtetl and go into the forests. Here they discuss Eretz Yisroel, sing Hebrew songs, and dream about a free Jewish life in their own land.

In those beautiful spring–days, which the young poet Menachem sang in praise, these are some of the verses:

> *Spring has arrived, the sun shines, the skies are blue*
> *The fields are in bloom, and early mornings are immersed in nature*
> *Blooms appear from the black earth,*
> *Looking and wondering: –God's world is great.*
> *The sparrows are arriving and singing without end...*

Berko and his friends wandered over hills and valleys, fields and forests.

An artistic soul hid in this young boy Berko. He used to draw, paint, sculpt, dabble in artistic photography and possibly, if he had been given the opportunity to study, he would have developed into an artist, a sculpturer. But instead of this, his life locked him inside a workshop for many hours, every day, [in the tailor workshop], and as a result, he escaped like a bird from a cage. In these outings, or in *the garden* of "HaShomer–HaTzair" he expressed his entire being through song– his grief, his sadness and his pain.

[Page 438]

Many evenings I remember, when we sat in "Garden" of "HaShomer–HaTzair" and sang songs that poor people sing:

> *There was a pauper*
> *He didn't have anything to eat and what to wear...*

And late at night these songs sung by the members drifted through the wind. They didn't only wander in the nearby village, but also to the surrounding villages: Pultusk, Ruzhan, Krasnasheslk; the Makower *"guards"*[loyal members] wandered about, they were known for their pranks which Berko organized.

And in the shtetl people would sing this popular song:

> *Let's go for a walk, a beautiful walk,*
> *The young guards, big and small are following,*
> *Berko is the commandant, Menachem helps him out,*
> *People go hiking in summer, because people do not go in winter…*

Years go by. I was a student in the University in Warsaw, and running from one lecture to another, I suddenly saw a familiar face–Berko.

Why are you running, Menachem? he asks me.

Looking at him, I questioned myself: Why am I running?

We roamed the streets of Warsaw and talked for hours about our days in Makow. Years went by again. Berko is already in Eretz Yisroel, in the kibbutz and suddenly the dreadful news: Dov Hendel was hit by an Arab bullet in the kibbutz.

In Makow we gathered together with all his friends and acquaintances. I went on the stage of the city theatre (there was a cinema already built at that time) I want to speak, but the words don't say anything. I feel only, that Berko is missing, that no one can replace him.

I pass through the streets of Makow later on, and I feel the sorrow in everything around me due to the death of Berko. It seems to me, the houses are lower, the sun doesn't shines like before, the Oszycz became small and shallow. The forests of the neighbourhood look poor and bare– Berko is missing here!

In the Land of Israel the remnants of the Makov community gathered together at Berko's grave in Kibbutz Ein–Shemer for the yearly memorial.

[Page 439]

I stand and look at the memorial stone, where the words are engraved "Dov Hendel".

The whole life of this person is concentrated in this stone. And standing at his grave of my young friend and soulmate, I felt, this stone and others like it–this is the foundation of building and freedom, the foundation for our state [of Israel] – our freedom.

May the earth of our homeland bring you strength, dear friend and brother.

May your memory be inscribed in the book of life.

Yisroel Pomeranc,
May his Memory be Blessed

Written by the Committee

Translated by Naomi Gal

*The late Israel Pomerantz, Son of Haim and Rachel
Died fulfilling his duty for IDF
On August 26th, 1951*

He was born in Maków in 1932. When the Germans fought in Poland, his parents and their family escaped to Russia and thus were saved from the Holocaust the Nazis brought forth, May their Name be Erased.

After the war, in 1946 they arrived, after many hardships, to Ulm in Germany. During the Independence War his older brother, who had arrived in Israel with Aliya B', was enlisted and participated in the bloody battles over Jerusalem. He made Aliya following his footsteps and settled in Ein–Harod Kibbutz, where he stayed until the whole family arrived in Israel.

Israel was a handsome youngster, talented and energetic, he worked during the day and studied at night. He was a loyal son to his parents and was liked by his friends, he sang and played music, was easy–going and content.

[Page 440]

In 1950 he joined the IDF and was accepted to the Air Force. Here too, he excelled in his studies and in his duties, and since he could play, he was part of IDF's Orchestra.

In 1951, on his way from furlough to his unit he was killed in a car accident, together with five of his IDF friends.

The pain and sorrow for the lives of these young people were great and Yisroel will never be forgotten by his friends and fellow–citizens of Maków for ever and ever.

[Page 441]

Second Lieutenant Rani Weisberg
May his Memory Blessed

Written by the Committee

Translated by Naomi Gal

He fell after the Six Days War while removing mines in Ramat Ha'Golan. The late Rani was born in Afula, both his parents were from Maków – Issachar and Zila Weisberg. His grandfather Dov–Berish owned the only printing–house in Maków, and he was the one to organize, with his student Yaakov, a Bible Circle.

Second Lieutenant Rani Weisberg

His great–grandfather, Menahem–Mendel Lefkowitz, the Rabbi from Parzniewice [Przasnysz], published an encyclopedia for Jewish Laws titled "Kehilat Menahem".

The late Rani inherited most of his families' (who perished in the Holocaust) characteristics and talents, from painting to woodcarving. He graduated from high school and his teacher said that he was "A young man radiating simplicity, modesty, and earnestness, generous who always craved the beautiful and useful; he excelled in his studies and in drawing, he was active among the other students and was liked by them. He was gifted and had an intellectual curiosity. He was interested in different sciences and used to come up with fast and accurate answers, diving into the depth of problems with wisdom and logic."

In the IDF he was in the Engineering Corps and during the Six Day War he was appointed as the intelligence officer of his regiment. After the war his soldiers received an order to go out to a difficult and dangerous mission, removing Syrian mines. The late Rani postponed the wedding furlough he was granted and headed out with his soldiers.

And then one of the mines exploded and put an end to his life, the smile remained on his face after his death. He left behind shocked and adoring soldiers and at home – his love and bereaved parents.

His blessed memory will be with us forever.

[Page 442]

The Late Rabbi Reb Pinkhas Ingergman
Perished in an "El-Al" plane, shot down over Bulgaria in 1955

by Rabbi Moshe Halevi Shulman, "Day- Morning Magazine"

Translated by Anita Frishman-Gabbay

My hands shake when I have to write that rabbi Pinkhas Ingberman is no longer among the living. The young and energetic Reb was full of life. Torah and wisdom always sprung from him. To recite the Torah was always his great pleasure. We expected quickly to celebrate his wedding. But instead of joyfully singing "over him" at his wedding, we brought him to be buried.

Still as a young boy, when he arrived in Pultusk, near Warsaw, to the Beth Yosef Yeshiva, to the Rosh Yeshiva rabbi HaGoan Reb Yitzhak Elfand, May God avenge his blood, he already had a reputation: The Makower Genius". His first teacher-rabbi was rabbi Reb Moshe Turner *Schlit'a*, today in Brooklyn. He tells that already then when Pinkhas Ingberman was 12 years old, he already displayed great talents with his sharp mind.

Later he arrives in Bialystock at the main yeshiva of "Beth Yosef" which had 36 branches all over Poland, 12 of them I founded. The head Rosh- Yeshiva was the well known *Gaon* Rabbi Avraham Yaffe *Shlit'a*, which is today the chief "Rosh-Yeshiva" of the Bialystoker Yeshiva "Beth Yosef" in Brooklyn.

When the young Pinkhas arrives in Bialystock, he draws the attention of all the 400 young boys who were then in the Yeshiva.

Although there was no lack of intelligent students in the Yeshiva, people obviously knew that Pinhkas Makower was an exceptional student. He was a genius in the full sense of the word. In Torah, from memory, he literally performed miracles and as a young lad, the Head of the Yeshiva *Schlit'a* said about him: "here grows a great Adam" and so he sat and studied with great perseverance and persistance for Torah innovations until the war broke out. Then together with the Yeshiva lads he was sent to Russia, to Siberia. He arrived in a work camp with a group of young Yeshiva boys, one being the son in law of the head of the Yeshiva, rabbi HaGoan Reb Yehuda Leib Nekritz *Shlit'a*, today R.M. In the yeshiva Beth Yosef in Brooklyn. In this work camp he was required to chop wood in the forests during the daytime, in the great freezing Siberian winters, enduring hunger and cold, not having the necessary clothing for such cold weather.

[Page 443]

Going to the forest he took several pages of Gemara with him, and when he completed these pages he exchanged them with a friend for other pages. When Friday arrived, he would make an *eruv* [a ritual halakhic enclosure made for the purpose of allowing activities which are normally prohibited on Shabbat, like carrying objects], so that he could go on the Sabbath from his village to another village, where the other Bialystoker Yeshiva lads were working. They got together to celebrate the Shabbat day in Torah and Mussar.

He took care not to fail in the desecration of the Sabbath or eat forbidden foods. We can say about him as King David eulogized Abner: " thy hands were not bound, nor thy feet put in fetters; as a man falleth before the children of iniquity, so didst thou fall. And all the people wept again over him". [1] (Samuel ll, 3: 34)

Also, for the young and saintly rabbi one can say: "with your hands thou hast written months of Torah and carried pages of Gemara; with your feet you walked to study Torah and you fell down at the hands of a criminal act which tore apart your blossoming young life".

After Liberation he arrives, in 1946, in America, to the Yeshiva Beth Yosef in Brooklyn, where he continues to teach for several years and becomes a rabbi in Plainfield, New Jersey. He remains there two years as a rabbi in "Tiffereth Israel"- Brisker synagogue in Brooklyn, where he earns a great reputation among the rabbis and students. The 35 year old Rabbi reached a level in his studies as seen in the older generation of rabbis.

We are certain that God will not remain silent for the innocent spilt blood "for the blood of his servants shall rise, vengeance shall return upon his adversaries, and he will be return to his people".

Translator's footnote:

1.   https://www.mechon-mamre.org/p/pt/pt08b03.htm

[Page 444 - Hebrew] [Page 446 - Yiddish]

The late Mindl Frydman–Rajczyk

by Yehuda Erez, Tel Aviv

Translated by Naomi Gal

I recognized her even before I saw her face. Even in a photo. This testifies to the special merits of her personality.

Mindl Rajczyk–Frydman

A disaster happened in my family, which darkened my life, although I made many efforts to hide it from people. And then one day I got a long letter from her, in juicy Yiddish and it was imbibed with her sort of feminine gentleness and love for people, that surprised me in both its nice form and its deep human content. Is it possible that in faraway America, whose people, they say, care only about business, and all they think about is accumulating dollars, could it be that there are people who feel other's pain and it can touch their hearts so deeply? And this humanly warm language, with an ingredient of soulfulness, born from the Jewish Shtetl that was so charitable and overflowing with sensitivity for others' sufferings – how was this maintained in a bustling city, where its wheels turn and smash the essence of a personality? And I – who am I for her? I am only a childhood friend of her relative, and I haven't seen this friend for dozens of years and just a short while ago we reconnected.

In her letter she invited me to visit the USA and stay for a while to change the atmosphere and release the anguish. All this without flowery language nor pathos. The simplicity of the words, so sincere, trustworthy, so captivating.

[Page 445]

I could not accept her cordial invitation at once. Many months had passed, years, until I had the privilege of seeing her in real life, this figure I conjured in my imagination based on the letters she sent me and her real image surpassed the one I imagined.

I saw her in her home, at the restaurant which supported her, surrounded by her big family, in her relationships with friends and acquaintances and at her public activities – American style, it was impossible not to respect, cherish and love her.

Her house was an open one, welcoming each and every guest. When I arrived, I found there another Israeli descendant of Maków, who spent most of his time in New York at her home. And before him there was another Israeli, one I recommended, and he had the house key and came and went at will, ate, drank and left when he wanted and his presence was felt… the refrigerator full of food and different goodies…and it went on for many months, until this man found himself a wife and made a home in America, but he did not return the key…

Needless to say, that I felt at home in this house, from the very first moment, as did each person who entered that place. This woman knew well the secret of welcoming guests!

Soon I saw her working at the restaurant, while it was still dark outside, she went to work and came back at night. The work was relentless, she had to take care of shopping, organizing the restaurant, bills, managing the workers, the clients – and day after day, hour after hour with no break. Where did she find the physical strength for it all, being a small, short woman and as it later became clear – the terminal disease, which shorthanded her life, and was already nesting inside her.

And after a day of labor – a long trip, to visit the old mother, her mother–in–law. And very often the parties of the "Farband" Circle in her home, if you haven't seen her preparations for these parties you haven't seen the sacred work done with love and trembling soul. She stood for hours and prepared different delicacies: tiny sandwiches in diverse geometrical forms, filled with varied cheeses, meat, sausage, all set up nicely on plates and decorated with many colorful vegetables – a feast for the eyes. All this set on tables decorated as well with greens and flowers and bottles, a real masterpiece. So, is it any wonder that there was a special ambiance that affected each one who entered the house? Needless to say, all expenditures came from the Frydman's pocket and the entire income – was consecrated to the working Land–of–Israel.

And when the party was over – a long time to rearrange and clean the house, till after midnight and the day after, before dawn, back to work.

She had an unconditioned love to the Land–of–Israel and admiration for its people, especially to its pioneers. More than once I thought, while watching her work, that if she worked as hard in our country, she would have made a good living no worse than there, and I thought that some of our friends in Israel do not appreciate the loyalty and dedication of our friends in America, whose work has a good dose of pioneering – although American Style. Mindl was one of the best friends of the working class of the Land–of–Israel.

[Page 446]

Her dream came true at last, she and Yehoshua visited Israel in 1960 and their happiness was *bonding*. I accompanied them when they toured the Upper Galilei and to other places. They spoke a lot about making Aliya. They went back to America but their hearts remained in Israel. We believed that they would come to us, become Israeli citizens and we would enjoy their good company – but then one day we received the bitter news that the good and generous Mindl had died.

A terminal disease ended her life, and she was taken from us.

[Page 449]

Shoshanna,
May Her Memory Be a Blessing

Israel Frankel

Translated by Anita Frishman Gabbay

Edited by Janie Respitz

The house of Anchel Kontziak, director of the Hebrew school in our town, was rooted in religious–nationalistic traditions. His children–talented and smart, were raised in the spirit of their father–served with all their skills to improve the conditions for the Jewish youth in our city. Kontziak's children learned Hebrew and were involved in all the youth organizations of Makow.

Shoshanna, the daughter of Anchel Kontziak was a beautiful girl with a delicate pale–rose complexion and a head full of black hair with piercing black eyes.

In 1918, when Meir Kantziak of Mlawa founded the "HaShomer HaTzair" in our town, Shoshanna immersed herself in this movement and was elected "Head Kibbutz Leader" and later secretary of "HaShomer HaTzair".

Despite her involvement, she continued her studies, completed her teachers' course and excelled in her grades. She was invited by the "Tarbut–Central" in Warsaw to work as a teacher in their Hebrew school system (which was then founded in Poland).

But Shoshanna didn't want to leave her home town and the youth of "HaShomer HaTzair", which respected and admired her. Shoshanna decided to remain in Makow and work in her father's school. She was a good teacher and educator. In addition, she had a beautiful voice and also a talent for singing. Her Hebrew and childrens' songs, which she learned at school and at the "HaShomer HaTzair" gatherings, were so popular in our town. Having artistic talents, she often performed at our Zionist evenings that took place in Makow.

In 1935, she, together with her husband, arrived in Ramat–Gan. She came to visit me in my home. Her husband was a native of the Land, whom she met and married in Poland.

Likable, happy and good humored–how fortunate for her dream to come to the Land of Israel. She told me of her plans to bring the rest of her family, who were still in Poland.

Her unpredicted death disrupted all her plans. She was torn away from us, still in her youth, after giving birth to her first child.

[Page 450]

This sad death affected the emigre community of Makow in the Land of Israel.

May these few lines serve as a heartful memory–for her daughter she left behind and who never got the chance to meet her. Shoshana, one of our best daughters of the nation of Israel, from the kehillah of Makow–Mazowiecki.

Honor her memory!

תוכנית המחזה „חשה היתומה" בבצוע החוג הדרמטי במאקוב, בשנת 1917

Program from the play "Chasia the Orphan" performed by the drama circle in Makow, 1917

[Page 451]

A Beloved Soul and an Enterprising Image
To the memory of Yahushua Makover

David Buchner / Tel–Aviv

Translated by Naomi Gal

Yahushua Makover of Blessed Memory
The first secretary of the Organization of Maków
descendants in Israel

A blessed soul, a man of many activities, one of the forgers of the youth's image in our city, was our friend, Yahushua Makover.

He was born to a family of laborers, grew up and was educated on the ideals of work, early in his life he joined the Working Youth of the Land–of–Israel.

At that time the youngsters in our city were agitated and all their organizations were swept away in the upheavals that took place. Some went to the right, others to the left – and not always in line with the origins of their status. Maków was one of the cities in which the youth was organized and aware, these were the years 1925–1926 and the young men and women roamed around with nothing to do, no profession and no future. They began their soul searching and the question was: Where to?

This question haunted them until some found their way to the land of America or to west–European countries but the majority of the youth were part of the Zionist movements and went to training camps, preparing to make Aliya.

The movement grew and developed despite the many years this youth had to wait without being able to make Aliya due to the hostile policy of the British Mandate. But slowly, step by step, we overcame all the obstacles with deep motivation and in every possible way, and quite a few of our city's youngsters made Aliya.

[Page 452]

* * *

Yehoshua was one of them. Due to his constant activity in the movement he was granted an Aliya certificate from the Halutz, although he did not do a training – something that was unprecedented back then.

Yehoshua was born to be a public activist, and from a young age managed, with great talent, the library of the JNF [Jewish National Fund] in our city, which was his "temple". He invested there all his strength and energy. He arrived at his evening shift, every evening, at the library which was situated in Mr. Plato's house. He had an outstanding memory, knew by heart the names of all the books and knew all the readers, and who read what. He was as well the secretary of the Fund of Land–of–Israel Workers in our city – one of the prominent Zionist's endeavors in Poland, which aim was to financially assist the Land–of–Israel workers. He was also the secretary of the Halutz and of "Freiheit" that were established back then and Yahushua was one of their founders.

He was among the first valuable activists in every Zionist endeavor, his great capability and his brilliant talent helped him with everything he tackled. He was as good as his word.

* * *

His Aliya and absorption in Israel deserve a chapter apart. It was not easy to find work in these days and the question was: what profession should he choose for himself? By nature, he despised easy and comfortable work. He wanted to be a real laborer and make a living with his sweat. He chose construction. His life was not easy but he was happy and proud of his work. His gifts and his strong will helped him to become in a short time one of the best professionals in construction and he was promoted to be a foreman. He insisted on accuracy and discipline and his bosses, like his co–workers, appreciated and respected him.

Since he was dedicated to his work body and soul, he found lots of satisfaction and did not notice that his health was deteriorating. All the efforts his family and friends made to help him find an easier job were to no avail until the bitter day arrived when he fell ill and never got up again.

* * *

Remembered are the days when he managed the secretariat of Maków descendants. His heart ached when he was hardly able to help his city's people when they arrived in Israel after the Holocaust because there was no money.

He was witty and clear minded. He insisted on his principals and although we did not always accept his views about matters of the world and in Israel, we respected him and tried to understand him.

He consecrated all his free time to reading, there was always a good book in his hands throughout all his years in Israel. He was a devoted and generous friend who was always willing to help. He was as well an exemplary father and husband.

The heart breaks because he was unable to see the future of his children, who are good and excelling students. It is painful to come to terms with the awful thought that he is no longer with us. His heart stopped forever. His dear family and his many friends and all Maków citizens lost a gentle and cherished man.

We will never forget him.

[Page 453]

Reb Eliezer – Dov Son of Reb Pinkhas
(Leyzer Shoykhet)

Yehuda Rozenman / New York

Translated by Janie Respitz

My friends in Israel reproached me: could you explain, Reb Leyzer Shoykhet was a well known personality in the old home, so why don't you write about him so people could read remember and know who he was?

Despite the fact that I am against children profiting from the name of their famous fathers, I agreed: these personalities in general, and particularly from Makow belong to everyone and we must write in order to be irradiated with their light for future generations.

Reb Eliezer was a ritual slaughterer, performed circumcisions, led Torah services, belonged to the Burial Society, headed the Society to Provide Clothing to the Poor, was an arbitrator and a peace – maker. Always ready to serve others. If you needed, he would even protect you from evil. If someone asked for help, Reb Leyzer Shoykhet was the first to arrive. He would already have his religious books and notes to lay under the patient's head, which helped to bring about true salvation…

I remember: someone once told my father they saw me skating on the river on a Saturday afternoon, which was the custom on winter days, he was furious. I remember the beating I received. "What does this mean" shouted my father, "God forbid, desecrating the Sabbath and not studying, standing by the river and watching spoiled children? A transgression, a great transgression".

[Page 454]

Or, when Shmuel Yosef Rozental, the rabbinic judge, would give a class at the Yeshiva where I studied, and then, Heaven forbid, told my father that I was not learning diligently, I did not only receive a beating but reprimanded me without stop. I must add that his helped.

What Jew served God more than Reb Leyzer Shoykhet, and not out of fear, but out of love? He loved to pray and perform good deeds. He found great satisfaction in this for himself and God. It could be said that Reb Leyzer Shoykeht did not have an "I". His greatest desire was to improve the situation of the poor and help anyone who stretched out a hand. He was also a member of the Burial Society. This meant: purifying the corpse, accompanying the deceased to his grave. He was also the town's leader of prayers, a position he held for 60 years. Who doesn't remember his heart rending praying? As if a heavy mountain was on his shoulders. This was how he felt leading services. He understood he had to ask, cry and persuade God to grant a healthy year for all those praying. I can still hear his chanting in my ears until today. It broke your heart, everyone cried.

Reb Leyser Shoykhet had his own choir, his four sons and Zalmen Podel who played the bass with Shloime the musician.

Reb Leyzer Shoykhet's personal friends were: Moishe Yosef Garfinkel (the baker), Shmuel Yosef Rozental (the rabbinic judge), and all the Talmud teachers who we studied with.

His sons: Khaim Shoykhet of blessed memory, a pious Jew, a ritual slaughterer and performed circumcisions;

Yehoshua Rozenman of blessed memory, a ritual slaughterer, a pious Jew, God fearing and a scholar;

Yisroel Yosef Rozenman of blessed memory, a ritual slaughterer, former secretary of the Ritual Slaughterers Society in New Your;

Yekhiel Rozenman of blessed memory, a businessman;

Dovid Rozenman of blessed memory killed with his family in the flames of Hitler's hell;

Yehuda Rozenman, the writer of these lines, and two sisters: Feyge – Soreh, married to Moishe – Zelik, the son of Yekhiel form Makow; and Nekhame, also married both live in New York.

[Page 455]

Lines to the image of our father

by Nekhama Sela–Lewkowicz, Yakov Lewkowicz / Tel–Aviv

Translated by Naomi Gal

From the depth of the past, we conjure the noble image of our father, with a big beard, large forehead and eyes radiating wisdom. I can especially recall a long December night, when the whole family was at the table and our father, of blessed memory, told us the story of his life and how and under which circumstances his personality was forged.

Our late father was born in 1878 in the city Różan on the river Narew in Łomża County. When he was two years old, he lost his father, so his mother, who was disabled, had to make a living by teaching. She taught the city's girls prayers and writing in Russian. Everybody called her "Sara Gittel the Educated" and indeed according to standards back then she was educated, she was familiar with Chumash and Rashi, and knew by heart all the chapters of the book of Psalms.

The Melameds discovered unusual gifts in our father. He surprised all since his childhood with his sharp mind. He had a thirst for knowledge from a tender age. He did not settle just for sacred studies and began learning secretly the state's language. He was once "caught" by two Yeshiva students. At once a rumor spread in town that the youngster had lost his faith and for a while, he was outcast. But society's attitude did not deter him and he went on studying Hebrew and Russian in secret. He felt the place was too confining for him and craved a larger space.

When he turned sixteen, he heard some whispered echoes from Lithuania about an awakening of the Jewish People and the establishment of a Zionist Movement. This rumor made him grow wings. In his mind's eyes he saw a path he could follow. He then decided to leave his city and go to a place where the blossoms of the revival were taking root. But since he had no means he was unable to do so and he was often vacillating between desperation and hope.

The turning point – enlisted to the army

When he was enlisted to the army it was a welcome turning point in his life. He gave up his right to avoid serving since he was an only child and luckily for him, he was sent to Kaunas, of which he has been dreaming all his youth. He was intoxicated by the atmosphere there and quickly integrated in the new society and made many new friends. He visited the teacher's Beit Midrash, explored new ways of teaching and was in favor of not discriminating against women who wanted to learn sacred studies.

After serving a year in the army his superiors noticed his talents and he was promoted to *feldwebel* [field usher]rank.

[Page 456]

Two years went by while he had peace of mind and good financial and social conditions, since he was with his own people. But it did not last and he was transferred to a remote spot, faraway from Jewish settlements. He suffered there and was starving due to the lack of Kosher slaughter. Realizing that he was weakening considerably he traveled to Vilnius to "Chofetz Chaim" (R' Yisrael Meir Kagan) to ask his advice. The Rabbi allowed him to eat non–kosher food but not to suck the bones. Still, despite the Rabbi's permission, our father avoided non–kosher food – till the end of his military service. There was with him during his service another Jew from Maków, Pianka's father, the head of the governmental school, he, too, avoided non–kosher food.

By the end of his military service father came back home a resilient man, rich with life experiences and deep knowledge that helped him reach his goals.

Twenty Yeshiva Students

When he was 26 years old, he married the daughter of Eliezer and Etta Albaster, the open–handed family that hosted every Shabbat twenty yeshiva students. Every Thursday evening, they baked, cooked, prepared, labored and worked for these Torah learners – the three daughters: our mother Chaia–Bathya, Tova and the late Zipporah, they, too, married teachers; one was Kalman the famous Sofer ST"M, the brother of Yisrael Stern, the well–known poet and writer. He founded the Shlomai Emunai Israel Association in Maków and was a great scholar, a gifted speaker and was busy day and night writing Torah books and dealing with Jewish ceremonial art.

The other one, the late Mordechai David, of blessed memory, was also a great scholar and highly educated, he was a teacher in the general Cheder. Our grandfather's only son, the late Alter Albaster, was one of the founders of the Zionist Movement in Maków.

Our late father stayed for three years at our grandfather's house. Throughout this time, he was busy writing petitions and appeals to the authorities and served sometimes as a lawyer. Each juridical prosses he undertook was successful. This gave him a good name among the city's dignitaries: Doctor Wielechowski, Hillel Sheinberg, Barenboim, Titonowitz, Austau, Segal, Raychik and others, they all sought his company and invited him to their houses to teach their sons Hebrew. These prominent people also helped him found the improved school and they participated in establishing the Mizrahi Movement in our city.

In the beginning of his teaching career our father encountered a strong objection from the Orthodox. They disliked his educational reforms. He took the child out of the narrow space of the Cheder and placed him in a large classroom on Ziloni Rink Street, with a blackboard, benches etc.' next to a big field that served for physical exercises every morning, before prayer. On Saturday's afternoons he taught them Pirkei Avot and took them on field trips to the forest, straightening their bent backs and planting in their hearts a love for flora and fauna. When they came back from these excursions, he organized them in rows and the sounds of Zion songs spread throughout the entire Jewish neighborhood.

These novelties created a great commotion, the Orthodox laid obstacles before every step our father took. More than once he came back from the synagogue "Amshinover Shtiebel" angry and bitter. They

(page 457)

made his life miserable and attacked him mercilessly. They instilled such rancor in their students' hearts that one of them even dared throw a stone at the window of our father's school, for whose survival he fought for so many years.

But his work was not in vain. He harvested many successes; the number of his students increased every year. Students flocked to his school from the neighboring cities like Przasnysz[Praschnitz] and Pultusk and from villages, too, and the school became crowded.

It is difficult to relate our father's joy when Lag B'Omer arrived. He adorned his students with blue–and–white ribbons, put a Magen–David on their hats and gave them *Zion* flags. Thus, they walked the city's streets – to the forest, with their traditional bows and arrows.

But father was not satisfied until he fully completed his mission. He also opened evening Hebrew classes for girls,

Among the girls who studied there, one, ten years old, excelled with her beautiful voice, she was Yenta Schneiderman, who later became a famous singer. Father loved singing and sang well reading music notes. He organized a mixed choir of girls and boys "Lithuania Style". When they found out, the orthodox raised hell and when he came to pray at the "Shtiebel" on Shabbat they showered him with curses and accusations, who knows what could have happened if Moshe–Yosef Garfinkel (the righteous) did not calm them down.

A few years later the "Aguda[h]"(a political movement of Orthodox Jewry) people followed our father's footsteps, they founded a general school under the management of Volvol Finezieg and Yakov Klein. Teachers were brought from Bialystok and Vilnius. The Hebrew language, which they rejected previously, now had an important place in their curriculum. The contentions with father dissipated and they now had a peace pact. The teachers from their school, David Levin and Portnoy, were father's best friends and frequent guests in our home.

When the general Cheder was established father saw it as trespassing on one side and as the fulfilling of his life's dream on the other. He was tremendously happy when he saw the Hebrew language conquering one barrier after an other and spreading to all the social classes. Finally, he decided that it was time to let other places enjoy the national Hebrew education. He traveled to Różan, his birthplace, and founded there a school as well as a branch in Goworowo. And so, he had one success after another preparing himself and his students for the sacred mission of making Aliya. He perceived teaching Hebrew as the first stage of redemption and hence, the coming of the Messiah. He lit this fire in everyone who approached him and he bequeathed this enthusiasm to his sons and the generation he educated.

His personality combined three titles: Rabbi, Teacher and Melamed.

[Page 458]

Our Home

Nekhama Sela–Lewkowicz & Yakov Lewkowicz

Translated by Naomi Gal

My late father's image conjures Maków landscape. The paths his feet trod, the river where he bathed or where he caught fish with his fishhook, the forest where he walked its length and width at dawn in all seasons of the year.

He loved nature, the sight of nature, the changes and transformations were an inspiration for him and lifted his spirits. He was a part of the Maków landscape and when he was in Mother Nature's arms, he completely immersed himself, his happiness and awe were whole.

When he saw a group of the Hashomer Hazair camped on one of the mountains, his face filled with light, when he heard the Hebrew language sounds from his trainees, he welcomed them with a big smile and a hearty Shalom greeting.

The unforgettable Alta Hendel, who was one of his best students, served as a group's head and delegated her superb qualities to hundreds of her trainees.

* * *

And here comes to memory the Maków "Shtiebel" where he prayed at dawn with his orthodox opponents, who in the evenings became his friends because the Talmud page brought them close together and when they were discussing a Talmud question their contention was forgotten. Here is Poperztchna Street, paralleled to Parazsnish Street, where our shack stood. From the outside it looked as if it was crumbling but inside it was a fortress of Torah and a meeting place for the wise. The teachers of "Yavne" School – the principal Rosenblum, Portnoy and David Levin found in our home a warm haven since for a whole year they were far from their homes and because of their meager salary were unable to be with their families. They led vivid discussions till midnight, joined by the uncles Kalman Stern, the Sofer ST"M and Mordechai David, the educated scholar. The discussions were peppered with sages' sayings, verses from the Zohar and more. They spoke also about worlds' topics and argued about politics. The lively conversation created a pleasant ambiance in the house.

* * *

We can still see before us the Shabbat in our house with all its glory and sacredness. We were at the table, light illuminating us all. Father of blessed memory, began as always with Shabbat's songs and ended with Zion songs – "With my Plow", "In the Middle of the Road", "El Hazipor" and others, with his "choir" of course. Our sister Rachel, of blessed memory, who sang well, was the first voice. Moshe and Yehuda – second voices.

[Page 459]

The singing grew stronger, burst outside and echoed in the air. People from all corners of the city crowded next to the windows and doors. The sounds of Zion songs penetrated their bones and filled their hearts with overpowering longings to Zion...

Our father was a trove of spiritual and practical capacities. In the attic of our house, he had carpenters' tools and frames – a real workshop where he was trained in all handicrafts, he made doors and windows for our house as well as a construction plan according to all engineering regulations and the municipality approved this plan. There is no knowing what our father could have achieved with his gifts, if only he was able to...

Light in the Night

by A Student

Translated by Anita Frishman Gabbay

Late at night. The small town of Makow is asleep. The small wooden houses on Czechonover Street, painted white, lights up the darkness. From the rocky bank the steps of a passerby can be heard. Only from one wooden house, a light appears through the window. This is the last house on Czechonover Street. This is where the "Cheder Metukan" of the Hebrew teacher R'Anschel Kotziak is located.

When the late passerby looks inside the room of the "Cheder", he sees, the teacher, R'Anschel, standing and writing with chalk small, clear, important words on the blackboard–a lesson for his students for the next day.

It is almost morning. It is the Yarzheit [memorial of a death] of Dr. Binjamin Zeev Herzl, of blessed memory, and R'Anschel wants to tell his students of the "Cheder Metukan" [this was a Hebrew school, but in the small Hasidic shtetl, Makow, it was easier to use the name "*Cheder Metukan*"] about the "*great Zionist leader*", who lit up like a star the *Dark Sky of Exile*".

R'Anschel creases his forehead, he wants to share as much information about this important leader and about the great values of Zion, but the blackboard is too small. There he writes small, clear letters, in order to squeeze in one more lesson [to plant into the hearts of his students].

[Page 460]

When he finished writing and washing his hands, he remembered, that he hadn't prayed his Maariv prayers today, so he sits down and silently whispers: "and to Jerusalem...".

Oy, Jerusalem, Jerusalem! How the Land of his fathers is beckoning!

R'Anschel goes to his dresser, takes out a thick book with papers and documents and rereads the letter from the Palestine–Office in Warsaw. The date: 1920. They acknowledge, due to the situation now in Eretz–Israel, the consideration[request] for his Aliyah and for his three sons. His wife and daughters, for the time being must remain in Poland. He deliberates with much anxiety, Aliyah is not possible as an entire family. So he remains for the time being in Makow, on the river Orzyc and continues to teach Jewish children Hebrew, Tanach, while planting the love for Eretz–Israel.

From the direction of Sloninover Way [tiny street], a crowing hen is heard, he then creeps silently into his house located in a neighbouring building–to rest after a hard day.

The life of R'Anschul Kotziak was not easy when he arrived in 1917 from Warsaw to Makow.

It was the time of the German occupation, of the First World War. In Warsaw there was a shortage of food, when the Makower landowner, R' Aba Berenboim, became aquainted with the teacher, he invited him to open a "Cheder Metukan" in Makow. The latter agreed.

R'Anschul came from Lithuania, studied at the Volozhin Yeshiva, wrote Hebrew songs and dreamed of studying philosophy. Instead, he arrived in the small Hasidic shtetl Makow. The trip from Warsaw to Makow was in a large carriage, which stopped in many muddy Polish towns. He arrived at the wood bridge, which brought him into the shtetl, then travelling across the large market square with the small–town houses and some ruins left over from the last war. R' Aba Berenboim received him graciously and the next morning, he met with other landowners of the city, who were interested in the "Cheder Metukan": Rekant, Sheinberg, Hendel, Montchkovsky and others.

Shortly afterwards, they rented a dwelling in a wooden house next to the river Ozycz. R'Anschel opened his "Cheder Metukan" and brought his family from Warsaw.

Spring. The fields are blooming. The sun is shining. It seems, that the largest part of the sun–rays swallow the sober–water of the Ozycz. The students–Chaim Berenboim, Moishe Sheinberg, Yankel Sobel, Eliezer Montchkovsky, Schmulik Kleinhoiz, Chaim Hendel, Yankel Goldstein, Avrahamel Riback and others run to the river. Also R' Anschul's young sons–Yerachmiel and Menachem–Mendele are among them.

[Page 461]

They are running barefoot in the water and are trying to catch the small fish that swim in the river. Then they run over the ruins of the former houses, to play hide and seek. The bell now rings. R' Anschel doesn't allow his students to linger–we must resume the Torah and other work.

Lag B'Omer, 1918, all the Jewish Cheders participate in the march to the Makower forest to celebrate. Jewish children with blue–white banners go through the streets, singing Jewish songs and also the song of S.L. Gordon *"the honeysuckle, the honeysuckle is a bow and arrow"*.

R'Anschul organized the first children's' Hebrew library in his "Cheder–Metukan. It was the first time these children went into a Hebrew library". He also emphasized speaking Hebrew in the street[in everday life]. The landowners wondered, how did these youngsters speak Hebrew so fluently?

The largest part of R'Anschel's students became involved in the Zionist Youth Organizations of Hashomer Hatzair and Halutz. Many made their way to the [Kibbutz] training camps and through them– made Aliyah to Eretz Israel.

Arriving in the Land they knew Hebrew language.

Although R'Anschul was a religious Jew, from "Mizrachi", he embraced the Zioinist ideology. With love he spoke about the pioneers, who are building the land with their blood and sweat.

R'Anschel was very active in the social life of Makow. His wife, Malka, who was an organizer of "Linat Tzedek", brought help to the sick and needy with the help of the other women of the shtetl.

The "Cheder Metukan" was a modern school, but in hindsight, when remembering "tuition", R'Anschul was indifferent. Makow was a poor shtetl and to earn a living was difficult. The parents of R'Anschul's students needed a loan[or to pay in installments]. But R'Anschul never sent a student home. When the money was due at the end of the month for the Cheder, that also maintained the teacher and melamdim, the *safe* was empty. In the thick book, lying in the drawer, the debt grew and the *obligations* remained. In 1927 when R'Anschul liquidated the Cheder and left Makow, he took the book of debts with him, which were never paid. He was the type of Jew where money was never an issue. He was proud that he instructed a generation of children in the Hebrew language and taught them the love and devotion for Eretz Israel.

[Page 462]

In 1927, after working in Makow for 10 years, he returned to live in the birth–town of his wife, Grajewo [Grayewo].

Until the Second World War, he continued with a Hebrew school in Grajewo. In 1939, when the Russian Army arrived, he was a Jew over 65 years, he continued to teach students in Yiddish subjects. When Russia and Nazi–Germany entered the war, Grajewo, on the first day, was invaded by Nazi hordes and the fate of the Grajewo Jews was the same as the fate of all the Jewish communities–a ghetto was created, then the road led to Aushwitz.

R'Anschul Kotziak departed on his last journey with all the Jews of Grajewo, with his son, the teacher Alter Kotziak and family, and his youngest daughter, Ruchl, of blessed memory (his wife Malka died in Grajewo before the war).

May these few lines serve as a tombstone [memorial] for the unknown grave of my teacher R'Anschul Kontziak, of blessed memory, who educated thousands of students to love the Nation of Israel and the Land of Eretz Israel that he himself was never able to achieve, which he spent his entire life striving to achieve.

May his Soul be Bound in the Bond of Eternal Life.

Note: See Grajewo[Grayewo, Grayeve] Yiskor Book, History of the Grajewo Ghetto, see Anshel Kotchak, same person as R'Anschul Kotsiak

[Page 463]

Memories of My Father's House

by Chaya–Gitl Prezberg, Tel Aviv

Translated by Anita Frishman Gabbay

After my grandfathers death he left 5 sons: Yacov–Meir, Sender(my father), Avraham, Eliezer, and Fishl(my husband's father). They inherited a large house on Popzethehne Street. In distributing an inheritance, often, many quarrels broke out between the heirs, which often passed through the courts and caused many years of brothers and sisters not speaking to one another. It was different between the 5 Prezberg brothers, which learned good values in their father's home. Honesty and love for the fellow man. They were devoted one to the other, they helped each other–not just in as friends, also after their weddings.

After sitting Shiva [ritual after a person dies], the brothers came to their grandmother's house, and in one evening , they divided the inheritance. Each were given the same, an apartment in the house, quietly distributed the merchandise in the warehouse, which was in the yard, and no one was upset.

A Lag B'Omer march from the Cheder "Yavneh", 1932

[Page 464]

One of the brothers sold his inheritance to his nephew [brother's son], and the remaining 4 brothers all lived under one roof, all working in the same business, which was inherited from my grandfather–"stores". It means, that each one with horse and wagon spent the week travelling from village to village, to noble houses near the city, selling cloth and head–scarves. They all earned the same.

It didn't happen, that one was envious of the other. The opposite, they often bought their cloth together, and were satisfied, each one, that they were able to work together. In the city and its surroundings, the Prezberg brothers were an example of living harmoniously together and with their neighbours– working and living together.

They were good–humored, quiet and religious Jews. Roaming an entire week among Christians, they strictly adhered to their Jewishness. My father carried his *talis* a0nd *tefilim* through the villages, together with his cup, bowl, spoon and knife, cooked for himself only dairy and eggs.

For his honesty, the nobility as well as the peasants, trusted and had confidence in him.

In the long winter evenings my father stayed at the peasants' homes, telling them stories from the Tanach and news from around the world. It was a difficult livelihood. Five days a week he went from place to place. He didn't sleep in a bed, our house from Sunday to Thursday had an air of loneliness.

My mother Rivka, a smart woman, who was knowledgeable in praying and reading the "tzainu v rainu", the passage of the week, told the neighbours: 'it is not a way to live, as a father is not home for his children the entire week".

In those days, our mother was lonely, cooked our meals and prepared the table, as all the Jews. We waited the entire week and so the children of the Prezberg brothers awaited their fathers every Thursday evening returning from their villages . Every Thursday, after lunch we prepared to greet our fathers. Summertime–we ventured further to greet them. We were overjoyed, when we saw our father's horse and wagon from a distance. Father stopped, embarrassed and kissed us and put us in the wagon, while asking questions about home. In order to speak, he loosened the reins of the horse, knowing the horse could navigate in the right direction.

[Page 465]

Thursday morning the atmosphere at home became livelier. Mother and the aunts arrived from the street with full baskets, cleaned the house, and busied themselves in the kitchen. Put on their Shabbat clothes, and awaited the men, who arrived before evening. It was a Shabbat–holiday atmosphere in the house with their arrival, until their departure Sunday morning.

When I started to read Mendele Mocher Sforim's "The Vinshfingerl"[The Wishing Ring], the story of Shabbos and the week of Moishele's poor father, Shmelik Tandenik, I identified with him, literally his heart–wrenching story was a version of mine. Although my father wasn't a poor man, my father also arrived for the Shabbat, and left after the Shabbat to roam the villages.

The five brothers, like I said, were pious Jews. But not fanatic. They allowed their children to study in a Cheder and a Yeshiva. The girls went to the Polish Folk–Schul[elementary] and in the "Cheder Metukan". We also had lessons in Hebrew. Moishe–Yehuda Prezberg, son of Eliezer Prezberg, was an active Zionist, speaker and representative of the "Keren Kayemet" in our town, (his sister Sura, and her husband Yechiel Prezberg are now living in Israel).

A group of Makower Halutzim [pioneers] making Aliyah to Eretz–Israel, 1925

[Page 466]

My father didn't interfere in my youth, I became involved in "Hachalutz Hatzair", where I became the head of the division. Chaim Goldstein, was a talented fellow, an energetic leader and a charismatic speaker. He perished in Warsaw. The secretary was Yacov–Chaim Sobel–today in New York. Known for his commitment to the *landsleit* [*fellow townsmen*] and for the "Welfare of the Makower Society in Israel".

I will never forget our gatherings– summer in the forest, on the hill, near the Orzyc river. There we read A.D. Gordon's letter from Eretz–Israel, sang Hebrew songs and speaking about Hachara [training] and Aliyah.

Not everyone who went through training–from Hachalutz or from Hashomer Hatzair–had the fortune in those days to receive certificates, in order to make Aliyah. Most of the Jewish youth, and also the Prezberg brothers, by the hands of the Nazis, may their name and memory be erased forever, were tortured, burned and gassed together with the other 6 million Jews.

Blessed shall be their memory!

[Page 467]

To Ben–Zion Hendel's Memory

by David Bukhner, Tel–Aviv

Translated by Naomi Gal

Ben–Zion Hendel was born and raised by parents who were Amshinov Hasidim. They were progressive Hasidim and his name testifies to the Zionist inclination in their home. He received a traditional education and studied in Cheder until he was sixteen years old. When the news about the establishment of the "Halutz" in Poland reached Maków, our city, and the information about the possibility of training and making Aliyah, he was one of the firsts who took off his traditional attire and registered to "Halutz". He was one of the first to engage in this new organization, at a time when our city's youngsters were active in existing organizations: the "Bund" and other Zionist movements. "Halutz" urged the youngsters to shake themselves free of idleness and life of degeneration.

After a short while Ben–Zion left for training, to Klesów which then was the center for training in Poland. He studied carpentry, a profession that did not thrill his parents, but Ben–Zion convinced them that this was a necessary profession for building the new state of Israel.

In 1929, when all of Israel's gates were locked by the British Mandate, he was one of the few who managed to make Aliyah. I remember the evening he said farewell to his "Halutz" friends and dozens of them accompanied him with songs and dances. The joy brought him to tears. When he arrived in Israel it was a time of harsh riots and he was one of the first to enlist for the country's defense. He lived on the other side of the rioters' nest in the Brenner neighborhood. He spent days and nights standing on guard and found work in his profession with Avraham Krinitzi (Ramat–Gan's mayor) who was one of the first employers in this branch. My city citizens who arrived in Israel after him found a welcoming home and a dedicated and loyal friend, willing to help in every way. When there was a resuscitation of work and construction, he moved to Rishon–Lezion, started a family and begun working independently. Ben–Zion loved his profession with all his heart. He was happy and proud and did not complain. He lived a modest life, and in his free time was active in Mapai, the association of the craftsmen and the Maków descendants committee. He was dedicated and willing to make any sacrifice. His home was open to all needy. He was happy with his family life despite the difficult times he had endured. He always had a big smile and used to pat you on the shoulder saying: "Things will get better, mate".

The news about his death astonished his many friends and fellow citizens. It is hard to believe that we will never again see his unforgettable and vivid personality in meetings and memorials.

May his soul be bound in the bundle of the living.

[Page 468]

A visit to the hometown Makow
Twenty–three years after the Holocaust

by Max Pianka. Ph.D.

Typed up by Genia Hollander

In February 1966, I received an invitation from the Polish Academy of Sciences for a two–week lecture tour in Poland. The invitation was also extended to my wife. I had misgivings about going to Poland, the grave of our people. However, this was to be a scientific tour and, after all, the Polish Government is considered by the Israeli Government to be friendly and a number of scientists from Israel have visited Poland. My wife and I decided to accept the invitation. We visited Poland in June, 1966. I delivered a number of lectures at the Universities of Warsaw, Lodz and at an Institute near Cracow. We were given a most friendly reception and covered a great deal of the country in a chauffeur–driven car.

While in Warsaw, I made it clear to my hosts that I would like to meet Jews and I was introduced to a charming Assistant Professor at the University who spoke excellent Yiddish and Hebrew. We went to the Yiddish Theatre to see Scholem Aleichem's "Schadchonim un Menschen". It was a delightful performance. One felt though as if visiting a museum. The audience used ear–phones for a simultaneous translation into Polish, it was obvious that the younger people did not speak Yiddish. In a Jewish restaurant, most of the dishes were "heimish" but the waiters did not speak Yiddish. There is practically no new Yiddish literature and the management of the Theatre has to rely on the old Yiddish classics only.

The feeling in Warsaw, just as it was during our visit to Makow, was that of unreality. It was heart–rending to see Warsaw and a score of small towns, especially Makow, without the hustle and bustle and the warmth of Jewish life. Our feelings of sadness and of nostalgia were overwhelming, beyond imagination…

The horror and tragedy of Auschwitz which has been turnedinto a Museum of atrocities, cannot be deleted from one's memory. My wife's parents perished there and, I believe, my Dear Mother too and many of our dear Makower Landsleit. We felt it is our duty to visit there and render to their sacred memory our act of solemn devotion, and "there" I said "Kaddish". Nothing can be forgotten, nothing can be forgiven…

[Page 469]

From Warsaw, we went by car via Ppltusk to visit the hometown Makow. I felt compulsively driven to re–visit the town where my childhood memories and the most memories of our town's people are buried. I would have felt lacking in my duty, how painful it was, to be in Poland and not go to Makow, so I went.

My pilgrimage brought me to the "Marek", the Market Place with a post in its centre carrying a bill with the name and plan of the town.

It is still a "Powiat" town with a population of over 4000 inhabitants. There is not a single Jew living there now.

The Ciechanowska Street, where so many Jewish families lived and traded, has changed appearance and name. Where our house stood, is now an empty lot. Where the "Yatkes" were, there is now a cinema: "Mazowsze".

Further up, in place of the "Talmud Tora", where so many of our children were educated according to our ageless tradition of orthodox Judaism, there are now some wooden dwellings. Where stood the Public School, my father's original "Szkola Powszechna", the centre of so many extramural cultural and social activities, which I remember, one of our visiting lecturers from Warsaw aptly referred to as: "The Makower University", there are now small shops.

We went across to where the Synagogue, our Shul and the Bet–Midrash were the site of the war–time Ghetto, whence our people were deported to their doom, there is now just an empty lot.

Miraculously, the row of houses near the river Orzyc is now somehow narrow and shallow.

We then turned to the Bazaar across the bridge. The school, which was built before the war on the Bazaar for the Jewish children, still stands intact. It houses now a high school. The headmaster occupies, in fact, the same office which my father occupied.

[Page 470]

Imagine my feelings when the choir of the school sang for us at the reception held for my wife and me, at which we were introduced to the pupils of the school as important guests of the Polish Academy of Sciences and the Ministry of Chemical Industry; the speaker referring to me as the son of the pre–war headmaster and beloved leader in our town. This was really poetic justice.

On the slope of a hill facing the river Orzyc is a graveyard of some Jews and non–Jews shot or hanged for minor offences by the Nazi. I was told that some survivors of our own Makower Jews who came back to Makow after the war, have transferred the bodies of the Jews from this common grave to the Beis Olem.

The Jewish cemeteries, the old Beis Olem and the new Beis Olem in Makow do not exist anymore; they are completely destroyed – there are now just empty lots. What a shame? …

The hydroelectric station "Turbina" on the river still stands but it is not functioning and the nearby baths, "Laznia" are still in operation. The water pumps in the Market Place "(Rynek)" are now electrically operated. The part of the town where the church is, remains intact, like nothing happened. All the houses are there just as I remembered them and the "Alejki" where we used to take our evening strolls are still there as a witness to the tragic division of our hometown into the Jewish and Christian parts, one of which is practically obliterated and the other still standing intact.

This is how Makow, our hometown, looked now, 23 years after the Holocaust, after the big "Hurban".

I was under the impression that I have visited a Cemetery, a Graveyard without graves.

Leaving the town, I had the feeling that the Ashes of our "Kedoshim" are still wandering in the air.

I heard an echo with an outcry calling: "Zachor – Tizkor" …"DO NOT FORGET"…

[Page 471]

[Page 472] Blank

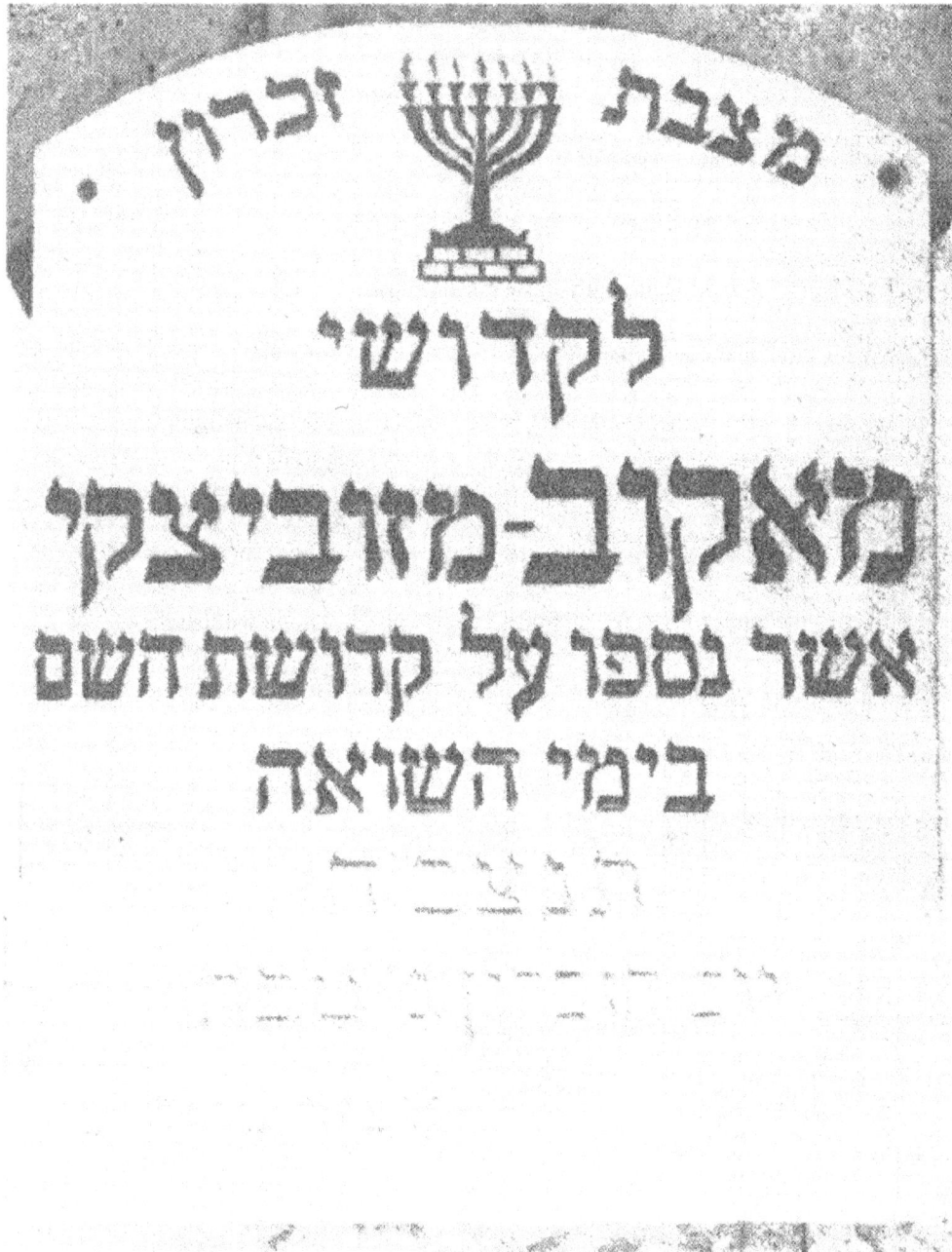

Monument to the martyrs of Makow in the holy city of Jerusalem

[Page 473]

Remembrance

Translated by Anita Frishman Gabbay

Let the Nation of Israel remember the holy community of Makow

Which was cruelly uprooted, destroyed and annihilated.

May they recall their murdered residents, victims of the evil regime,

Who were tortured physically and spiritually in the death camps.

May they recall all those who were deported to desolate lands, leaving no trace

Who were massacred in marketplaces and roads, hauled to their destruction in death wagons

Who were buried alive, burned, slaughtered, drowned and strangled

Whose honor was violated, and whose blood was spilled, by impure hands, in Sanctification of the Divine Name.

May the Nation of Israel remember it's dear children, pure ones, the children of pure ones

Who were robbed from their parents' bosom by beasts in human disguise and taken like sheep to slaughter

Who were beheaded and murdered, in all manner of unnatural deaths

And piled in heaps in the open–

Infants and babies who were broken against stone walls, who were tossed down from walls

Whose lives were cut off in their infancy by cruel hands.

May the Nation of Israel remember the pure children, and the splendor of the worlds

And may they not forget the evil and the atrocities

As long as they live upon the earth.

Blessed be their Memory!

[Page 474] Blank
[Pages 475-504]

List of Martyrs from Maków Mazowiecki, Poland

Translated by Shalom Bronstein

Family name(s)	First name(s)	Maiden name	Gender	Name of spouse	Additional family	Remarks	Page
א Alef							
OVLODZINER	Ya'akov Leib		M				475
OVLODZINER	Chaya Sheindel		F				475
OVLODZINER	Shlomo		M				475
OVLODZINER	Moshe		M		His family		475
OVLODZINER	Kaltzieh	LEVKOWITCH	F		His family		475
ADLER	Avraham Mechel		M		His family	From Chorzele. In Maków Mazowiecki during the war; he perished together with his family	475
AHARONOVITCH					The entire family	Listing states - the AHARONOVITCH family with no personal names	475
UNGER	Chaim Ya'akov		M		His family		475
UNGER	Efraim Fishel		M				475
UNGER	Hinda		F				475
UNGER	Antshel		M				475
UNGER	Mendel		M				475
UNGER	Arieh		M				475
UNGER	Breina		F				475
UNGER	Gittel		F				475
UNGER	Chava		F				475

AZRILEVITCH	Raphael Hersh		M			475
AZRILEVITCH	Sarah		F			475
AZRILEVITCH	Pinchas		M			475
AZRILEVITCH	Tzirl		F			475
AZRILEVITCH	Azriel		M			475
AZRILEVITCH	Nechama		F			475
AZRILEVITCH	Ya'akov Moshe		M			475
AZRILEVITCH	Tzirl		F			475
AZRILEVITCH	Yonatan		M			475
AZRILEVITCH	Shmuel Yosef		M			475
AZRILEVITCH	Frimet		F			475
AZRILEVITCH	Simcha		M			475
AZRILEVITCH	Sarah Rivkah		F			475
INGBERMAN	Menachem Mannes		M			475
INGBERMAN	Chava Breindel		F			475
INGBERMAN	Perl		F			475
INGBERMAN	Yehudit		F			475
INGBERMAN	Sarah		F			475
INGBERMAN	Pinchas		M		He is listed as Rabbi Pinchas INGBERMAN	475
INGBERMAN	David		M			475
INGBERMAN	Leah		F			475
INGBERMAN	Moshe		M			475
INGBERMAN	Chana Feiga		F			475
EISENMAN	Pelteh		F	His family		475
EISENMAN				The entire family	Listing states - the EISENMAN family with no personal names	475
EISENSTADT	Naftali		M			475

EISENSTADT	Baila Rachel	F		475
EISENSTADT	Chaya	F		475
EISENSTADT	Yosef	M		475
ITZKOVITCH	Yitzhak	M		475
ITZKOVITCH	Sarah Leah	F		475
ITZKOVITCH	Freydel WISHINSKI	F	Children - number not given	476
ITZKOVITCH	Perl	F		476
ITZKOVITCH	Yenta	F	Her husband	476
ITZKOVITCH	Rachel	F		476
ITZKOVITCH	Fishel	M		476
ITZKOVITCH	Chana Rivkah	F		476
ITZKOVITCH	Perl	F		476
ITZKOVITCH	Yenta	F		476
ITZKOVITCH	Abba	M	His family	476
ITZKOVITCH	Yosef Leib	M		476
ITZKOVITCH	Reizel	F		476
ITZKOVITCH	Henne	F		476
ALBECK	Shlomo Henech	M		476
ALBECK	Rachel Leah	F		476
ALBECK	Leibel	M		476
ALBECK	Chaim	M		476
ALBECK	Simcha	M		476
ALBECK	Masheh	F		476
ALBECK	Nechama	F		476
ALTER	Zeinvel	M	His family	476
ALTER	Yosef Leib	M		From Warsaw. In Maków Mazowiecki during the war	476

ALTER	Ita	ORLICK	F		In Warsaw during the war	476
ALTER	Moshe		M			476
ALTER	Avraham		M			476
ALTER	David		M			476
ALTER	Yitzhak		M			476
ALTER	Rachel		F			476
ALTER	Chana		F			476
ALTER	Esther		F			476
OSTRY	Meir		M			476
OSTRY	Breina		F			476
OSTRY	Nechama		F			476
OSTRY	Gittel		F		Her husband & 1 child	476
OSTASHEVER	Berish		M		His family	476
OPPENHEIM	Pinchas		M			476
OPPENHEIM	Bluma		F			476
OPPENHEIM	Shmuel		M			476
OPPENHEIM	Peseh		F			476
ORLOVSKY	Hershel		M			476
ORLOVSKY	Devorah		F			476
ORLOVSKY	Sarah Esther		F			476
ORLOVSKY	Chava		F			476
ORLOVSKY	Nachman		M			476
ORLOVSKY	Yosef		M			476
ORLICK	Ya'akov Chanoch		M			476
ORLICK	Adeleh Aidel		F			476
ORLICK	Shmuel David		M			476
ORLICK	Shlomo Zalman		M			476
ORLICK	Feiga		F			476

ORLICK	Yitzhak		M			476
ORLICK	Roiza		F			476
ORLICK	Chana Chava		F	Shmuel		476
ORLICK	Shmuel		M	Chana Chava		476
ORLICK	Dina		F		Her family	476
ORLICK	Chaim		M			476
ORLICK	Rachel		F			476
ORLICK	Velvel		M			476
ORLICK	Perl		F			476
ORLICK	David		M			476
ORLICK	Basha		F			476
ORLICK	David		M			477
ORLICK	Chaim		M			477
ORLICK	Racheltshe		F		1 child	477
ORLICK	Moshe		M			477
ORLICK	Chava		F	Yechiel	Children - number not given	477
ORLICK	Yechiel		M	Chava	Children - number not given	477
ORLICK	Aharon		M			477
ORLICK	Gittel		F			477
ORLICK	Meir		M			477
ORLICK	Chana		F			477
ORLICK	Rivkah		F			477
ORLICK	Vaveh		?			477
ORLICK	Tobeh		F			477
ROSENBAUM	Sarah	ORLICK	F		Her husband & children	She is listed by her maiden name ORLICK; her husband's name is ROSENBAUM, no personal name given	477

ORLICK	Mordecai Ber		M		477
ORZSHECH	Yisrael Leib		M		477
ORZSHECH	Chana Rachel		F		477
ORZSHECH	Chaya Devorah		F		477
ORZSHECH	Ya'akov		M		477
ORZSHECH	Meir Mordecai		M		477
ASHENMIL	Shmuel Avraham		M		477
ASHENMIL	Rachel		F		477
ASHENMIL	Freydel		F		477

ב Bet

BOTZIAN	Velvel		M	His family	477
BOTZIAN	Binyamin		M	His family	477
BORENSTEIN	Roiza	KATZ	F	Her family	477
BORENSTEIN	Michael		M		477
BORENSTEIN	Shifra		F	Her family	477
BORENSTEIN	Shayeh		M	His family	477
BORENSTEIN	Gershon		M	His family	477
BARSHT	Mendel		M		477
BARSHT	Mindel		F	Children - number not given	477
BORENSTEIN	Yankel		M	His family	477
BORENSTEIN	Yehuda Leib		M	His family	477
BORDOVITCH	Moshe Meir		M		477
BORDOVITCH	Niche		F	Children - number not given	477
BORDOVITCH	Simcha		M	His family	477
BORDOVITCH	Chaya		F		477

BARAB	Feivel		M		477
BUCHNER	Avraham Yitzhak		M		477
BUCHNER	Golda		F		477
BUCHNER	Yisrael Chaim		M		477
BUCHNER	Feiga		F		477
BUCHNER	Yisrael Feivel		M		477
BUCHNER	Bracha	BORENSTEIN	F	Her family	477
BULMAN	Aharon		M	His family	477
BORSTEIN	Shlomo		M		477
BORSTEIN	Zvia Leah	GARFINKLE	F	Children - number not given	478
BORSTEIN	Fishel		M	His family	478
BAZSHOZA	Chanoch Henech		M		478
BAZSHOZA	Margalit		F		478
BAZSHOZA	Avraham		M		478
BAZSHOZA	Sarah		F		478
BAZSHOZA	Minyeh		F		478
BEATSH	Yitzhak		M		478
BEATSH	Tabeh		F		478
BEATSH	Peseh		F		478
BEATSH	Devorah		F		478
BEATSH	Chaim		M		478
BEATSH	Freyda		F		478
BEATSH	Shmuel		M		478
BEILIS	Fishel		M		478
BEILIS	Baila		F		478
BEILIS	Avigdor		M		478
BEILIS	Moshe		M		478
BEILIS	Temma		F		478
BLACHOVITSH	David		M	His family	478

BLANK		.			The entire family	List states BLANK family with no personal names or other information given	478
BLUM	Hershel		M				478
BLUM	Henech		M				478
BLUM	Rivkah		F				478
BLUM	Esther		F				478
BLUM	Lartzyeh		F	Perkal			478
BLUM	Perkal		M	Lartzyeh			478
BLUM	Yitzhak		M				478
BLUM	Shimshon		M				478
BLUM	Gittel		F				478
BLUM	Mordecai		M			Father's name Shimshon	478
BLUM	Devorah		F				478
BLUM	Feiga		F				478
BLUM	Moshe		M				478
BLUM	Maniyoshe		F				478
BLUM	Mordecai		M			Father's name Feivel	478
BLUM	Saratshe	TENENBAUM	F				478
BLUM	Blimtzia		F				478
BLUM	Shmuel Leib		M				478
BLUM	Yoel		M				478
BLUM	Avraham		M				478
BLUM	Tzime Zisia		F				478
BLUM	Rachel		F				478
BLUM	Itzel		M				478
BLUM	Devorah		F				478
BLUM	Chaya Rivkah		F				478
BLUM	Aharon		M		His family		478

BLUM	David		M	His family	478
BLUM	Baruch		M	His family	478
BLUM	Moshe		M	His family	478
BLUM	Feivel		M	His family	478
BLUM	Feila	ROSENBAUM	F	Her son	478
BLUM	Yosel		M		478
BLUM	Ita		F		478
BLENKITNER	Berel		M		478
BLENKITNER	Roiza		F		478
BLENKITNER	Peseleh		F		479
BLENKITNER	Shlomo		M		479
BLENKITNER	Batya		F		479
BLENKITNER	Peseh		F		479
BLENKITNER	Chanaleh		F		479
BERGAZIN	Leah		F		479
BERGAZIN	Chaya		F		479
BERGAZIN	Feiga		F		479
BERGAZIN	Rachel		F		479
BERGAZIN	Mendel		M		479
BERGAZIN	Arieh		M		479
BERGAZIN	Simcha		M		479
BENDER	Simcha Hersh		M		479
BENDER	Miriam		F		479
BENDER	Chaya		F		479
BELDIKER	Azriel Mordecai		M	His wife	479
BELDIKER	Hersh Meir		M	His family	479
BERNBAUM	Abba		M		479
BERNBAUM	Mordecai		M		479
BERNBAUM	Sarah		F		479
BERENHOLTZ	Arieh		M		479
BERENHOLTZ	Esther		F		479

BERGSON	Yosef	M	His family	479
BERGSON	Berel	M	His family	479
BEHER	Chaim Meir	M	His family	479
BEHER	Yechiel	M		479
BEHER	Bracha	F		479
BEHER	Sarah Feiga	F		479
BERLINSKY	Meir	M	His family	479
BERLINSKY	Nechama	F		479
BERMAN	Fishel	M	His family	479
BERMAN	Ya'akov	M	His family	479
BRATZKI	Yisrael	M	His family	479
BOTSHAN	Gedalia	M		479
BOTSHAN	Feiga	F		479
BORNSTEIN	Chava	F		504
BORNSTEIN	Hershel	M		504
BORNSTEIN	Hertzka	M		504
BORNSTEIN	Bina	F		504
BORNSTEIN	Moshe	M		504

א Gimmel

GOGOL	Meir Mannes	M		479
GOGOL	Temma Gittel	F		479
GOGOL	Moshe	M		479
GOGOL	Malka	F		479
GOGOL	Peseh	F		479
GOGOL	Shlomo	M		479
GOGOL	Pinchas	M		479
GOGOL	Chaim	M		479
GOGOL	Sarah Gittel	F		479
GOGOL	Ya'akov	M		479

GOGOL	Miriam		F			479
GOGOL	Yitzhak		M	His family		479
GOGOL	Leibel		M			479
GAVARTSHIK	Chaim Davidl		M			479
GAVARTSHIK	Reizel		F			479
GOTTESMAN	Esther Leah	LILIENTHAL	F	With her family		480
GOTTESMAN	Chaim Motel		M	His family	He was a rabbi	480
GOLDSTEIN	David Leib		M			480
GOLDSTEIN	Reizel		F			480
GOLDSTEIN	Ya'akov Chaim		M			480
GOLDSTEIN	Peseh	ALBECK	F			480
GOLDSTEIN	Sarah	KATZ	F			480
GOLDSTEIN	Yitzhak		M	His family		480
GOLDVASSER	Fishel		M			480
GOLDVASSER	Henne		F			480
GOLDVASSER	Ya'akov		M			480
GOLDVASSER	Kruseh		F			480
GOLDVASSER	Hinda		F			480
GOLDVASSER	Chaim David		M			480
GOLDVASSER	Chana Gittel		F			480
GOLDVASSER	Sima		F			480
GOLDVASSER	Ya'akov		M			480
GOLDVASSER	Freydel		F			480
GOLDVASSER	Yosef		M			480
GOLDBAUM	Yechiel		M	His family		480
GOLDBAUM	Itsha Meir		M			480
GOLDBAUM	Shasha		F			480
GOLDBAUM	Avraham		M			480
GOLDBAUM	Menucha		F			480

GOLDBAUM	Neche		F		ˋ	480
GOLDBAUM	Leibel		M			480
GOLDBAUM	Ya'akov Zalman		M			480
GALINA	Hershel		M			480
GALINA	Rachel		F		Children - number not given	480
GARFINKLE	Moshe Yosef		M			480
GARFINKLE	Mirl		F			480
GARFINKLE	Baruch David		M			480
GARFINKLE	Yisrael Yitzhak		M			480
GARFINKLE	Feiga Rivkah	REITSHIK	F			480
GARFINKLE	Henech Chanoch		M			480
GARFINKLE	Tzime Michleh		F			480
GARFINKLE	Mirl		F			480
GARDBEIN					The entire family	480
NAVYAZDA	Yosef		M			480
NAVYAZDA	Rachel		F			480
NAVYAZDA	Zlateh		F			480
GUTLEIZER	Matityahu		M			480
GUTLEIZER	Shasha		F			480
GAZSHECHYENIAZSH	Zalman		M		His family	480
GLOGAVER	Fishel		M		His family	480
GLOGAVER	Eliezer		M			480
GLOGAVER	Henne	ITZKOVITCH	F			480
GLOGAVER	Hershel		M			480
GLOGAVER	Moshe David		M			480
GLOGAVER	Yehuda Leib		M		His wife	480

GLOGAVER	Azriel	M		480
GRADAVITSH	Eliezer	M	His family	480
GRADZITZKY	Chaya Malka	F		480
GRAMB	Avraham Yitzhak	M	Children - number not given	480
GRAMB	Moshe Aharon	M		480
GRAMB	Fabeh	F		480
GRAMB	Sarah Leah	F		480
GRAMB	Gershon Henech	M		481
GRAMB	Yitzhak	M		481
GRANIEVITSH	Shlomo	M		481
GRANIEVITSH	Esther	F		481
GRANIEVITSH	Leah Lutsha	F		481
GRANIEVITSH	Chaim	M		481
GRANIEVITSH	Ya'akov	M		481
GROSSMAN	Yoelke	M		481
GROSSMAN	Nechama	F		481
GROSSMAN	Shmuel Ya'akov	M		481
GROSSMAN	Mindel	F	Children - number not given	481
GRODEK	Yehezkel	M	His family	481
GREENSPAN	Sender	M		481
GREENSPAN	Liftshe	F		481
GREENSPAN	Moshe	M		481
GREENSPAN	Chava	F	With her family	481
GREENBERG	Fishel	M		481
GREENBERG	Zisa	F		481
GREENBERG	Asher Yosef	M		481

GREENBERG	Leah		F		481
GREENBERG	Perl		F		481
GREENBERG	Rachel		F		481
GREENBERG	Bluma		F		481
GREENBERG	Reuven		M	His family	481
GREENBERG	Natan		M	His family	481
GREENBERG	Hershel		M	His family	481
GREENBERG	Yitzhak		M	His family	481
GERLITZ	David		M		481
GERLITZ	Zisha		F		481
GERLITZ	Sarah	RIBACK	F		481
GLICKSBERG	Hersh Ber		M		481
GLICKSBERG	Sheindel		F		481
GLICKSBERG	Sarah		F		481
GLICKSBERG	Chava		F		481
GLICKSBERG	Chaya Liba		F		481
GLICKSBERG	Frimet		F		481
GLICKSBERG	Leibel		M		481
GLICKSBERG	Rivtsheh		F		481
GELUDE	Shlomo		M	His family	481
GETZELOVITSH	Hersh Yitzhak		M		481
GETZELOVITSH	Malka		F		481

ד **Dalet**

DOBRES	Itzel		M		481
DOBRES	Feigel		F		481
DOBRES	Chaya Sarah		F		481
DOBRES	Leahke		F		481
DOBRES	Devorah		F		481
DOBRES	Yehudit		F		481
DOBRES	Nisan		M		481
DAVIDOVITSH	Moshe		M	His family	481

DOMB	Feiga	F			481
DOMB	Avraham	M	His family		482
DOMB	Velvel	M		He was a shochet (slaughterer of animals)	482
DOMB	Mishke	F	Children - number not given		482
DOMB	Mendel	M			482
DOMB	Shlomo Zalman	M			482
DOMB	Sarah	F			482
DOMB	Chaya	F			482
DOMB	Yitzhak	M			482
DOMBEK	Ya'akov	M			482
DOMBEK	Sarah	F			482
DOMBEK	Temma	F			482
DOMBEK	Dareh	F			482
DOMBEK	Feiga	F			482
DZIENKOVITSH	Ya'akov Meir	M			482
DZIENKOVITSH	Rachel Leah	F			482
DZIENKOVITSH	Saratshe	F			482
DZIENKOVITSH	Tzirl	F			482
DZIENKOVITSH	Rivkah	F			482
DZIENKOVITSH	Temma	F			482
DZIENKOVITSH	Shmulik	M			482
DZIENKOVITSH	Yentel	F			482

הּ Hey

HOLTZKENER	Yitzhak	M			482
HOLTZKENER	Rachel Leah	F			482
HOCHMAN	Henech	M		Father's name Shlomo. Her mother's maiden name was SEGAL	482

					and first name Sheindel	
HIBEL	Nachum		M			482
HIBEL	Tzirl		F	Her daughter		482
HIBEL	Shepsel		M	His family		482
HIBEL	Fishel		M	His family		482
HILERT	Henech		M			482
HILERT	Chaya Devorah		F			482
HENDEL	Hillel		M			482
HENDEL	Sarah Blima		F			482
HENDEL	Alteh		F			482
HENDEL POLACK	Shmuel Zelig		M			482
HENDEL	Estherel	SOBOL	F			482
HENDEL	Ida		F			482
HENDEL	Henne		F			482
HENDEL	Devorah Gittel		F			482
HENDEL	Yosel		M			482
HENDEL	Leah		F			482
HENDEL	Shmulik		M			482
HENDEL	Chaya	MALACH	F	Her husband		482
HENDEL	Golda		F			482
HENDEL	David		M		He was a rabbi	482
HENDEL	Nechama	GARFINKLE	F	Children - number not given		482
HENDEL	Ya'akov David		M			482
HENDEL	Basha		F			482
HENDEL	Avraham		M			482
HENDEL	Baila		F			482
HERTZBERG	David		M			483

HERTZBERG	Feiga	F		483
HERTZBERG	Leibel	M		483
HERTZBERG	Sender	M	His family	483
HERTZBERG	Shlomo	M	His family	483
HERTZBERG	Shalom Eliyahu	M	His family	483
HERTZBERG	Hinda	F		483
HERTZBERG	Bashka	F		483
HERTZBERG	Rivkah	F		483
HERTZBERG	Chava	F		483
HERTZBERG	Chana	F		483
HERTZBERG	Natan	M	His family	483
HERTZBERG	Chaim Aharon	M	His family	483
HERTZBERG	Mordecai	M	His family	483

ו Vav

WOLFOVITSCH	Velvel	M		483
WOLFOVITSCH	Etta	F		483
WOLFOVITSCH	Mordecai	M	His family	483
WOLFOVITSCH	David	M	His family	483
WOLFISH	Shlomo	M		483
WOLFISH	Tzirl	F		483
WOLFISH	Temma	F		483
WOLFISH	Ya'akov Meir	M		483
WONSIAK	Moshe Leib	M		483
WONSIAK	Esther Leah	F		483
WONSIAK	Yosel	M	His family	483
WONSIAK	Baila Rachel	F		483
WONSKALASER	Avraham	M		483
WONSKALASER	Sheintshe	F		483
WONSKALASER	Meir	M		483

VARSHAVER	Aharon		M		484
VARSHAVER	Rachel		F	Children - number not given	483
VARSHAVER	Mendel		M		483
VARSHAVER	Gittel		F		483
VIATRAK	Fishel		M		483
VIATRAK	Chava		F		483
VIATRAK	Simcha		M		483
VIATRAK	Chaya		F	Children - number not given	483
VIATRAK	Leibush		M		483
VIATRAK	Sarah		F	Children - number not given	483
VIATRAK	Shmuel		M		483
VIATRAK	Sarah		F	Children - number not given	483
VIGODA	Aharon Yitzhak		M		483
VIGODA	Tzima		F		483
VIGODA	Esther		F		483
VIGODA	Rivkah		F		483
VIGODA	Yehezkel		M		484
VIGODA	Yenta		F		484
VILTSHEVSKY	Hersh		M		484
VILTSHEVSKY	Neche		F		484
VILENBERG	Yosel		M		484
VILENBERG	Gittel		F		484
VILENBERG	Moshe		M	His family	484
VILENBERG	Moshe		M		484
VILENBERG	Sheva		F		484
VILENBERG	Vashveh		F		484
VILENBERG	Itsha		F		484

VILENBERG	Feiga Leah		F			484
VILENBERG	David		M			484
VILENBERG	Bezalel		M			484
VILENBERG	Freyda		F			484
VILENBERG	Yisrael		M			484
VILENBERG	Golda		F			484
VILENBERG	Moshe		M			484
VILENBERG	Esther		F			484
VILENBERG	Ayzik		M			484
VISGARBER	Melech		M			484
VISGARBER	Chana Leah		F			484
VISGARBER	Mordecai		M			484
VISGARBER	Breina		F		Children - number not given	484
WEISSBERG	Hershel		M			484
WEISSBERG	Chayatshe	VILENBERG	F			484
WEISSBERG	Dov Berish		M			484
WEISSBERG	Baruch		M			484
WEISSBERG	Feiga		F			484
WEISSBERG	Etel		F		Her family	484
WEISSBERG	Mendel		M	Basha Platke		484
WEINTRAUB	Shmuel		M			484
WEINTRAUB	Baila		F			484
WEINTRAUB	Henech		M			484
WEINTRAUB	Mordecai David		M			484
WEINTRAUB	Velvel		M			484
WEINSTOCK	Perl		F			484
WEISAKER	Noach		M		His family	484
WEISSMAN	Henech		M			484
WEISSMAN	Leahtshe	BARSHTASH	F		Children - number not given	484

WEISSMAN	Yechielke		M			484
WISHINIA	Ya'akov David		M			484
WISHINIA	Yehudit		F			484
WISHINIA	Baila		F			484
WISHINIA	Roiza		F			484
WISHINIA	Rivkah		F			484
WISHINIAK	Moshe		M	His family		484
VENGERKA	Chone Bines		M	His family		484
VENGERKA	Leibel		M	His family		484
VENGDOVER	Ya'akov		M			484
WEISSALEK	Meir		M	His family		484
WEISSALEK	Yitzhak		M			484
WEISSALEK	Chava		F	Children - number not given		484
WEINSTEIN	Avraham		M			484
WEINSTEIN	Nechemiah		M			484

⌶ Zayin

SOMERFELD	Simcha Bines		M	His family		485
SOMERFELD	Yosef Mendel		M	His family		485
SOMERFELD	Chaim Shmuel		M			485
SOMERFELD	Chaya Esther	GARFINKLE	F	With her family		485
SOMERFELD	David		M			485
SOMERFELD	Tzima		F	Children - number not given		485
ZAKLITZEVER	Zanvel		M	His family		485
ZAKLIKOVSKY	Yisrael		M			485
ZAKLIKOVSKY	Sarah		F		She was a university student	485

SACKS	Chaya Sarah		F		485
SACKS	Feivel		M		485
ZAGRIZIK	Leibel		M	His family	485
SEGAL	Pinchas		M		485
SEGAL	Bailtshe	SOBOL	F		485
SEGAL	Racheleh		F		485
SEGAL	Ya'akov		M		485
SEGAL	Rivkah		F	Her daughter	485
SILVERBERG	Yitzhak		M		485
SILVERBERG	Blima		F		485
SILVERBERG	Avraham Yosef		M		485
SILVERBERG	Chaya		F	Children - number not given	485
SILVERBERG	Shlomo		M		485
SILVERBERG	Sarah		F	Children - number not given	485
SILVERBERG	Sarah Perl		F		485
SILVERBERG	Sima		F		485
SILVERBERG	Menachem		M		485
SILVERBERG	Ya'akov David		M	Children - number not given & his wife	485
ZILBERMAN	Chava		F	Children - number not given	485
ZHOTKEVITSCH	Eliezer		M		485
ZHOTKEVITSCH	Rachel		F		485
ZHEFKA				The entire family	485
ZHELOZNER	Avraham Yosef		M	His family	485
ZHELOZNER	Yisrael Chaim		M		485

ZHELOZNER	Yachtshe	LODVIANOVITCH	F			485
ZHELOZNER	Yehoshua		M			485
ZHELOZNER	Chaim Yitzhak		M	The entire family	Occupation - melamed (teacher of young children)	485

ט Tet

TORDES RICKOVER	Yitzhak		M			486
TORDES	Basha	RICKOVER	F			486
TORDES	David		M			486
TORDES	Yishayahu		M			486
TAUB	Wolf		M	His family		486
TAUB	Litman		M			486
TAUB	Avraham		M			486
TAUB	Efraim		M			486
TAUB	Yechiel		M			486
TAUB	Sarah		F			486
TAUB	Breina		F			486
TAFT	Mannes		M			486
TOPER	Feivel		M	His family		486
TORUK	Wolf		M	His family		486
TEITELBAUM	Mendel Moshe		M	His family		486
TCHMIEL	Yitzhak		M			486
TCHMIEL	Chaya Blima		F			486
TCHMIEL	Avigdor		M	His family		486
TCHMIEL	Moshe		M	His family		486
TCHMIEL	Leibel		M	His family		486
TCHMIEL	Avraham		M	His family		486
TCHMIEL	Feiga		F			486
TCHMIEL	Etel		F			486
TCHERVONOGURA	Avraham		M			486
TCHERVONOGURA	Yoel		M			486
TCHERVONOGURA	Yitzhak		M			486

TCHERVONOGURA	Chaya Sarah	REISHIK	F			486
TUTSHIN	Chaya Etta		F		She was the wife of a rabbi	486

ק Yod

YACHLONTCHIK	Yehezkel		M			486
YACHLONTCHIK	Perl	ITZKOVITCH	F			486
YACHLONKA	Shmuel		M		His wife's maiden name was SKORNIK; wife's 2nd husband. Mother's name Perl	486
YANOVER	Karpel		M	His family		486
YANOVER	Baruch David		M	His family		486
YANOSAVITCH	Velvel		M	His family		486
YANOSAVITCH	Shalom Yona		M	His family		486
YUSTMAN	Binyamin		M	His family		486
YEDVOVNIK	Ya'akov		M			486
YEDVOVNIK	Chaya Ita	PERLBERG	F			486
YEDVOVNIK	Leibel		M			486
YEDVOVNIK	Shmulka		M			486
YEDVOVNIK	Mordecai		M			487
YEDVOV	Yitzhak Meir		M			487
YEDVOV	Rachel		F			487
YEDVOV	Itka		F			487
YEDVOV	Maleh		F			487
YEDVOV	Arieh		M			487
YEDVOV	Sarah		F			487
YEDVOV	Shmuel David		M			487
YEROZOLIMSKY	Raphael		M	His family		487
YEROZOLIMSKY	David		M	His family		487
YEROZOLIMSKY	Shmuel		M			487

YEROZOLIMSKY	Esther		F		487
YEROZOLIMSKY	Yosef		M	His family	487
YISMACH	Mordecai Shmuel		M		487
YISMACH	Rivkah Leah		F		487
YISMACH	David		M		487
YISMACH	Moshe Aharon		M		487
YISMACH	Mechel		M		487
YISMACH	Gittel	HENDEL	F		487
YISMACH	Rachel		F		487

כ Kaf

KAHANA	Eliezer		M	His family	487
KVITAIKA	Baila		F	Her family	487
KVITAIKA	Ya'akov David		M		487
KVITAIKA	Liba		F		487
KVITAIKA	Elkana		M	His family	487
KVITAIKA	Yankel		M	His family	487
KVITAIKA	Yitzhak		M	His family	487
KONAVITCH	Hershel		M		487
KONAVITCH	Gittel		F	Her family	487
KILINOVITCH	Shimon Chaim		M		487
KILINOVITCH	Sheva		F		487
KILINOVITCH	Ben-Zion		M		487
KILINOVITCH	Esther		F		487
KATZ	Yankel		M		487
KATZ	Zisa		F		487
KATZ	Mordecai		M	His family	487
KATZ	Fishel		M		487
KATZ	Chaim		M	His family	487
KATZ	Feine		F	Her family	487

KATZ	Fishel	M	His family	487
KATZ	Avremel	M		487
KATZ	Chaim	M		487
KATZ	Tzipeh	F		487
KATZ	Chenke	F		487
KATZ	Pinchas	M		487
KATZ	Freyda Rachel	F		487
KATZ	Zalman Menashe	M	His family	487
KATZ	Aharon	M		487
KATZ	Basha	F		488
KATZ	Leibel	M		488
KATZ	Berel	M		488
KATZ	Chaim	M		488
KATZ	Pinchas	M		488
KATZ	Mordecai	M		488
KATZ	Chaya Bracha	F		488
KATZ	Roiza	F		488
KATZ	Breina	F		488
KATZ	David	M		488
KATZ	Rachel	F		488
KATZ	Yechiel	M		488
KATZ	Mordecai	M		488
KATZ	Shifra	F		488
KATZ	Avraham	M	His family	488
KATZ	Moshe	M	His family	488
KASHONOVER	Efraim Yosef	M		488
KASHONOVER	Feiga	F		488
KASHONOVER	Shmuel Yosef	M		488
KASHONOVER	Yehezkel	M		488

KASHONOVER	Shlomo Ya'akov		M		488
KASHON	Ezra		M		488
KASHON	Chaya Leah	PIASETZKY	F		488
KASHON	Moshe		M		488

ל Lamed

LADIGA				The entire family	488
LAMANIETZ	Yechiel		M	His family	488
LAMANIETZ	Shmuel		M	His family	488
LASEK	Avraham		M		488
LASEK	Chaya Silka		F		488
LASEK	Sarah		F		488
LASEK	Henech		M		488
LASEK	Yochanan		M		488
LASEK	Mordecai Pesach		M	His family	488
LASEK	Ya'akov		M		488
LASEK	Shayneh Esther		F		488
LASKA	Matityahu		M		488
LASKA	Saratshe		F		488
LASKA	Yoel David		M		488
LASKA	Moshe		M		488
LASKA	Etke		F		488
LASKA	Henne		F		488
LASKA	Golda		F		488
LODVIANOVITCH	Miriam		F	Children - number not given	488
LODVIANOVITCH	Matityahu		M	His family	488
LODVIANOVITCH	Perl		F		488
LODVIANOVITCH	Yosel		M		488

LODVIANOVITCH	Saratshe		F		488
LODVIANOVITCH	Ya'akov Bertshe		M	His family	488
LODVIANOVITCH	Shmuel		M	His family	489
LODVIANOVITCH	Yosel		M		489
LODVIANOVITCH	Shlomo		M		489
LODVIANOVITCH	Gittel	GALINA	F	Her family	489
LODVIANOVITCH	Devorah		F	Her family	489
LODVIANOVITCH	Roiza	ZOLANTSH	F	Her family	489
LODVIANOVITCH	Frimet	GREENBERG	F	Her family	489
LIBOVITCH	Ya'akov Shmuel		M		489
LIBOVITCH	Minkeh		F		489
LIBOVITCH	Chaya		F		489
LUKAVITZKY	Yona		M	His family	489
LILIENTHAL	Chaim Leib		M		489
LILIENTHAL	Rachel		F		489
LILIENTHAL	Meir		M		489
LILIENTHAL	Simcha Binem		M		489
LILIENTHAL	Avraham Velvel		M		489
LILIENTHAL	Breina		F		489
LICHTEMSTEIN	Ya'akov		M		489
LICHTEMSTEIN	Tzirl		F		489
LICHTEMSTEIN	Ben-Ami		M		489
LICHTEMSTEIN	Carmi		M		489
LICHTEMSTEIN	Eliezer		M		489
LICHTEMSTEIN	Sarah		F		489
LICHTEMSTEIN	Meir Fishel		M		489
LICHTEMSTEIN	Pinchas		M		489
LICHTEMSTEIN	Shlomo Yudel		M		489
LICHTEMSTEIN	Hershke		M		489

LICHTEMSTEIN	Chaim Aharon		M		489
LICHTEMSTEIN	Chaya Esther		F	Children - number not given	489
LICHTEMSTEIN	Itsha Meir		M		489
LICHTEMSTEIN	Freyda Hinda		F		489
LICHTEMSTEIN	Arkeh		M		489
LICHTEMSTEIN	Miriam		F		489
LICHTEMSTEIN	Motel		M	His wife & 1 child	489
LICHTEMSTEIN	Rachel		F		489
LICHTEMSTEIN	Pinchas		M		489
LICHTEMSTEIN	Sarah		F		489
LICHTEMSTEIN	Fishel		M		489
LICHTEMSTEIN	Chava	KATZ	F		489
LICHTEMSTEIN	Leib		M		489
LICHTEMSTEIN	Sarah		F		489
LICHTIG	Eliezer		M	His family	489
LICHTIG	Avraham Michal		M		489
LICHTIG	Mendel		M		489
LIFSHITZ	Pinchas		M		489
LIFSHITZ	Freydel		F		489
LIFSHITZ	Ya'akov		M	His family	489
LIFSHITZ	Feiga	FRAM	F	Her husband	489
LIFSHITZ	Eliezer		M		489
LIPOVITCH	Peyshe		M		490
LIPOVITCH	Sima		F	Children - number not given	490
LIPOVITCH	Minkeh		F	Her family	490
LEV	Ya'akov Moshe		M	His family	490
LEVINGER	Moshe		M		490

LEVINGER	Sarah		F			490
LEVINGER	Roiza		F			490
LEVINGER	Esther		F			490
LESMAN	Zecharia		M			490
LESMAN	Chaya Saratshe		F			490
LESMAN	Henech		M			490
LESMAN	Reuven		M			490
LESMAN	Meir Wolf		M			490
LESER					Only family name given; no other details	490
LASHER	Hershel		M		The entire family	490
LASHER	Leibel		M		His family	490
LASHER	Feiga Leah		F			490
LASHER	Fishel		M			490
LASHER	Shayneh		F			490
LASHER	Fishel		M		His family	490

מ Mem

MALA	Berel		M			490
MODRIKAMIYEN	Shlomo		M		His family	490
MODRIKAMIYEN	Reuven		M		His family	490
MALACH	Avraham		M		His family	490
MALACH	Rivkah	KRAKOVER	F		Children - number not given	490
MALACH	Binyamin		M		His family	490
MONTLACK	Chaim		M			490
MONTLACK	Reizel		F		Children - number not given	490
MANTCHKOVSKY	Yehoshua		M			490
MANTCHKOVSKY	Esther Miriam		F			490
MANTCHKOVSKY	Gronia		M	Fela		490

MANTCHKOVSKY	Fela		F	Gronia			490
MANTCHKOVSKY	Bella		F			She was a child	490
MONSHTIK	Chaim Eliyahu		M		His family		490
MONSHTIK	Moshe Hersh		M				490
MONSHTOK	Yechiel		M				490
MONSHTOK	Saratshe		F		Children - number not given		490
MONSHTOK	Binyamin		M		His family		490
MONKOZSH	Fishel		M				490
MONKOZSH	Mindel		F				490
MONKOZSH	Tabeh		F				490
MONKOZSH	Yitzhak		M				490
MONKOZSH	Elka		F				490
MONKOZSH	Esther		F				490
MONKOZSH	Yosel		M				490
MOSKOVITCH	Yehuda Leib		M				490
MOSKOVITCH	Fishel		M				491
MOSKOVITCH	Chaya Rachel		F				491
MOSKOVITCH	Sarah Esther		F				491
MOSKOVITCH	Moshe Aharon		M				491
MOSKOVITCH	Ya'akov		M				491
MAKOVER	Yishayahu		M				491
MAKOVER	Reizel		F				491
MAKOVER	Hershel		M				491
MAKOVER	Leibel		M				491
MAKOVER	Khinkeh		F		Children - number not given		491
MAKOVER	Ya'akov		M		His family		491
MAKOVER	Yosef		M				491

MAKOVER	Chaya		F			491
MAKOVER	Matkeh		F			491
MAKOVER	Shmulik		M			491
MAKOVER	Aharon		M			491
MINTZ	Aharon		M			491
MINTZ	Bailtshe		F	Children - number not given		491
MINTZ BLUM	Velvel		M	7 children		491
MINONA	Shmuel		M	His family		491
MINONA	David		M	His family		491
MINONA	Sender		M	His family		491
MAROTZKY	Leibel		M	His family		491

ב Nun

NODVARNY	Bertshe		F	His family		491
NOVISKY	Esther		F			491
NOVODVARSKY	Bendet		M			491
NOVODVARSKY	Chana		F			491
NOVODVARSKY	Rashkeh		F			491
NOVODVARSKY	Chaya Esther		F			491
NOVODVARSKY	Leibel		M			491
NOVAK	Leizer		M	His family		491
NEIMAN	Yanes		M	His family		491
NEIMAN	Freyda		F			491
NEIMAN	Tova	STOLINTZ	F			491
NEIMARK	Meir		M	His family		491
NEIMARK	Miriam		F			491

ס Samech

SOBOL	Moshe		M	His family		491
SOBOL	Fishel		M	His family		491
SOBOL	Yishayahu		M		Father's name Avraham	491

SOBOL	Chava	F			491
SOBOL	Devorah	F			492
SOBOL	Avraham	M			492
SOBOL	Shlomo	M			492
SOBOL	Yishayahu	M		Father's name Hirsh Meir	492
SOBOL	Chana	F	Children - number not given		492
SOBOTKA	Baila	F			492
SOFIAN	Freyda	F	Her family		492
SOLOMON	Reuven	M	His family		492
SOLOMON	Zanvel	M	His family		492
SOLOMON	Fishel	M	His family		492
SOSKIN				Only family name given; no other details; they were elderly (?)	492
SOSKIN	Masheh	F			492
SOSKIN	Yashek	M			492
SOSKIN	Yosef	M			492
STUDENT	Mendel	M			492
STUDENT	Perl	F			492
STUDENT	Manya	F			492
STUDENT	Hershel	M			492
STUDENT	Chana	F			492
STUDENT	Feivel	M			492
STUDENT	Leah	F			492
SMOLIOZSH	Yankel	M			492
SMOLIOZSH	Zisha	F	Children - number not given		492
SEMPH	Naftali	M			492
SEMPH	Miriam Rivkah	F			492
SEMPH	Shaul	M			492

SEMPH	Mindel	F		492
SEMPH	Moshe	M		492
SENDLER	Avraham	M	His family	492
SKOLEH	Moshe	M		493
SKOLEH	Leah Gittel	F		493
SKOLEH	Yitzhak	M		493
SKOLEH	Malka	F		493
SKOLEH	Avraham	M		493
SKOLEH	Feiga Rachel	F		493
SKOLEH	Masheh	F		493
SKOLEH	Chana	F		493
SKOZA	Aharon	M		493
SKOZA	Chana	F		493
SKOZA	Leah	F		493
SKOZA	Ya'akov	M		493
SKOZA	Leibush	M		493
SKOZA	Esther	F		493
SKOZA	Shmuel	M		493
SKORA	Shmulka	M		493
SKORA	Genendel	F		493
SKORA	Yosef	M		493
SKORA	Moshe	M		493
SKORA	Rachel	F		493
SKORNIK	Yankel	M		493
SKORNIK	Zlatkeh	F		493
SKORNIK	Perl	F		493
SKAZSHINIAK	Shayeh	M	His family	493
SKAZSHINIAK	Mendel	M	His family	493
SKAZSHINIAK	Moshe	M	His family	493
SKAZSHINIAVLAGER	Yankel	M	His family	493
SKAZSHINIAVLAGER	Pinchas	M	His family	493
SEREBRENIK	Ita	F		493

ע Ayin

EVGENIOSH	Gershon		M	His family	493
IVRI	Yisrael Chaim		M		493
IVRI	Henne Rivkah		F		493
IVRI	Hershel		M	His family	493
IVRI	Chana Feiga		F		493
IVRI	Chaya		F		493
EPSTEIN	Alter		M	His family	493
EPSTEIN	Chaya		F		493

פ Peh

FEGAL	Chaya Feiga		F		492
FEGAL	Ita		F		492
FEGAL	Chaim Baruch		M	His family	492
FEGAL	Devorah		F		492
FEGAL	Moshe		M	His family	492
FEGAL	Fishel		M		492
FEGAL	Liba		F		492
FEGAL	Tuvia		M		492
FEGAL	Chaya		F		492
FEGAL	Hershel		M	His family	492
FEGAL	Yisrael		M	His family	492
FEGAL	Moshe		M		492
FEGAL	Tabeh		F		492
FEGAL	Shmuel		M		492
FEGAL	Ya'akov Meir		M		492
FEGAL	Gittel		F		492
FEGAL	Ya'akov Mordecai		M		492
FEGAL	Traneh		F	Her family	492

FEGAL	Chaim Leizer		M		492
FEGAL	Chavatshe		F		492
FEGAL	Yitzhak Itshe		M		492
FEGAL	Golda	KLEINER	F		492
FEGAL	Rita		F		492
FEGAL	Fishel		M	From Kraśnicza Wola(?); In Maków Mazowiecki during the war	492
FEGAL	Basha		F		492
FOGELMAN	Zalman		M	His family	494
FODEMBOVITSH	Aharon Leizer		M	His family	494
FODEMBOVITSH	Rivkah		F		494
PETTER	Leibel		M	His family	494
POLYVADA	Yudel		M	His family	494
POLISHOK	Ita		F		494
POMERANIETZ	Yosef		M		494
POMERANIETZ	Ya'akov		M		494
POMERANIETZ	Basha	HERTZBERG	F		494
POMERANIETZ	Nisan		M		494
POMERANIETZ	Yitzhak		M		494
POMERANIETZ	Rivkah	ZEWALSKA	F		494
POMERANIETZ	Yisrael		M		494
FASS	Chone		M		494
PASKOVITCH	Yitzhak		M	His family	494
PASKOVITCH	Yehuda Leib		M	His family	494
PASKOVITCH	Avraham		M		494
FOX	Yitzhak		M	His family	494
FOX	Yosef		M		494
FOX	Melech		M		494
FOX	Chaya		F		494
FOX	Chana		F		494

FOX	Esther	F		494
FOX	Moshe	M		494
FOX	Sheindel	F		494
FOX	Feivel	M		494
FOX	Breina	F		494
FORMANSKY	Yankel	M		494
FORMANSKA	Aidel	F		494
PIANKA	Shmuel	M		494
PIANKA	Chaya	F		494
PIANKA	Izia	M		494
PIANKA	Yitzhak	M	His family	494
PIANKA	Rakeh	F		494
PIANKA	Rachel Leah	F	Children - number not given	494
PIANKA	Efraim	M		494
PIANKA	Basha Devorah	F	Her family	494
PIANKA	Meir	M	His family	494
PIANKA	Yudel	M		494
PIANKA	Naftali	M		494
PIASETZKY	Avraham Eliyahu	M		494
PIASETZKY	Sarah Rivkah	F		494
PIASETZKY	Shmuel	M		494
PIASETZKY	Frimetshe	F		494
PIASETZKY	Itka	F		494
PIASETZKY	Shlomo	M	His family	494
PIASETZKY	Yankel	M	His family	495
PIASETZKY	Rachel	F		495
PIASETZKY	Avraham Fishel	M		495
PIASETZKY	Hersh Moshe	M		495
FIGA	Ya'akov	M		495

FIGA	Roiza	F	Her family		495
FIGA	Arieh	M	His family		495
FIGA	Simcha	M	His family		495
PYEKARTSHIK	Sheima	M			495
PYEKARTSHIK	Tzipeh	F			495
PYEKARTSHIK	Esther	F			495
PYEKARTSHIK	Meir	M			495
PYEKARTSHIK SEGAL	Elka	F			495
PILAR	Levi Yitzhak	M			495
PILAR	Gittel	F	Children - number not given		495
PILOT			The entire family	Only family name given; no other information on names	495
FILER PERLBERG	Avraham Fishel	M			495
FILER	Hersh Moshe	M			495
FEINTZEIG	Velvel	M			495
FEINTZEIG	Mindel	F	Her family		495
FEINTZEIG	Yehezkel	M	His family		495
FINKELMAN	Ya'akov	M			495
FINKELMAN	Basha	F			495
FINKELMAN	David	M			495
FINKELSTEIN	Chaim Ya'akov	M	His family		495
FISHNER	Hershel	M	His family		495
FISHNER	Abba	M	His family		495
FISHMAN			The entire family	Only family name given; no other information on names	495
PLAIDA	Hersh Itshe	M			495
PLAIDA	Roiza	F	Her family		495

PLATAU	Yechiel Meir		M		495
PLATAU	Zivia		F		495
PLATAU	Lutsha		F		495
PLATAU	Chana Bluma		F		495
PLATA	Meir		M		495
PLATA	Breina		F		495
PLATA	Batel		F		495
PLATKA	Baruch Mordecai		M		495
PLATKA	Leah		F		495
PLATKA	Shmuel Leizer		M		495
PLATKA	Rivkah Rachel	GARFINKLE	F	Children - number not given	495
PLATKA	Basha		F	1 child	495
PLATKA	Ita Golda		F		495
PLATKA	Yisrael		M		495
FELDBERG	Efraim Fishel		M		495
FELDBERG	Yachet		F		495
FELDBERG	Avraham Hirsh		M		495
FELDBERG	Aharon Binyamin		M		495
FELDBERG	Chaya Sarah		F		495
FETZINIASH	Yisrael Meir		M		495
FETZINIASH	Chaya Necha		F	Her family	495
PERLEMUTTER	Ya'akov		M		495
PERLEMUTTER	Sheindel		F		495
PERLEMUTTER	Itzel		M		496
PERLBERG	Frimet		F		496

PERLBERG	Racheltshe Rachtshe	F		496
PERLBERG	Raphael Reuven	M		496
PERLBERG	Sarah	F		496
PERLBERG	Yona	M		496
PERLBERG	Noteh	M		496
FRIEDMAN	Matieh	F	His family	496
FRIEDMAN	Esther Ita	F		496
FRIEDMAN	Chanatshe SEGAL	F		496
FRIEDMAN	Yona Moshe	M		496
FRIEDMAN	Yechiel	M		496
FRIEDMAN	Chaya Gittel	F		496
FRIEDMAN	Roiza Feiga	F		496
FRIEDMAN	Avraham	M		496
PRESBERG	Fishel	M	His family	496
PRESBERG	Chaim Leizer	M	His family	496
PRESBERG	Gedalia	M		496
PRESBERG	Liftshe	M		496
PRESBERG	Feiga	F		496
PRESBERG	Leizer Cheikel	M		496
PRESBERG	Shmuel	M		496
PRESBERG	Leib Zelig	M		496
PRESBERG	Moshe Yehuda	M		496
PRESBERG	Rivkah	F		496
PRESBERG	Chaya	F		496
PRESBERG	Sender	M		496
PRESBERG	Malka	F		496
PRESBERG	Hendel	F		496
PRESBERG	Mindel	F		496

PRESBERG	Michleh		F			496
PRESBERG	Avraham		M			496
PRESBERG	Yitzhak		M			496
PRESBERG	Toiba Ita		F			496
PRESBERG	Blima		F			496
PERELBERG	Chana Blima		F			496
PERELBERG	Ber		M			496
PERELBERG	Sheindel		F			496
PERETZ	Ya'akov		M	His family		496
PERKAL	Yechiel		M	His family		496
PERKAL	Reuven		M	His family		496
PERSH	Rachel		F	Her family		496
FRANENBERG	Moshe		M			496
FRANENBERG	Rachel		F			496
FRANENBERG	Avraham Mordecai		M			496
FRANENBERG	Tzirl		F			496
FRANENBERG	Sarah Tabeh		F			496
FRANENBERG	Yankel		M			496
FRANENBERG	Yitzhak Hirsh		M	His family		496
FRANK	Sarah		F			496
FRANK	Zalman		M		From Przasnysz. In Maków Mazowiecki during the war	496
FRANK	Rachel		F		From Przasnysz. In Maków Mazowiecki during the war	496
FRANK	Menasha		M			496
FRIEDLOV	Etta Gittel	PIEKROTSHIK	F			497
FRIEDLOV	Esther		F			497
FRIED	Eliezer		M			497
FRIED	Leah		F			497

FRIED	Gavriel Pesach	M		497
FRIED	Feiga	F		497
FRIED	Liba	F		497
FRIED	Chaya Hinda	F		497
FRIED	Simcha	M	His family	497
PRESBERG	Eliezer David	M		497
PRESBERG	Henye	F		497
PRESBERG	Moshe Yehuda	M		497
PRESBERG	Feiga Rivkah	F		497
PRESBERG	Yitzhak	M		497
PRESBERG	Yosef	M		497
PRESBERG	Fishel	M		497
PRESBERG	Esther Malka	F		497
PRESBERG	Yitzhak	M		497
PRESBERG	Avraham Abba	M		497
PRESBERG	Ya'akov	M		497
PRESBERG	Pesach	M		497
FRENKEL	Meir	M	His family	497
FRENKEL	Ya'akov	M	His family	497
FRENKEL	Avraham Yudel	M		497
FRENKEL	Yitzhak Itshe Meir	M		497
FRENKEL	Reitzeh	F		497
FRENKEL	Moshe	M		497
FRENKEL	Dina	F		497
FRENKEL	Ya'akov	M		497
FRENKEL	Leah	F		497
FRENKEL	Zev Valdek	M		497

FRENKEL	Meir		M			497
FRENKEL	Fela		F			497
FRENKEL	Niyoshe		F			497
FRENKEL PALMAN	Chaya Fela		F			497
FRENKEL EIBESHITZ	Sarah		F			497
FRENKEL EIBESHITZ	Adanek		M		Mother's name Sara	497
FRANENBERG	Moshe		M			504
FRANENBERG	Rachel		F			504
FRANENBERG	Avraham		M			504
FRANENBERG	Tzirl		F			504
FRANENBERG	Sarah Tova		F			504
FRANENBERG	Ya'akov		M			504
FRANENBERG	David		M			504

צ Tzadik

ZUCKER	Gittel		F			497
ZUCKER	Ya'akov		M			497
ZUCKERMAN	Shmuel Gershon		M			497
ZUCKERMAN	Esther Rivkah		F			497
ZUCKERMAN	Nechama	KUMEH	F			497
TZIGEL	Yitzhak		M	His family		497
ZION	Moshe		M			497
ZION	Sheindel	SKORNIK	F			497
ZION	Rodeh		F			497
ZION	Sarah		F			497
ZION	Yechiel Alter		M			497
TZIVINER	Alter Moshe		M			497
TZITRONOVITCH				The entire family	Only family name is listed	497
TZIBELON	Naftali		M	His family		497
TZIECHONOVER	Racheltshe	Rachtshe	F			498

TZIECHONOVER KIRSCHENBAUM	Rivkah		F			498
TZIECHONOVER	Chana Hadassah		F			498
TZIKORIO	Azriel		M			498
TZEGLO				The entire family	Only family name is listed	498
TZERTNER	Ya'akov Leib		M	His family		498
TZENTURA				The entire family	Only family name is listed	498

ק Kof

KOVER	Yitzhak		M			498
KOVER	Neshe		F	Her family		498
KOVER	Avremel		M			498
KOTZIAK	Anshel		M	His family		498
KALOSKY	Shalom		M	His family		498
KALINSKY				The entire family	Only family name is listed	498
KOPLOVITCH	Gedalia		M			498
KOPLOVITCH	Golda		F			498
KOPLOVITCH	Yitzhak		M			498
KOPLOVITCH	Liba	RICKOVER	F			498
KOPLOVITCH	David		M			498
KOPLOVITCH	Moshe		M			498
KOPLOVITCH	Benish		M			498
KOPLOVITCH	Shimon		M			498
KOPLOVITCH	David		M			498
KOPLOVITCH	Henech		M	His family		498
KALENDER	Shalom		M	His family		498
KAMIEN	Simcha Binem		M			498
KAMIEN	Perl		F			498
KAMIEN	Mordecai David		M	His family		498

KANAREK	Moshe		M	His family		498
KANTOR	Yehezkel		M			498
KANTOR	Yenta		F	Children - number not given		498
KANTOR	Yosel		M			498
KARASH				The entire family	Only family name is listed	498
KARLINSKY	Hershel		M	His family		498
SHOKTON	Noteke		M	His family		498
KULAS	Yitzhak		M			498
KULAS	Henneye		F			498
KULAS	Mindel		F			498
KULAS	Yerachmiel		M			498
KULAS	Sarah		F			498
KORNIK	Michael		M	His family		498
KORNIK	Shmuel David		M	His family		498
KORNIK	Hershel		M	His family		498
KORNIK	Feivel		M			498
KORNIK	Drezl		F			498
KORNIK	Rashkeh		F			498
KORNIK	David Berel		M	His family		499
KEET	Shmuel Yosef		M	His family		499
KEET	Moshe		M	His family		499
KEET	Shayneh Rachel		F	Her family		499
KIRSCHENBAUM	Hinda	RICKOVER	F			499
KIRSCHENBAUM	David		M			499
KIRSCHENBAUM	Aharon		M			499
KIRSCHENBAUM	Velvel		M			499
KIRSCHENBAUM	Rivkah		F			499
KIRSCHENBAUM	Chaya		F			499
KIRSCHENBAUM	Yosef		M			499

KIRSCHENBAUM	Rachel	F		499
KIRSCHENBAUM	Avraham	M		499
KLEINHAUS	Gittel	F		499
KLEINHAUS	Bella	F		499
KLEINHAUS	Moshe	M		499
KLEINHAUS	Haika	F		499
KLEINHAUS	Gittel	F	Her family	499
KLEINHAUS	Leahtshe	F	Her family	499
KLEINHAUS	Racheltshe Rachtshe	F	Her family	499
KLEINHAUS	Feiga	F		499
KLEINHAUS	Vavkeh	F		499
KLEINER	Ya'akov	M		499
KLEINER	Esther	F		499
KLEINER	Leibel	M		499
KLEINER	Berish	M		499
KLEINER	Perl Chaya	F		499
KLEINER	Mindel	F		499
KLEINER	Freyda Beiltshe	F		499
KLEINER	Gittel	F		499
KLEINER	Chaim Shalom	M		499
KLEINER	Mendel	M		499
KLEINER	Freyda	F	Children - number not given	499
KAMIATEK	Moshe	M	His family	499
KRONGARD	Yitzhak	M		499
KRONGARD	Chaya Sarah	F		499
KRONGARD	Henne	F		499
KRONGARD	Fishel Mordecai	M		499
KRAKOVER	Yosef	M		499

KRAKOVER	Feiga Sarah		F			499
KRAKOVER	Moshe David		M			499
KANAPEL ITZKOVITSH	Chaya		F	Children - number not given		499
KOVEL	David		M		From Chorzele. In Maków Mazowiecki during the war	499
KOVEL	Feivel		M		From Chorzele. In Maków Mazowiecki during the war	499
KOVEL	Liba		F		From Chorzele. In Maków Mazowiecki during the war	499
KOVEL	Yetta		F		From Chorzele. In Maków Mazowiecki during the war	499
KOVEL	Leah		F		From Chorzele. In Maków Mazowiecki during the war	499
KAUFMAN	Shmuel Avraham		M			499
KAUFMAN	Chaya Esther		F			499
KAUFMAN	Moshe Ber		M			499
KAUFMAN	Feiga Pese		F			499

ר Resh

RAGOZA	Avraham		M			500
RAGOZA	Golda		F			500
RAGOZA	Temma		F			500
RAGOZA	Yitzhak Itshe Ya'akov		M			500
RAGOZA	Sarah Esther		F			500

ROZSHANER	Mordecai	M			500
ROZSHANER	Hinda	F	Children - number not given		500
ROZSHANER	Shlomo	M	His family		500
ROZSHANER	Moshe	M			500
ROZSHANER	Hadassah Hodes	F			500
ROZSHANER	Yishayahu Shaya	M			500
ROZSHANER	Feiga Leah	F	Her family		500
ROZSHANEK	Ezra	M			500
ROZSHANEK	Rela	F			500
ROZSHANEK	Etta	F			500
ROZSHANEK	Avraham	M			500
ROZSHANEK	Rivkah	F			500
ROZSHANEK	Ya'akov Binyamin	M			500
ROZSHANEK	Hershke	M			500
ROSENBERG	Hershel	M	His family		500
ROSENBERG	Shmuel Shamshons	M			500
ROSENBERG	Sarah	F			500
ROSENBERG	Chaim David	M	His family		500
ROSENBERG	Moshe	M			500
ROSENBERG	Bracha	F	Children - number not given		500
ROSENBERG	David Yosef	M	His family		500
ROSENBERG	Shimshon	M			500
ROSENBERG	Yudel	M	His family		500
ROSENBERG	Shmuel	M	His family	His occupation was - scribe	500
ROSEN	Shimon Meir	M	His family		500
ROSENTHAL	Feiga	F			500

ROSENTHAL	David		M	His wife	500
ROSENTHAL	Avraham		M		500
ROSENTHAL	Reizel		F		500
ROSENTHAL	David		M		500
ROSENTHAL	Shmulik		M		500
ROSENTHAL	Shmuel Yosef		M	His family	500
ROSENTHAL	Chava	YISMACH	F		500
ROSENTHAL	Feiga		F		500
ROSENTHAL	Freyda		F		500
ROSENTHAL	David		M	His family	500
ROSENMAN SHOCHAT	Chaim		M		500
ROSENMAN SHOCHAT	Eliezer		M		500
ROSENMAN	Zvia		F		500
ROSENMAN SHOCHAT	Eliezer		M	His family	500
ROSENMAN SHOCHAT	Yisrael Yosef		M		500
ROSENMAN SHOCHAT	Yechiel		M		500
ROSENMAN SHOCHAT	Yishayahu		M		500
ROSENSTEIN	Avraham Zanvel		M		501
ROSENSTEIN	Etta		F	Her family	501
ROSENBLUM	David Hersh		M	His wife	501
ROSENBLATT	Moshe		M		501
ROSENBLATT	Gedalyahu		M		501
ROSENBLATT	Sarah		F		501
ROSENBLATT	Meir		M		501
ROTER	Bluma Rachel		F		501
ROTER	Shlomo		M	His brothers	501

ROTSTEIN	Yisrael		M			501
ROTSTEIN	Sarah Feiga	GARFINKLE	F	Children - number not given		501
ROLNIK	Fishel		M	His family		501
ROLNIK	Avraham		M	His family		501
ROKITA				The entire family	Only family name is listed	501
ROMANER	Meir		M	His family		501
ROSHINIAK	Ya'akov Meir		M			501
ROSHINIAK	Rachel		F			501
ROSHINIAK	David		M			501
ROSHINIAK	Frimet		F			501
ROSHINIAK	Hinda		F			501
RUBIN	Eliezer		M			501
RUBIN	Hinda		F			501
RUBIN KATZ	Pinchas		M			501
RUBIN	Liba		F	1 child		501
RUBIN	Moshe Nisan		M			501
RUBIN	Baila Feiga		F			501
RUBIN	Binyamin		M			501
RUBIN	Rachel		F			501
RUBIN	Avraham Yehuda		M		He was a child. Mother's name Rachel	501
RUBIN	Michleh	RADZONOVSKI	F			501
RUBIN	Pinchas		M			501
RUBIN	Liba		F			501
RUBIN	Masheh		F		She was a child. Mother's name Liba	501
RUBIN	Yerachmiel		M			501
RUDEK	Kalman		M			501
RUDEK	Chaya		F			501
RUDEK	Aharon		M			501

RUDEK	Hershel		M		Children - number not given	501
RIBACK	Hershel		M		Children - number not given	501
RIBACK	Hershel		M		Children - number not given	501
RIBACK	Chava		F			501
RIBACK	Nisan		M		His family	501
RIBACK	Moshe		M			501
RIBACK	Leahtshe		F			501
RIBACK	Leibush		M			501
RIBACK	Baila		F			501
RIBACK	Yechiel		M			501
RIBACK	Hadassah Hodes		F			501
RIBACK	Shmuel		M			501
RIBACK	Reizel		F			501
RIBACK	Elka		F			501
RIZIKA	Butsha		F			501
RIZIKA	Feiga		F			501
RIZIKA	Bailtshe		F			501
RIZIKA	Naomi		F			501
RIZIKA	Natan		M		His family	502
RIZER	Leahtshe		F			502
REITSHIK	Freydka		F		Children - number not given	502
REITSHIK	Shalom		M			502
REITSHIK	Kreindel		F		Her family	502
REITSHIK	Shmuel		M			502
REITSHIK	Yehuda Meir		M			502
REITSHIK	Yankel		M			502
REITSHIK	Avraham		M			502

REITSHIK	Rivkah	F		502
REITSHIK	Chava	F		502
REITSHIK	Ya'akov	M		502
REITSHIK	Velvel	M		502
REITSHIK	Moshe	M		502
REITSHIK	Avraham	M		502
REITSHIK	Esther	F		502
RICKOVER	David	M		502
RICKOVER	Sarah Rivkah	F		502
RICKOVER	Natan	M		502
RICKOVER	Chava	F		502
RICKOVER	David	M		502
RICKOVER	Eliyahu	M		502
RICKOVER	Henne	F		502
RISHELEVSKY	Eliyahu David	M	His family	502

ש Shin

SOMOVITCH	Yosef	M		502
SOMOVITCH	Devorah	F		502
SOMOVITCH	Avraham	M		502
SOMOVITCH	Itzel	M		502
SOMOVITCH	Manya	F		502
SOMOVITCH	Shimon	M		502
SOMOVITCH	Yenta	F		502
SHULDENREIN	Yitzhak Shlomo	M		502
SHULDENREIN	Chaya	F		502
STERN	Kalman	M	His occupation was - scribe	502
STERN	Tabeh	F	Children - number not given	502
SHEINBERG	Avraham Hillel	M		502

SHEINBERG	Yachet		F		502
SHEINBERG	David		M		502
SHEINBERG	Devorah Ita		F		502
SHEINBERG	Rivtzieh		F		502
SHEINBERG	Leib		M		502
SHEINBERG	Eliyahu		M		502
SHLOMOVITCH	Zvi Zev		M		502
SHLOMOVITCH	Hinda	SHELSKY	F		502
SHLOMOVITCH	Ya'akov		M		502
SHLOMOVITCH	Hinda	GOGOL	F		502
SHLOMOVITCH	Eliezer David		M		502
SHLOMOVITCH	Meir Mannes		M		502
SHLOMOVITCH	Leibel		M		502
SHLOMOVITCH	Matus		M		502
SHLOMOVITCH	Feiga		F		502
SHLOMOVITCH	Feiga	ROSHINIAK	F		502
SHLIOZER	Ya'akov		M		503
SHLIOZER	Esther Leah		F	Children - number not given	503
SHLIOZER	Nachman		M	Children - number not given	503
SHMULEVITCH	Alter		M	His family	503
SHMULEVITCH	Yudel		M	His family	503
SHNIAROVSKY	Binyamin		M		503
SHNIAROVSKY	Sarah Ette		F		503
SHNIAROVSKY	Ya'akov Meir		M		503
SHNIAROVSKY	Henne Gittel		F		503
SHNIAROVSKY	Wolf		M		503
SHNIAROVSKY	Sarah Dreizel		F		503

SHNIAROVSKY	Basha	F			503
SHNIAROVSKY	David	M			503
SHNIAROVSKY	Leizer	M	His family		503
SCHNEIDERMAN	Feiga	F			503
SCHNEIDERMAN	Yenta	F			503
SCHNEIDERMAN	Brontshe	F			503
SCHNEIDERMAN	Anshel	M			503
SCHNEIDERMAN	Yosef	M			503
SCHNEIDERMAN	Chana	F			503
SCHNEIDERMAN	Shalom	M			503
SCHNEIDERMAN	Eliyahu	M			503
SCHNEIDERMAN	Meir	M			503
SHELSKY	Feivel	M	His family		503
SHELSKY	Yudel	M			503
SHELSKY	Ya'akov David	M			503
SHREMER	Yishayahu	M			503
SHREMER	Ita Devorah	F			503
SHREMER	Yosef Pinchas	M			503
SHREMER	Keila Perl	F			503
SHREMER	Leibel	M			503
SHREMER	Mordecai	M			503
SHREMER	Saratshe	F	Children - number not given		503
SHREMER	Fabeh	F			503
SHER	Yisrael	M		In Maków Mazowiecki during the war	503
SHER	Blima	F			503
SHERMAN	Rachel Leah	F			503

ת Tav

| TEOMIN | Feintshe | | F | | Her family | | 503 |

NAME INDEX

Addendum to:
Memorial Book of the Community of
(Maków Mazowiecki, Poland)

Sons of Makow Remembered
in USA and Canada

Hyman G. Rickover

Hyman G. Rickover (January 27, 1900 – July 8, 1986) was an admiral in the U.S. Navy. He directed the original development of naval nuclear propulsion and controlled its operations for three decades as director of the U.S. Naval Reactors office. In addition, he oversaw the development of the Shipping port Atomic Power Station, the world's first commercial pressurized water reactor used for generating electricity. Rickover is also one of four people who have been awarded two Congressional Gold Medals.

Rickover is known as the "Father of the Nuclear Navy," and his influence on the Navy and its warships was of such scope that he "may well go down in history as one of the Navy's most important officers." He served in a flag rank for nearly 30 years (1953 to 1982), ending his career as a four-star admiral. His years of service exceeded that of each of the U.S. Navy's five-star fleet admirals—Leahy, King, Nimitz and Halsey—all of whom served on active duty for life after their appointments. Rickover's total of 63 years of active-duty service make him the longest-serving naval officer, as well as the longest-serving member of the U.S armed forces in history.

Having become a Naval engineering duty officer (EDO) in 1937 after serving as both a surface ship and submarine-qualified unrestricted line officer, his substantial legacy of technical achievements includes the United States Navy's continuing record of zero reactor accidents.

Early life and education

Rickover was born Chaim Godalia Rickover to Abraham and Rachel (Unger) Rickover, a Polish Jewish family from Maków Mazowiecki in Congress Poland. His parents changed his name to "Hyman" which is derived from Chayyim, meaning "life". He did not use his middle name Godalia (a form of *Gedaliah*), but he substituted "George" when at the Naval Academy: https://en.wikipedia.org/wiki/Hyman_G._Rickover - cite_note-auto2-9

Rickover made passage to New York City with his mother and sister in March 1906, fleeing anti-Semitic Russian pogroms during the Revolution of 1905. They joined Abraham, who had made earlier trips there beginning in 1897 to become established. Rickover's family lived initially on the East Side of Manhattan but moved two years later to North Lawndale, Chicago, which was a heavily Jewish neighborhood at the time, where Rickover's father continued work as a tailor. Rickover took his first paid job at age nine, earning three cents an hour (equivalent to $0.9 in 2021) for holding a light as his neighbor operated a machine. Later, he delivered groceries. He graduated from grammar school at 14.

Rickover attended John Marshall Metropolitan High School in Chicago and graduated with honors in 1918. He then held a full-time job as a telegraph boy delivering Western Union telegrams, through which he became acquainted with Congressman Adolph J. Sabath, a Czech Jewish immigrant. Sabath nominated Rickover for appointment to the United States Naval Academy. Rickover was only a third alternate for appointment, but he passed the entrance exam and was accepted.

Naval career through World War II

Rickover's naval career began in 1918 at the Naval Academy; at this time, attending military academies was considered active-duty service, due in part to World War I. On 2 June 1922, Rickover graduated 107th out of 540 midshipmen and was commissioned as an ensign. He joined the destroyer *La Vallette* on 5 September 1922. Rickover impressed his commanding officer with his hard work and efficiency, and was made engineer officer on 21 June 1923, becoming the youngest such officer in the squadron.

He next served on board the battleship *Nevada* before earning a Master of Science degree in electrical engineering from Columbia University in 1930 by way of a year at the Naval Postgraduate School and further coursework at Columbia. At the latter institution, he met Ruth D. Masters, a graduate student in international law, whom he married in 1931 after she returned from her doctoral studies at the Sorbonne in Paris. Shortly after marrying, Rickover wrote to his parents of his decision to become an Episcopalian, remaining so for the remainder of his life

Rickover had a high regard for the quality of the education he received at Columbia, as demonstrated in this excerpt from a speech he gave at the university some 52 years after attending:

Columbia was the first institution that encouraged me to think rather than memorize. My teachers were notable in that many had gained practical engineering experience outside the university and were able to share their experience with their students. I am grateful, among others, to Professors Morecroft, Hehre, and Arendt. Much of what I have subsequently learned and accomplished in engineering is based on the solid foundation of principles I learned from them.

Rickover preferred life on smaller ships, and he also knew that young officers in the submarine service were advancing quickly, so he went to Washington and volunteered for submarine duty. His application was turned down due to his age, at that time 29 years. Fortunately for Rickover, he ran into his former commanding officer from *Nevada* while leaving the building, who interceded successfully on his behalf. From 1929 to 1933, Rickover qualified for submarine duty and command aboard the submarines *S-9* and *S-48*: https://en.wikipedia.org/wiki/Hyman_G._Rickover - cite_note-24 While aboard S-48 he was addressed a letter of commendation from the Secretary of the Navy "for rescuing Augustin Pasis... from drowning at the Submarine Base, Coco, Solo, Canal Zone."[While at the Office of the Inspector of Naval Material in Philadelphia, Pennsylvania in 1933, Rickover translated *Das Unterseeboot* (*The Submarine*) by World War I German Imperial Navy Admiral Hermann Bauer. Rickover's translation became a basic text for the U.S. submarine service.

On 17 July 1937, he reported aboard the minesweeper *Finch* at Tsingtao, China, and assumed what would be his only ship-command with additional duty as Commander, Mine Division Three, Asiatic Fleet. The Marco Polo Bridge Incident had occurred ten days earlier, and in August, *Finch* stood out for Shanghai to protect American citizens and interests from the conflict between Chinese and Japanese forces. On 25 September, Rickover was promoted to lieutenant commander, retroactive to 1 July. In October, his designation as an engineering duty officer became effective, and he was relieved of his three-month command of *Finch* at Shanghai on 5 October 1937.

Rickover was assigned to the Cavite Navy Yard in the Philippines, and was transferred shortly thereafter to the Bureau of Engineering in Washington, D.C. Once there, he took up his duties as assistant chief of the Electrical section of the Bureau of Engineering on 15 August 1939.

On 10 April 1942, after America's entry into World War II, Rickover flew to Pearl Harbor to organize repairs to the electrical power plant of USS *California*. Rickover had been promoted to the rank of commander on 1 January 1942, and in late June of that year was made a temporary captain. In late 1944 he appealed for a transfer to an active command. He was sent to investigate inefficiencies at the naval supply depot at Mechanicsburg, Pennsylvania, then was appointed in July 1945 to command of a ship repair facility on Okinawa. Shortly thereafter, his command was destroyed by Typhoon Louise, and he subsequently spent some time helping to teach school to Okinawan children.

Later in the war, his service as head of the Electrical Section in the Bureau of Ships brought him a Legion of Merit and gave him experience in directing large development programs, choosing talented technical people, and working closely with private industry. *Time* magazine featured him on the cover of its January 11, 1954 issue. The accompanying article described his wartime service:

Sharp-tongued Hyman Rickover spurred his men to exhaustion, ripped through red tape, drove contractors into rages. He went on making enemies, but by the end of the war he had won the rank of captain. He had also won a reputation as a man *who gets things done.*

Naval Reactors and the Atomic Energy Commission

See also: Naval Reactors

In December 1945, Rickover was appointed Inspector General of the 19th Fleet on the west coast, and was assigned to work with General Electric at Schenectady, New York, to develop a nuclear propulsion plant for destroyers. In 1946, an initiative was begun at the Manhattan Project's Clinton Laboratory (now the Oak Ridge National Laboratory) to develop a nuclear electric generating plant. Realizing the potential that nuclear energy held for the Navy, Rickover applied. Rickover was sent to Oak Ridge through the efforts of his wartime boss, Rear Admiral Earle Mills, who became the head of the Navy's Bureau of Ships that same year.

Rickover became an early convert to the idea of nuclear marine propulsion, and was the driving force for shifting the Navy's initial focus from applications on destroyers to submarines. Rickover's vision was not initially shared by his immediate superiors: he was recalled from Oak Ridge and assigned "advisory duties" with an office in an abandoned ladies' room in the Navy Building. He subsequently went around several layers of superior officers, and in 1947 went directly to the Chief of Naval Operations, Fleet Admiral Chester Nimitz, also a former submariner. Nimitz immediately understood the potential of nuclear propulsion in submarines and recommended the project to the Secretary of the Navy, John L. Sullivan. Sullivan's endorsement to build the world's first nuclear-powered vessel, USS *Nautilus*, later caused Rickover to state that Sullivan was "the true father of the Nuclear Navy."

Subsequently, Rickover became chief of a new section in the Bureau of Ships, the Nuclear Power Division reporting to Mills, and began work with Alvin M. Weinberg, the Oak Ridge director of research, to initiate and develop the Oak Ridge School of Reactor Technology and to begin the design of the pressurized water reactor for submarine propulsion. In February 1949 he was assigned to the Atomic Energy Commission's Division of Reactor Development, and then assumed control of the Navy's effort within the AEC as Director of the Naval Reactors Branch. This twin role enabled him to lead the effort to develop *Nautilus*.

The decision to originally select Rickover as head of development of the nation's nuclear submarine program ultimately rested with Admiral Mills. According to Lieutenant General Leslie Groves, director of the Manhattan Project, Mills was anxious to have a very determined man involved. He knew that Rickover was "not too easy to get along with" and "not too popular," but in his judgement Rickover was the man on whom the Navy could depend "no matter what opposition he might encounter".

While his team and industry were completing construction of the *Nautilus*, Rickover was promoted to the rank of rear admiral in 1953, however this was anything but routine, and occurred only after an extraordinary chain of events:

Admiral Rickover aboard USS *Nautilus*, the world's first nuclear-powered vessel. *"I did not recruit extraordinary people. I recruited people who had extraordinary potential—and then I trained them."*

"[Rickover's] peers in the Navy's engineer branch thought to get rid of him through failure of promotion above captain. This would entail automatic retirement at the thirty-year mark. But someone made the case to the U.S. Senate, charged by the Constitution with formal confirmation of military promotions. In that year, 1953, two years before *Nautilus* first went to sea, the Senate failed to give its usual perfunctory approval of the Navy admiral promotion list, and the press was outraged because Rickover's name was not on it. ... Ultimately an enlightened Secretary of the Navy, Robert B. Anderson, ordered a special selection board to sit. With some shuffling of feet it did what it had been ordered to do.... Ninety-five percent of Navy captains must retire regardless of how highly qualified because there are only vacancies for 5 percent of them to become admirals, and although vindictiveness has sometimes played a part in determining who shall fail of selection for promotion (thus also violating the system), never before or since have pressures from outside the Navy overturned this form of career-termination."

Regardless of the challenges faced in developing and operating brand-new technology, Rickover and the team did not disappoint: the result was a highly reliable nuclear reactor in a form-factor that would fit into a submarine hull with no more than a 28-foot (8.5 m) beam. This became known as the S1W reactor. *Nautilus* was launched and commissioned with this reactor in 1954.

Later Rickover oversaw the development of the Shipping port Atomic Power Station, the first commercial pressurized water reactor nuclear power plant. Kenneth Nichols of the AEC decided that the Rickover-Westinghouse pressurized-water reactor was *"the best choice for a reactor to demonstrate the production of electricity"* with Rickover *"having a going organization and a reactor project under way that now had no specific use to justify it."* This was a reference to the first core used at Shipping port originating from a cancelled nuclear-powered aircraft carrier. This was accepted by Lewis Strauss and the Commission in January 1954.

Rickover was promoted to vice admiral in 1958, the same year that he was awarded the first of two Congressional Gold Medals. He exercised tight control for the next three decades over the ships, technology, and personnel of the nuclear Navy, interviewing and approving or denying every prospective officer being considered for a nuclear ship. Over the course of Rickover's career, these personal interviews numbered in the tens of thousands; over 14,000 interviews were with recent college-graduates alone. The interviewees ranged from midshipmen and newly commissioned ensigns destined for nuclear-powered submarines and surface combatants, to very senior combat-experienced Naval Aviator captains who sought command of nuclear-powered aircraft carriers. The content of most of these interviews has been lost to history, though some were later chronicled in several books on Rickover's career, as well as in a rare personal interview with Diane Sawyer in 1984.

In 1973, though his role and responsibilities remained unchanged, Rickover was promoted to the rank of four-star admiral. This was the second time (after Samuel Murray Robinson) in the history of the U.S. Navy that an officer with a career path other than an operational line officer achieved that rank. Also, fairly uniquely—and because his responsibilities did not include direct command and control of combatant naval units—technically he was appointed to the grade of admiral on the retired list so as to provide some clarity on this issue. This was also done to avoid affecting the maximum-authorized number of admirals (O-10) on the "active list."

As head of Naval Reactors, Rickover's focus and responsibilities were dedicated to reactor safety rather than tactical or strategic submarine warfare training. However, this extreme focus was well known during Rickover's era as a potential hindrance to balancing operational priorities. One way that this was addressed after Rickover retired was that only the very strongest, former at-sea submarine commanders have held Rickover's now unique eight-year position as NAVSEA-08, the longest chartered tenure in the U.S. military. From Rickover's first replacement, Kinnaird R. McKee, to today's head of Naval Reactors, James F. Caldwell Jr., all have held command of nuclear submarines, their squadrons and ocean fleets, but none have been a long-term Engineering Duty Officer such as Rickover. In keeping with Rickover's promotion to four-star admiral, those who were subsequently selected for assignment to Director, Naval Reactors are promoted to this same rank, but also on active-duty status.

Historian Francis Duncan, who for over eight years was granted generous access to diverse numbers and levels of witnesses—including U.S. presidents—as well as Rickover himself, came to the conclusion that the man was best understood with respect to a guiding principle that Rickover invoked foremost for both himself and those who served in the U.S. Navy's nuclear propulsion program: "exercise of the concept of responsibility." This is further evidenced by Rickover listing *responsibility* as his first principle in his final-years paper and speech, *Thoughts on Man's Purpose in Life*.

Safety Record

Rickover's stringent standards are largely credited with being responsible for the U.S. Navy's continuing record of zero reactor accidents (defined as the uncontrolled release of fission products to the environment resulting from damage to a reactor core). He made it a point to be aboard during the initial sea trial of almost every nuclear submarine completing its new-construction period. Following the Three Mile Island accident on March 28, 1979, Admiral Rickover was asked to testify before Congress in the general context of answering the question as to why naval nuclear propulsion had succeeded in achieving a record of zero reactor-accidents, as opposed to the dramatic one that had just taken place.

The accident-free record of United States Navy reactor operations stands in some very stark contrast to those of the Soviet Union, which had fourteen known reactor accidents. As stated in a retrospective analysis in October 2007:

U.S. submarines far outperformed the Soviet ones in the crucial area of stealth, and Rickover's obsessive fixation on safety and quality control gave the U.S. nuclear Navy a vastly superior safety record to the Soviet one.

Views on Nuclear Power

Given Rickover's single-minded focus on naval nuclear propulsion, design, and operations, it came as a surprise to many in 1982, near the end of his career, when he testified before the U.S. Congress that, were it up to him what to do with nuclear powered ships, he "would sink them all." At a congressional hearing Rickover testified that:

I do not believe that nuclear power is worth it if it creates radiation. Then you might ask me why do I have nuclear powered ships. That is a necessary evil. I would sink them all. I am not proud of the part I played in it. I did it because it was necessary for the safety of this country. That's why I am such a great exponent of stopping this whole nonsense of war. Unfortunately limits—attempts to limit war have always failed. The lesson of history is when a war starts every nation will ultimately use whatever weapon it has available. ... Every time you produce radiation, you produce something that has a certain half-life, in some cases for billions of years. ... It is important that we control these forces and try to eliminate them.

— *Economics of Defense Policy: Hearing before the Joint Economic Committee, Congress of the United States, 97th Cong., 2nd sess., Pt. 1 (1982)*

A few months later, following his retirement, Rickover spoke more specifically regarding the questions "Could you comment on your own responsibility in helping to create a nuclear navy? Do you have any regrets?":

I do not have regrets. I believe I helped preserve the peace for this country. Why should I regret that? What I accomplished was approved by Congress—which represents our people. All of you live in safety from domestic enemies because of security from the police. Likewise, you live in safety from foreign enemies because our military keeps them from attacking us. Nuclear technology was already under development in other countries. My assigned responsibility was to develop our nuclear navy. I managed to accomplish this.

Focus on education

President Kennedy and Rickover, White House, February 11, 1963 *"...in addition to the multilateral POLARIS force, we discussed education and how he and I were brought up as boys."*

When he was a child still living in Russian-occupied Poland, Rickover was not allowed to attend public schools because of his Jewish faith. Starting at the age of four, he attended a religious school where the teaching was solely from the *Tanakh*, i.e., *Old Testament*, in Hebrew. Following his formal education in the United States, Rickover developed a decades-long and outspoken interest in the educational standards of the US as being a national security issue, particularly as compared during the Cold War era to Soviet Russia.

An example of his passion for education from his 1959 *Report on Russia* https://en.wikipedia.org/wiki/Hyman_G._Rickover - cite_note-74 in the context of comparative educational systems:

"There is no room here (in nuclear powerplant development) for lofty theories which do not work out in practice. We would not get anywhere if we had the loose, hazy thinking you encounter when you bring out the obvious failures of the American educational system. ... there are times when it is irresponsible to avoid criticizing something which one knows to be wrong and dangerous for the Nation as a whole. I feel that every one who has a position of responsibility in this country and who can see and understand what is happening not only has the right, he has the obligation and the duty to speak. ... This is why I feel so strongly about education—about our failure to give our children as good an education as they deserve and need. ... It is my considered opinion that there is no problem that faces the Congress or the country that is as important."

Rickover believed that US standards of education were unacceptably low. His first book centered on education was a collection of essays calling for improved standards of education, particularly in math and science, entitled *Education and Freedom* (1959). In it, he stated that "education is the most important problem facing the United States today" and "only the massive upgrading of the scholastic standards of our schools will guarantee the future prosperity and freedom of the Republic." A second book, *Swiss Schools and Ours* (1962) was a scathing comparison of the educational systems of Switzerland and America. He argued that the higher standards of Swiss schools, including a longer school day and year, combined with an approach stressing student choice and academic specialization produced superior results.

Recognizing that "nurturing careers of excellence and leadership in science and technology in young scholars is an essential investment in the United States national and global future," following his retirement Rickover founded the Center for Excellence in Education in 1983. Additionally, the Research Science Institute (formerly the Rickover Science Institute), founded by Rickover in 1984, is a summer science program hosted by the Massachusetts Institute of Technology for high school seniors from around the world.

Public image

Rickover has been called "the most famous and controversial admiral of his era." He was hyperactive, blunt, confrontational, insulting, and a workaholic, always demanding of others without regard for rank or position. Moreover, he had "little tolerance for mediocrity, none for stupidity." Even while a captain, Rickover did not conceal his opinions, and many of the officers whom he regarded as unintelligent eventually rose to be admirals and were assigned to the Pentagon. Rickover frequently found himself in bureaucratic combat with these senior naval officers, to the point that he almost missed becoming an admiral; two selection boards passed him over for promotion, and it took the intervention of the White House, U.S. Congress, and the Secretary of the Navy before he was promoted.

Rickover's military authority and congressional mandate were absolute with regard to the U.S. fleet's reactor operations, but his controlling personality was frequently a subject of internal Navy controversy. He was head of the Naval Reactors branch, and thus responsible for signing off on a crew's competence to operate the reactor safely, giving him the power to effectively remove a warship from active service, which he did on several occasions. The view became established that he sometimes exercised power to settle scores. Author and former submariner Edward L. Beach Jr. referred to him as a "tyrant" with "no account of his gradually failing powers" in his later years.

Death

Headstone of Admiral Hyman G. Rickover, Arlington National Cemetery

Rickover died at his home in Arlington, Virginia, on July 8, 1986, at age 86. He was buried on July 11 in a small, private ceremony at Arlington National Cemetery. On July 14, memorial services were led by Admiral James D. Watkins at the Washington National Cathedral, with President Carter, Secretary of State George Shultz, Secretary

Lehman, senior naval officers, and about 1,000 other people in attendance. At the request of the admiral's widow, President Carter read Milton's sonnet *When I Consider How My Light is Spent*.

Secretary of the Navy Lehman said in a statement:

"With the death of Adm. Rickover, the Navy and this nation have lost a dedicated officer of historic accomplishment. In his 63 years of service, Adm. Rickover took the concept of nuclear power from an idea to the present reality of more than 150 U.S. naval ships under nuclear power, with a record of 3,000 ship-years of accident-free operations."

And the then-Chief of Naval Operations:

"Most important," Admiral Watkins said, "he was a teacher. He set the standards. They were tough. That is the legacy and the challenge he left to all who study his contributions."

Rickover is buried in Section 5 at Arlington National Cemetery. His first wife Ruth is buried with him and the name of his second wife Eleonore is inscribed on his gravestone. Eleonore passed away on July 5, 2021, and is to be buried in Arlington Cemetery. Rickover is survived by Robert Rickover, his sole son by his first wife.

Honors

The *Los Angeles*-class submarine USS *Hyman G. Rickover* (SSN-709) was named for him. It was commissioned two years before his death, and was, at that time, one of only two Navy ships to be named after a living person since 1900 (there have been 16 more since). The submarine was launched on August 27, 1983, sponsored by his second wife Eleonore, commissioned on July 21, 1984, and deactivated on December 14, 2006. In 2015, the Navy announced a *Virginia*-class submarine named USS *Hyman G. Rickover* (SSN-795) in his honor. The submarine's christening took place on July 31, 2021.

Rickover Hall at the United States Naval Academy houses the departments of Mechanical Engineering, Naval Architecture, Ocean Engineering, Aeronautical and Aerospace Engineering. Rickover Center at Naval Nuclear Power Training Command is located at Joint Base Charleston, where Navy personnel begin their engineering training. In 2011, the U.S. Navy Museum included Rickover as part of the *Technology for the Nuclear Age: Nuclear Propulsion* display for its Cold War exhibit, which featured the following quotation:

"Good ideas are not adopted automatically. They must be driven into practice with courageous impatience."

Other things named in his honor include the Admiral Hyman Rickover Fellowship at M.I.T., Hyman G. Rickover Naval Academy, and Rickover Junior High School.

References: Wikipedia

David Azrieli

David Joshua Azrieli (Azrylewicz), b. 1922 in Makow Mazowiecki

This life story is based mostly on David Azrieli's biography "One Step Ahead", written by David's daughter Danna Azrieli, as she was told by her father. The book was published by Yad Vashem, Jerusalem in 2001 and translated to Hebrew and Russian.

Life Before the War

David Joshua Azrieli was born in Makow Mazowiecki in 1922 to Rafael-Hirsh Azrylewicz and Haia-Sarah nee Gerwer (Gerber).

Rafael Azrylewicz was raised in a tailors' family in the region of Makow Mazowiecki and was very successful thanks to his professional skills. He owned a prosperous sewing workshop with several employees.

Among his clients were wealthy Germans who came especially from Prussia and Germany to sew their clothes by the famous tailor.

The Azrylewicz couple had three sons and one daughter:
Ephraim, their first born, was born in 1920.
David-was born in 1922.
Pinchas-was born in 1924.
Tzirele-was born in 1936.

In David Azrieli's autobiography, written by his daughter Danna, he talks about, contrary to his eldest brother Ephraim who showed an interest in his father's business, that he himself was not interested in the clothing business. David preferred reading political articles, listening to the radio and playing sports games. In his happy childhood he used to ride a bicycle throughout Makow Mazowiecki and join children's groups who presented theatrical shows in house yards. He also loved playing football with his younger brother Pinchas, sliding on the frozen river in winter, swimming and kayaking during the summer.

After finishing elementary school in Makow Mazowiecki, David was accepted to study at the Teachers Seminary in Warsaw and at the age of 14 he left his parents' home to study there. David returned to Makow at the end of that year as an appropriate high school (gymnasium) was open in his hometown and there was no longer any need to travel to the big city.

During the 1930s, with the increasing winds of war in Europe, young David sensed that a real danger for the Jewish people was approaching. His mother Haia Sarah also worried about the signs of a coming war and expressed her desire to immigrate to Palestine. She claimed that the Jewish people needed a country of their own to be safe from their enemies. On the other hand, David's father, Rafael-Hirsh was optimistic and believed the European democratic countries would succeed in coping with the rising Nazism.

From time to time the question came up whether the family should leave Makow Mazowiecki for a safer place but David's father, Rafael, remembered the events of World War I and was hopeful that the end of the war would come soon enough.

Life During Wartime

A month before the war broke out, David's brother Ephraim was recruited to the Polish army. On the 3rd of September 1939 (two days after the war broke out) the Azrylewicz Family gathered and decided that David and Pinchas should flee from Makow Mazowiecki, for fear that they would remain under Nazi occupation and would probably not be able to continue their studies.

On the 4th of September 1939, David and Pinchas left with the intention to escape eastwards, reach Romania and from there sail to Palestine. Their first station was Pultusk from which they continued to Wyszkow.

The entire road was covered with scattered corpses of cows and horses killed by the German bombings, a dreadful sight, which left an unforgettable impression on young David.

From Wyszkow they both continued to Wengrow (Wegrow). Exhausted, they were received warmly by the Jewish community and the following day, literally with the Germans moving eastward, they continued their run toward Brzecs (Brest) and Pinsk, where they boarded a train going east.

On their way the train was strafed several times by machine guns from the airplanes and David was shot in his right arm, fracturing the bone of his right forearm. As a result of his injury, David and his brother were unable to continue their journey through Romania to Israel and were forced to alter their plans, thus stopping in Luniec (Luninets).

Upon their arrival at Luniec (Luninets) they were taken in by a warm Jewish family named Beker (with whom David kept in touch with). Due to his wound David had to be taken to the nearest hospital in Rowne.

On September 17th 1939, right after the Molotov Ribbentrop Pact was signed, according to this agreement, Rowne was included in the eastern part of Poland ruled by the Soviets. Medical teams arrived to treat the wounded refugees and soldiers who were flowing into town and thus David received proper medical treatment.

Meanwhile, Ephraim was released from the army and moved with his girlfriend Miriam to Bialystock, which was in an area under Russian rule. Relatives and family acquaintances from Makow Mazowiecki also arrived in Bialystock, prompting David and Pinchas to also move there.

In Bialystock they joined Ephraim and Miriam and lived together as a family. Pinchas and David registered at school to complete their studies, Ephraim worked a variety of jobs and the four of them led a relatively peaceful life.

During that period, David endangered himself by crossing the border and back three times, from East to West Poland, reaching his parents' house in Makow Mazowiecki. The first time he tried, without success, to persuade his parents to come to Bialystock. The second time he went to bring supplies for the winter but was robbed on the way and came back empty handed. The third time, in February 1940, when his mother decided to see her children, and risked crossing the border and then getting back to Makow Mazowiecki.

At the end of April 1940, the Soviets introduced a new plan, every refugee who didn't want to return to territories under German occupation would receive status as a Russian citizen. They would receive a passport and had to move further eastwards at least 200 km from the border.

David decided to remain in the Soviet Union. His family and relatives, including his two brothers, chose to return to Makow Mazowiecki.

Pinchas, his brother, was caught by Soviet policemen and since then disappeared. Ephraim and Miriam were sent to Siberia (as part of a misleading Soviet plan, which sends all people who wish to return to occupied Poland, to hard labour camps in Siberia).

On his way eastward, David returned to Luniec where he found work as an accountant in a flour mill in Gavrileici, a remote village deep in the swamps of Pinsk. From there he was able to visit the Beker family, which for him was a substitute to his family. David lived in that village for over a year leading a rather comfortable routine, but nevertheless feeling lonely and disconnected. David was able to contact Ephraim in Siberia but continuously worried about his younger brother. The whereabouts of Pinchas were totally unknown.

In June 1941, five days after the breach of the Molotov Ribbentrop Pact by the Germans, David decided to continue running eastward in order to get further away from the fast-approaching war. He crossed the border, was caught and almost sent back to Poland. Miraculously he managed to jump onto a cargo train that was evacuating equipment eastward and was saved from being sent back into the hands of the Nazi's.

Following a three-day journey on another train, the passengers (mostly refugees), were divided into groups and were sent to work in a kolkhoz (governmental agricultural farm).

David was sent to a Sovchoz not far from Rostov in the Ukraine, where he worked as a blacksmith's apprentice.

In the summer of 1941, after the occupation of Kiev by the Germans, David left with a friend eastward towards Stalingrad and made his journey on the Volga River in the direction of Siberia.

During all that time David had hopes of finding his brothers, Ephraim and Pinchas, on one of the trains or on the road among the Polish citizens who were released from the labour camps in Siberia. Yet, in vain, he never did find them. It turned out that Ephraim and Miriam had decided to go southwest of the Volga River, while most refugees had gone south to Tashkent; nothing was heard from Pinchas.

He tried to enlist in the Anders Polish army and to his astonishment he was drafted in spite of the fact that Jewish applicants were mostly rejected due to health reasons or as a result of the well-known anti-Semitic approach of general Anders.

Together with a Jewish friend he met in his military unit, they learned to survive in that hostile, antisemitic military environment. They both had one goal: to leave Russia as army soldiers and arrive to the land of Israel (then Palestine). Having this goal constantly in mind helped them overcome the humiliation and abuse inflicted on them by the soldiers and commanders.

After completing basic training, Adam and David's military unit sailed to Pahlevi port [Bandar-e Anzali] in Iran. There, they both decided, with the help of a local Jewish family, to leave the army and somehow reach Israel (Palestine). The mentioned Jewish family provided David with a train ticket. After a long journey of stress and adventures, David arrived in Baghdad. With the help of the Jewish underground, which was operating at the time in Iraq, David and his friend were smuggled into Palestine disguised as British soldiers. They rode on buses returning to Palestine from Iraq, their journey lasted 5 days.

In September 1942, the exhausting journey of David Azrilewicz from Makow Mazowiecki, which began in September 1939, came to its final end.

Life in Israel-Palestine till the end of the War of Independence

David and his friend were received very warmly at Kibbutz Maoz Haim.
They received a tent to live in, to them it was like a magnificent house. They worked in the fields of a Jewish Kibbutz surrounded by their own people; this gave them a sense of freedom and spiritual uplift.

In March 1943, after receiving their mandatory identity cards from the Jewish agency, both parted from the kibbutz. His friend began studying literature at the Hebrew university in Jerusalem while David moved to Haifa, where he began preparing himself to study at the Technion-Institute. David considers the day he received notification of his acceptance at the Technion to be one of the most memorable of his life.

David also started corresponding with his Uncle Nathan who lived in England and Uncle Sam who lived in South Africa. Sam provided some financial support for David's studies. His two other uncles, in Paris and Antwerp, with whom he was unable to make contact, eventually perished. He was fortunate to contact his family in the United States. His social life also blossomed after integrating into a group of friends, also refugees, from Poland. Together they created a 'company' as a substitute for their families who had disappeared in the turbulent war in Europe.

Towards 1945, documented photographs and information about the Holocaust of the Polish and European Jews began to appear, David and his friends kept nurturing hopes that their families were still alive.

It was only in the winter of 1946, following an intensive inquiry, David found out that his mother and sister had perished in Birkenau, while his father was murdered in Auschwitz. This knowledge shocked him so severely, that he fell into a deep depression and became ill.
Several months later David received comforting news from his uncle Nathan in England, that his brother Ephraim along with his wife Miriam and their son Moty, had survived the Holocaust. They were staying in a 'displaced persons' camp in Germany.
In 1947, David's brother Ephraim and his family arrived in Israel, and finally David had a real family in the country.
David enlisted in the 'Haganah'. In March 1948 and enrolled in an officer's course. When the Independence War broke out in May of that year, he was posted in one of the fighting companies of the 7th brigade.
David was wounded in the battle at 'Latrun', he received a rare appointment as education officer in the Air Force. When the war ended (September 1949), David was released from the army.

Life in Canada - David as Businessman and Philanthropist

In February 1950, David (who had changed his surname to a Hebrew name - Azrieli) was sent by the Jewish agency to a Jewish community in Cape Town, South Africa, as a youth instructor and Hebrew teacher. That mission enabled him to meet his Uncle Sam who lived in Johannesburg.

The trip to South Africa was the beginning of a new chapter in David's life. He travelled all over the world, living in England and the USA until 1954 when he settled down in Montreal, Canada.

In Canada he met Stephanie (Lefort) his wife to be. They got married in 1957 and had four children: Rafi [Rafael], Sharon, Naomi and Danna.

In 1956, he completed a Bachelor of Arts at the Thomas More Institute (now part of Bishop's University) in Montreal. In 1997, at the age of 74, he earned a Master of Architecture from Carleton University.

In 1958, David established the "Azrieli Group" and began building the first shopping mall in Israel, 'Canyon-Ayalon' in Ramat-Gan. Later he went on to build several notable commercial centres and skyscrapers in Israel.

Above all, David Azrieli built the "Hashalom-Azrieli Center' in Tel Aviv, which is, as he said, "the highlight of all my achievements".

As an architect and developer his success and influence extended from Canada to Israel, most notably in the transformation of the Tel Aviv skyline with the three towers of the Azrieli centre. He has had a major impact in both countries through his philanthropic work with the Azrieli foundation. David Azrieli received many honorary degrees and awards from a number of institutions both in Canada and Israel. He is a member of the Order of Canada and a Chevalier of L'Ordre National du Quebec and received the Israel Prime Minister's Jubilee Award. David Azrieli is ranked the 8th richest man in Canada and #374 on the Forbes world billionaires list.

This Jewish boy, born in Makow Mazowiecki Poland, lived a life of fear and escape, lost his family in the Holocaust and whose dream was to immigrate to Israel, managed to triumph over the evil intentions of the Nazis and their collaborators.

Against all odds, he managed to survive the inferno, build a career as a world-renowned designer and builder, raise a family and become one of the most important philanthropists, both in Canada and Israel.

Reference: "One step Ahead" by Danna Azrieli

Awards and recognition

- Member of the Order of Canada (1984)
- Chevalier to the Ordre national du Quebec (1999)
- Honorary doctorate from Concordia University (1975), Yeshiva University (1983), Technion-Israel Institute of Technology (1985), Tel Aviv University(1996), Carleton University (2003), Weizmann Institute of Science (2012)
- Israeli Prime Minister's Jubilee Award (1998)
- Honorary Fellow of the City of Jerusalem (2001)
- Queen Elizabeth II's Golden Jubilee Medal (2002)
- Queen Elizabeth II's Diamon

Makow Mazowiecki: Chaja-Sara, Rafael-Hirsz and David, Efraim and Pinchas Azrylewicz (about 1920s)

WARSAW: David Azrylewicz and collegues (1935)

Makow Mazowiecki: Azrylewicz Family
Seated: Mordechai and Tzirel
From right: Rafael- Hirsz, Szmuel- Josef, Frimet, Azriel

Makow Mazowiecki: The Gerber family (1920s)
Second from left in the first row Chaja Sara A., David and Efraim in Makow M.

Azrieli Family Foundation in Makow Mazowiecki.
Sitting: Stephanie Azrieli

Visit in 2013; Naomi Azrieli in Makow Mazowiecki standing in front of her grandparents' house (and father David Azrieli) in the Market (Rynek) Square.

References: Poland Virtual Shtetl

Pinchus [Paul] Sharon [Shuldenrajn]

Submitted by Bruce Shuldenrein

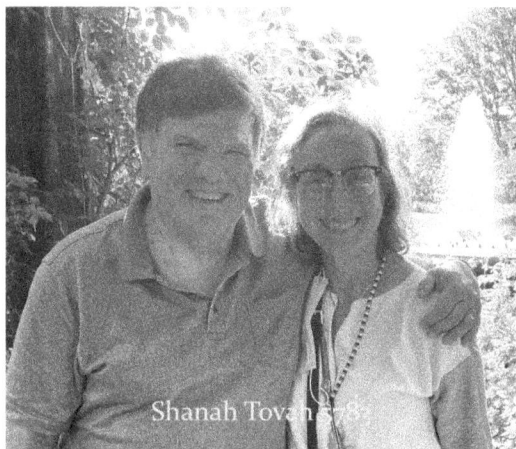

Shanah Tovah 5784

"For I still live, still exist,
but my repose - is with the slaughtered"
Yitzhak Lamdan

"כי אני עוד חי, קיים, אך מנוחתי - בנרצחים"
יצחק למדן

פול (פנחס) שרון (שולדנריין)

(פולין, 1912 – ארצות-הברית, 1998)

Paul (Pinkus) Sharon (Szuldenrajn)

(Poland, 1912 – United States, 1998)

נולד בוורשה. גדל במקוב מזובייצקי. למד באקדמיה לאמנות בוורשה ועבד כמאייר בהוצאת הספרים "סנטרל". עם פרוץ המלחמה עבד בסוכנות הידיעות הפולנית ואחר כך ברח לברית-המועצות. בתום המלחמה עבר למחנה העקורים בציילסהיים, שם נישא ב-1946 ליוג'ניה וויימן, ניצולת שואה מווילנה. עבד בוועדה הפולנית לחקר פשעי הנאצים ואייר כרזות בנושא השואה. ב-1948 היגר עם אשתו לניו יורק ועסק באיור כרזות פרסומות.

Born in Warsaw, he was raised in Makow Mazowiecki. He studied at the Warsaw Academy of Arts and worked as an illustrator for the *Central* publishing house. Following the outbreak of the war he worked for the Polish Express Agency ATE, and afterwards fled to the Soviet Union. Following the war, he went to the Zeilsheim DP camp, where in 1946 he married Eugenia Weimann, a Holocaust survivor from Vilna. He worked for the Central Historical Commission in Poland, and illustrated posters on the subject of the Holocaust. In 1948, he immigrated with his wife to the United States, where he worked in commercial poster design.

"Zchor et Asher Asau Lcho Amalek." This is a lithograph produced about 1946. Yad Vashem has a copy and at least as of a few years ago, it was on their permanent display in the last room of the museum dedicated to Shearith HaPleita.

Historical poster from 1947-1948 commemorating all the horrors that the Jews had gone through by the Goyim throughout time.

The poster comes with impressive illustration by Pinchas Schuldenrein, depicting the persecutions suffered by the Jewish people throughout the ages along with the books which were subsequently written on the subject: The enslavement in Egypt and the Passover Haggadah / The devastation of the temple and the Book of Lamentations / The events of 1648-49 and the book of Yaven Metzulah / The expulsion from Spain and the book Emek Habakha.

The historical events are linked by clock hands, under which appears a drawing of a skeleton pointing to the symbolic number "6,000,000", a feather (for writing) and a line commanding: "Sammelt un Vorzeichnet" – collect and write-down, referring to the role of the Central Historical Committee in documenting the history of the Jews at the time of the Holocaust.

The artist Pinchas Schuldenrein was born in Poland and studied in the Warsaw Academy of Arts. After the Holocaust he established an art studio in the area of the displaced-persons camp in Zeilsheim with the aid of the JDC, where he created his famous work "Yizkor". He gave some art lessons to children in the displaced-persons camps and his work was influenced by the Holocaust. In 1947 he immigrated to the USA and settled in New York. A few years later he changed his name to Paul Sharon. In New York he worked as an independent graphic artist and for the Schlesinger Brothers, until his death in 1998.

Other credits regarding Pinchas' works were "Virtues of Memory" published by Yad Vashem and "Anachnu Poh", also published by Yad Vashem.

Camp Art

by Joseph Rubin

Yizkor, which means "Remember," is one of the more dramatic items contributed to the Holocaust Archives of the Jewish Heritage Collection. The poster was donated by Charlotte Shayne, formerly of Columbia and Walhalla, South Carolina. It came into her hands in 1946 while she was an assistant to Rabbi Philip S. Bernstein, advisor in Jewish affairs to the Theater Commander of the U.S. Army of Occupation in Frankfurt, Germany. One day an unknown young woman from the Zeilsheim UNRRA (United Nations Relief and Rehabilitation Administration) near Frankfurt arrived unexpectedly in Shayne's office and presented her with the print.

Pinchas Schuldenrein, the poster's creator, grew up in Makow Mazowiecki, Poland, and attended the Warsaw Academy of Art. After World War II he met historian Koppel S. Pinson, then educational director of the American Joint Distribution Committee. Pinson helped Schuldenrein, who had lost all of his work during the war, establish a studio outside Zeilsheim. Art materials were extremely scarce, but in a bombed-out airport Schuldenrein found materials in sufficient quantity to tackle the challenge of conveying the terrors of the Holocaust through art.

In the months that followed he taught art to Jewish children in Displaced Persons (DP) camps and created paintings depicting what he had seen and endured. Reproduced in both poster and postcard form, *Yizkor* was distributed throughout UNRRA camps with the assistance of the Central Historical Commission of the Central Committee of Liberated Jews in American-occupied Germany. Schulderein's poster *Remember Amalek* won first prize in a contest among DP artists sponsored by the Central Commission, and his *Vehigadita Levincha*, or "You will tell your children," took top honors in a poster competition sponsored by the United Jewish Appeal. The prize was awarded by none other than UJA General Chairman Henry Morgenthau, Jr.

In 1947 Schuldenrein immigrated to the United States. When he became an American citizen several years later, he changed his name to Paul Sharon. He worked in New York as a commercial and graphic artist for himself and Shulsinger Brothers until his death in 1998. Today, the original *Yizkor* painting is owned by the artist's son, Dr. Bruce Sharon, of Skokie, Illinois.

Yizkor represents in grisly symbolism the artist's homage to the six million Jews murdered by the Nazis. The title

Pinchas Schuldenrein created the poster, Yizkor, from his original painting while he was interned in the DP camp at Zeilsheim, Germany. Approximately 14 ½ by 20 ½ inches, ink on paper, ca. 1946.

appears in calligraphic uppercase Hebrew across the top, flanked by the dates 5700 to 5705 (1940–1945), written in ornate Torah script. The figure "6000000" sits in a pool of blood with candles at either end dripping not wax but tears of grief. Within the outline of the block numerals the artist painted a mosaic of Nazi atrocities.

The whole—the number with candles on either side, the blackness above and red below—suggests a coffin of six million souls awaiting burial. Adding a phrase of consolation and warning to the outrage portrayed by the imagery, Schuldenrein quoted from *Tehillim* (Psalms) and the *Av HaRachamim* prayer in modern Hebrew script: *Ki doresh dammim otam zachar*, "For he who exacts retribution for spilled blood remembers them."

"Vehigadita Levincha," a lithographic poster produced around the same time as the "Amalek". This piece won first prize in a post-war art competition.

"Katzetnick." The subject is a mutual friend of my father and Joseph's father.

Additional artworks:

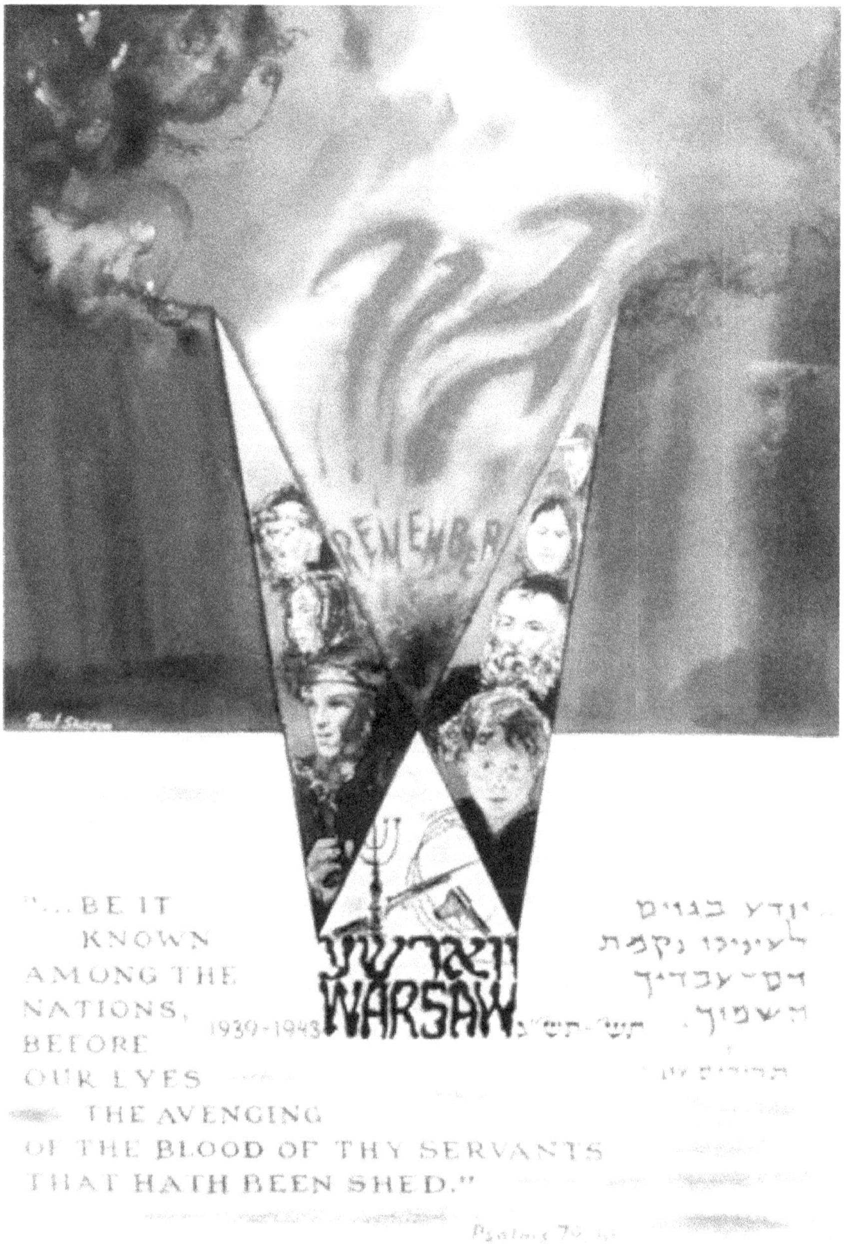

REMEMBER
WARSAW
1939-1943
"...BE IT KNOWN AMONG THE NATIONS, BEFORE OUR EYES THE AVENGING OF THE BLOOD OF THY SERVANTS THAT HATH BEEN SHED."
יודע בגוים לעינינו נקמת דם־עבדיך השפוך.

YAD VASHEM

The Holocaust Martyrs' and Heroes' Remembrance Authority

יד ושם

רשות הזיכרון לשואה ולגבורה

ירושלים, ט״ז סיון, תשס״ח

19 יוני, 2008

לכבוד

Bruce Shawn

שלום רב,

אני מתכבד להעניק לך את האלבום:

אנחנו פה

ניצולי השואה במדינת ישראל

בשמי ובשם עורכי האלבום והוצאת יד ושם, אני מבקש להביע הערכתנו העמוקה של תרומתך לאלבום, תרומה ייחודית שהעשירה אותו, וסייעה להופכו ליצירה בעלת ערך היסטורי וספרותי. ההדים הראשונים לגבי האלבום, ממומחים, מבקרים וכלל הציבור, חיובים ונלהבים. חן- חן לך על חלקך בכך.

בברכה ובתודה מקרב לב,

גבי הדר

מנהלת ההוצאה לאור

אבנר שלו

יו״ר הנהלת יד ושם

ת.ד. 3477, ירושלים 91034, טל. 02-6443455, פקס. 02-6443452 .P.O.B. 3477, JERUSALEM 91034, TEL. 02-6443455, FAX. 02-6443452

www.yadvashem.org